중등 필수 영문법 +
객관식·서술형 드릴 및
실전문제 풀이

핵심 영문법 복습 +
서술형 유형별/단계별
집중 훈련

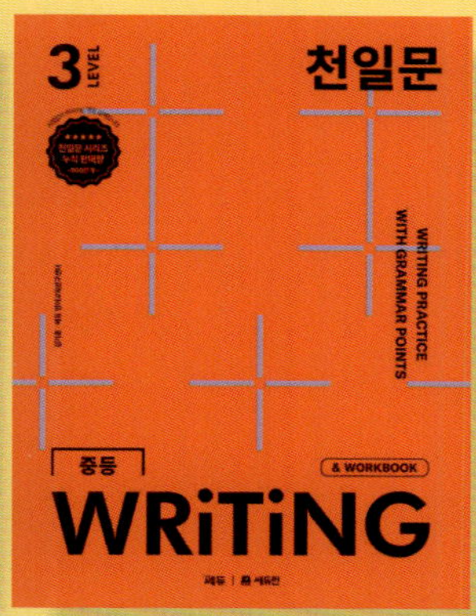

<천일문 중등 WRITING>은 <거침없이 Writing>의 개정 교재입니다.

✳ 연계 학습 예시 *뒷장의 Syllabus를 확인해 보세요.

천일문 중등 GRAMMAR LEVEL 1	POINT
Chapter 01 be동사	
Unit 1 be동사의 긍정문	1~4
Unit 2 be동사의 부정문과 의문문	5~6
Chapter 02 일반동사	
Unit 1 일반동사의 현재형	1~2
Unit 2 일반동사의 과거형	3~4

천일문 중등 WRITING LEVEL 1	POINT
Chapter 01 be동사와 일반동사	
Unit 1 be동사	1~2
Unit 2 일반동사의 현재형과 과거형	3~4

- 권별 목차가 연계되어 있어 <천일문 중등 GRAMMAR> 학습 후 <천일문 중등 WRITING>으로 서술형 집중 훈련이 가능합니다.
- <천일문 중등 WRITING>은 서술형 내신 기출문제 분석에 초점을 맞춰 내용을 구성하여, <천일문 중등 GRAMMAR> 구성과는 약간의 차이가 있을 수 있습니다.

Syllabus

천일문 중등 GRAMMAR LEVEL 1		POINT
Chapter 01 be동사		
Unit 1	be동사의 긍정문	1~4
Unit 2	be동사의 부정문과 의문문	5~6
Chapter 02 일반동사		
Unit 1	일반동사의 현재형	1~2
Unit 2	일반동사의 과거형	3~4
Unit 3	일반동사의 부정문과 의문문	5~8
Chapter 03 현재진행형과 미래 표현		
Unit 1	현재진행형	1~3
Unit 2	미래 표현	4~5
Chapter 04 조동사		
Unit 1	조동사의 기본 형태와 can/may	1~6
Unit 2	must/have to/should	7~8
Chapter 05 명사와 관사		
Unit 1	셀 수 있는 명사와 셀 수 없는 명사	1~3
Unit 2	관사	4~5
Unit 3	There is/are	6
Chapter 06 대명사		
Unit 1	인칭대명사와 재귀대명사	1~3
Unit 2	지시대명사와 it	4~6
Unit 3	one, some, any	7~9
Chapter 07 형용사, 부사, 비교		
Unit 1	형용사	1~4
Unit 2	부사	5~8
Unit 3	비교급과 최상급	9~12
Chapter 08 여러 가지 문장 종류		
Unit 1	명령문, 제안문, 감탄문	1~4
Unit 2	의문사 의문문	5~9
Unit 3	부가의문문, 부정의문문	10~12
Chapter 09 문장의 여러 형식		
Unit 1	SVC	1~2
Unit 2	SVOO	3~4
Unit 3	SVOC	5~6
Chapter 10 to부정사와 동명사		
Unit 1	to부정사의 명사적 쓰임	1~3
Unit 2	to부정사의 부사적, 형용사적 쓰임	4~5
Unit 3	동명사의 쓰임	6~10
Chapter 11 전치사		
Unit 1	장소, 위치, 방향 전치사	1~2
Unit 2	시간을 나타내는 전치사	3~4
Unit 3	여러 가지 전치사	5~6
Chapter 12 접속사		
Unit 1	and/but/or	1~2
Unit 2	여러 가지 접속사	3~4

천일문 중등 WRITING LEVEL 1		POINT
Chapter 01 be동사와 일반동사		
Unit 1	be동사	1~2
Unit 2	일반동사의 현재형과 과거형	3~4
Unit 3	일반동사의 부정문과 의문문	5~6
Chapter 02 현재진행형과 미래 표현		
Unit 1	현재진행형	1~2
Unit 2	미래 표현	3~4
Chapter 03 조동사		
Unit 1	can, may	1~4
Unit 2	must, have to, should	5~6
Chapter 04 명사와 대명사		
Unit 1	명사	1~3
Unit 2	인칭대명사와 재귀대명사	4~5
Unit 3	지시대명사와 부정대명사	6~9
Chapter 05 형용사, 부사, 비교		
Unit 1	형용사	1~2
Unit 2	부사	3~4
Unit 3	비교급과 최상급	5~6
Chapter 06 여러 가지 문장 종류		
Unit 1	명령문, 제안문, 감탄문	1~3
Unit 2	의문사 의문문	4~6
Unit 3	부가의문문	7
Chapter 07 문장의 여러 형식		
Unit 1	SVC(2형식)	1
Unit 2	SVOO(4형식)	2~3
Unit 3	SVOC(5형식)	4
Chapter 08 to부정사		
Unit 1	to부정사의 명사적 쓰임	1~2
Unit 2	to부정사의 부사적 쓰임	3
Unit 3	to부정사의 형용사적 쓰임	4
Chapter 09 동명사		
Unit 1	명사로 쓰이는 동명사	1~2
Unit 2	자주 쓰이는 동명사 표현	3
Chapter 10 전치사와 접속사		
Unit 1	전치사	1~3
Unit 2	접속사	4~6

펴낸이   김기훈   김진희

펴낸곳   ㈜쎄듀 / 서울시 강남구 논현로 305 (역삼동)

발행일   2024년 11월 1일 초판 1쇄

내용 문의   www.cedubook.com

구입 문의   콘텐츠 마케팅 사업본부

Tel. 02-6241-2007

Fax. 02-2058-0209

등록번호   제22-2472호

ISBN   978-89-6806-443-2

978-89-6806-442-5(SET)

CEDU(쎄듀)는 A **C**omprehensive **E**nglish e**DU**cation(종합적 영어교육)의 약자입니다.

천일문

LEVEL 1

WRITING PRACTICE
WITH GRAMMAR POINTS

중등

WRITING

저자

김기훈

現 ㈜쎄듀 대표이사

現 메가스터디 영어영역 대표강사

前 서울특별시 교육청 외국어 교육정책자문위원회 위원

저서 천일문 〈STARTER·입문편·기본편·핵심편·완성편〉 / 천일문 중등 GRAMMAR
리딩그라피 / 리딩 플랫폼 / 리딩 릴레이 / Reading Q / Listening Q
미리 수능 영어 / 천일문 VOCA / 쓰작 / 잘 풀리는 영문법
어휘끝 / 어법끝 / 첫단추 / 파워업 / ALL씀 서술형
수능영어 절대유형 시리즈 / 수능실감 등

쎄듀 영어교육연구센터

쎄듀 영어교육연구센터는 영어 콘텐츠에 대한 전문지식과 경험을 바탕으로
최고의 교육 콘텐츠를 만들고자 최선의 노력을 다하는 전문가 집단입니다.

인지영 수석연구원 · **최세림** 선임연구원 · **홍세라** 연구원 · **전진영** 연구원 · **박소민** 연구원

교재 개발에 도움을 주신 분들

김경희 선생님(미카영어) **김은정** 선생님(일산 이제이 잉글리쉬) **김정미** 선생님(앰버랩영어교습소)

김지연 선생님(송도탑영어학원) **박혜선** 선생님(써니잉글리쉬) **방성모** 선생님(방성모영어학원)

이동현 선생님(쌤마스터입시학원) **이화연** 선생님(써니사이드학원) **전혜경** 선생님(JHK영어)

정지안 선생님(쌤영어수학학원) **조양희** 선생님(뮤엠영어 신도림동아점)

마케팅 콘텐츠 마케팅 사업본부

영업 문병구

제작 정승호

인디자인 편집 올댓에디팅

표지 디자인 모스그래픽

내지 디자인 스튜디오에딩크

일러스트 박아름

영문교열 James Clayton Sharp

Foreword

많은 학생이 영문법을 공부한 후 객관식 문항은 순조롭게 풀다가도 서술형만 만나면 멈칫하는 순간을 경험합니다. 감으로 풀거나 답을 찍는 요령이 통하지 않거니와, 문법 단순 암기에서 한 단계 나아가 표현하고자 하는 영어 문장을 자유자재로 써낼 정도로 체득해야 문제없이 쓸 수 있기 때문입니다. 따라서 서술형 문제들은 만점 정복의 가장 결정적인 승부 포인트라 할 수 있으며 그 중요성이 날이 갈수록 강조되고 있습니다.

〈천일문 중등 WRITING〉은 〈거침없이 Writing〉의 개정판으로, 초판 교재의 특장점은 유지함과 동시에 〈천일문 중등 GRAMMAR〉와 브랜드를 통일시켜 목차 연계성을 더 높였습니다. 단순한 쓰기 형태의 문제만 모은 형식적인 대비서가 되는 것을 지양하고, 서술형을 명확한 타깃으로 삼아 최적의 학습 방향과 실질적 효과를 제공하도록 심혈을 기울였습니다.

새로워진 〈천일문 중등 WRITING〉의 특장점을 소개합니다.

+1 최신 개정 교육과정 반영 및 전국 내신 서술형 기출 문제 완벽 분석

새롭게 최신 2022 개정 교육과정을 반영했으며, 총 10,000여 개의 내신 서술형 문제를 수집하여 가장 많이 출제되는 포인트 중심으로 학습하도록 구성했습니다. 학습 포인트 별로 자주 등장하는 서술형 기출 유형까지 포함하여 실전 대비에 최적화된 훈련이 가능합니다.

+2 〈천일문 중등 GRAMMAR〉와 연계되는 핵심 문법 설명과 단계별 서술형 문항 수록

〈천일문 중등 GRAMMAR〉와 연계 학습이 가능하도록 서술형 대비에 꼭 필요한 핵심 문법 설명을 수록하였으며, 이와 함께 학습한 문법 사항을 쓰기에 적용하는 방법도 제시했습니다. 영작의 가장 기초가 되는 배열과 영작 연습 문제로 충분히 기초를 쌓고, 나아가 실전 응용문제까지 다양하게 접하도록 구성함으로써 서술형을 완벽하게 대비할 수 있습니다.

+3 논술형 수행평가 연습 문제로 장문 영작까지 내신 완벽 대비

기존 내신 서술형 문제는 단문 영작이 주를 이루었지만, 점점 영어 글쓰기의 중요성이 높아짐에 따라 수행평가의 비중도 높아지고 있습니다. 이에 〈천일문 중등 WRITING〉은 실전 글쓰기 실력을 향상할 수 있는 논술형 수행평가 연습문제를 제공합니다. 학습한 문법 사항 중 가장 실용적인 쓰임의 언어형식으로 '예시 글 구성 → 예시 글의 구조 분석 → 학습자 스스로 글의 뼈대 구상 → 개개인의 독창적인 글 완성 → 자세하고 명확한 평가 기준으로 채점'까지 가능하게 하였습니다.

서술형을 어떻게 대비해야 할지 고민하던 학생들도 〈천일문 중등 WRITING〉으로 기본부터 차근차근 학습한다면 어느 순간 서술형에 대해 두려움이 사라지고 정답을 거침없이 써 내려가는 자신 스스로를 발견할 것입니다. 노력이 결실을 맺어 영어의 실력자가 되는 그날까지 여러분을 응원합니다.

저자

Preview

1 본책

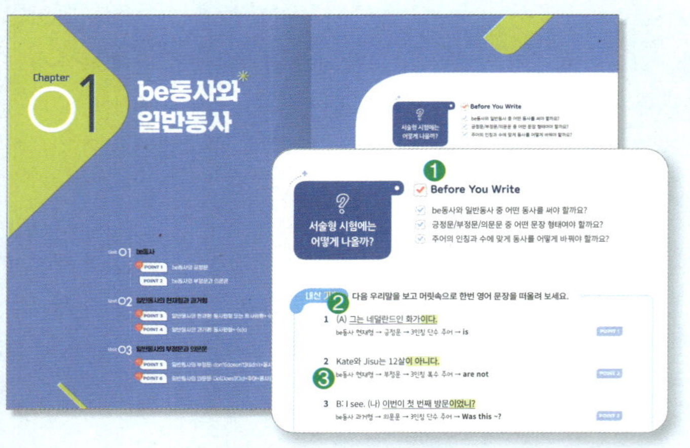

기출 예제로 살펴보는 Chapter Preview

1 해당 챕터 학습 전 미리 점검하는 주요 영작 포인트
2 실제 기출 영작 문제에 제시된 우리말 중 어느 부분이 정답의 단서가 되는지 확인
3 정답 도출 과정 제시

효과적인 POINT별 학습

1 중요 핵심 문법을 POINT별로 구성 및 내신 기출 빈도수에 따라 [빈출] 표시
2 우리말 어순과 영어의 어순이 비교 가능한 대표 예문
3 영작 시 꼭 알아야 하는 주요 문법 사항
4 [주의!] 기출에 자주 등장하거나 주의해야 할 문법 사항
5 [MORE+] 실력 향상을 위한 기출 심화 개념
6 [대표 기출 문제] 내신에 자주 출제되는 대표 기출 문제와 그 문제를 푸는 해결 단서 제공
7 [함정 피하기] 서술형 문제를 풀 때 주의해야 할 감점 요인 정리

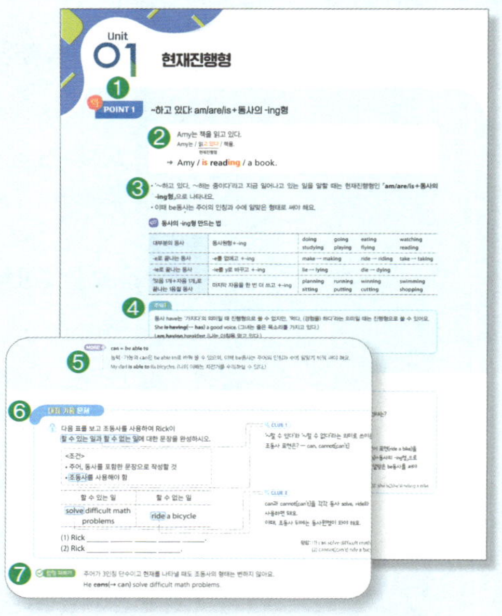

단계적 학습을 위한 문제 구성

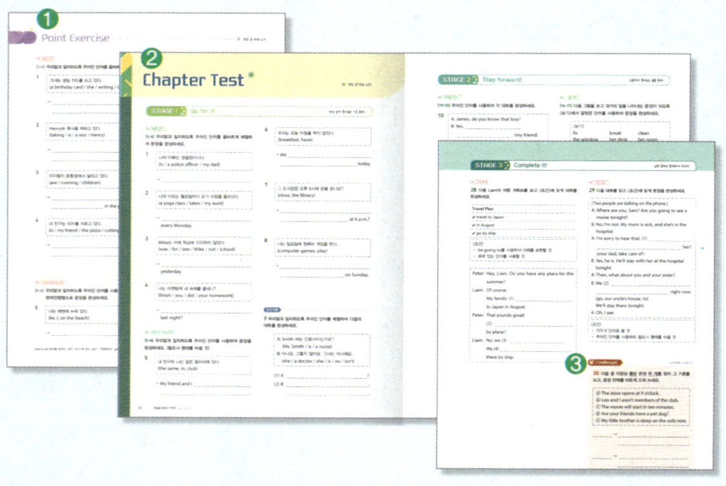

1 [Point Exercise] 학습한 포인트들을 바로 점검하는 연습 문제
2 [Chapter Test] 전국 내신 서술형 기출 문제의 출제 유형을 총망라한 단계별 실전 문제
- STAGE 1 기본 배열, 영작 문제
- STAGE 2 STAGE 1보다 한 단계 높은 응용 문제
- STAGE 3 고난도 서술형
3 [Challenge!] 앞서 배운 챕터 3개에서 학습한 내용을 점검해보는 누적 문제

중등 내신 대비를 위한 **논술형 수행평가 연습 문제** (총 10회)

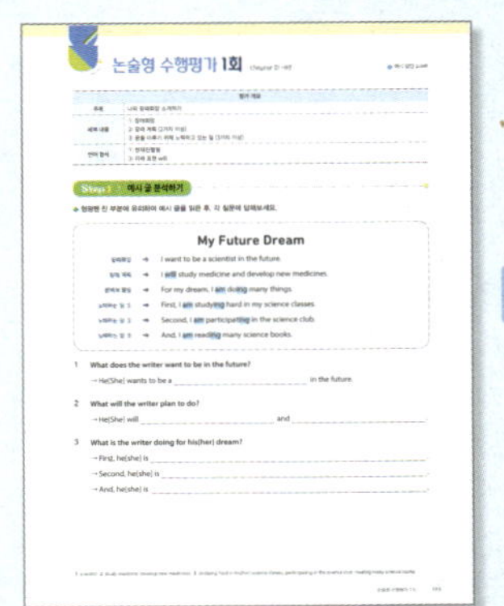 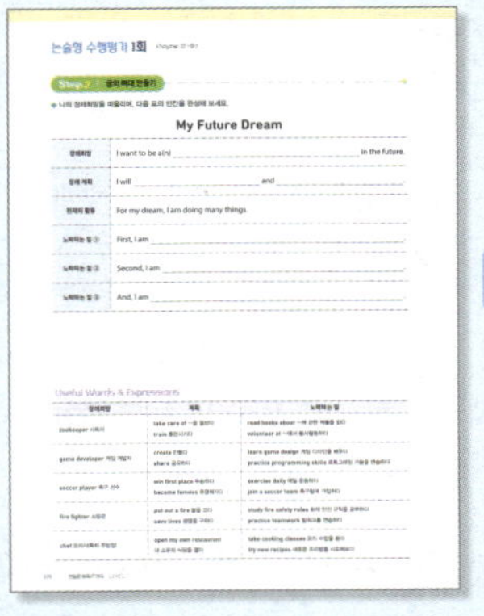 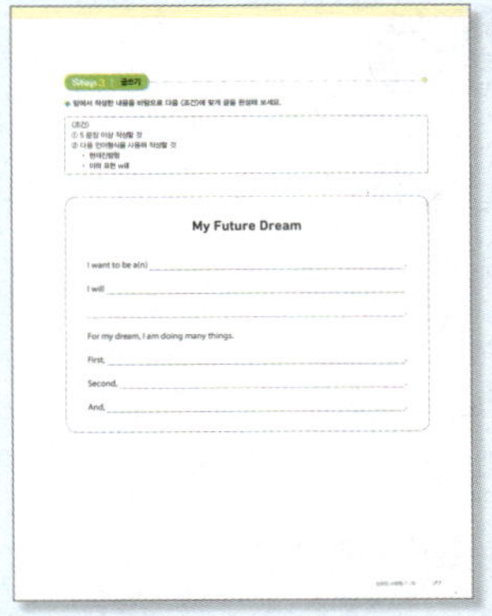 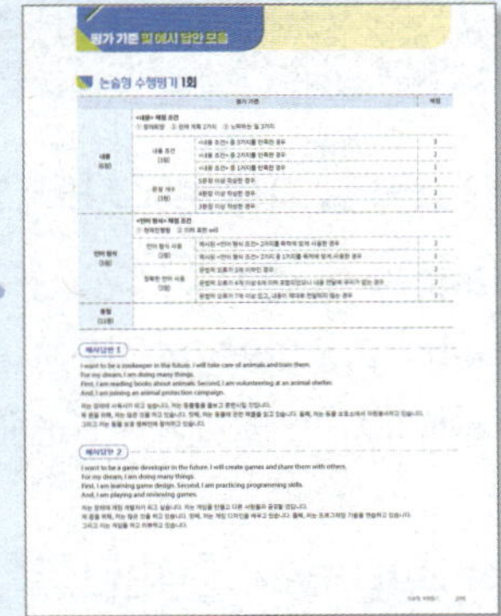

Step 1 예시 글 분석
- 전국 중학교 영어 내신 수행평가를 분석하여 포맷 구성
- 학습한 여러 언어 형식을 사용하여 기본 영작 연습

Step 2 글의 뼈대 구성
- 스스로 아이디어 구상 및 글의 뼈대 작성
- 주제별 유용한 어휘 및 표현 함께 제공

Step 3 나만의 글 작성
- 제시된 〈조건〉에 맞춰 실전 글쓰기 연습
- Step 2에서 완성한 뼈대에 맞춰 자신만의 글 완성

평가 기준 및 예시 답안
- 누구나 손쉽게 채점 가능한 간결하고 명확한 평가 기준
- 초보 학습자의 부담을 줄여주는 예시 답안 제공

② 워크북

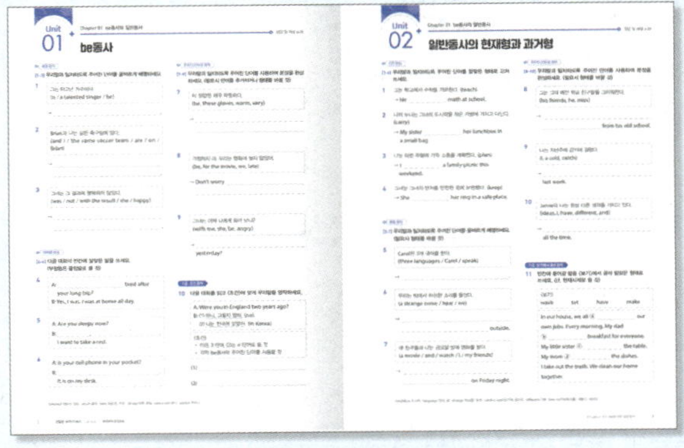 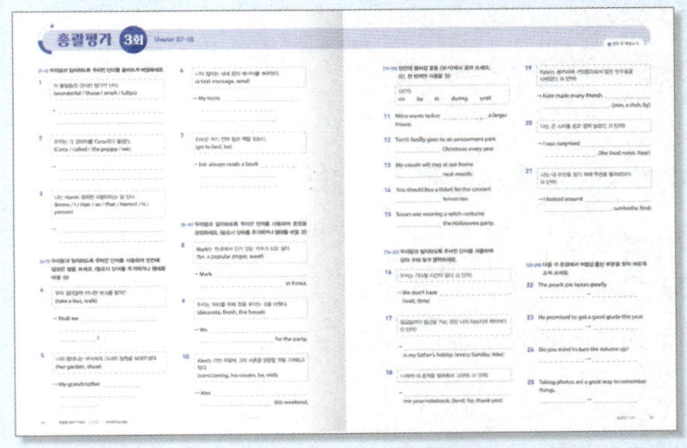

- 완벽 복습 가능한 유닛별 연습 문제
- 각 유닛에서 가장 많이 출제되는 기출 문제 함께 수록

- 총괄평가 3회분 수록 (챕터 3~4개씩 묶어 출제)
- 앞서 익힌 문법 사항의 누적 학습
- 기본 영작, 응용 영작, 고난도 심화 문제로 구성

③ 부가서비스 (www.cedubook.com)

모든 자료는 www.cedubook.com에서 다운로드 가능합니다.

 **1. 어휘리스트   2. 어휘테스트**

- 교강사 여러분께는 위 부가서비스를 비롯하여, 문제 출제 활용을 위한 한글 파일,
  수업용 PDF 파일, 챕터별 추가 문제를 제공해드립니다. (파일 신청 및 문의는 book@ceduenglish.com)

Contents*

Chapter 01

be동사와 일반동사

✓ Before You Write

서술형 시험에는
어떻게 나올까?

- ☑ be동사와 일반동사 중 어떤 동사를 써야 할까요?
- ☑ 긍정문/부정문/의문문 중 어떤 문장 형태여야 할까요?
- ☑ 주어의 인칭과 수에 맞게 동사를 어떻게 바꿔야 할까요?

내신 기출 다음 우리말을 보고 머릿속으로 한번 영어 문장을 떠올려 보세요.

1 (A) 그는 네덜란드인 화가<u>이다.</u>
be동사 현재형 → 긍정문 → 3인칭 단수 주어 → **is**   POINT 1

2 Kate와 Jisu는 12살<u>이 아니다.</u>
be동사 현재형 → 부정문 → 3인칭 복수 주어 → **are not**   POINT 2

3 B: I see. (나) 이번이 첫 번째 방문<u>이었니?</u>
be동사 과거형 → 의문문 → 3인칭 단수 주어 → **Was this ~?**   POINT 2

4 그는 토요일마다 그의 차를 <u>세차한다.</u> (wash)
일반동사 현재형 → 긍정문 → 3인칭 단수 주어 → **washes**   POINT 3

5 B: 우리는 어르신들을 위해 노래를 <u>불러드렸어.</u>
일반동사 과거형 → 긍정문 → **sang**   POINT 4

6 B: Yes, they are. They play soccer very well, too.
But (그들은 배드민턴과 야구와 농구를 <u>하지 않는다.</u>)
일반동사 현재형 → 부정문 → 3인칭 복수 주어 → **do not play**   POINT 5

7 A: (그는 재미있는 책과 영화를 <u>좋아하니?</u>)
일반동사 현재형 → 의문문 → 3인칭 단수 주어 → **Does he like ~?**   POINT 6

정답: **1** He is[He's] a Dutch painter. **2** Kate and Jisu are not[aren't] 12 years old. **3** Was this your first visit? **4** He washes his car every Saturday.
5 We sang songs for the elderly. **6** they do not[don't] play badminton, baseball, or basketball. **7** Does he like interesting books and movies?

Unit 01 be동사

POINT 1   be동사의 긍정문

> James는 키가 크다.
> James는 / ~이다 / 키가 큰.
> 주어(3인칭 단수) be동사 현재형
>
> → **James / is / tall.**

- be동사의 현재형은 '~이다/~하다/(~에) 있다'의 의미로, 주어의 상태를 설명하거나 위치를 나타내요.
- be동사 뒤에는 '무엇', '상태' 또는 '어디'에 해당하는 말이 와요.
- 주어의 수와 인칭에 따라 am/are/is 중 적절한 것을 쓰는 것이 중요해요.

주어			be동사 현재형	줄임말
인칭	수	인칭대명사		
1인칭 (나/우리)	단수	I	am	I'm
	복수	We	are	We're
2인칭 (너/너희)	단수·복수	You	are	You're
3인칭 (그, 그녀, 그것, 그(것)들)	단수	He/She/It	is	He's/She's/It's
	복수	They	are	They're

> Sophia와 나는 교실 안에 있었다.
> Sophia와 나는 / 있었다 / 교실 안에.
> 주어(1인칭 복수) be동사 과거형
>
> → **Sophia and I / were / in the classroom.**

주어가 A and B 형태의 복수이면 be동사도 복수형을 써야 해요.
B 자리에 오는 I를 보고 was를 쓰지 않도록 주의하세요.

- be동사의 과거형은 was, were 두 가지로 나타낼 수 있어요.

be동사 현재형	am, is	are
be동사 과거형	was	were

대표 기출 문제

🔒 우리말과 같은 뜻이 되도록 빈칸에 알맞은 동사를
어법에 맞게 쓰시오.

> 그는 야구 선수이다.
> = He ___________ a baseball player.

CLUE 1
'~이다'의 의미로 주어의 상태를 설명할 때 쓰이는
동사는? – be동사의 현재형!

CLUE 2
주어가 3인칭 단수인 He이므로, 이에 알맞은 be동사
의 현재형을 써야 해요.

정답: is

Point Exercise

정답 및 해설 p.02

○● 배열 영작

[1-4] 우리말과 일치하도록 주어진 단어를 올바르게 배열하세요.

1
네 책은 탁자 위에 있다.
(your book / on the table / is)

→ _______________________________.

2
나는 학교에 지각했다.
(late for / was / school / I)

→ _______________________________.

3
그녀의 방은 깨끗하고 정돈되어 있다.
(neat / and / is / her room / clean)

→ _______________________________.

4
이 신발은 너무 작다.
(too / these shoes / small / are)

→ _______________________________.

○● 주어진 단어로 영작

[5-11] 우리말과 일치하도록 주어진 단어를 사용하여 문장을 완성하세요. (필요시 형태를 바꿀 것)

5
너는 매우 똑똑하구나!
(be, smart, very, you)

→ _______________________________

6
Justin은 어제 아팠다. (be, sick)

→ _______________________________
yesterday.

7
파스타는 내가 가장 좋아하는 음식이다.
(be, pasta, favorite food, my)

→ _______________________________

8
Sam과 Jane은 영국 출신이다.
(be, England, from, and)

→ _______________________________

9
그의 개는 정말 귀엽다.
(be, his dog, cute, so)

→ _______________________________

10
나의 반 친구들은 다정하고 재미있다.
(be, and, funny, my classmates, friendly)

→ _______________________________

11
Kate와 나는 그때 가장 친한 친구였다.
(be, and, best, friends, I)

→ _______________________________
_______________________________ at that time.

○● 기출·조건 영작

12 우리말과 일치하도록 〈조건〉에 맞게 문장을 완성하세요.

Alex와 나는 공원에 있었다.

〈조건〉
• the park, and, in, be, I를 사용할 것
• 필요시 단어의 형태를 바꿀 것

→ _______________________________
____

neat 정돈된, 단정한 friendly 다정한, 상냥한

　be동사의 부정문과 의문문

과학은 내가 가장 좋아하는 과목이 아니다.

과학은 / ~이 아니다 / 내가 가장 좋아하는 과목.
　주어　　be동사의 부정문

→ **Science** / **is not[isn't]** / my favorite subject.

- be동사의 부정문(~이 아니다/~하지 않다/(~에) 있지 않다)은 **be동사 바로 뒤에 not**을 붙이며, 아래 표와 같이 줄임말 형태로 잘 쓰여요.

I	am not	
He/She/It	is not[isn't]	was not[wasn't]
We/You/They	are not[aren't]	were not[weren't]

- 다만, am과 not을 줄여 amn't의 형태로는 쓰지 않아요.
- 주어와 be동사를 줄인 형태(I'm not/He's not/You're not 등)로도 쓸 수 있어요.

A: 네가 가장 좋아하는 과목은 영어니?　　　　　B: 응, 맞아. / 아니, 그렇지 않아.

네가 가장 좋아하는 과목은 ~이니 / 영어?
　　　　　　　　be동사의 의문문

→ A: **Is your favorite subject** / English?　B: Yes, **it is**. / No, **it isn't**.

- be동사의 의문문(~이니?/~하니?/(~에) 있니?)은 「**be동사＋주어 ~?**」의 순서로 씁니다.
- 응답은 Yes/No로 하며, 의문문에서 묻는 대상은 적절한 대명사와 be동사를 사용해 대답해야 해요.
- 부정의 응답에서 「be동사＋not」은 보통 줄여 씁니다.

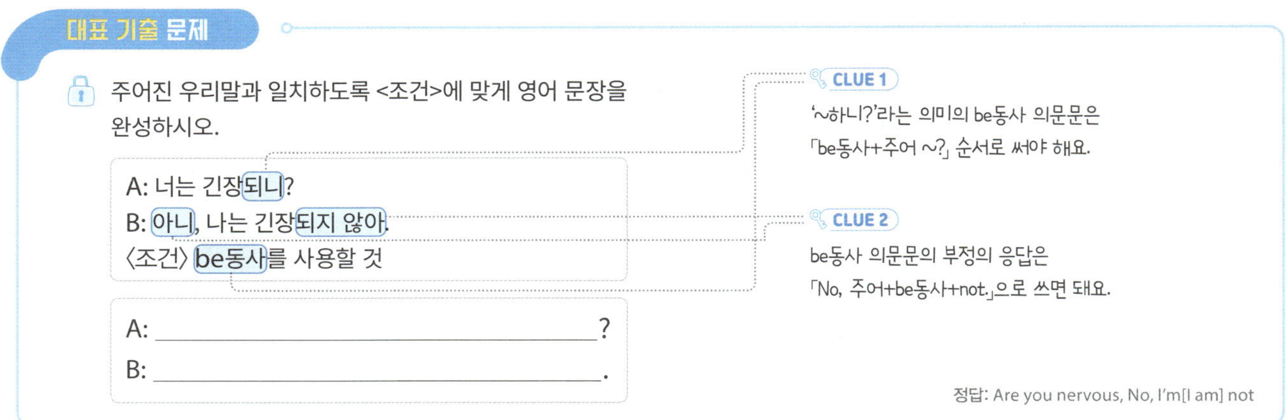

대표 기출 문제

🔒 주어진 우리말과 일치하도록 <조건>에 맞게 영어 문장을 완성하시오.

A: 너는 긴장되니?
B: 아니, 나는 긴장되지 않아.
〈조건〉 be동사를 사용할 것

A: ______________________ ?
B: ______________________ .

CLUE 1
'~하니?'라는 의미의 be동사 의문문은
「be동사＋주어 ~?」 순서로 써야 해요.

CLUE 2
be동사 의문문의 부정의 응답은
「No, 주어+be동사+not.」으로 쓰면 돼요.

정답: Are you nervous, No, I'm[I am] not

✅ **함정 피하기**　be동사의 의문문에서 be동사는 뒤에 나오는 주어의 수와 인칭에 맞게 써야 해요.
또한, 응답할 때 주어는 알맞은 대명사로 바꿔 답해야 해요.
A: **Are** Jin and Peter in the classroom? B: No, **they** aren't. (A: Jin과 Peter는 교실에 있니? B: 아니, 그렇지 않아.)

Point Exercise

빈칸 완성

[1-4] 우리말과 일치하도록 빈칸에 들어갈 알맞은 말을 쓰세요.

1

그들은 인기 있는 배우들이 아니다.

→ They _______________ popular actors.

2

그 가방은 내 것이 아니다.

→ The bag _______________ mine.

3

그 영화는 재미있지 않았다.

→ The movie _______________ interesting.

4

Dean과 Andy는 운동장에 있니?

→ _______________ Dean and Andy on the playground?

대화문 완성

[5-8] 다음 대화의 빈칸에 알맞은 응답을 쓰세요.
(부정형은 줄임말로 쓸 것)

5

A: Are they English teachers?
B: _____________, _____________ _____________.
   They are math teachers.

6

A: Is Ellie at home now?
B: _____________, _____________ _____________.
   She's at school now.

7

A: Is the man a singer?
B: _____________, _____________ _____________.
   He is my favorite singer.

8

A: Were Ted and Alice at the concert?
B: _____________, _____________ _____________.
   They enjoyed the concert.

주어진 단어로 영작

[9-10] 우리말과 일치하도록 주어진 단어를 사용하여 문장을 완성하세요. (필요시 형태를 바꿀 것)

9

너는 오늘 오후에 한가하니?
(you, this afternoon, free)

→ _________________________________

____

10

Paul과 Frank는 내 사촌들이 아니다.
(my, and, cousins)

→ _________________________________

____

기출: 그림 영작

11 다음 그림을 보고 〈보기〉와 같이 대화를 완성하세요.

〈보기〉
A: Is Mr. Harrison angry?
B: (1) No, he isn't.
   (2) He is surprised.

A: Are Bella and her friend sad?
B: (1) _________________________. (3 단어)
   (2) _________________________. (3 단어)

---

popular 인기 있는, 대중적인 mine 내 것 interesting 흥미로운, 재미있는 playground 운동장, 놀이터 enjoy 즐기다 surprised 놀란

Unit 02 일반동사의 현재형과 과거형

POINT 3 일반동사의 현재형: 동사원형 또는 동사원형+-(e)s

나는 매운 음식을 좋아한다.
나는 / **좋아한다** / 매운 음식을.
주어(1인칭 단수) 일반동사 현재형

→ I / **like** / spicy food.

그는 주말마다 자전거를 탄다.
그는 / **탄다** / 자전거를 / 주말마다.
주어(3인칭 단수) 일반동사 현재형

→ He / **rides** / a bike / on weekends.

- 주어의 동작이나 상태를 설명하는 일반동사의 현재형은 주어가 1, 2인칭이거나 3인칭 복수(friends, teachers ...)일 때는 **동사원형**을 써요.
- 주어가 3인칭 단수(My friend, A teacher ...)일 때는 **보통 일반동사 뒤에 -s나 -es**를 붙여요.
- 철자에 따라 3인칭 단수 현재형이 다른 형태로 변하기도 하므로 자주 쓰이는 동사의 변화형들은 꼭 외워두세요.

일반동사의 3인칭 단수 현재형

대부분의 동사	+-s	cleans	picks	takes	likes
-o, -s, -x, -ch, -sh로 끝나는 동사	+-es	goes teaches	does watches	misses washes	fixes brushes
「자음+y」로 끝나는 동사	-y를 i로 바꾸고 +-es	carries	studies	cries	
「모음+y」로 끝나는 동사	+-s	plays	buys	says	enjoys
불규칙 변화	have → has				

대표 기출 문제

주어진 우리말과 일치하도록 <보기>에서 골라 각각 알맞은 형태로 쓰시오.

〈보기〉 go   like   eat   have

(1) He ___________ to Daehan Middle School.
　　(그는 대한중학교에 다닌다.)

(2) Jessica ___________ a beautiful smile.
　　(Jessica는 아름다운 미소를 갖고 있다.)

CLUE 1
현재형 '학교에 다니다'라는 의미의 영어 표현(go to school)을 3인칭 단수 주어(He)에 알맞게 쓰려면 동사 go 뒤에 -es를 붙여 써야 해요.

CLUE 2
현재형 '가지고 있다'라는 뜻의 일반동사(have)를 3인칭 단수 주어(Jessica)에 알맞은 형태로 써야 해요. 이때 have는 불규칙 변화형인 점에 주의하세요.

정답: (1) goes (2) has

Point Exercise

정답 및 해설 p.02

[1-4] 우리말과 일치하도록 주어진 단어를 사용하여 빈칸에 알맞은 말을 쓰세요.

1 그는 산책한다. (take)

→ He ________________ a walk.

2 그녀는 숙제를 한다. (do)

→ She ________________ her homework.

3 Susan은 매일 아침 침대를 정돈한다. (make)

→ Susan ________________ her bed every morning.

4 그 아기는 하루 종일 운다. (cry)

→ The baby ________________ all day long.

[5-7] 우리말과 일치하도록 주어진 단어를 올바르게 배열하세요. (필요시 형태를 바꿀 것)

5
> 나의 엄마와 나는 함께 저녁 식사를 요리한다.
> (and I / cook / my mom / dinner)

→ ________________________________ ________________________ together.

6
> 그 개는 긴 귀를 가지고 있다.
> (ears / have / long / the dog)

→ ________________________________ .

7
> 그녀는 영어를 아주 열심히 공부한다.
> (English / study / she)

→ ________________________________ ________________________ very hard.

[8-10] 우리말과 일치하도록 주어진 단어를 사용하여 문장을 완성하세요. (필요시 형태를 바꿀 것)

8
> 많은 사람들이 밝은 날에는 선글라스를 쓴다.
> (many, sunglasses, wear, people)

→ ________________________________

________________________ on bright days.

9
> Miller 씨는 그의 자동차를 한 달에 한 번 세차한다.
> (wash, his car, Mr. Miller)

→ ________________________________

________________________ once a month.

10
> 그녀의 언니는 아이들에게 한국어를 가르친다.
> (teach, Korean, her sister)

→ ________________________________

________________________ to the children.

11 다음 〈조건〉에 맞게 주어진 글을 바꿔 쓸 때, 빈칸에 알맞은 문장을 쓰세요.

> 〈조건〉
> • (1)은 4 단어, (2)는 6 단어로 쓸 것
> • 필요시 형태를 바꿔 쓸 것

> I am Emma. I like music. I play the piano.
> Sometimes, I go to concerts with friends.
>
> ↓
>
> This is my friend Emma. She likes music.
> (1) ________________________________ .
> (2) Sometimes, ________________________
> ________________________________ .

take a walk 산책을 하다 make one's bed 침대를 정돈하다 all day long 하루 종일 once 한 번 sometimes 때때로, 가끔

POINT 4   일반동사의 과거형: 동사원형+-(e)d

나는 어제 내 방을 청소했다.
나는 / 청소했다 / 내 방을 / 어제.
　　　일반동사 과거형

→ **I** / **cleaned** / my room / yesterday.

- 일반동사를 사용하여 과거에 일어난 일을 '~했다'라고 나타낼 때는 **주어의 인칭과 수에 관계없이** 일반동사의 과거형을 써요.
- 일반동사의 과거형은 대부분 **동사원형에 -(e)d**를 붙여 만들어요.

📢 일반동사의 과거형 만드는 법

대부분의 동사	+-ed	watch**ed**　　want**ed**　　call**ed**　　finish**ed**
-e로 끝나는 동사	+-d	like**d**　　moved　　danc**ed**
「자음+y」로 끝나는 동사	-y를 i로 바꾸고 +-ed	stud**ied**　　tr**ied**　　worr**ied**
「모음+y」로 끝나는 동사	+-ed	play**ed**　　stay**ed**　　enjoy**ed**
「모음 1개+자음 1개」로 끝나는 동사	마지막 자음을 한 번 더 쓰고 +-ed	stop**ped**　　plan**ned**　　drop**ped** *강세가 앞에 오는 2음절 이상의 동사는 +-ed (visited[vízitid], entered[éntərd])

📢 일반동사 불규칙 과거형 (☞ p.172 동사 변화형)

모음이 바뀌는 동사	see – **saw** run – **ran** swim – **swam** come – **came**	give – **gave** speak – **spoke** write – **wrote** wake – **woke**	take – **took** ride – **rode** break – **broke** eat – **ate**	meet – **met** get – **got** find – **found** know – **knew**
단어 끝이 바뀌는 동사	have – **had** make – **made**	hear – **heard** lose – **lost**	build – **built** send – **sent**	lend – **lent** spend – **spent**
모음이 바뀌고 단어 끝이 d, t로 바뀌는 동사	feel – **felt** leave – **left** sleep – **slept**	keep – **kept** buy – **bought** think – **thought**	teach – **taught** catch – **caught** do – **did**	tell – **told** pay – **paid** say – **said**
기타 동사	go – **went**			
원형 = 과거형	hit – **hit**	cut – **cut**	put – **put**	read[ri:d] – **read**[red]

대표 기출 문제

🔒 다음 대화에서 주어진 단어를 이용하거나 변형하여 우리말 문장을 영어 문장으로 쓰시오.

A: What's up?
B: 나는 어제 나쁜 꿈을 꿨어.

Answer: ______________________________ .
　　　(have a bad dream)

CLUE 1
'어제 ~했다'라는 과거에 일어난 일을 나타내므로 일반동사의 과거형을 써야 해요.

CLUE 2
동사 have의 과거형은? — had

정답: I had a bad dream yesterday

Point Exercise

[1-4] 우리말과 일치하도록 주어진 단어를 사용하여 빈칸에 알맞은 말을 쓰세요.

1 그는 시험을 위해 수학을 공부했다. (study)

→ He _______________ math for the test.

2 우리는 수영장에서 수영을 했다. (swim)

→ We _______________ in the pool.

3 Mason은 도서관에 갔다. (go)

→ Mason _______________ to the library.

4 나는 엄마를 위해 카드를 썼다. (write)

→ I _______________ a card for my mom.

[5-7] 다음 주어진 문장을 〈보기〉와 같이 과거형 문장으로 바꿔 쓰세요.

〈보기〉
I watch a movie on Saturday.
→ I watched a movie on Saturday.

5 My sister enjoys her walk in the park.

→ _______________

____

6 Tom reads a book before bedtime.

→ _______________

____

7 We eat some ice cream after lunch.

→ _______________

____

[8-9] 우리말과 일치하도록 주어진 단어를 사용하여 문장을 완성하세요. (필요시 형태를 바꿀 것)

8
Tina는 지난주에 친구들과 함께 사진을 찍었다.
(a picture, take)

→ _______________

with her friends last week.

9
나는 버스에 내 우산을 두고 내렸다.
(leave, I, my umbrella)

→ _______________

on the bus.

10 Dan의 어제 오후 일과표를 보고 과거의 일을 나타내는 문장이 되도록 빈칸에 알맞은 말을 쓰세요.

시간	할 일
12:30	have lunch
2:00	meet his friends

(1) Dan _______________ at 12:30.

(2) Dan _______________ at 2:00.

11 다음 글을 읽고 주어진 단어를 ⓐ~ⓓ에 알맞은 형태로 쓰세요.

I ⓐ _______________ (wake up) late yesterday. I ⓑ _______________ (brush) my teeth and ⓒ _______________ (wash) my face. I ⓓ _______________ (run) to school. However, there was no one in the classroom. It was Sunday yesterday!

---

pool (= swimming pool) 수영장 walk 산책, 걷기 bedtime 잘 시간, 취침 시간 take a picture 사진을 찍다 leave ~을 두고 오다

Unit 03 일반동사의 부정문과 의문문

POINT 5 일반동사의 부정문: don't[doesn't]/didn't+동사원형

나는 추운 날씨를 좋아하지 않는다.

나는 / 좋아하지 **않는다** / 추운 날씨를.

주어(1인칭 단수) 일반동사 현재형의 부정문

→ I / **do not[don't]** like / cold weather.

• 일반동사 현재형의 부정문은 「**do[does] not+동사원형**」 형태로 써요. 각각 don't와 doesn't로 줄여 쓸 수 있어요.

She **doesn't like** hot weather. 그녀는 더운 날씨를 좋아하지 않는다.

1, 2인칭 주어 3인칭 복수 주어	동사	3인칭 단수 주어	동사
I/You/We They …	do not[don't] ~.	He/She/It …	does not[doesn't] ~.

나는 그 영화를 보지 않았다.

나는 / 보지 **않았다** / 그 영화를.

일반동사 과거형의 부정문

→ I / **did not[didn't]** see / the movie.

• 일반동사 과거형의 부정문은 동사원형 앞에 did not을 붙여 「**did not[didn't]+동사원형**」으로 써요.

모든 주어 (인칭과 수에 상관없이)	동사
I/You/We/They/He/She/It …	did not[didn't] ~.

대표 기출 문제

🔒 다음 주어진 표현을 이용하여 <보기>와 같이 부정문을 완성하시오.

〈보기〉 I / like / fast food
→ I don't like fast food.

my sister / eat / anything / at night
→ _______________________

CLUE 1
일반동사 현재형의 부정문
— 「don't[doesn't]+동사원형」

CLUE 2
주어가 3인칭 단수(my sister)이므로, 부정문은
「doesn't+동사원형」으로 써야 해요.

정답: My sister doesn't eat anything at night.

✓ 함정 피하기 주어에 상관없이 don't, doesn't, didn't 뒤에는 항상 동사원형이 오는 것에 주의하세요.
Jessica **doesn't has** a pen. (✕) → *Jessica* **doesn't have** a pen. (○) (Jessica는 펜을 가지고 있지 않다.)
He **didn't ate** breakfast this morning. (✕) → *He* **didn't eat** breakfast this morning. (○)
(그는 오늘 아침에 아침 식사를 하지 않았다.)

Point Exercise

정답 및 해설 p.02

문장 전환

[1-10] 다음 주어진 문장을 부정문으로 바꿔 쓸 때 빈칸에 알맞은 말을 쓰세요. (단, 줄임말을 쓸 것)

1 I remember his name.

→ I ________________ his name.

2 He likes steak and pasta.

→ He ________________ steak and pasta.

3 Our school has a swimming pool.

→ Our school ________________ a swimming pool.

4 Jenny and Bill live in London.

→ Jenny and Bill ________________ in London.

5 My brother gets up early.

→ My brother ________________ early.

6 Mr. Brown exercises every day.

→ Mr. Brown ________________ every day.

7 I cleaned my room this afternoon.

→ I ________________ my room this afternoon.

8 Last week, she visited the museum.

→ Last week, she ________________ the museum.

9 Liam wore a black coat today.

→ Liam ________________ a black coat today.

10 Olivia and I went to school together.

→ Olivia and I ________________ to school together.

주어진 단어로 영작

[11-13] 우리말과 일치하도록 주어진 단어를 사용하여 문장을 완성하세요. (필요시 형태를 바꿀 것)

11
Jack은 지난주에 나에게 전화하지 않았다. (me, call)

→ ________________

________________ last week.

12
Kate는 밤에 TV를 보지 않는다. (watch, TV)

→ ________________

________________ at night.

13
Dave와 Jason은 어제 파티에 오지 않았다. (come, the party, to, and)

→ ________________

________________ yesterday.

기출: 어법 오류 수정

14 다음 밑줄 친 부분을 어법상 알맞게 고쳐 완전한 문장으로 다시 쓰세요. (시제는 바꾸지 말 것)

(1) My mom and dad doesn't drink coffee.

→ ________________

____

(2) The dog doesn't sleeps in its bed.

→ ________________

____

(3) I didn't bought a gift for my sister.

→ ________________

____

get up 일어나다 museum 박물관, 미술관

POINT 6 — 일반동사의 의문문: Do[Does]/Did + 주어 + 동사원형 ~?

A: 그녀는 매일 개를 산책시키나요?　B: 네, 그래요. / 아니요, 그렇지 않아요.
그녀는 산책시키나요 / 그녀의 개를 / 매일?
일반동사 현재형의 의문문

→ A: **Does** *she* **walk** / her dog / every day?
　 B: Yes, *she* **does**. / No, *she* **doesn't**.

- 일반동사 현재형의 의문문은 '~하니?'라는 의미로, **주어 앞에 Do나 Does**를 써서 나타내요.
- 주어가 3인칭 단수일 때는 Does를 써야 해요.

일반동사의 의문문			긍정의 대답	부정의 대답
Do	I/you/we/they/3인칭 복수 주어		Yes, 주어+do.	No, 주어+don't.
Does	3인칭 단수 주어(he/she/it/단수명사)	+동사원형 ~?	Yes, 주어+does.	No, 주어+doesn't.
Did	모든 주어(주어의 인칭과 수에 상관없이)		Yes, 주어+did.	No, 주어+didn't.

A: 너는 그 축구 경기를 봤니?　B: 응, 그래. / 아니, 보지 않았어.
너는 봤니 / 그 축구 경기를?
일반동사 과거형의 의문문

→ A: **Did** *you* **watch** / the soccer game?
　 B: Yes, *I* **did**. / No, *I* **didn't**.

- 일반동사 과거형의 의문문은 주어의 인칭과 수에 상관없이 **주어 앞에 Did**를 써요.

대표 기출 문제

다음 주어진 표현을 활용하여 대화의 빈칸에 들어갈 알맞은 문장을 쓰시오.

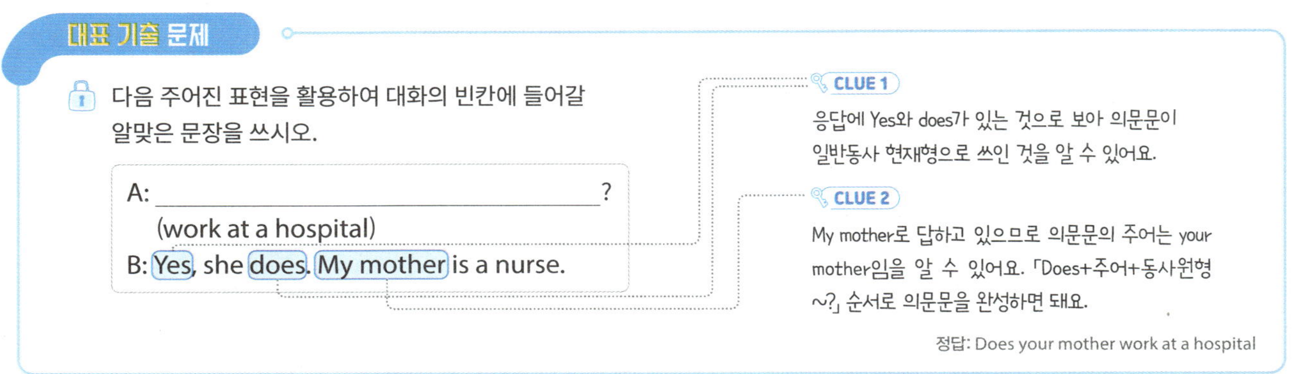

A: ________________________ ?
　(work at a hospital)
B: Yes, she does. My mother is a nurse.

CLUE 1
응답에 Yes와 does가 있는 것으로 보아 의문문이 일반동사 현재형으로 쓰인 것을 알 수 있어요.

CLUE 2
My mother로 답하고 있으므로 의문문의 주어는 your mother임을 알 수 있어요. 「Does+주어+동사원형 ~?」 순서로 의문문을 완성하면 돼요.

정답: Does your mother work at a hospital

함정 피하기 일반동사 의문문에서 주어가 3인칭 단수일 때도 「Does+주어」 뒤에는 항상 동사원형을 써야 해요.
「Did+주어」 뒤에도 동사의 과거형을 쓰지 않아야 합니다.
Does *he* **has** a pen? (✕) → **Does** *he* **have** a pen? (○) (그는 펜을 가지고 있니?)
Did *you* **went** to school by bus? (✕) → **Did** *you* **go** to school by bus? (○) (너는 학교에 버스를 타고 갔니?)

Point Exercise

[1-4] 우리말과 일치하도록 주어진 단어를 올바르게 배열하세요.

1
> 당신은 도움이 좀 필요하신가요?
> (you / any help / need / do)

→ _______________________________________ ?

2
> 그녀는 매일 뉴스를 보나요?
> (watch / does / she / the news)

→ _______________________________________

_______________________________ every day?

3
> 너와 Linda는 이번 주말에 계획이 있니?
> (you / plans / have / do / and Linda)

→ _______________________________________

_______________________ for this weekend?

4
> 너는 지난주 금요일에 쇼핑하러 갔니?
> (you / did / shopping / go)

→ _______________________________________

_______________________________ last Friday?

[5-6] 다음 주어진 문장을 의문문으로 바꿔 쓰세요.

5 Bella worries about the history exam.

→ _______________________________________

____

6 He got the tickets for the concert.

→ _______________________________________

____

[7-10] 다음 대화의 빈칸에 알맞은 응답을 쓰세요.

7
> A: Do you have sunglasses?
> B: __________, __________ __________.
> I have to buy some.

8
> A: Does she speak any other languages?
> B: __________, __________ __________.
> She speaks French, too.

9
> A: Does Charlie take a bus to school?
> B: __________, __________ __________.
> He walks to school.

10
> A: Did the students go on a picnic today?
> B: __________, __________ __________.
> They will go tomorrow.

11 자연스러운 대화가 되도록 주어진 단어를 사용하여 질문을 완성하세요.

(1) A: _______________________________________

____

(she, my phone number, know)

B: Yes, she does. She will call you.

(2) A: _______________________________________

____

(break, the glass, you)

B: No, I didn't. My brother did it.

---

go shopping 쇼핑하러 가다 exam 시험 other (그 밖의) 다른 language 언어, 말 French 프랑스어 go on a picnic 소풍 가다

Chapter Test *

정답 및 해설 p.03

STAGE 1) Go for it!

자신 있게 풀어보는 기초 문제!

○ 배열 영작

[1-4] 우리말과 일치하도록 주어진 단어를 올바르게 배열하여 문장을 완성하세요.

1
> 나의 아빠는 경찰관이시다.
> (is / a police officer / my dad)

→ _______________________________.

2
> 나의 이모는 월요일마다 요가 수업을 들으신다.
> (a yoga class / takes / my aunt)

→ _______________________________
every Monday.

3
> Mike는 어제 학교에 지각하지 않았다.
> (was / for / late / Mike / not / school)

→ _______________________________
yesterday.

4
> 너는 어젯밤에 네 숙제를 끝냈니?
> (finish / you / did / your homework)

→ _______________________________
last night?

○ 주어진 단어로 영작

[5-8] 우리말과 일치하도록 주어진 단어를 사용하여 문장을 완성하세요. (필요시 형태를 바꿀 것)

5
> 내 친구와 나는 같은 동아리에 있다.
> (the same, in, club)

→ My friend and I _______________________________
_______________________________.

6
> 우리는 오늘 아침을 먹지 않았다.
> (breakfast, have)

→ We _______________________________
_______________________________ today.

7
> 그 도서관은 오후 6시에 문을 닫나요?
> (close, the library)

→ _______________________________
_______________________________ at 6 p.m.?

8
> 나는 일요일에 컴퓨터 게임을 한다.
> (computer games, play)

→ _______________________________
_______________________________ on Sunday.

최신 기출

9 우리말과 일치하도록 주어진 단어를 배열하여 다음의 대화를 완성하세요.

> A: Smith 씨는 간호사이신가요?
>   (Ms. Smith / is / a nurse)
> B: 아니요, 그렇지 않아요. 그녀는 의사예요.
>   (she / a doctor / she / is / no / isn't)

(1) A: _______________________________ ?

(2) B: _______________, _______________________.
_______________________________.

대화문 완성

[10-15] 주어진 단어를 사용하여 각 대화를 완성하세요.

10
A: James, do you know that boy?
B: Yes, ____________ ____________
____________ ____________. (my friend)
We are in the same class.

11
A: Are you a high school student?
B: ____________, ____________ ____________.
(no) I'm a middle school student.

12
A: Does Susan play the violin?
B: No, ____________ ____________
____________ ____________ ____________.
(the violin, play) She plays the drums.

13
A: ____________ ____________ ____________
____________ ____________ last week?
(in Seoul, your sister)
B: No, she wasn't. She was in Busan.

14
A: Is Olivia in the bathroom?
B: No, she isn't. She ____________
____________ ____________ ____________
____________. (the living room, in)

15
A: ____________ ____________ ____________
____________ ____________ yesterday?
(see, a movie)
B: Yes, I did. I saw it with my family.

그림 영작

[16-17] 다음 그림을 보고 과거의 일을 나타내는 문장이 되도록
〈보기〉에서 알맞은 단어를 사용하여 문장을 완성하세요.

〈보기〉		
fix	break	clean
the window	her desk	her room

16 Mia ____________________________ yesterday.

17 Minho ____________________________ a week
ago.

최신 기출

18 다음 그림은 Andy의 가족이 지난 주말에 캠핑에 가서
한 일을 나타내요. 주어진 단어를 사용하여 글을 완성하세요.

Last week, Andy's family went camping. Andy's
dad (1) ____________________________.
(the guitar, play) Emily sang a song with her
dad. But Andy (2) ____________________________
____________________________ with them. (sing)
He (3) ____________________________ in the lake. (swim)

[19-27] 다음 각 문장에서 어법상 **틀린** 부분을 찾아 바르게 고쳐 쓰세요.

19 I amn't tired now.

_______________ → _______________

20 Does she visits her grandma on weekends?

_______________ → _______________

21 Kevin washs his hands before meals.

_______________ → _______________

22 My brother don't wears gloves in winter.

_______________ → _______________

23 Jane and I am in the subway now.

_______________ → _______________

24 I finded some old photos in the drawer.

_______________ → _______________

25 Is your father drive to work?

_______________ → _______________

26 Do you borrow a book last week?

_______________ → _______________

27 Is the students nervous before the exam?

_______________ → _______________

[28-31] 다음 각 문장을 괄호 안의 지시대로 바꿔 쓰세요.

28
> John does the homework at home.
> (의문문으로)

→ _______________

29
> She grows flowers in the garden.
> (부정문으로)

→ _______________

30
> I heard the news yesterday.
> (부정문으로)

→ _______________

31
> Your friends were in the mall.
> (의문문으로)

→ _______________

최신 기출

32 다음은 Amy에 관한 소개 글이에요. 어법상 틀린 문장 <u>두 개</u>를 찾아 그 문장 전체를 바르게 고쳐 쓰세요.

> Amy is 14 years old. She are a middle school student. She lives with her parents and her dog, Molly. She likes art, but she don't likes math. She paints every day.

(1) _______________

(2) _______________

○━ (도표 영작)

33 다음 일과표를 보고 〈보기〉와 같이 빈칸에 알맞은 말을 넣어 문장을 완성하세요.

Schedule	I	Janet
cook breakfast	○	○
read a newspaper after breakfast	○	×
study Chinese at school	×	○
watch TV at night	×	×

〈보기〉
I <u>cook</u> breakfast.
Janet <u>cooks</u> breakfast.

(1) I _________________ a newspaper after breakfast.

Janet _________________

a newspaper after breakfast.

(2) I _________________

Chinese at school.

Janet _________________ Chinese at school.

(3) I _________________

TV at night.

Janet _________________

TV at night.

○━ (어법 오류 수정)

34 다음은 Cindy가 친구에게 받은 편지입니다. 다음 ⓐ~ⓔ 중 어법상 **틀린 두 개**를 찾아 그 기호를 쓰고, 문장 전체를 바르게 고쳐 쓰세요.

Dear Cindy,

　How are you doing? Thank you for your Christmas card. ⓐ <u>Did you really make it?</u> I liked your drawing on the card.

　On Christmas, ⓑ <u>I went to Disneyland</u> with my family. The next day, ⓒ <u>we eated delicious seafood</u> at the beach. ⓓ <u>We also stayed at a nice hotel</u> near the beach.

　ⓔ <u>Did you had a good time</u> on Christmas, too? Tell me about it! I miss you so much.

Love,
Sara

_________ → _________________

_________ → _________________

현재진행형과 미래 표현

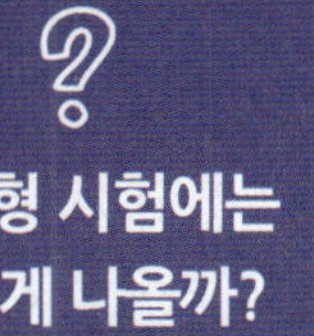

✅ Before You Write

- ☑ '(지금) ~하고 있다, ~하는 중이다'와 '(앞으로) ~할 것이다'는 각각 동사를 어떻게 활용해서 나타낼까요?
- ☑ 긍정문/부정문/의문문 중 어떤 문장 형태여야 할까요?
- ☑ 동사는 주어의 인칭과 수에 맞게 어떤 형태로 써야 할까요?

내신 기출 다음 우리말을 보고 머릿속으로 한번 영어 문장을 떠올려 보세요.

1 나는 지금 숙제를 하는 중이다. (my, do, now)
현재진행형 → 긍정문 → 1인칭 단수 주어 → **I am doing**   `POINT 1`

2 그는 지금 수영을 하고 있지 않다.
현재진행형 → 부정문 → 3인칭 단수 주어 → **He is not swimming ~?**   `POINT 2`

3 (2) 그녀는 지금 춤을 추는 중이니?
현재진행형 → 의문문 → 3인칭 단수 주어 → **Is she dancing ~?**   `POINT 2`

4 Q: What will you be in the future?
A: 나는 축구 선수가 될 거야.
미래 표현 → 긍정문 → **I will be**   `POINT 3`

5 You will feel great and (A) 쉽게 병에 걸리지 않을 것입니다.
미래 표현 → 부정문 → **will not get**   `POINT 3`

6 It is Sungmin's favorite animal in the shop.
③ 우리는 다음 주말에 이 가게를 방문할 것이다. (going to)
미래 표현 → 긍정문 → 1인칭 복수 주어 → **We are going to visit**   `POINT 4`

정답: **1** I am[I'm] doing my homework now. **2** He is not[isn't] swimming now. **3** Is she dancing now? **4** I will[I'll] be a soccer player.
5 will not[won't] get sick easily **6** We are[We're] going to visit this shop next weekend.

Unit 01

현재진행형

POINT 1 ~하고 있다: am/are/is+동사의 -ing형

> Amy는 책을 읽고 있다.
> Amy는 / 읽고 있다 / 책을.
>   현재진행형
>
> → Amy / **is** read**ing** / a book.

- '~하고 있다, ~하는 중이다'라고 지금 일어나고 있는 일을 말할 때는 현재진행형인 「**am/are/is+동사의 -ing형**」으로 나타내요.
- 이때 be동사는 주어의 인칭과 수에 알맞은 형태로 써야 해요.

📣 동사의 -ing형 만드는 법

대부분의 동사	동사원형+-ing	doing　going　eating　watching studying　playing　flying　reading
-e로 끝나는 동사	-e를 없애고 +-ing	make → making　ride → riding　take → taking
-ie로 끝나는 동사	-ie를 y로 바꾸고 +-ing	lie → lying　die → dying
「모음 1개+자음 1개」로 끝나는 1음절 동사	마지막 자음을 한 번 더 쓰고 +-ing	planning　running　winning　swimming sitting　putting　cutting　shopping

주의

동사 have는 '가지다'의 의미일 때 진행형으로 쓸 수 없지만, '먹다, (경험을) 하다'라는 의미일 때는 진행형으로 쓸 수 있어요.
She ~~is having~~(→ **has**) a good voice. (그녀는 좋은 목소리를 가지고 있다.)
I **am having** breakfast. (나는 아침을 먹고 있다.)
We **are having** a good time. (우리는 좋은 시간을 보내고 있다.)

대표 기출 문제

🔒 주어진 한글 뜻과 일치하도록 문장을 완성하시오.

A: What is Jinny doing?
B: ______________________________ .
(그녀는 자전거를 타고 있다.)

CLUE 1
A의 질문에서 사용된 동사의 형태는?
— be동사+동사의 -ing형

CLUE 2
'자전거를 타다'라는 의미의 영어 표현(ride a bike)을 현재진행형 「be동사(am/are/is)+동사의 -ing형」으로 써야 해요. 이때 주어(She)에 알맞은 be동사를 써야 합니다.

정답: She is[She's] riding a bike

Point Exercise

배열 영작

[1-4] 우리말과 일치하도록 주어진 단어를 올바르게 배열하세요.

1
> 그녀는 생일 카드를 쓰고 있다.
> (a birthday card / she / writing / is)

→ ____
____ .

2
> Henry는 휴식을 취하고 있다.
> (taking / is / a rest / Henry)

→ ____
____ .

3
> 아이들이 운동장에서 달리고 있다.
> (are / running / children)

→ ____
______________________________ in the playground.

4
> 내 친구는 피자를 자르고 있다.
> (is / my friend / the pizza / cutting)

→ ____
____ .

주어진 단어로 영작

[5-8] 우리말과 일치하도록 주어진 단어를 사용하여
현재진행형으로 문장을 완성하세요.

5
> 나는 해변에 누워 있다.
> (lie, I, on the beach)

→ ____

6
> 그는 신문을 읽고 있다.
> (read, he, a newspaper)

→ ____
____

7
> 그녀의 건강이 좋아지고 있다.
> (health, get better, her)

→ ____
____

8
> 몇몇 사람들이 벤치에 앉아 있다.
> (some people, sit)

→ ____
______________________________ on the bench.

기출 그림 영작

9 다음 그림을 보고 〈보기〉에서 알맞은 표현을 골라 현재
진행형으로 문장을 완성하세요.

(1)   (2)

> 〈보기〉
> listen to music   watch TV
> go to a movie   talk on the phone

(1) The boy ______________________________ .

(2) Suji and her friend ______________________________
____ .

take a rest 휴식을 취하다, 쉬다 lie 누워 있다, 눕다; 거짓말하다 get better (병 등이) 좋아지다 bench 벤치 go to a movie 영화 보러 가다 talk on the phone 전화로 이야기하다

 현재진행형의 부정문과 의문문

그는 지금 교복을 입고 있지 않다.
그는 / 입고 있지 않다 / 그의 교복을 / 지금.
_{현재진행형 부정문}

→ He / **is not[isn't] wearing** / his school uniform / now.

- '~하고 있지 않다, ~하는 중이 아니다'라는 의미의 현재진행형 부정문은 **be동사 뒤에 not**을 붙여,
「**am/are/is not＋동사의 -ing형**」으로 나타내요.

A: Mia는 음악을 듣고 있니?　　　　　　　B: 응, 맞아. / 아니, 그렇지 않아.
　　Mia는 듣고 있니 / 음악을?
　_{현재진행형 의문문}

→ A: **Is** Mia **listening** / to music?　B: Yes, she **is**. / No, she **isn't**.

is listening to music의 줄임말

📢 **현재진행형의 의문문과 대답**

의문문	대답
Am/Are/Is＋주어＋동사의 -ing형 ~? (~하고 있니?, ~하고 있는 중이니?)	Yes, 주어＋am/are/is.　「be동사+not」은 보통 줄임말을 써요. No, 주어＋am/are/is＋not.

대표 기출 문제

🔒 주어진 한글 뜻과 일치하도록 문장을 완성하시오.

> Brian has a test tomorrow. But he _________
> _________ _________ (공부하고 있지 않다) now
> because he is tired. (study)

CLUE
'~하고 있지 않다'라는 현재진행형의 부정문 형태는?
— 「be동사(am/are/is)+not+동사의 -ing형」

정답: is not studying

🔒 다음 괄호 안의 단어를 사용하여 알맞은 형태로 바꾸시오.

> A: Is Jack _____________? (swim)
> 　(Jack은 수영을 하고 있니?)
> B: No, he _____________.
> 　(아니, 그렇지 않아.)

CLUE 1
'~하고 있니?'라고 묻는 말이므로 현재진행형 의문문
으로 써요.
— 「be동사(Am/Are/Is)+주어+동사의 -ing형 ~?」

CLUE 2
No로 시작하는 부정의 대답이므로, 주어(he)에 알맞
은 be동사의 부정형으로 응답하면 돼요.

정답: swimming, isn't

Point Exercise

◯ 배열 영작

[1-5] 우리말과 일치하도록 주어진 단어를 올바르게 배열하세요.

1
> 그 아기는 지금 울고 있니?
> (the baby / is / crying)

→ ___________________________________
___________________________________ now?

2
> 그는 오늘 그의 안경을 쓰고 있지 않다.
> (his glasses / not / he / wearing / is)

→ ___________________________________
___________________________________ today.

3
> Rachel은 피아노를 연습하고 있지 않다.
> (not / Rachel / the piano / is / practicing)

→ ___________________________________
___________________________________ .

4
> 그들은 지금 경기에 이기고 있지 않다.
> (winning / are / the game / they / not)

→ ___________________________________
___________________________________ now.

5
> 너는 네 숙제를 하고 있니?
> (are / doing / you / homework / your)

→ ___________________________________
___________________________________ ?

◯ 주어진 단어로 영작

[6-9] 우리말과 일치하도록 주어진 단어를 사용하여 문장을 완성하세요. (필요시 형태를 바꿀 것)

6
> Tom이 저녁 식사를 요리하고 있니?
> (cook, dinner)

→ ___________________________________

7
> Nancy는 그림을 그리고 있지 않다.
> (draw, pictures)

→ ___________________________________

8
> 내 친구들은 테니스를 치고 있지 않다.
> (play, my, tennis, friends)

→ ___________________________________

9
> 그들은 버스를 기다리고 있니?
> (wait for, they, a bus)

→ ___________________________________

◯ 기출: 대화문 완성

10 우리말과 일치하도록 주어진 단어를 사용하여 다음의 대화를 완성하세요.

> A: Kate는 도서관에서 공부를 하고 있니? (study)
> B: 아니, 그렇지 않아. 그녀는 점심을 먹고 있어.
>   (have, lunch)

A: ___________________________________ in the library?

B: No, ___________________________________ .
___________________________________ .

practice 연습하다   wait for ～을 기다리다

미래 표현

POINT 3 ~할[일] 것이다: will+동사원형

수업은 오전 9시에 시작할 것이다.
수업은 / 시작할 것이다 / 오전 9시에.

→ The class / **will** start / at 9 a.m.

• 우리말의 '~할[일] 것이다'는 앞으로 일어나리라고 생각되는 일을 말할 때 쓰는 표현이에요.
• 영어에서는 **will**을 사용하여 표현할 수 있는데, will 다음에는 항상 **동사원형**을 써야 해요.
• will은 인칭대명사 주어와 함께 쓰일 때 'll로 줄여 쓸 수 있어요.

나는 네 생일을 잊지 않을 거야.
나는 / 잊지 않을 것이다 / 네 생일을.

→ I / **will not[won't]** forget / your birthday.

A: 미나는 3월에 16살이 되니?　　B: 응, 맞아. / 아니, 그렇지 않아.
미나는 ~이 되니 / 16살 / 3월에?

→ A: **Will** Mina **be** / sixteen / in March?
　 B: Yes, she **will**. / No, she **won't**.

📢 will의 부정문과 의문문

부정문	의문문
will not[won't]+동사원형 (~하지 않을 것이다)	Will+주어+동사원형 ~? (~할 거니?) – Yes, 주어+will. / No, 주어+won't.

대표 기출 문제

🔒 밑줄 친 우리말과 뜻이 같도록 다음의 단어를 이용하여
완전한 문장으로 쓰시오.

Tomorrow, Mike는 친구와 함께 놀 것이다.
(play, will, friends, his, with)
→ Tomorrow, ＿＿＿＿＿＿＿＿＿＿＿＿＿＿ .

CLUE 1
앞으로 일어날 일(~할 것이다)은 will을 사용해 나타
낼 수 있어요.

CLUE 2
will 다음에 오는 동사(play)의 형태는? — 동사원형

정답: Mike will play with his friends

✅ 함정 피하기　will 다음에 동사원형 이외의 형태를 쓰지 않도록 주의하세요.
She will ~~goes~~(→ go) to the library. She will ~~to go~~(→ go) to the library. (그녀는 도서관에 갈 것이다.)
Will you ~~are~~(→ be) at home tonight? (너는 오늘 밤에 집에 있을 거니?)

Point Exercise

배열 영작

[1-5] 우리말과 일치하도록 주어진 단어를 올바르게 배열하세요.

1
> Harry는 공원에서 자전거를 빌릴 것이다.
> (a bike / will / borrow / Harry)

→ ___________________________
___________________________ in the park.

2
> Hazel은 그녀의 마음을 바꾸지 않을 거야.
> (change / Hazel / not / her mind / will)

→ ___________________________
___________________________ .

3
> 그 가게는 5분 뒤에 문을 닫을 것이다.
> (will / the door / the store / close)

→ ___________________________
___________________________ in 5 minutes.

4
> 그들은 제시간에 도착할까?
> (arrive / they / on time / will)

→ ___________________________
___________________________ ?

5
> 우리는 이 순간을 잊지 않을 것이다.
> (forget / we / this / not / will / moment)

→ ___________________________
___________________________ .

주어진 단어로 영작

[6-9] 우리말과 일치하도록 주어진 단어와 will을 사용하여 문장을 완성하세요. (필요시 형태를 바꿀 것)

6
> Mike는 이번 주말에 가방을 살 것이다. (a bag, buy)

→ ___________________________
this weekend.

7
> 걱정하지 마. 그녀는 늦지 않을 거야.
> (be, she, late)

→ Don't worry. ___________________________
____

8
> 나는 오늘 이 검은색 코트를 입지 않을 것이다.
> (wear, I, black coat, this)

→ ___________________________
___________________________ today.

9
> 너는 미술 동아리에 가입할 거니?
> (join, the art club, you)

→ ___________________________

기출: 대화문 완성

10 우리말과 일치하도록 주어진 단어와 will을 사용하여 다음의 대화를 완성하세요.

> A: 너는 포크를 사용할 거니? (a fork, use)
> B: 아니, 그러지 않을 거야.
>   나는 젓가락을 사용할 거야. (chopsticks, use)

A: ___________________________

B: No, ___________________________ .
____

change one's mind 마음[생각]을 바꾸다 on time 제시간에 moment 순간 club 동아리, 클럽 chopsticks 젓가락

~할[일] 것이다, ~할 예정이다: be going to+동사원형

나는 영화를 볼 예정이다.
나는 / 볼 예정이다 / 영화를.

→ I / **am going to** watch / a movie.

- '~할[일] 것이다, ~할 예정이다'는 예정된 계획을 나타내요. 이와 같이 미래에 일어날 일, 예정된 계획이나 의도를 나타낼 때는 「**be going to+동사원형**」으로도 표현해요.

그녀는 우리 계획에 동의하지 않을 것이다.
그녀는 / 동의하지 않을 것이다 / 우리 계획에.

→ She / **is not[isn't] going to** agree / with our plan.

A: 너는 곧 점심을 먹을 예정이니?   B: 응, 그래. / 아니, 그렇지 않아.
너는 먹을 예정이니 / 점심을 / 곧?

→ A: **Are** you **going to** eat / lunch / soon?
B: Yes, I **am**. / No, I**'m not**.

📢 be going to의 부정문과 의문문

부정문	의문문
be동사+not+going to+동사원형 (~하지 않을 예정이다)	be동사+주어+going to+동사원형 ~? (~할 예정이니?) – Yes, 주어+be동사. / No, 주어+be동사+not.

대표 기출 문제

🔒 주어진 단어를 활용하여 문장을 완성하시오.

그녀는 이번 주말에 쇼핑을 갈 예정이다.
(shopping / to / going / be / go)

→ She (   ) (   ) (   ) (   ) (   )
this weekend.

CLUE 1
'~할 예정이다'라는 우리말로 보아 미래의 일!

CLUE 2
주어진 단어로 나타낼 수 있는 미래 표현은?
— 「be going to+동사원형」

정답: is going to go shopping

✅ **함정 피하기** 미래 표현 「be going to go(갈 것이다)」와 진행형 「be동사+going to(~에 가는 중이다)」를 혼동하지 않도록 주의해야 해요.
그는 파티에 갈 것이다. → He **is going to go** to the party. <미래 표현>
그는 파티에 가고 있다. → He **is going to** the party. <현재진행형>

Point Exercise

○ **배열 영작**

[1-5] 우리말과 일치하도록 주어진 단어를 올바르게 배열하세요.

1

우리는 기타 수업을 함께 들을 것이다.
(take / are / to / going / we / a guitar class)

→ ______________________________________

______________________________________ together.

2

Mark와 그의 친구들은 오늘 축구를 하지 않을 것이다.
(not / to / soccer / going / are / play)

→ Mark and his friends ______________________

______________________________________ today.

3

그들은 오늘 밤에 외식하지 않을 것이다.
(going / they / to / are / eat out / not)

→ ______________________________________

______________________________________ tonight.

4

우리 팀이 그 퀴즈 대회에서 우승할 것이다.
(the quiz contest / win / is / our team / to / going)

→ ______________________________________

______________________________________ .

5

Lucas는 그의 파티에 많은 사람을 초대할 예정이니?
(going / people / Lucas / many / to / is / invite)

→ ______________________________________

______________________________________ to his party?

○ **주어진 단어로 영작**

[6-8] 우리말과 일치하도록 주어진 단어와 be going to를 사용하여 문장을 완성하세요. (필요시 형태를 바꿀 것)

6

Teddy는 한국의 축제에 대해 이야기할 예정이다.
(talk about, Korean festivals)

→ ______________________________________

____

7

나는 오늘 산에 오르지 않을 것이다.
(climb, I, the mountain)

→ ______________________________________

______________________________________ today.

8

그녀는 일주일 동안 여기서 머무를 예정이니?
(stay, she, here)

→ ______________________________________

______________________________________ for a week?

기출: 조건 영작

9 다음 대화를 읽고 〈조건〉에 맞게 우리말을 영작하세요.

A: Sangho, what are you going to do this weekend?
B: 나는 미술관에 갈 거야. There are a lot of famous paintings there.

〈조건〉
• 9 단어로 쓸 것
• to, go, the art museum을 사용할 것

→ ______________________________________

____

---

eat out 외식하다 contest 대회, 시합 art museum 미술관

Chapter Test [*]

정답 및 해설 p.05

STAGE 1 · Go for it!

자신 있게 풀어보는 기초 문제!

빈칸 완성

[1-4] 우리말과 일치하도록 주어진 단어를 사용하여 빈칸에 알맞은 말을 쓰세요. (필요시 형태를 바꿀 것)

1
> 오리들이 호수에서 수영을 하고 있다. (swim)

→ Ducks ______________ ______________
in a lake.

2
> 그는 샤워를 하고 있지 않다. (take)

→ He ______________ ______________
______________ a shower.

3
> 그녀는 뉴욕시를 방문할 예정이다. (visit)

→ She ______________ ______________
______________ ______________
New York City.

4
> 나는 금요일에 저녁을 먹으러 나갈 것이다. (go out)

→ I ______________ ______________
______________ for dinner on Friday.

배열 영작

[5-7] 우리말과 일치하도록 주어진 단어를 배열하여 문장을 완성하세요. (필요시 형태를 바꿀 것)

5
> 그는 체육관에서 운동을 하고 있니?
> (exercise / at the gym / be / he)

→ ______________
______________ ?

6
> Tim은 파티에 오지 않을 것이다.
> (not / the party / come / Tim / will / to)

→ ______________
______________ .

7
> 그들은 새집으로 이사할 예정이다.
> (to a new house / going / they / be / to / move)

→ ______________
______________ .

최신 기출

8 우리말과 일치하도록 주어진 단어를 배열하여 다음의 대화를 완성하세요. (필요시 형태를 바꿀 것)

> A: What is Claire doing now?
> B: <u>그녀는 그녀의 반 친구들을 위해 바닥을 청소하는 중이야.</u>
>   (be / she / the floor / clean / her / for / classmates)
> A: Oh, she's really nice.

→ ______________
______________ .

대화문 완성

[9-13] 주어진 단어를 사용하여 각 대화를 완성하세요.

9
A: What is John doing in his room now?
B: He ______________________________.
(draw, a picture)

10
A: What are Jiwon and Suji doing now?
B: They ______________________________
______________________________.
(kick, a soccer ball)

11
A: What are you going to do after school?
B: I ______________________________
______________________________.
(ride, a bike, be)

12
A: What will Sumin do on Sunday?
B: She ______________________________
______________________________.
(cook, with, will, her mom)

13
A: What is your dad going to do tomorrow?
B: He ______________________________
______________________________.
(fix, be, my computer)

그림 영작

[14-15] 다음 그림을 보고 주어진 단어를 사용하여 질문에 답하세요.

14
A: What is she doing now?
B: ______________________________
______________________________ (listen to)

15
A: What are they doing now?
B: ______________________________
______________________________ (play)

최신 기출

16 〈보기〉에서 알맞은 단어를 골라 will 또는 won't를 사용하여 콘서트 관객 유치를 위해 홍보하는 글을 완성하세요. (단, 한 번씩만 쓸 것)

〈보기〉
be   play   sing   take place

The concert (1) ___________ ___________
___________ in the school gym. Nate and
Sam (2) ___________ ___________ the
guitar. Jenny (3) ___________ ___________
some popular songs. You (4) ___________
___________ bored. You'll love it!

[17-21] 다음 각 문장을 괄호 안의 지시대로 바꿔 쓰세요.

17
> He makes cookies for the Christmas party.
> (현재진행형으로)

→ _______________________________

____

18
> Jenny is going to return my book on
> Saturday. (부정문으로)

→ _______________________________

____

19
> I drink a cup of tea after lunch.
> (현재진행형으로)

→ _______________________________

____

20
> The English class will begin at 10 a.m.
> (의문문으로)

→ _______________________________

____

21
> Our school is going to finish early today.
> (의문문으로)

→ _______________________________

____

[22-26] 다음 각 문장에서 어법상 **틀린** 부분을 찾아 바르게 고쳐 쓰세요.

22 Sally's little brother is stand behind her now.

_____________ → _____________

23 My parents is going to buy a new car.

_____________ → _____________

24 Is Janet come here now?

_____________ → _____________

25 He is going not to visit his grandmother this weekend.

_____________ → _____________

26 Will your sister goes to your school next year?

_____________ → _____________

27 다음 글의 밑줄 친 문장을 〈조건〉에 맞게 올바른 문장으로 고쳐 쓰세요.

> Right now, I'm playing a game on my phone. I actually don't exercise much, so I'm gaining weight. I will change my lifestyle.
> First, (1) I start exercising this summer. (2) I eat junk food like hamburgers and coke.

〈조건〉
· (1)은 be going to를, (2)는 will을 사용해 글의 흐름에 맞게 쓸 것
· (1)은 7 단어, (2)는 9 단어로 쓸 것

(1) _______________________________

____

(2) _______________________________

____

◦〔도표 영작〕

28 다음 Liam의 여행 계획표를 보고 〈조건〉에 맞게 대화를 완성하세요.

Travel Plan

✔ travel to Japan

✔ in August

✔ go by ship

〈조건〉
- be going to를 사용하여 미래를 표현할 것
- 표에 있는 단어를 사용할 것

Peter: Hey, Liam. Do you have any plans for this
summer?

Liam: Of course.
My family (1) _________________
to Japan in August.

Peter: That sounds great!
(2) _________________
by plane?

Liam: No, we (3) _________________.
We (4) _________________
there by ship.

◦〔조건 영작〕

29 다음 대화를 읽고 〈조건〉에 맞게 문장을 완성하세요.

(Two people are talking on the phone.)
A: Where are you, Sam? Are you going to see a
movie tonight?
B: No, I'm not. My mom is sick, and she's in the
hospital.
A: I'm sorry to hear that. (1) _________________
_________________ her?
____
(your dad, take care of)
B: Yes, he is. He'll stay with her at the hospital
tonight.
A: Then, what about you and your sister?
B: We (2) _________________
_________________ right now.
(go, our uncle's house, to)
We'll stay there tonight.
A: Oh, I see.

〈조건〉
- 각각 6 단어로 쓸 것
- 주어진 단어를 사용하되 필요시 형태를 바꿀 것

⚡ **Challenge!**   누적 문제 Ch 01-02

30 다음 중 어법상 틀린 문장 두 개를 찾아 그 기호를
쓰고, 문장 전체를 바르게 고쳐 쓰세요.

ⓐ The store opens at 9 o'clock.
ⓑ Leo and I aren't members of the club.
ⓒ The movie will start in ten minutes.
ⓓ Are your friends have a pet dog?
ⓔ My little brother is sleep on the sofa now.

_______ → _________________
____

_______ → _________________
____

Chapter 03 조동사

?
서술형 시험에는 어떻게 나올까?

✅ Before You Write

- ☑ 문장의 의미에 따라 어떤 조동사를 써야 할까요?
- ☑ 조동사 뒤에 오는 동사는 어떤 형태로 써야 할까요?
- ☑ 긍정문/부정문/의문문 중 어떤 문장 형태여야 할까요?

내신 기출 다음 우리말을 보고 머릿속으로 한번 영어 문장을 떠올려 보세요.

1 B: 아니, 나는 테니스(tennis)를 칠 수 있어.
<can 사용하기>
→ (2) No, I can't, but ＿＿＿＿＿＿＿＿＿＿＿ tennis.
can (능력) → 긍정문 → **can play**　　`POINT 1`

2 B: Yes, please. Can I try on this jacket?
M: Yes, of course. (A) 당신은 어떤 상품이든 입어볼 수 있어요 in our shop.
can (허가) → 긍정문 → **can try on**　　`POINT 2`

3 A: 창문을 닫아줄래? It's a little cold.
• 다음 단어들을 반드시 사용할 것 (can, the window)
can (요청) → 의문문 → **Can you close ~?**　　`POINT 3`

4 여러분이 믿지 못할 수도 있지만,
→ You ＿＿＿＿＿ ＿＿＿＿＿ ＿＿＿＿＿ this,
may (추측) → 부정문 → **may not believe**　　`POINT 4`

5 (1) 너는 번화한 거리에서 조심해야만 한다.
(streets, must, busy, on, careful, be)
→ You ＿＿＿＿＿＿＿＿＿＿＿＿＿＿＿.
must (의무) → 긍정문 → **must be**　　`POINT 5`

6 밤에는 우유를 마시지 않는 것이 좋다. (should, drink)
→ You ＿＿＿＿＿＿＿＿＿＿＿ at night.
should (조언) → 부정문 → **should not drink**　　`POINT 6`

정답: **1** I can play **2** You can try on any items **3** Can you close the window? **4** may not believe **5** must be careful on busy streets
6 should not[shouldn't] drink

can, may

 **POINT 1**

~할 수 있다: can

그는 영어를 잘 말할 수 있다.
그는 / 말할 수 있다 / 영어를 / 잘.
　　　can+동사원형

→ He / **can** speak / English / well.

- '~할 수 있다'라는 **능력·가능**을 나타낼 때 조동사 can을 쓸 수 있어요. can과 같은 조동사 뒤에는 반드시 **동사원형**을 써야 해요.
- '~할 수 없다'라고 부정문을 쓸 때는 「cannot[can't]+동사원형」을 씁니다.
  I **can't swim** at all. 나는 수영을 전혀 못 해.

A: 너는 영어를 잘 말할 수 있니?　　　　　B: 응, 할 수 있어. / 아니, 할 수 없어.
　너는 말할 수 있니 / 영어를 / 잘?
　　Can+주어+동사원형

→ A: **Can** you speak / English / well?　　B: Yes, I **can**. / No, I **can't**.

- '~할 수 있니?'라고 의문문을 만들 때는 「Can+주어+동사원형 ~?」의 형태로 씁니다.

MORE+ **can = be able to**
능력·가능의 can은 be able to로 바꿔 쓸 수 있으며, 이때 be동사는 주어의 인칭과 수에 알맞게 바꿔 써야 해요.
My dad **is able to** fix bicycles. (나의 아빠는 자전거를 수리하실 수 있다.)

대표 기출 문제

🔒 다음 표를 보고 조동사를 사용하여 Rick이 할 수 있는 일과 할 수 없는 일에 대한 문장을 완성하시오.

<조건>
- 주어, 동사를 포함한 문장으로 작성할 것
- 조동사를 사용해야 함

할 수 있는 일	할 수 없는 일
solve difficult math problems	ride a bicycle

(1) Rick ________ ________ ________ ________ ________.
(2) Rick ________ ________ ________ ________.

CLUE 1
'~할 수 있다'와 '~할 수 없다'라는 의미로 쓰이는 조동사 표현은? — can, cannot[can't]

CLUE 2
can과 cannot[can't]을 각각 동사 solve, ride와 함께 사용하면 돼요.
이때, 조동사 뒤에는 동사원형이 와야 해요.

정답: (1) can solve difficult math problems
(2) cannot[can't] ride a bicycle

✓ **함정 피하기** 주어가 3인칭 단수이고 현재를 나타낼 때도 조동사의 형태는 변하지 않아요.
He ~~cans~~(→ can) solve difficult math problems.

Point Exercise

[1-4] 우리말과 일치하도록 〈보기〉에서 알맞은 단어를 골라 can과 함께 문장을 완성하세요.

〈보기〉

run   play   swim   sing

1 지호는 수영할 수 있다.

→ Jiho ________________ ________________.

2 나의 오빠는 피아노를 매우 잘 칠 수 있다.

→ My brother ________________ ________________ the piano very well.

3 그녀는 빠르게 달릴 수 없다.

→ She ________________ ________________ fast.

4 너는 무대에서 노래할 수 있니?

→ ________________ you ________________ on the stage?

[5-7] 우리말과 일치하도록 주어진 단어를 올바르게 배열하세요.

5 우리는 공항에 버스를 타고 갈 수 있다.
(can / to / go / we / the airport)

→ ____
____ by bus.

6 그녀는 일본어를 아주 잘 말할 수 있다.
(can / speak / very well / she / Japanese)

→ ____
____.

7 Nate는 모임에 올 수 있니?
(can / come / Nate / to the meeting)

→ ____?

[8-10] 우리말과 일치하도록 주어진 단어를 사용하여 문장을 완성하세요. (필요시 단어를 추가할 것)

8 그는 이 책을 하루 만에 읽을 수 있다.
(read, this book, in a day)

→ ____
____

9 미나는 그 문제를 풀 수 있니?
(solve, the question, Mina)

→ ____

10 나는 내 휴대 전화를 찾을 수 없다.
(find, cell phone, my)

→ ____

11 다음 대화문을 〈조건〉에 맞게 영작하세요.

〈조건〉
• 조동사 can을 사용할 것
• play, badminton, tennis를 사용할 것

(1) A: 너는 배드민턴을 칠 수 있니?

→ ____

(2) B: 아니, 할 수 없어. 나는 테니스를 칠 수 있어.

→ No, ________________________.

stage 무대 airport 공항 Japanese 일본어 meeting 모임, 회의 solve (문제 등을) 풀다, 해결하다 cell phone 휴대 전화

~해도 된다: can, may

너는 여기 앉아도 돼.
너는 / 앉아**도 된다** / 여기에.
can[may]+동사원형

→ You / **can sit** / here.
= may sit

- 조동사 can은 '~해도 된다'라는 **허가**의 의미도 가지고 있어요. 이때 can 대신 may를 쓸 수도 있습니다.

너는 도서관에서 먹으면 안 된다.
너는 / 먹으**면 안 된다** / 도서관에서.
cannot[may not]+동사원형

→ You / **cannot[can't] eat** / in the library.
= may not eat

- '~하면 안 된다'라는 **금지**를 나타내려면, 「cannot[can't]+동사원형」 또는 「may not+동사원형」의 형태로 쓰면 됩니다.

A: 당신의 컴퓨터를 사용해도 되나요?   B: 네, 됩니다. / 아니요, 안 됩니다.
사용**해도 되나요** / 당신의 컴퓨터를?
Can[May]+주어+동사원형

→ A: **Can I use** / your computer?   B: Yes, you **can**. / No, you **can't**.
= May I use   = may   = may not

- '~해도 되나요?'라고 **허가**를 구할 때는 「Can[May]+주어+동사원형 ~?」의 어순으로 써야 해요.

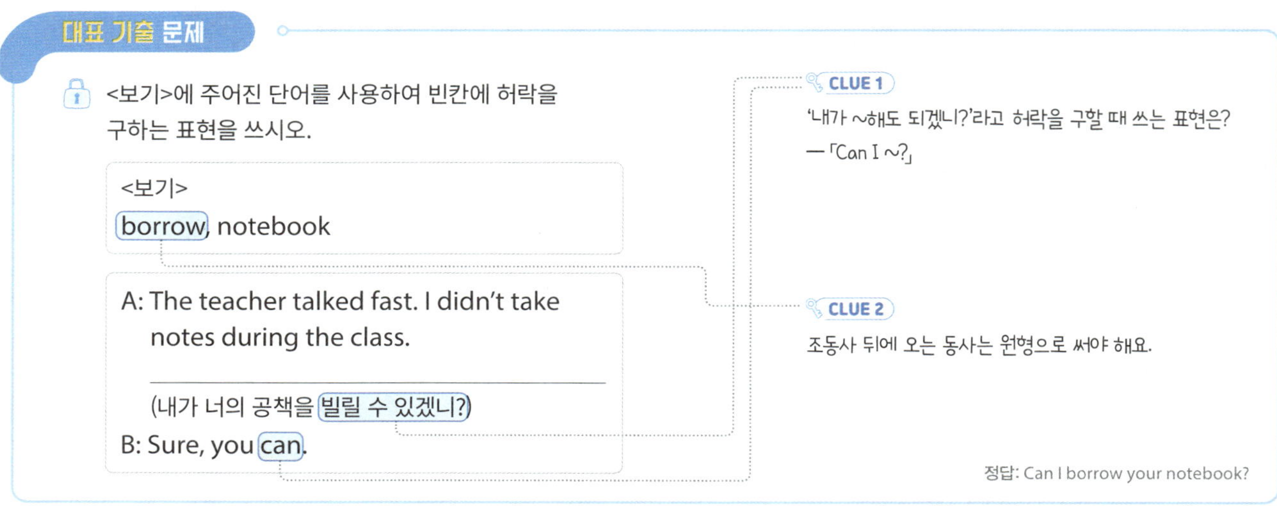

Point Exercise

[1-5] 우리말과 일치하도록 〈보기〉에서 알맞은 단어를 골라 주어진 조동사와 함께 문장을 완성하세요.

> 〈보기〉
> take   swim   go   ask   sit

1 너는 잠깐 휴식을 취해도 된다. (may)

→ You ______________ ______________ a break for a while.

2 너는 여기에 앉으면 안 된다. (can)

→ You ______________ ______________ here.

3 방문객들은 이 구역에서 수영하면 안 됩니다. (may)

→ Visitors ______________ ______________ ______________ in this area.

4 부탁을 하나 드려도 되나요? (may)

→ ______________ I ______________ you a favor?

5 화장실에 가도 될까요? (can)

→ ______________ I ______________ to the bathroom?

[6-7] 우리말과 일치하도록 주어진 단어를 올바르게 배열하세요.

6 너는 극장에서 시끄럽게 하면 안 된다.
(not / noise / may / make / you)

→ ______________________________
______________________________ at the theater.

7 죄송하지만, 반려동물을 식당 안으로 데려오실 수 없습니다.
(your / bring / pet / cannot / you)

→ I'm sorry, but ______________________________
______________________________ into the restaurant.

[8-9] 우리말과 일치하도록 주어진 단어를 사용하여 문장을 완성하세요. (필요시 단어를 추가할 것)

8 너는 언제든지 나에게 전화해도 돼.
(call, me, can)

→ ______________________________
anytime.

9 너는 수업 중에 나가면 안 된다.
(during the class, leave, may)

→ ______________________________
____

10 다음 그림을 보고 주어진 단어를 사용하여 가게의 점원에게 허가를 구하는 문장을 완성하세요.

→ ______________________________ ?
(this T-shirt, try on, I)

take (휴식을) 취하다 ask 부탁하다, 요청하다 for a while 잠시, 잠깐 favor 부탁 make noise 시끄럽게 하다 anytime 언제든지 leave 떠나다 try on 입어 보다

~해 줄래요?, ~해 주시겠어요?: Can[Could] you ~?

문을 닫아줄래요?
닫아줄래요 / 문을?
Can[Could]+주어+동사원형

→ **Can you close** / the door?
= Could you close

- 「Can[Could] you+동사원형 ~?」은 '~해 줄래요?, ~해 주시겠어요?'라고 **요청**의 의미를 나타내는 표현이에요.
- 이때 can 대신 could를 쓰면 더 정중한 표현이 돼요.

POINT 4   ~일[할]지도 모른다: may

당신은 재킷이 필요할지도 모른다. 밖은 춥다.
당신은 / 필요할지도 모른다 / 재킷이.
may+동사원형

→ You / **may need** / a jacket. It's cold outside.

내일은 날씨가 춥지 않을지도 모른다.
날씨가 / ~이 아닐지도 모른다 / 추운 / 내일.
may not+동사원형

→ The weather / **may not be** / cold / tomorrow.

- 「may+동사원형」은 '~일[할]지도 모른다'와 같은 불확실한 일에 대한 **추측**의 의미도 나타낼 수 있어요.
- '~이 아닐지도 모른다, ~하지 않을지도 모른다'는 부정의 의미는 「may not+동사원형」으로 나타내요.

대표 기출 문제

ⓐ에 들어갈 수 있는 적절한 표현을 영어 여섯 단어로 쓰시오.

G: ⓐ (내 부탁을 들어줄 수 있니)?
B: What is it, Mina?
G: Well, can you please do the dishes?
B: I'd like to, but I'm very busy today.

→ ___________________________________

CLUE 1
'~해 줄 수 있니?'라고 무언가 요청할 때 쓰는 표현은?
— 「Can[Could] you+동사원형 ~?」

CLUE 2
'A의 부탁을 들어주다'라는 영어 표현(do A a favor)
과 조동사를 사용해 문장을 완성하면 돼요.

정답: Can[Could] you do me a favor?

Point Exercise

배열 영작

[1-6] 우리말과 일치하도록 주어진 단어를 올바르게 배열하세요.

1
저를 도와주시겠어요?
(you / can / me / help)

→ _______________________, please?

2
Samuel은 지금 집에 있을지도 몰라.
(be / at home / may)

→ Samuel _______________________

_______________________ now.

3
잠시 기다려 주시겠어요?
(you / a moment / can / wait)

→ _______________________

_______________________, please?

4
그들은 같은 동아리에 가입할지도 몰라.
(may / the same club / they / join)

→ _______________________

_______________________.

5
불 좀 꺼줄래?
(turn off / you / can / the lights)

→ _______________________

_______________________?

6
그 아기는 아직 배가 고프지 않을지도 몰라.
(not / the baby / may / hungry / be)

→ _______________________

_______________________ yet.

주어진 단어로 영작

[7-10] 우리말과 일치하도록 주어진 단어와 can 또는 may를 사용하여 문장을 완성하세요.

7
너는 오늘 오후에 우산이 필요할지도 모른다.
(an umbrella, need)

→ _______________________

this afternoon.

8
Lucas는 오늘 과학 수업에 늦을지도 몰라.
(be, the science class, late for)

→ _______________________

_______________________ today.

9
그녀는 내일 학교에 오지 않을지도 몰라.
(come, to school)

→ _______________________

_______________________ tomorrow.

10
저를 지하철역으로 데려다 주시겠어요?
(you, take, me)

→ _______________________

to the subway station?

기출: 대화문 완성

11 우리말과 일치하도록 주어진 단어와 can을 사용하여 다음의 대화를 완성하세요.

A: Fred, 날 위해 이 책들을 도서관에 반납해 줄래?
   (to the library, these books, return)
B: Sure! I'm heading to the library now.

→ Fred, _______________________

_______________________ for me?

moment 잠깐, 잠시 turn off (전기 등을) 끄다 be late for ~에 늦다 head to ~로 향하다, ~로 가다

POINT 5 ~해야 한다: must, have to

너는 규칙들을 따라야 한다.
너는 / 따라야 한다 / 규칙들을.
　　　must[have to]+동사원형

→ You / **must[have to] follow** / the rules.

- '~해야 한다'라는 뜻으로 **의무**를 나타낼 때는 조동사 **must**를 사용하며, 같은 의미의 **have[has] to**로 바꿔 쓸 수 있어요.
- 과거시제일 때 must는 과거형이 없기 때문에 had to로 나타냅니다.
  She **had to go** home early yesterday. 그녀는 어제 집에 일찍 가야 했다.

너는 아무것도 걱정할 필요가 없다.
너는 / 걱정할 필요가 없다 / 아무것도.
　　don't have to+동사원형　　→ do[does] not have to로 쓸 수도 있으나 주로 don't[doesn't] have to로 써요.

→ You / **don't have to worry** / about anything.

- '~하면 안 된다'라고 **강한 금지**를 나타낼 때 부정형 **must not**을 쓰는데, 이때는 have to의 부정형으로 바꿔 쓸 수 없어요.
  You **must not tell** lies. 너는 거짓말을 해서는 안 된다.
- **don't[doesn't] have to**는 '~할 필요가 없다'라는 **불필요**를 나타내므로, must not과는 의미가 다릅니다.

> **주의**
>
> 주어가 3인칭 단수인 경우 has to와 doesn't have to로 써야 해요.
> She **have to** go now. (×) → She **has to** go now. (○) (그녀는 지금 가야 한다.)
> She **don't have to** go now. (×) → She **doesn't have to** go now. (○) (그녀는 지금 갈 필요가 없다.)

대표 기술 문제

🔒 must나 have to를 사용하여 다음 표지판의 의미를 영어로 쓰시오.

너는 여기서 자전거를 타면 안 된다.
→ You ________________________________ .

CLUE 1
must와 have to 모두 '~해야 한다'라는 의미지만, '~하면 안 된다'라는 의미를 표현하려면? — must not
don't have to는 '~할 필요가 없다'라는 의미로 쓰여요.

CLUE 2
must not 뒤에는 동사원형이 와야 하므로 must not ride로 쓰면 돼요.

정답: must not ride a bike here

Point Exercise

[1-5] 우리말과 일치하도록 〈보기〉에서 알맞은 단어를 골라 must 또는 have to를 사용하여 문장을 완성하세요.

〈보기〉
miss   do   follow   study   wear

1 우리는 안전벨트를 매야 한다.
→ We ____________ ____________
seat belts.

2 나는 저녁 식사 후에 설거지를 해야 한다.
→ I ____________ ____________
____________ the dishes after dinner.

3 그는 의사의 조언을 따라야 한다.
→ He ____________ ____________
the doctor's advice.

4 너는 지금 공부해야 한다.
→ You ____________ ____________
____________ now.

5 Nancy는 수업을 빠지면 안 된다.
→ Nancy ____________ ____________
____________ the class.

[6-10] 우리말과 일치하도록 주어진 단어를 사용하여 문장을 완성하세요. (필요시 단어를 추가하거나 형태를 바꿀 것)

6
너는 충분한 물을 마셔야 한다.
(drink, water, have, you, enough)

→ ________________________________
____

7
나의 언니는 용돈을 아껴야 한다.
(save, my sister, her pocket money, have)

→ ________________________________
____

8
나는 내일 일찍 일어날 필요가 없다.
(early, have, get up, I)

→ ________________________________
________________________________ tomorrow.

9
Tom은 밤늦게까지 공부해야 했다.
(late, study, have)

→ ________________________________ at night.

10
너는 모임에 늦으면 안 된다.
(be, must, you, late)

→ ________________________________
for the meeting.

11 다음 그림을 보고 〈보기〉에서 알맞은 조동사를 골라 주어진 단어와 함께 문장을 완성하세요.
(필요시 형태를 바꾸고 현재시제로 쓸 것)

〈보기〉
have to   don't have to   must not

→ Nara ________________________________.
(her room, clean)

---

miss 놓치다 follow 따르다 seat belt 안전벨트 advice 조언, 충고 pocket money 용돈 get up 일어나다

~해야 한다, ~하는 것이 좋다: should

너는 휴식을 좀 취해야 한다.
너는 / 취해야 한다 / 약간의 휴식을.
should+동사원형

→ You / **should get** / some rest.

- '~해야 한다, ~하는 것이 좋다'라는 의미를 나타낼 때, 조동사 should를 사용할 수 있어요.
- should는 일상생활에서 건강, 관계, 생활 습관 등에 관한 조언을 할 때 자주 사용돼요.
- 즉, should는 must, have to보다는 가벼운 정도의 **의무나 충고, 또는 조언**을 나타낸다고 보면 됩니다.

너는 단것을 너무 많이 먹지 말아야 한다.
너는 / 먹지 말아야 한다 / 너무 많은 단것을.
should not[shouldn't]+동사원형

→ You / **should not[shouldn't]** eat / a lot of sweets.

- 어떤 행동을 피하거나 금지하는 것이 좋다고 조언할 때, '~하지 말아야 한다'라는 의미의 should not [shouldn't]를 사용해요.

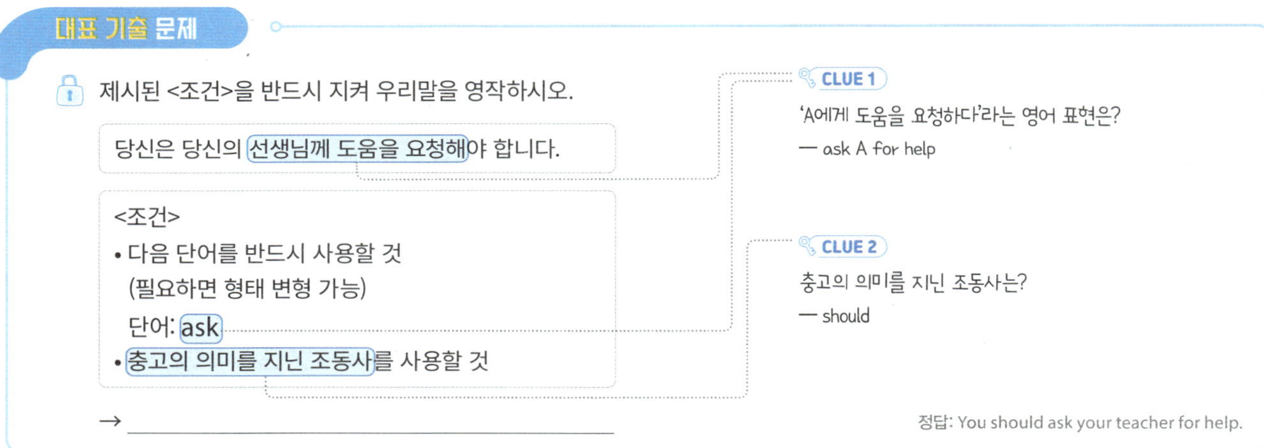

대표 기출 문제

제시된 <조건>을 반드시 지켜 우리말을 영작하시오.

당신은 당신의 선생님께 도움을 요청해야 합니다.

<조건>
- 다음 단어를 반드시 사용할 것
  (필요하면 형태 변형 가능)
  단어: ask
- 충고의 의미를 지닌 조동사를 사용할 것

→ ______________________________

CLUE 1
'A에게 도움을 요청하다'라는 영어 표현은?
— ask A for help

CLUE 2
충고의 의미를 지닌 조동사는?
— should

정답: You should ask your teacher for help.

Point Exercise

[1-5] 우리말과 일치하도록 〈보기〉에서 알맞은 단어를 골라 should 또는 shouldn't를 사용하여 문장을 완성하세요.

〈보기〉
eat　　watch　　exercise　　go　　buy

1 우리는 매일 운동하는 것이 좋다.
→ We ＿＿＿＿＿＿＿＿＿＿＿ every day.

2 나는 새 교복을 사야 한다.
→ I ＿＿＿＿＿＿＿＿＿＿＿ a new school uniform.

3 그는 하루 종일 TV를 보지 말아야 한다.
→ He ＿＿＿＿＿＿＿＿＿＿＿ TV all day.

4 어린아이들은 일찍 잠자리에 드는 것이 좋다.
→ Young children ＿＿＿＿＿＿＿＿＿＿＿ to bed early.

5 너는 밤늦게 많은 음식을 먹지 말아야 한다.
→ You ＿＿＿＿＿＿＿＿＿＿＿ large meals late at night.

[6-10] 우리말과 일치하도록 주어진 단어와 should를 사용하여 문장을 완성하세요. (필요시 단어를 추가할 것)

6
나는 그에게 약속을 지켜야 한다.
(keep, my promise)

→ ＿＿＿＿＿＿＿＿＿＿＿ to him.

7
너는 돈을 낭비하지 말아야 한다. (waste, money)

→ ＿＿＿＿＿＿＿＿＿＿＿

8
그녀는 남동생의 숙제를 도와줘야 한다.
(help, her brother)

→ ＿＿＿＿＿＿＿＿＿＿＿ with his homework.

9
우리는 도서관에 음식을 가져가면 안 된다.
(bring, to the library, food)

→ ＿＿＿＿＿＿＿＿＿＿＿

10
사람들은 여기서 큰 소리로 말하면 안 된다.
(people, here, talk loudly)

→ ＿＿＿＿＿＿＿＿＿＿＿

11 주어진 단어와 should 또는 shouldn't를 사용하여 각 상황에 알맞은 조언을 완성하세요.

(1) The hallway is very slippery. Be careful.
→ You ＿＿＿＿＿＿＿＿＿＿＿ .
(in the hallway, run)

(2) It is raining heavily outside.
→ You ＿＿＿＿＿＿＿＿＿＿＿ .
(a raincoat, wear)

---

school uniform 교복　all day 하루 종일　meal 식사, 끼니　keep one's promise 약속을 지키다　waste 낭비하다　loudly 큰 소리로　hallway 복도　slippery 미끄러운　careful 조심하는, 주의 깊은　heavily (양·정도가) 심하게, 아주 많이　raincoat 우비

Chapter Test [*]

정답 및 해설 p.07

STAGE 1) Go for it!

자신 있게 풀어보는 기초 문제!

배열 영작

[1-4] 우리말과 일치하도록 주어진 단어를 배열하여 문장을 완성하세요.

1
> 나를 위해 문을 잡아줄래?
> (the door / can / hold / you)

→ ___________________________________

___________________________________ for me?

2
> 나는 내일 나의 삼촌 댁에 가야 한다.
> (should / to / my uncle's house / go / I)

→ ___________________________________

___________________________________ tomorrow.

3
> Linda는 식사를 거르면 안 된다.
> (not / meals / Linda / skip / must)

→ ___________________________________

___________________________________ .

4
> 그는 오늘 오후에 수학을 공부해야 한다.
> (to / has / study / he / this afternoon / math)

→ ___________________________________

___________________________________ .

주어진 단어로 영작

[5-7] 우리말과 일치하도록 주어진 단어를 사용하여 문장을 완성하세요.

5
> 제가 당신에게 나중에 전화해도 될까요?
> (later, call, may)

→ ___________________________________

6
> 우리는 자연을 보호해야 한다.
> (protect, have, nature)

→ ___________________________________

____

7
> 당신은 빙판길에서 조심해야 한다.
> (on, careful, be, icy roads, must)

→ ___________________________________

____

최신 기출

8 다음은 Chris와 Sophia가 할 수 있는 것과 할 수 없는 것을 나타낸 표예요. 표를 보고 〈보기〉와 같이 문장을 완성하세요.

	○	×
Chris	swim	ice-skate
Sophia	play soccer	play baseball

〈보기〉
Chris <u>can swim</u>, but he <u>can't ice-skate</u>.

→ Sophia ___________ ___________

___________ , but she ___________

___________ ___________ .

● 보기에서 골라 영작

[9-12] 빈칸에 들어갈 말을 〈보기〉에서 골라 쓰세요.
(단, 한 번씩만 사용할 것)

〈보기〉
have to　　must not　　may　　can

9
A: I'm so hungry now.
　______________ you cook
　something for me?
B: Of course. What do you want?

10
A: ______________ I use your pen?
B: Sure. Which one do you need, the black
　one or the blue one?

11
A: Erica, will you go shopping with me this
　afternoon?
B: I'm sorry, I ______________ go see
　a doctor.

12
A: Mom, can I eat a hamburger?
B: Dan, you ______________ eat
　fast food. It's bad for your health.

● 그림 영작

[13-14] 〈보기〉와 같이 주어진 단어와 must를 사용하여
각 표지판이 나타내는 내용을 쓰세요.

〈보기〉

You <u>must not bring pets</u> into the shop.
(pets, bring)

13 
You ______________
on the street. (throw, trash)

14 
You ______________
on the boat. (a life jacket, wear)

● 최신 기출

15 다음 대화를 읽고 〈조건〉에 맞게 우리말을 영작하세요.

〈조건〉
・ can과 may를 각각 한 번씩 사용할 것
・ 주어진 단어를 사용할 것

A: (1) <u>나는 네 생일 파티에 일찍 오지 못할지도 몰라.</u>
B: It's okay. (2) <u>나중에 나에게 메시지를 보내줄래?</u>
A: Sure.

(1) ______________
to your birthday party. (early, come)

(2) ______________
to me later? (send, a message)

[16-20] 다음 각 문장을 괄호 안의 지시대로 바꿔 쓰세요.

16
Emily can eat raw fish. (의문문으로)

→ ____________________

____

17
Jinsu has to wait for his friend for an hour.
(과거시제로)

→ ____________________

____

18
You may go into this room. (부정문으로)

→ ____________________

____

19
She should come here before 8 p.m.
(부정문으로)

→ ____________________

____

20
Leo must bring his textbook tomorrow.
(과거시제로)

→ ____________________

____________________ yesterday.

[21-23] 〈보기〉와 같이 should를 사용하여 주어진 문제 상황에 대한 충고의 문장을 완성하세요. (단, Problem의 문장을 사용할 것)

〈보기〉
Problem: Susan didn't turn off the TV again.
Advice: You <u>should turn off the TV.</u>

21
Problem: Kate plays computer games too much.

Advice: You ____________________

____________________.

22
Problem: Amy didn't wash the dishes again.

Advice: You ____________________

____________________.

23
Problem: Suho goes to bed late at night.

Advice: You ____________________

____________________.

최신 기출

24 다음 대화를 읽고 상황에 알맞은 문장을 〈조건〉에 맞게 영작하세요.

〈조건〉
· must, have to, must not, don't have to 중 하나를 사용할 것
· 주어진 단어를 사용할 것

Jane: Does every classroom have lockers for students?
Nina: Yes. They can keep their books in them. So, ____________________

____________________ from home.
(carry, heavy books, students)

○● 도표 영작

25 다음 표에 제시된 각 고민에 대한 알맞은 조언을 〈조건〉에 맞게 완성하세요.

Worries
(1) I spend too much money on shopping every month.
(2) I have a math test next Friday.
(3) I always watch TV in my free time.
(4) I gained too much weight.

〈조건〉
- 주어와 동사를 포함하는 완전한 문장으로 쓸 것
- 주어진 조동사를 사용하고, 필요시 단어를 추가하거나 형태를 바꿀 것
- 〈보기〉에 있는 모든 단어를 반드시 사용할 것
- 표에 제시된 고민들의 번호에 각각 맞게 쓸 것

〈보기〉
many sweets, too often, find, eat, hobby, another, go shopping, study hard

(1) You ___________________________

___________________________ .

(should)

(2) You ___________________________

___________________________ .

(have to)

(3) You ___________________________

___________________________ .

(should)

(4) You ___________________________

___________________________ .

(must)

○● 어법 오류 수정

26 다음 ⓐ~ⓔ 중 어법상 **틀린** 것을 찾아 그 기호를 쓰고, 바르게 고쳐 쓰세요.

> Suji's class will go on a field trip to Gyeongju next week. They ⓐ should study about the Kingdom of Silla before the field trip.
> Next Wednesday, students ⓑ must come to school before 8 a.m. They will visit Gyeongju by train. They ⓒ have to bring their lunch because they'll eat at one of the famous restaurants in Gyeongju. They ⓓ cannot tour alone and ⓔ must follow their teacher. The students are going to visit many nice places. Everyone will have fun together.

___________ → ___________

🎯 **Challenge!**

누적 문제 Ch 01-03

27 다음 대화에서 어법상 틀린 **두 개**를 찾아 그 기호를 쓰고, 바르게 고쳐 쓰세요.

> A: Matt, what are you doing now?
> B: Hi, Tom. ⓐ We're make an English magazine, and ⓑ we need some help.
> A: Sure. What can I do for you?
> B: ⓒ Can you write an English poem?
> A: No, I can't. But, ⓓ Jenny can writes it. ⓔ She will help you.
> B: Okay. Thanks.

___________ → ___________

___________ → ___________

Chapter 04 명사와 대명사

✅ Before You Write

- ☑ 셀 수 있는 명사와 셀 수 없는 명사를 구분할 수 있나요?
- ☑ 명사의 수나 양은 어떤 표현으로 나타낼 수 있을까요?
- ☑ 「There+be동사」 뒤에 오는 명사의 수에 맞게 be동사를 알맞은 형태로 쓸 수 있나요?
- ☑ 우리말을 보고 여러 대명사 중 알맞은 것을 사용할 수 있나요?

내신 기출 다음 우리말을 보고 머릿속으로 한번 영어 문장을 떠올려 보세요.

1 For Eva, breakfast is (B) 우유 한 잔 and bread with toppings.
셀 수 없는 명사 → 담는 그릇으로 수량 표현 → **a glass of milk** `POINT 2`

2 교실에 두 명의 아이들이 있습니다.
「There+be동사」 현재형 긍정문 → 뒤에 복수명사(two children) → **There are** `POINT 1·3`

3 1970년대에는 대구에 많은 극장이 있지 않았다.
→ There ________________ in Daegu in the 1970s.
「There+be동사」 과거형 부정문 → 뒤에 복수명사(many theaters) → **(There) were not** `POINT 1·3`

4 이것들은 우리들에 관한 나의 시이다.
알맞은 지시대명사와 인칭대명사 → **These are my** poems about **us.** `POINT 4·6`

5 "ⓑ 나는 물에 비친 나 자신을 볼 수 있어요,"
주어(나) = 목적어(나 자신) → 재귀대명사 → **myself** `POINT 5`

6 목요일입니다.
요일 표현 → 뜻이 없는 주어 It 사용 → **It is** `POINT 7`

7 (2) 그녀의 교실에는 아무도 없었다.
(was / nobody / there)
____________ ____________ ____________ in her classroom.
「There+be동사」 과거형 → 뒤에 단수 취급하는 대명사(nobody) → **There was nobody** `POINT 3·9`

정답: **1** a glass of milk **2** There are two children in the classroom. **3** were not[weren't] many theaters **4** These are my poems about us.
5 I can see myself in the water **6** It is[It's] Thursday. **7** There was nobody

Unit 01 명사

 셀 수 있는 명사

나는 개 한 마리와 고양이 두 마리가 있다.
나는 / 있다 / **개** 한 마리와 **고양이** 두 마리가.

→ I / have / **a dog** and **two cats**.

- 사람이나 사물, 동물, 장소 등의 이름을 나타내는 명사 중 하나, 둘, 셋, … 이렇게 셀 수 있는 것들을 '셀 수 있는 명사'라고 불러요.
- 셀 수 있는 명사가 하나를 가리킬 때는 앞에 **관사 a나 an**을 붙이고, 둘 이상 여럿을 가리킬 때는 대부분 명사 뒤에 **-s나 -es**를 붙여 **복수형**으로 나타내요.

📢 셀 수 있는 명사의 복수형 만드는 법

대부분의 명사	+-s	books	apples	friends	cups
-s, -x, -ch, -sh로 끝나는 명사	+-es	buses	boxes	watches	dishes
「자음+o」로 끝나는 명사	+-es	potatoes tomatoes heroes *예외: pianos, photos, memos			
「자음+y」로 끝나는 명사	y를 i로 바꾸고 +-es	baby → babies story → stories *「모음+y」로 끝나는 명사 +-s days boys toys monkeys ways			
-f, -fe로 끝나는 명사	f, fe를 v로 바꾸고 +-es	knife → knives leaf → leaves *예외: roof → roofs			
불규칙	man → men woman → women child → children tooth → teeth foot → feet mouse → mice				
형태가 같은 경우	fish → fish sheep → sheep deer → deer				

대표 기출 문제

우리말과 같은 뜻이 되도록 괄호 안의 말을 알맞은 형태로 고치시오.

봐! 코알라 한 마리가 나무에서 자고 있어.
코알라들은 보통 하루에 열여섯 시간 정도 잠을 자.

Look! ⓐ (koala) is sleeping in the tree.
ⓑ (koala) usually sleep for about 16 hours a day.

CLUE 1
'동물 한 마리'를 나타내는 말에 올 수 있는 형태는?
— 「a/an+셀 수 있는 명사」

CLUE 2
'여럿의 동물'을 나타내는 말에 올 수 있는 형태는?
— 「셀 수 있는 명사+-s/-es」

정답: ⓐ A koala ⓑ Koalas

함정 피하기

1 셀 수 있는 명사의 단수형 앞에는 대부분 관사 a를 붙이지만, 명사의 첫소리가 모음일 때는 an을 붙여야 해요.
an apple (사과 한 개)   **an** egg (달걀 한 개)   **an** hour (한 시간)

2 우리말에서는 '고양이들 두 마리'처럼 명사에 '들'을 붙이는 경우가 많지 않으므로, 영작할 때 '-(e)s'를 빠뜨리지 않도록 주의해야 해요.

Point Exercise

[1-10] 다음 빈칸에 주어진 단어를 알맞은 형태로 쓰세요.

1 Three _______________ are in the picture.
(rabbit)

2 Two _______________ are on the road. (bus)

3 The girl brought an _______________ for him.
(orange)

4 She invited five _______________ to her home.
(child)

5 We have only an _______________. (hour)

6 My brother gave six _______________ to me.
(pencil)

7 He is going to buy ten _______________. (fish)

8 A bear can stand on two _______________. (foot)

9 Four _______________ are eating pizza. (woman)

10 They need eight _______________ for their meal.
(knife)

[11-15] 우리말과 일치하도록 주어진 단어를 사용하여 문장을
완성하세요. (필요시 형태를 바꿀 것)

11

우리는 아파트에 방이 세 개 있다.
(we, room, have, three)

→ _______________________________________
in our apartment.

12

Wendy는 감자 다섯 개가 필요하다.
(potato, five, need)

→ _______________________________________

13

그는 여동생 한 명과 남동생 두 명이 있다.
(two, he, sister, a, brother, and, have)

→ _______________________________________

14

그 아기는 이가 네 개 있다.
(the baby, tooth, four, have)

→ _______________________________________

15

그녀는 상자들을 옮기고 있다.
(box, carry, she)

→ _______________________________________

16 다음 표에서 Brandon이 아침과 점심에 먹은 것을 보고
〈조건〉에 맞게 문장을 완성하세요.

Breakfast	달걀 1개, 바나나 2개
Lunch	샌드위치 2개

〈조건〉
- 개수는 반드시 영문으로 쓸 것
- 동사는 과거형으로 쓸 것
- 주어진 단어를 사용하되 필요시 형태를 바꿀 것

(1) Brandon _______________________________________
_______________________________________ for breakfast.
(have, and, egg, banana)

(2) Brandon _______________________________________
_______________________________________ for lunch.
(sandwich, have)

  셀 수 없는 명사

오늘 날씨가 정말 좋다.
날씨가 / 정말 좋다 / 오늘.

→ The **weather** / is really nice / today.

- 셀 수 없는 명사는 커피, 설탕처럼 일정한 형태가 없거나 아름다움, 건강함처럼 눈에 보이지 않는 개념을 나타내요.
- 셀 수 없는 명사는 명사 앞에 a, an을 붙일 수 없고, 복수형으로도 쓰일 수 없어요.
- 셀 수 없는 명사가 주어로 쓰일 때 동사는 항상 단수 형태를 써요.

주의 혼동하기 쉬운 셀 수 없는 명사

bread(빵), money(돈), news(뉴스), homework(숙제), furniture(가구), baggage(수하물) 등

그는 하루에 커피 두 잔을 마신다.
그는 / 마신다 / 커피 **두 잔**을 / 하루에.

→ He / drinks / **two cups of** coffee / a day.

- 셀 수 없는 명사는 담는 그릇이나 모양 등 단위를 나타내는 표현을 단수형 또는 복수형으로 써서 그 양을 나타내요.

셀 수 없는 명사의 수량 표현

a cup(컵[잔]) **of** tea/coffee	**a glass**(잔) **of** water/milk/juice
a bottle(병) **of** water/wine/juice	**a bowl**(그릇) **of** rice/soup/salad
a piece[sheet](장) **of** paper	**a slice[piece]**(조각) **of** pizza/cheese/cake
a loaf(덩이) **of** bread	**a bar**(막대) **of** chocolate/soap

MORE + gloves(장갑), shoes(신발), socks(양말), skates(스케이트)처럼 두 개가 한 쌍을 이루는 명사를 셀 때도 단위 표현을 사용해요.
a pair of gloves (장갑 한 켤레), **two pairs of** socks (양말 두 켤레)

대표 기출 문제

밑줄 친 우리말과 같게 주어진 단어를 사용하여 문장을
완성하시오.

녹차 세 잔과 케이크 두 조각을 주세요.

→ We'll have ___________________________
___________________________. (green tea, cake)

CLUE 1
녹차는 셀 수 없지만, 녹차가 담긴 '잔(cup)'의 단위를
사용해 셀 수 있어요.

CLUE 2
'케이크'는 여러 덩어리로 나뉠 때,
'조각(slice 또는 piece)'의 단위로 셀 수 있어요.

정답: three cups of green tea and two slices[pieces] of cake

함정 피하기 단위 표현이 아닌 셀 수 없는 명사를 복수형으로 만들지 않도록 주의해야 해요.
two loaf of breads (×) → two **loaves of** bread (○) (빵 두 덩이)

Point Exercise

빈칸 완성

[1-6] 우리말과 일치하도록 주어진 단어를 사용하여 빈칸에 알맞은 말을 쓰세요. (단, 수를 나타내는 말은 영문으로 쓸 것)

1 밥 네 그릇 (rice)

→ ______________________________

2 빵 세 덩이 (bread)

→ ______________________________

3 주스 열 병 (juice)

→ ______________________________

4 치즈 다섯 조각 (cheese)

→ ______________________________

5 우유 두 잔 (milk)

→ ______________________________

6 케이크 두 조각 (cake)

→ ______________________________

조건 영작

[7-11] 우리말과 일치하도록 〈조건〉에 맞게 문장을 완성하세요.

〈보기〉

piece of	bar of	cup of
bowl of	bottle of	

〈조건〉
- 〈보기〉에서 알맞은 말을 골라 한 번씩만 쓸 것 (필요시 형태를 바꿀 것)
- 수를 나타내는 말은 영문으로 쓸 것
- 주어진 단어를 사용할 것

7 차 한 잔 드시겠어요? (tea)

→ Would you drink ______________________________ ?

8 모든 그룹은 종이 다섯 장을 받게 될 것이다. (paper)

→ Every group will get ______________________________

______________________________ .

9 그녀는 매일 물 세 병을 마신다. (water)

→ She drinks ______________________________

______________________________ every day.

10 그 호텔은 모든 객실에 비누 한 개를 제공한다. (soap)

→ The hotel provides ______________________________

______________________________ in every room.

11 그는 저녁으로 샐러드 한 그릇을 먹었다. (salad)

→ He had ______________________________

______________________________ for dinner.

기출: 문맥에 맞게 영작

12 다음 글을 읽고 주어진 단어를 사용하여 마지막 질문에 알맞은 답변을 쓰세요.

It is a very hot day. You and your friend are very thirsty. You come home and see your brother in the kitchen. What would you say to him?

→ ______________________________

______________________________ to us?

(can, give, glass, two, water)

provide 제공하다, 주다   thirsty 목마른

POINT 3   ~가[이] 있다: There is/are

방 안에 강아지 한 마리가 있다.
~가[이] 있다 / 강아지 한 마리 / 방 안에.
There is   단수명사   장소 부사구

→ **There is** / **a puppy** / in the room.

방 안에 강아지들이 있다.
~가[이] 있다 / 강아지들 / 방 안에.
There are   복수명사   장소 부사구

→ **There are** / **puppies** / in the room.

- Chapter 01에서 be동사가 '(~에) 있다'라는 의미를 나타낼 수 있다고 배웠어요.
- 하지만 영어에서는 '~가[이] 있다'라는 의미를 나타낼 때 「**There is[are]＋명사**」를 쓰는 경우가 훨씬 더 많아요. 이때, be동사는 뒤에 나오는 명사의 수에 따라 결정돼요.
- '~가[이] 있었다'라는 의미의 과거형은 「**There was[were]＋명사**」로 나타내요.

There is[was]	＋단수명사/셀 수 없는 명사
There are[were]	＋복수명사

- '~가[이] 없다'라는 뜻의 부정문과 '~가[이] 있니?'라는 뜻의 의문문은 다음 표와 같이 나타내요.

부정문	**There is[was] not** (= There isn't[wasn't])
	There are[were] not (= There aren't[weren't])
의문문	**Is[Was] there ~?** — Yes, **there is[was]**. / No, **there isn't[wasn't]**.
	Are[Were] there ~? — Yes, **there are[were]**. / No, **there aren't[weren't]**.

There is not a library in this town. 이 마을에는 도서관이 없다.

A: **Is there** a library in this town? 이 마을에는 도서관이 있니?

B: Yes, **there is**. / No, **there isn't**. 네, 있어요. / 아니요, 없어요.

대표 기출 문제

🔒 괄호 안에 주어진 단어를 사용하여 한글 뜻과
일치하도록 문장을 완성하시오.

책상 위에 많은 만화책들이 있다. (there)

→ _______________________________

_______________________________ .

CLUE 1

there를 이용하여 '~이 있다'라는 의미를 어떻게
나타낼 수 있을까?
— There is[are]＋명사

CLUE 2

주어(많은 만화책들)가 복수명사이므로 복수동사
are를 써야 해요.

정답: There are many[a lot of, lots of] comic books on the desk

Point Exercise

정답 및 해설 p.09

[1-4] 우리말과 일치하도록 빈칸에 알맞은 말을 〈보기〉에서 골라 쓰세요.

〈보기〉

There is	There are
There was	There were

1 수조에 물고기 한 마리가 있다.

→ ________________ ________________ a fish

in the tank.

2 건물 앞에 차가 한 대 있었다.

→ ________________ ________________ a car

in front of the building.

3 바구니 안에 사과가 많이 있다.

→ ________________ ________________ many apples

in the basket.

4 하늘에 많은 별들이 있었다.

→ ________________ ________________ a lot of stars

in the sky.

[5-9] 우리말과 일치하도록 주어진 단어를 사용하여 문장을 완성하세요. (필요시 형태를 바꿀 것)

5
냄비에 수프가 있다.
(soup, in the pot, there)

→ ________________________________

____

6
네 주머니에 표가 있니?
(a, in your pocket, there, ticket)

→ ________________________________

____

7
욕실에 큰 거미 한 마리가 있었다.
(a big spider, there, in the bathroom)

→ ________________________________

____

8
내 방에는 컴퓨터가 없다.
(computer, a, in my room, there)

→ ________________________________

____

9
그 동물원에는 많은 동물들이 있었니?
(many, there, in the zoo, animal)

→ ________________________________

____

10 다음 그림을 보고 〈조건〉에 맞게 문장을 완성하세요.

(1) 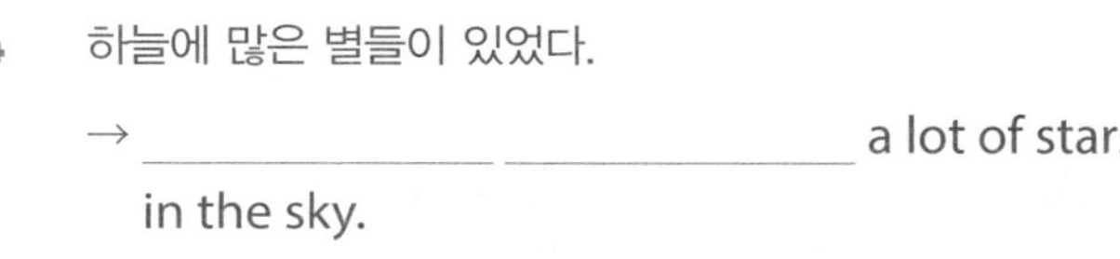 (2) 

〈조건〉
- 현재시제를 사용할 것
- 주어진 단어를 사용할 것

(1) ________________________________

____

(the table, two, there, cup, on)

(2) ________________________________

____

(the river, there, over, a bridge)

---

tank 어항, 수조 pot 냄비; 항아리, 단지 pocket 주머니 bathroom 욕실, 화장실

인칭대명사와 재귀대명사

POINT 4 역할에 따라 형태가 변하는 인칭대명사

나는 그녀를 나의 생일 파티에 초대했다.
나는 / 초대했다 / 그녀를 / 나의 생일 파티에.

→ **I** / invited / **her** / to **my** birthday party.

- '나, 너, 그, 그녀, 그것'처럼 사람이나 사물의 이름을 대신하는 말을 **인칭대명사**라고 부릅니다.
  이러한 대명사는 문장에서의 역할에 따라 형태가 바뀌어요.
- 인칭대명사가 문장에서 '~은[는], ~이[가]'와 같이 주어 역할이면 주격,
  '~의'라고 소유의 의미를 나타내면 소유격, '~을[를], ~에게'로 목적어 역할을 하면 목적격을 써요.
- 또한, '~의 것'이라는 의미로 「소유격+명사」를 대신하는 소유대명사의 종류도 알아두어야 해요.
  This isn't my book. It is **yours**(= your book). 이것은 나의 책이 아니다. 그것은 네 것이다.

📣 인칭대명사 종류와 격 변화

	단수				복수			
	주격 (~은[는], ~이[가])	소유격 (~의)	목적격 (~을[를], ~에게)	소유대명사 (~의 것)	주격	소유격	목적격	소유대명사
1인칭	I	my	me	mine	we	our	us	ours
2인칭	you	your	you	yours	you	your	you	yours
3인칭	he	his	him	his	they	their	them	theirs
	she	her	her	hers				
	it	its	it	-				

주의!

단수명사 앞에 소유격 대명사가 올 경우, 관사 a나 an과 함께 쓸 수 없어요.
This is **a my** book. (✕) → This is **a** book. (○), This is **my** book. (○)

대표 기출 문제

🔒 다음 우리말을 영어로 쓰시오.

Ella: 이건 내 것이 아니야. 이거 네 거니?
→ Ella: This is not ___ⓐ___.
　　　Is this ___ⓑ___?

CLUE 1
빈칸 ⓐ에는 '내 것, 나의 것'이라는 의미에 알맞은
소유대명사를 쓰면 돼요.

CLUE 2
빈칸 ⓑ에는 '네 것, 너의 것'이라는 의미의
소유대명사를 쓰면 돼요.

정답: ⓐ mine ⓑ yours

Point Exercise

정답 및 해설 p.09

[1-6] 우리말과 일치하도록 빈칸에 알맞은 말을 쓰세요.

1

이 멋진 자전거는 나의 것이다.

→ This nice bike is ______________.

2

우리는 곧 우리의 휴가 계획을 세워야 해.

→ ______________ should plan ______________
vacation soon.

3

그는 우리에게 감사 편지를 보냈다.

→ ______________ sent ______________
a thank-you letter.

4

카멜레온은 그것들의 색깔을 바꿀 수 있다.

→ Chameleons can change ______________
colors.

5

Jake는 나를 그의 독서 동아리에 초대했다.

→ Jake invited ______________ to
______________ reading club.

6

우리는 샌드위치를 가져와서 공원에서 그것들을 먹었다.

→ We brought sandwiches and ate
______________ in the park.

[7-11] 다음 괄호 안의 대명사를 어법상 알맞은 형태로 고쳐
쓰세요.

7 Can I borrow (you) umbrella?

→ ______________

8 His parents don't know (I) name.

→ ______________

9 My sister gave (she) books to me.

→ ______________

10 I made cookies. I will give (they) to him.

→ ______________

11 The red backpack is (she). That's not mine.

→ ______________

12 친구를 소개하는 다음 글을 읽고, 밑줄 친 부분 중 어법
상 틀린 곳을 찾아 그 기호를 쓰고 바르게 고쳐 쓰세요.

(1)

I would like to introduce ⓐ my friend. ⓑ He
name is Nate. ⓒ He lives in Canada. I met
ⓓ him five years ago in Seoul.

______________ → ______________

(2)

ⓐ My name is Sara. I have a best friend.
ⓑ Her name is Jenny. But ⓒ we are very
different. I like music, but Jenny likes sports.
I don't like animals, but Jenny loves ⓓ it.

______________ → ______________

vacation 휴가, 방학 thank-you letter 감사 편지 chameleon 카멜레온 club 동아리, 클럽 would like to-v ~하고 싶다 different 다른

POINT 5　재귀대명사: -self/-selves

나는 거울에 비친 나 자신을 보았다.
나는 / 보았다 / 나 자신을 / 거울 속의.
　주어　　　　　목적어

→ **I** / saw / **myself** / in the mirror.

우리는 항상 우리 자신을 사랑해 주어야 한다.
우리는 / 사랑해 주어야 한다 / 우리들 자신을 / 항상.
　주어　　　　　　　목적어

→ **We** / should love / **ourselves** / at all times.

- 문장의 목적어가 '~(들) 자신'이라는 의미로 주어와 같은 대상을 가리킬 때, 목적어 자리에 '-self[-selves]' 형태의 재귀대명사를 쓸 수 있어요.

인칭 ＼ 수	재귀대명사 (~(들) 자신)	
	단수	복수
1인칭	I - my**self**	we - our**selves**
2인칭	you - your**self**	you - your**selves**
3인칭	he - him**self** she - her**self** it - it**self**	they - them**selves**

MORE+　강조를 위한 재귀대명사의 쓰임

재귀대명사는 '직접, 스스로, 자체'라는 의미로 문장의 주어나 목적어를 강조할 때도 쓸 수 있어요.
이때 재귀대명사는 강조하는 말(주어, 목적어) 바로 뒤나 문장 맨 뒤에 써요.
I **myself** made this cake. (= *I* made this cake **myself**.) 〈주어 강조〉 (내가 이 케이크를 직접 만들었다.)
She liked *the song* **itself**. 〈목적어 강조〉 (그녀는 그 노래 자체를 좋아했다.)

대표 기출 문제

다음 우리말을 참고하여 주어진 문장의 어색한 부분 한 곳을 바르게 고쳐 전체 문장을 다시 쓰시오.

그 소녀는 자기 자신을 선생님에게 소개했다.
→ The girl introduced her to the teacher.

→ ______________________________
　______________________________

CLUE 1
문장에서 목적어인 '자기 자신'은 누구를 가리키는 걸까요?
— 주어 '그 소녀(The girl)'

CLUE 2
주어와 목적어가 같은 대상을 가리키므로 목적어를 알맞은 재귀대명사의 형태로 고쳐 쓰면 돼요.

정답: The girl introduced herself to the teacher.

Point Exercise

정답 및 해설 p.10

배열 영작

[1-5] 우리말과 일치하도록 주어진 단어를 올바르게 배열하세요.

1

나는 내 자신이 자랑스럽다.
(proud of / I / myself / am)

→ __________________________

__________________________ .

2

너는 지금 너 자신에게 집중해야 해.
(yourself / you / focus on / should)

→ __________________________

__________________________ now.

3

우리는 우리 자신을 믿어야 한다.
(we / believe in / have to / ourselves)

→ __________________________

__________________________ .

4

Peter는 거울에 비친 자신의 모습을 바라보았다.
(looked at / himself / Peter / in the mirror)

→ __________________________

__________________________ .

5

그녀는 그 실수에 대해 자신을 탓했다.
(blamed / the mistake / herself / for / she)

→ __________________________

__________________________ .

주어진 단어로 영작

[6-9] 우리말과 일치하도록 주어진 단어를 사용하여 문장을 완성하세요. (필요시 형태를 바꿀 것)

6

그들은 자신들의 사진을 찍었다.
(a picture of, take)

→ __________________________

____

7

그 소년은 커튼 뒤에 자신을 숨겼다.
(the boy, hide)

→ __________________________

behind the curtains.

8

너희들은 너 자신들을 보살펴 주어야 한다.
(take care of, should)

→ __________________________

____

9

나는 깨진 유리 조각에 나 자신을 베였다.
(cut, on the broken glass)

→ __________________________

기출: 문맥에 맞게 영작

10 다음 글을 읽고 우리말과 일치하도록 주어진 단어를 사용해 문장을 완성하세요.

Tina had an art class today. 그녀는 캔버스에 자기 자신을 그렸다. She showed her drawing to the class. Everyone praised her for her drawing. She was very happy.

→ __________________________

__________________________ (draw, on canvas)

---

be proud of ~을 자랑스러워하다 focus on ~에 집중하다 believe in ~을 믿다 mirror 거울 blame ~을 탓하다 hide 감추다, 숨기다 take care of ~을 보살피다 praise 칭찬하다 canvas 캔버스 천

Unit 03 지시대명사와 부정대명사

POINT 6 특정한 대상을 가리키는 this/that, these/those

이것은 그녀의 펜이 아니다.   저것이 그녀의 펜이다.
이것은 / ~이 아니다 / 그녀의 펜.   저것이 / ~이다 / 그녀의 펜.

→ **This** / is not / her pen.   **That** / is / her pen.

- this(이것, 이 사람)와 that(저것, 저 사람)은 말하는 사람과 가까이 있거나 멀리 있는 대상을 가리키는 대명사예요.
- 가리키는 대상이 여럿일 때는 these(이것들, 이 사람들) 또는 those(저것들, 저 사람들)를 써요.
- this/that, these/those 뒤에 명사가 오면 '이 ~(들)' 또는 '저 ~(들)'이라는 뜻으로, 명사를 꾸며 주는 형용사처럼 쓰여요.
  Those *boxes* are heavy. 저 상자들은 무겁다.

POINT 7 뜻이 없는 주어 It

지금은 12시 30분이다.
~이다 / 12시 30분 / 지금.

→ **It** is / twelve thirty / now.

- 위 예문의 우리말 뜻에는 주어가 없어요. 이런 경우, 우리말을 영어로 옮길 때 뜻이 없는 주어 It을 쓰는데, 이를 **비인칭 주어**라 불러요. 보통 날씨, 온도, 시간, 날짜, 요일, 계절, 거리 등을 나타낼 때 많이 쓰여요.

🔊 비인칭 주어 It이 쓰이는 경우

날씨	**It** is very cold in December. 12월에는 몹시 춥다.
시간	**It** is twelve o'clock. 12시 정각이다.
날짜	**It's** September 2nd. 9월 2일이다.
거리	**It** is a long way from New York City to L.A. 뉴욕에서 L.A.까지는 멀다.

대표 기출 문제

🔒 다음 <보기>의 밑줄 친 우리말을 4 단어로 영작하시오.
(숫자도 영어로 쓰시오.)

<보기>
I ran my first marathon yesterday.
<u>5시간이 걸렸어</u>.

→ _______________________________ .

CLUE
얼마나 시간이 걸리는지 영어로 나타낼 때 무엇을 주어로 쓸까? — 비인칭 주어 It

정답: It took five hours

Point Exercise

정답 및 해설 p.10

[1-4] 우리말과 일치하도록 빈칸에 알맞은 말을 〈보기〉에서 골라 쓰세요.

> 〈보기〉
> this   that   these   those

1 저것은 Harper의 휴대 전화이다.

→ ＿＿＿＿＿＿ is Harper's cell phone.

2 이것은 나의 가족사진이다.

→ ＿＿＿＿＿＿ is my family photo.

3 이 책들은 내 것이 아니다.

→ ＿＿＿＿＿＿ books are not mine.

4 저 귀여운 햄스터들 좀 봐!

→ Look at ＿＿＿＿＿＿ cute hamsters!

[5-9] 우리말과 일치하도록 주어진 단어를 올바르게 배열하세요.

5
> 오늘 날씨가 따뜻하다.
> (warm / is / today / it)

→ ＿＿＿＿＿＿＿＿＿＿ .

6
> 저것들은 네 펜이니?
> (those / pens / are / your)

→ ＿＿＿＿＿＿＿＿＿＿ ?

7
> 이 신발은 나에게 너무 꽉 낀다.
> (too tight / these / are / shoes)

→ ＿＿＿＿＿＿＿＿＿＿

    for me.

8
> 저기 있는 저 사람이 Richard야.
> (Richard / that / over there / is)

→ ＿＿＿＿＿＿＿＿＿＿ .

9
> 도서관까지는 한 시간이 걸린다.
> (it / to the library / takes / hour / an)

→ ＿＿＿＿＿＿＿＿＿＿ .

[10-11] 괄호 안의 단어를 사용하여 질문에 대한 답을 쓰세요.

10 A: When is your birthday?

    B: ＿＿＿＿＿＿＿＿＿＿＿

    (July 30th)

11 A: How's the weather today?

    B: ＿＿＿＿＿＿＿＿＿＿＿

    (rainy)

12 다음 표를 보고 〈보기〉와 같이 문장을 완성하세요.

City	Date	Day	Time
Paris	March 28th	Thursday	11:00 p.m.
Seoul	March 29th	Friday	7:00 a.m.

> 〈보기〉
> Date: In Paris, it is March 28th.
> In Seoul, it is March 29th.

(1) Day: In Paris, ＿＿＿＿＿＿＿＿＿ .

    In Seoul, ＿＿＿＿＿＿＿＿＿ .

(2) Time: In Paris, ＿＿＿＿＿＿＿＿＿ .

    In Seoul, ＿＿＿＿＿＿＿＿＿ .

cell phone 휴대 전화   photo 사진   hamster 햄스터   tight 꽉 끼는, 딱 붙는   over there 저쪽에

some, any: 정확하지 않은 수량

A: 케이크를 좀 드시겠어요?
드시겠어요 / 케이크를 좀?

B: 네. 조금만 주세요.
네. 주세요 / 조금만.

→ A: Would you like / **some** cake?
B: Yes, please. Give me / **some**.

↗ 우리말 번역에서 종종 생략되므로 any의 역할과 의미는 문장 안에서 파악해야 해요.

A: 너는 오늘 (어떤) 특별한 계획이라도 있니?
너는 있니 / (어떤) 특별한 계획이라도 / 오늘?

B: 아니, 나는 전혀 없어.

→ A: Do you have / **any** special plans / today?
B: No, I don't have **any**.

• some과 any는 둘 다 막연한 수나 양을 나타내는데, 명사 앞에서 형용사처럼 쓰이기도 해요.

some	any
긍정문/긍정의 대답을 기대하는 의문문	의문문/부정문
((긍정문)) 약간(의), 몇몇(의)	((의문문)) 몇몇의, 약간의, 조금
	((부정문)) 조금도 ~하지 않는, 전혀[하나도] ~없는

-one, -body, -thing: 정해져 있지 않은 사람, 사물

누군가 밖에서 널 기다리고 있어.
누군가 / (~을) 기다리고 있어 / 너를 / 밖에서.

→ **Someone** / *is* waiting for / you / outside.

• -one, -body, -thing으로 끝나는 대명사는 불특정한 사람이나 사물을 가리켜요.
• 이 대명사들이 주어로 쓰일 때는 뒤에 3인칭 단수형의 동사가 오는 것에 주의하세요.

everyone[everybody] (모든 사람, 모두)	someone[somebody] (어떤 사람, 누군가)	anyone[anybody] (누군가, 누구라도)	no one[nobody] (아무도 ~않다)
everything (모든 것)	something (무언가)	anything (무언가, 무엇이든)	nothing (어떤 것도 ~아니다)

대표 기출 문제

🔒 밑줄 친 (B)를 의미에 맞게 영작하시오.
단, 주어진 두 단어를 반드시 사용하시오.

Soon, (B) 대회에 참가한 모든 사람이 그녀를 격려한다. (up, the)

→ ______________________________________

CLUE 1
우리말에 따르면 주어 자리에는 '모든 사람'이라는 의미의 대명사(everyone[everybody])가 와야 해요.

CLUE 2
-one, -body로 끝나는 대명사는 단수 취급하므로, 그 뒤에 오는 '격려한다'라는 의미의 동사(cheer up)도 단수형으로 써야 해요.

정답: everyone[everybody] in the contest cheers her up.

Point Exercise

정답 및 해설 p.10

[1-4] 우리말과 일치하도록 주어진 단어를 올바르게 배열하세요.

1

쿠키 좀 먹을래?
(do / cookies / want / you / some)

→ ______________________________ ?

2

극장에 있는 모든 사람들이 웃었다.
(laughed / in the theater / everyone)

→ ______________________________ .

3

나는 오늘 숙제가 하나도 없다.
(have / I / homework / don't / any)

→ ______________________________
today.

4

탁자 위에는 아무것도 없다.
(anything / isn't / on the table / there)

→ ______________________________ .

[5-8] 다음 각 문장에서 어법상 <u>틀린</u> 부분을 찾아 바르게 고쳐 쓰세요.

5 Can I have any water, please?

______________ → ______________

6 Nobody know everything.

______________ → ______________

7 I don't have some plans for this weekend.

______________ → ______________

8 Everybody in my class like him.

______________ → ______________

[9-11] 우리말과 일치하도록 주어진 단어를 사용하여 문장을 완성하세요. (필요시 형태를 바꿀 것)

9

주방에서 무언가 맛있는 냄새가 난다.
(something, smell)

→ ______________________________
delicious in the kitchen.

10

나는 지금 돈이 하나도 없다.
(money, any, have)

→ I ______________________________
right now.

11

상자 안에는 아무것도 없었다.
(be, there, nothing)

→ ______________________________
in the box.

12 다음 글을 읽고 어법상 <u>틀린</u> 부분을 찾아 바르게 고쳐 쓰세요.

Today, we are talking about our favorite animals. Everyone share their favorite animals. My best friend, Minho shows a picture of his cat. It is very cute!

______________ → ______________

theater 극장, 영화관 right now 지금 당장 share 함께 나누다, 공유하다

Chapter Test *

정답 및 해설 p.10

STAGE 1) Go for it!

자신 있게 풀어보는 기초 문제!

배열 영작

[1-4] 우리말과 일치하도록 주어진 단어를 배열하여 문장을 완성하세요.

1

> 어제는 매우 흐렸다.
> (was / cloudy / very / it)

→ ____________________________________

yesterday.

2

> 이 영화는 아주 흥미로워. 너도 그것을 봐야 해.
> (is / this / interesting / movie / very)

→ ____________________________________

____________________________________.

You should watch it.

3

> 내 여동생은 주스 세 병을 샀다.
> (bottles / little sister / juice / bought / of / three / my)

→ ____________________________________

____________________________________.

4

> 운동장에는 다섯 명의 남자아이들이 있다.
> (there / the playground / boys / are / five / in)

→ ____________________________________

____________________________________.

빈칸 완성

[5-7] 우리말과 일치하도록 주어진 단어를 사용하여 빈칸에 알맞은 말을 쓰세요. (필요시 형태를 바꿀 것)

5

> Leah는 밥 두 그릇을 먹었다. (bowl, rice)

→ Leah ate ____________ ____________

____________ ____________.

6

> 누군가가 문을 두드리고 있다. (knock)

→ ____________ ____________

____________ on the door.

7

> 그는 지금 동전이 하나도 없다. (coins, have)

→ He ____________ ____________

____________ now.

최신 기출

8 우리말과 일치하도록 주어진 단어를 배열하여 다음의 대화를 완성하세요. (필요시 형태를 바꿀 것)

> Diana: Mom, are there any cookies left?
> Mom: No, (1) 우리는 쿠키가 하나도 없단다.
> But (2) 케이크가 좀 있어. How about that?

(1) ____________________________________.
(don't / have / cookies / any / we)

(2) ____________________________________.
(some / be / there / cake)

○─ 대화문 완성

[9-13] 주어진 단어를 사용하여 각 대화를 완성하세요.

9
> A: What did you buy at the supermarket?
> B: ____
>   at the supermarket. (five, tomato, buy)

10
> A: Minjun, how was your first day at school?
> B: It was great. Everyone was nice and
> ____
>   to the class. (introduce, I)

11
> A: It's really cold today. Do you want some
>   tea?
> B: Yes, please. _________________________
> ____?
>   (have, green tea, can, a cup of)

12
> A: What time is it now, Jane?
> B: ____
>   right now. (ten o'clock)

13
> A: Are there many movie theaters in your
>   town?
> B: No, _________________________. (there)
>   There is only one in my town.

○─ 그림 영작

14 다음 그림을 보고 주어진 단어를 사용하여 〈보기〉와 같이 문장을 완성하세요.

> 〈보기〉
> <u>There are three girls</u> on the picnic mat. (girl)

(1) ____
   under the tree. (dog)

(2) ____
   on the bench. (child)

(3) ____
   in the pond. (duck)

최신 기출

15 우리말과 일치하도록 〈조건〉에 맞게 문장을 완성하세요.

> 〈조건〉
> • 〈보기〉에서 알맞은 말을 골라 주어진 단어와
>   함께 사용할 것
> • (1)은 5 단어, (2)는 3 단어, (3)은 4 단어로 쓸 것

> 〈보기〉
> this   those   these   it

(1) 오늘은 3월 20일이다. (today, March 20th)
   → ____ .

(2) 여보세요, 저는 Tom입니다. (Tom)
   → Hello, _________________________________ .

(3) 이 양말은 짝이 안 맞다. (socks, match)
   → ____ .

[16-20] 빈칸에 들어갈 말을 〈보기〉에서 골라 알맞은 형태로 쓰세요. (단, 한 번씩만 사용할 것)

〈보기〉
loaf   bar   piece   glass   sheet

16 Joseph bought five ______________ bread at the bakery.

17 My sister drinks two ______________ milk every day.

18 I bought a ______________ chocolate at the store.

19 The restaurant prepared a hundred ______________ cake.

20 You need a pencil, an eraser, and a ______________ paper for the test.

21 우리말과 일치하도록 주어진 단어를 사용하여 다음의 대화를 완성하세요.

A: I'm so hungry. (1) 냉장고에 음식이 좀 있니?
B: Just a second. I'll check. Hmm…
  (2) 피자 두 조각이랑 주스가 좀 있어.
A: That's great! I can eat that!

(1) ____ ?
   (food, in the fridge, any, there)

(2) ____ .
   (pizza, some, there, juice)

[22-27] 다음 각 문장에서 어법상 **틀린** 부분을 찾아 바르게 고쳐 쓰세요.

22 Snails have over a thousand tooth.
______________ → ______________

23 This book on the table is not my.
______________ → ______________

24 I ate two piece of pizza in the afternoon.
______________ → ______________

25 That is August 15th today.
______________ → ______________

26 Can you solve this math problems?
______________ → ______________

27 A: Logan, do you have any pens?
B: Sorry, I don't have some.
______________ → ______________

28 다음 대화를 읽고 〈조건〉에 맞게 우리말을 영작하세요.

A: My family got a cat recently.
B: That's great! I also have a cat.
A: Oh, I got a question. Do you give your cat a bath?
B: Not really. 고양이들은 그들 자신을 깨끗하게 할 수 있어.

〈조건〉
• 4 단어로 쓸 것 • 주어진 단어를 사용하되 필요시 형태를 바꿀 것

→ ____
   (can, cat, clean)

심화 문제로 완벽하게 마무리!

도표 영작

29 이번 주 날씨를 보고 〈보기〉에서 알맞은 단어를 골라 〈조건〉에 맞게 문장을 완성하세요.

MON	TUE	WED	THU	FRI

〈보기〉

windy   sunny   cloudy   rainy

〈조건〉
• 미래 표현으로는 will을 사용할 것

(1) It is Monday today.

____ now.

(2) ____

on Tuesday.

(3) ____

on Wednesday.

(4) ____

on Thursday.

(5) ____

on Friday, too.

어법 오류 수정

30 다음 ⓐ~ⓔ 중 어법상 <u>틀린 두 개</u>를 찾아 그 기호를 쓰고, 바르게 고쳐 쓰세요.

My friends and I joined the art club at school. At ⓐ <u>ours club</u>, we draw pictures of people, places, and things. We sometimes ⓑ <u>go to parks</u> and draw trees, flowers, and animals. It is a lot of fun!

We show our pictures to ⓒ <u>everyone at the school festival</u> every year. ⓓ <u>These are our favorite event</u> of the year. Does it sound interesting to you? Then, please come to our club and ⓔ <u>draw some pictures</u> with us.

________ → ________________________

________ → ________________________

Challenge!

누적 문제 Ch 02-04

31 다음 중 어법상 <u>틀린 문장 두 개</u>를 찾아 그 기호를 쓰고, 문장 전체를 바르게 고쳐 쓰세요.

ⓐ She don't has to come here.
ⓑ We caught a lot of fish in the sea.
ⓒ It's about 2 kilometers from here to the station.
ⓓ There aren't much milk in the refrigerator.
ⓔ We're going to bake some cookies at home.

________ → ________________________

____

________ → ________________________

Chapter 05

형용사, 부사, 비교

✅ Before You Write

- ☑ 우리말의 어느 부분을 형용사나 부사로 나타낼 수 있을까요?
- ☑ 형용사는 명사를 꾸밀 때와 보어 역할일 때 각각 어디에 위치할까요?
- ☑ 부사는 의미와 역할에 따라 어느 자리에 써야 할까요?
- ☑ 비교급과 최상급은 어떤 형태로 써야 할까요?

내신 기출 다음 우리말을 보고 머릿속으로 한번 영어 문장을 떠올려 보세요.

1 ⓔ 그 강은 아주 진흙투성이가 되었다.
주어를 보충 설명 → 형용사 → **became muddy** `POINT 1`

2 그림을 보고 many나 much 둘 중 하나를 사용하여 영어로 문장을 완성하시오.
There (   ) (   ) (   ). (책들이 많이 있습니다.)
셀 수 있는 명사(book)의 복수형 앞 → **many books** `POINT 2`

3 (A) 왕은 공주를 따뜻하게 맞이했다.
The __________ __________ __________ __________ __________.
동사(greeted) 수식 → 부사 → **warmly** `POINT 3`

4 나는 가끔씩 점심 식사 전에 손을 씻는다.
→ I __________ __________ __________ __________ before __________.
빈도부사 → 일반동사(wash) 앞 → **sometimes wash** `POINT 4`

5 (A) Sally는 그녀의 친구들보다 더 빠르게 헤엄쳤다.
비교급 → 대부분의 형용사+-er → **faster than** `POINT 5`

6 (3) Mr. Steelbot은 세계에서 가장 힘이 센 로봇이다. (powerful)
→ Mr. Steelbot __________________________ robot in the world.
최상급 → 2음절 이상의 형용사 → **the most powerful** `POINT 6`

정답: **1** The river became very muddy. **2** are many books **3** king greeted the princess warmly[king warmly greeted the princess]
4 sometimes wash my hands, lunch **5** Sally swam faster than her friends. **6** is the most powerful

형용사

POINT 1 명사를 꾸미거나 주어를 보충 설명할 때

좋은 책은 훌륭한 친구이다.
좋은 책은 / ~이다 / 훌륭한 친구.

→ A **good** *book* / is / a **great** *friend*.

- 형용사란 사람이나 사물, 동물의 생김새나 크기, 모양, 수량 등을 설명해 주는 말이에요.
- 형용사는 명사 앞에 쓰여서 그 명사에 대해 자세히 꾸며줄 수 있어요.
- 단, -thing, -body, -one으로 끝나는 대명사를 꾸밀 때는 형용사를 대명사 뒤에 써야 합니다.
  I planned *something* **special** for my parents. 나는 부모님을 위해 특별한 무언가를 계획했다.

이 쿠키들은 맛있다.
이 쿠키들은 / ~하다 / 맛있는.
　주어　　　be동사　보어(형용사)

→ **These cookies** / are / **delicious**.

그 선물은 그를 행복하게 했다.
그 선물은 / (~하게) 했다 / 그를 / 행복한.
　주어　　　　동사　　　목적어　보어(형용사)

→ **The gift** / made / **him** / **happy**.

- 형용사는 be동사 뒤에서 주어를 보충 설명하거나, make, keep 등의 동사 뒤에서 목적어를 보충 설명해주
  는 역할을 해요. 이렇게 보충 설명하는 역할을 하는 형용사를 '보어'라고 해요. (☞ Ch 07 문장의 여러 형식)

대표 기출 문제

🔒 다음 문장을 우리말과 일치하도록 잘못된 곳을 찾아
올바른 문장으로 고쳐 쓰시오.

한지는 전통적인 한국의 종이이다.
Hanji is tradition Korean paper.

→ ______________________________________

CLUE 1

명사구 Korean paper 앞에 명사인 tradition이 위치
해 있어요.

CLUE 2

'전통적인'이라는 의미로 명사(구)를 앞에서 꾸며줄
수 있는 것은 형용사예요.

정답: Hanji is traditional Korean paper.

Point Exercise

[1-4] 주어진 단어를 알맞은 위치에 넣어 문장을 다시 쓰세요.

1

She buys bread every day. (fresh)

→ _______________________________________

____

2

A pianist visited Seoul. (famous)

→ _______________________________________

____

3

Daniel gave a present to me. (special)

→ _______________________________________

____

4

Jane should not drink anything. (cold)

→ _______________________________________

____

[5-8] 우리말과 일치하도록 주어진 단어를 올바르게 배열하세요.

5

우리의 새 학기는 3월에 시작한다.
(starts / semester / new / our)

→ _______________________________________

_______________________ in March.

6

그 아이들은 맛있는 햄버거를 먹었다.
(delicious / the children / hamburgers / ate)

→ _______________________________________

_______________________________________.

7

귀여운 소년들이 예쁜 꽃을 들고 있다.
(boys / are / pretty / cute / holding / flowers)

→ _______________________________________

_______________________________________.

8

그의 대답은 그녀를 화나게 했다.
(answer / angry / made / her / his)

→ _______________________________________.

9 다음 그림을 보고 〈보기〉에서 알맞은 형용사를 골라 주어진 단어와 함께 문장을 완성하세요.

〈보기〉
tall   colorful   strong   heavy

(1) Jiho is _______________________. (boy)

(2) Yuna is _______________________. (girl)

(3) Peter is holding _______________________

_______________________. (umbrella)

(4) Leah is carrying _______________________

_______________________. (something)

special 특별한 semester 학기 colorful (색이) 다채로운

POINT 2 — many, much, (a) few, (a) little을 써야 할 때

도로에 많은 차가 있다.
(~가) 있다 / 많은 차가 / 도로에.

many+셀 수 있는 명사의 복수형

→ There are / **many *cars*** / on the road.

우리는 지금 시간이 많지 않다.
우리는 없다 / 많은 시간이 / 지금.

much+셀 수 없는 명사

→ We don't have / **much *time*** / now.

- 형용사 중에는 many, much, (a) few, (a) little 등과 같이 수나 양의 많고 적음을 나타내는 것들이 있어요.
- 이때 뒤에 오는 명사가 셀 수 있는 명사인지, 셀 수 없는 명사인지에 따라 알맞은 형용사를 사용해야 합니다.

📢 수량을 나타내는 형용사

	셀 수 있는 명사의 복수형 앞	셀 수 없는 명사 앞
많은	**many** friends	**much** time
	a lot of[lots of] friends/time	
약간의, 조금 있는	**a few** friends	**a little** time
거의 없는	**few** friends	**little** time

대표 기출 문제

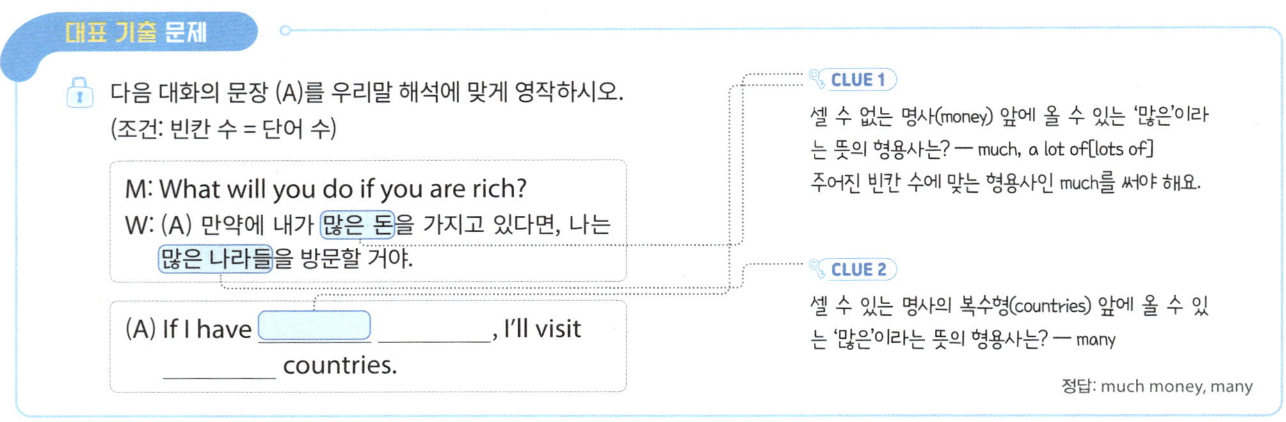

🔒 다음 대화의 문장 (A)를 우리말 해석에 맞게 영작하시오.
(조건: 빈칸 수 = 단어 수)

M: What will you do if you are rich?
W: (A) 만약에 내가 많은 돈을 가지고 있다면, 나는 많은 나라들을 방문할 거야.

(A) If I have _________ _________, I'll visit _________ countries.

CLUE 1
셀 수 없는 명사(money) 앞에 올 수 있는 '많은'이라는 뜻의 형용사는? — much, a lot of[lots of]
주어진 빈칸 수에 맞는 형용사인 much를 써야 해요.

CLUE 2
셀 수 있는 명사의 복수형(countries) 앞에 올 수 있는 '많은'이라는 뜻의 형용사는? — many

정답: much money, many

✅ **함정 피하기** 셀 수 있는 명사와 함께 쓰이는 many, a few, few 등은 뒤에 명사의 복수형이 와야 해요.
There are **many flower**(→ flowers) in the garden. (그 정원에는 많은 꽃들이 있다.)
I have **a few question**(→ questions). (저는 질문이 몇 개 있어요.)

Point Exercise

정답 및 해설 p.12

[1-3] 우리말과 일치하도록 주어진 단어를 올바르게 배열하세요.

1
> 이번 여름에는 비가 많이 오지 않았다.
> (rain / wasn't / much / there)

→ ______________________________
______________________________ this summer.

2
> 그녀는 가방에 많은 간식을 가지고 있다.
> (lots / she / has / snacks / of)

→ ______________________________
______________________________ in her bag.

3
> 나는 내 남동생을 위해 음식을 조금 남겨두었다.
> (my little brother / a little / for / I / food / left)

→ ______________________________
______________________________ .

[4-7] 우리말과 일치하도록 〈보기〉에서 알맞은 말을 골라 주어진 단어를 사용하여 문장을 완성하세요.
(단, 한 번씩만 쓸 것)

〈보기〉
little   much   a few   many

4
> 그녀는 James에게 꽃 몇 송이를 사줄 것이다.
> (will, flower, buy)

→ ______________________________
______________________________ for James.

5
> 서울에서 인천까지 많은 시간이 걸리지 않는다.
> (doesn't, take, it, time)

→ ______________________________
______________________________ from Seoul to Incheon.

6
> 그는 스포츠에 관심이 거의 없다.
> (interest, have, in sports)

→ ______________________________
____

7
> 그 서점은 많은 아동용 책을 판매한다.
> (sell, children's book, the bookstore)

→ ______________________________
____

8 우리말과 일치하도록 〈조건〉에 맞게 문장을 완성하세요.

〈조건〉
- 〈보기〉에서 알맞은 말을 골라 쓸 것
- 주어진 단어를 함께 사용하되, 필요시 형태를 바꿀 것

〈보기〉
many   much   few   little

(1)
> 교실 안에 학생들이 거의 없었다.
> (student, be, there)

→ ______________________________
______________________________ in the classroom.

(2)
> 나의 집 근처에는 고양이들이 많다.
> (cat, be, there)

→ ______________________________
near my house.

snack 간식   interest 관심, 흥미

POINT 3 동사, 형용사, 부사, 문장 전체를 꾸며줄 때

Jim은 매우 어려운 퀴즈들을 빠르게 풀었다.
Jim은 / 풀었다 / 매우 어려운 퀴즈들을 / 빠르게.
　　　동사　　부사　형용사　　　　　부사

→ Jim / *solved* / *very difficult* quizzes / **quickly**.

- 형용사가 명사와 함께 쓰이는 반면, 부사는 동사, 형용사, 다른 부사 또는 문장 전체를 더 자세하게 설명하고 꾸며 주는 역할을 해요.

  Luckily, *I passed the test* **so** *easily*. 운 좋게도, 나는 그 시험을 아주 쉽게 통과했다.

📢 부사의 형태

대부분의 부사	형용사+-ly	slow**ly**	loud**ly**	soft**ly**	beautiful**ly**
「자음+y」로 끝나는 형용사	-y를 i로 바꾸고+-ly	happ**ily**	luck**ily**	bus**ily**	eas**ily**
-le로 끝나는 형용사	e를 없애고+-y	terrib**ly**	gent**ly**	simp**ly**	
형용사와 형태가 같은 부사	late(늦은/늦게)	fast(빠른/빨리)	high(높은/높게)	hard(단단한, 어려운/열심히)	
-ly가 붙으면 뜻이 달라지는 부사	lately(최근에)	highly(매우)	hardly(거의 ~않다)		

📢 부사의 역할과 위치

역할	위치
동사를 꾸밀 때	주로 동사의 뒤 또는 문장 끝
형용사를 꾸밀 때	형용사 바로 앞
다른 부사를 꾸밀 때	다른 부사 바로 앞
문장 전체를 꾸밀 때	주로 문장 맨 앞

대표 기출 문제

🔒 주어진 단어를 활용하여 의미가 일치하는 문장을 바르게 완성하시오.

그들은 영원히 행복하게 살았다. (live)

→ They ＿＿＿＿＿＿＿＿＿ ever after.

CLUE 1
'행복하게'라는 말이 동사 live를 더 자세히 설명해 줄 수 있어요.

CLUE 2
동사를 꾸미거나 설명할 때는 부사(happily)를 사용해야 해요.

정답: lived happily

Point Exercise

배열 영작

[1-5] 우리말과 일치하도록 주어진 단어를 올바르게 배열하세요.

1

너는 사람들 앞에서 분명하게 말해야 한다.
(should / speak / clearly / you)

→ ______________________________

______________________ in front of people.

2

그 작가의 책은 나에게 매우 어렵다.
(book / difficult / the writer's / very / is)

→ ______________________________

______________________ for me.

3

내 개는 매우 크게 짖었다.
(loudly / my / so / barked / dog)

→ ______________________________

______________________ .

4

운 좋게도, 나는 빈 좌석을 쉽게 발견했다.
(an empty seat / luckily / easily / found)

→ ____________ , I ____________

______________________ .

5

우리는 그 공연을 정말 열심히 준비했다.
(the performance / hard / we / really /
prepared for)

→ ______________________________

______________________ .

주어진 단어로 영작

[6-9] 우리말과 일치하도록 주어진 단어를 사용하여 문장을 완성하세요. (필요시 형태를 바꿀 것)

6

그 커튼은 내 방과 완벽하게 어울린다.
(matches, the curtain, perfect)

→ ______________________________

______________________ with my room.

7

그는 기타를 아름답게 연주했다.
(beautiful, the guitar, played)

→ ______________________________

____

8

Paul은 내 질문에 아주 침착하게 대답했다.
(very, my, answered, question, calm)

→ ______________________________

____

9

기쁘게도, 나는 경기에서 우승했다.
(first place, won, in the race, happy)

→ ______________________________

____

기출: 조건 영작

10 우리말과 일치하도록 〈조건〉에 맞게 문장을 완성하세요.

〈조건〉
• 7 단어로 쓸 것
• the questions, solve, very, easy를 사용할 것
• 필요시 형태를 바꿀 것

나는 그 문제들을 매우 쉽게 풀 수 있다.

→ ______________________________

---

clearly 분명하게 loudly 큰 소리로 bark (개가) 짖다 empty 비어 있는 seat 좌석, 자리 performance 공연 prepare for ~을 준비하다 match 어울리다 perfect 완벽한
calm 차분한, 침착한 win first place 우승하다

POINT 4 · 얼마나 자주 일어나는지를 나타낼 때

학교는 항상 오전 9시에 시작한다.
학교는 / 항상 시작한다 / 오전 9시에.

→ School / **always starts** / at 9 a.m.
빈도부사+일반동사

이 시간에는 교통이 대개 혼잡하다.
교통이 / 대개 혼잡하다 / 이 시간에는.

→ The traffic / **is usually** heavy / at this time.
be동사+빈도부사

너는 절대로 네 꿈을 포기해서는 안 된다.
너는 / 절대 포기하면 안 된다 / 네 꿈들을.

→ You / **should never** give up / your dreams.
조동사+빈도부사

- always(항상), usually(보통) 등과 같이 어떤 일이 얼마나 자주 일어나는지를 나타내는 부사를 **빈도부사**라고 합니다.
- 빈도부사는 문장에서 정해진 위치에 써야 하는데, 일반동사가 쓰인 문장에서는 **일반동사 앞**에, be동사나 조동사가 쓰인 문장에서는 **be동사/조동사 뒤**에 써야 해요.

빈도부사의 종류와 의미

0% ——————————————————→ 100%

never (전혀 ~않다) < **sometimes** (때때로, 가끔) < **often** (자주) < **usually** (보통, 대개) < **always** (항상, 늘)

대표 기출 문제

제시된 조건을 반드시 지켜 우리말을 영작하시오.

> 나의 강아지는 항상 문제를 일으킨다.

- 다음 단어들을 반드시 사용할 것 (필요하면 형태 변형 가능)
  단어: make, trouble

→ _______________________________________ .

CLUE 1
'항상'이라는 의미의 빈도부사는?
— always

CLUE 2
문장의 동사 make는 일반동사이므로 always를 make 앞에 써야 해요.

정답: My dog always makes trouble

Point Exercise

[1-4] 우리말과 일치하도록 주어진 단어를 올바르게 배열하세요.

1
> 보라는 그녀의 오빠와 가끔 영화를 본다.
> (a movie / watches / sometimes)

→ Bora ___________________________________

___________________________ with her brother.

2
> John은 일요일에 보통 집에 있다.
> (at home / usually / is)

→ John ___________________________________

on Sunday.

3
> 나는 아침 식사를 절대 거르지 않을 것이다.
> (will / breakfast / skip / never / I)

→ ___________________________________ .

4
> 나의 부모님은 나를 항상 자랑스러워하신다.
> (always / my / proud / are / parents / of me)

→ ___________________________________

___________________________________ .

[5-8] 우리말과 일치하도록 〈보기〉에서 알맞은 말을 골라 주어진 단어를 사용하여 문장을 완성하세요.

> 〈보기〉
> always　　　never　　　usually　　　often

5
> 이 나라에서는 보통 비가 오지 않는다.
> (rain, doesn't, it)

→ ___________________________________

___________________________ in this country.

6
> 우리는 선생님의 말씀을 항상 주의 깊게 듣는다.
> (our teacher, listen to)

→ ___________________________________

___________________________ carefully.

7
> 너는 저 해변 근처에서 돌고래들을 자주 볼 수 있다.
> (can, dolphins, see)

→ ___________________________________

___________________________ near that beach.

8
> 내 친구들은 학교에 절대 지각하지 않는다.
> (late, my friends, for school, are)

→ ___________________________________

9 다음 표를 보고 〈보기〉와 같이 문장을 완성하세요.
(단, 현재시제를 사용할 것)

	always	usually	often	never
get up early		○		
(1) be busy	○			
(2) ride a bike				○
(3) play the violin			○	

> 〈보기〉
> She <u>usually gets up early</u>.

(1) My dad ___________________________________ .

(2) Nick ___________________________________ .

(3) They ___________________________________ .

skip 거르다, 빼먹다

비교급과 최상급

비교급+than ~

오늘은 어제보다 더 춥다.
오늘은 / 더 춥다 / 어제보다.

→ Today / is **colder** / **than** yesterday.

소리는 빛보다 더 느리게 이동한다.
소리는 / 이동한다 / 더 느리게 / 빛보다.

→ Sound / travels / **more slowly** / **than** light.

• '~보다 더 …한[하게]'라는 의미는 「**형용사[부사]의 비교급+than ~**」으로 나타냅니다. 비교급은 두 대상을 비교하는 것이므로, 비교의 대상 앞에는 '~보다'라는 의미의 **than**을 써야 해요.
• 비교급은 주로 형용사나 부사 뒤에 **-er**이나 **-r**을 붙이는데, 그 밖의 규칙을 따르거나 불규칙한 형태로 변하는 것들은 반드시 암기해 두어야 합니다.

📢 비교급 만드는 방법

대부분의 형용사/부사	+-er	tall – tall**er**	fast – fast**er**
-e로 끝나는 형용사/부사	+-r	nice – nicer	wise – wiser
「자음+y」로 끝나는 형용사/부사	y를 i로 고치고 +-er	happy – happ**ier**	busy – bus**ier**
「모음 1개+자음 1개」로 끝나는 형용사/부사	마지막 자음을 한 번 더 쓰고 +-er	hot – hot**ter**	big – big**ger**
2음절 이상의 형용사/부사	more +	popular – **more** popular	
불규칙하게 변하는 형용사/부사	good/well – **better** bad – **worse**	many/much – **more** little – **less**	

대표 기출 문제

🔒 다음 우리말 문장을 주어진 단어의 비교급을 사용하여 완성하시오.

(1) Jack이 Tom보다 키가 더 크다. (tall)

→ Jack is _____________ than Tom.

(2) 흰색 가방이 초록색 가방보다 더 무겁다. (heavy)

→ The white bag is _____________ the green one.

CLUE 1

'키가 더 큰'이라는 의미를 나타내려면 형용사 tall을 비교급(taller)으로 써요.

CLUE 2

'더 무거운'이라는 의미를 나타내려면 형용사 heavy를 비교급(heavier)으로 써요. 비교급 뒤에 '~보다'에 해당하는 than도 빠뜨리지 않아야 해요.

정답: (1) taller (2) heavier than

Point Exercise

정답 및 해설 p.13

배열 영작

[1-3] 우리말과 일치하도록 주어진 단어를 올바르게 배열하세요.

1

Gary는 Paul보다 더 빠르게 달린다.
(Paul / runs / than / faster)

→ Gary ___________________________

___________________________ .

2

어떤 나라들에서는 물이 석유보다 더 비싸다.
(is / expensive / oil / than / more)

→ In some countries, water ___________

___________________________ .

3

나는 나의 언니보다 노래를 더 잘할 수 있다.
(sing / can / better / my sister / than)

→ I ___________________________

___________________________ .

주어진 단어로 영작

[4-6] 우리말과 일치하도록 주어진 단어를 사용하여 문장을 완성하세요. (필요시 형태를 바꿀 것)

4

Susan은 Jina보다 더 일찍 일어난다.
(early, get up)

→ ___________________________

____

5

그 팀은 지난해보다 더 못했다.
(do, last year, bad, the team)

→ ___________________________

____

6

에펠탑은 루브르 박물관보다 더 유명하다.
(be, famous, the Eiffel Tower, the Louvre Museum)

→ ___________________________

____

어법 오류 수정

[7-8] 다음 각 문장에서 어법상 **틀린** 부분을 찾아 바르게 고쳐 쓰세요.

7 The kite flew high than the trees.

_______________ → _______________

8 Homemade food is healthyer than fast food.

_______________ → _______________

기출: 도표 영작

9 다음 표를 보고 〈보기〉와 같이 주어진 단어를 사용하여 문장을 완성하세요.

	Bag A	Bag B	Bag C
크기	Medium	Large	Small
무게	1 kg	0.5 kg	0.7 kg
인기	★	★★★	★★★★

〈보기〉
Bag A is smaller than Bag B. (small)

(1) Bag A ___________________________ .
(big)

(2) Bag C ___________________________ .
(heavy)

(3) Bag B ___________________________ .
(popular)

expensive 비싼 famous 유명한 homemade 집에서 만든 healthy 건강에 좋은 popular 인기 있는

the+최상급(+명사)+in[of] ~

> 영어는 모든 시험 중에서 가장 쉬웠다.
> 영어는 / 가장 쉬웠다 / 모든 시험 중에서.
>
> → English / was **the easiest** / **of** all the exams.

> 그는 그 팀에서 가장 훌륭한 선수이다.
> 그는 / 가장 훌륭한 선수이다 / 그 팀에서.
>
> → He / is **the best** player / **in** the team.

- '~ 중에서 가장 …한[하게]'라는 의미는 「**the＋형용사[부사]의 최상급(＋명사)＋in[of] ~**」으로 나타냅니다. 최상급은 셋 이상의 대상을 비교하는 것이므로, '~ 중에서'라는 의미의 범위를 나타내는 'in[of] ~'와 함께 쓰여요.
- 최상급은 **형용사와 부사 뒤에** 주로 **-est**나 **-st**를 붙여요. 그 밖의 규칙을 따르거나 불규칙적으로 변하는 것들은 반드시 암기해 두세요.

📢 **최상급 만드는 방법**

대부분의 형용사/부사	+-est	tall – tall**est**	fast – fast**est**
-e로 끝나는 형용사/부사	+-st	nice – nice**st**	wise – wise**st**
「자음+y」로 끝나는 형용사/부사	y를 i로 고치고 +-est	happy – happ**iest**	busy – bus**iest**
「모음 1개+자음 1개」로 끝나는 형용사/부사	마지막 자음을 한 번 더 쓰고 +-est	hot – hot**test**	big – big**gest**
2음절 이상의 형용사/부사	most +	popular – **most** popular	
불규칙하게 변하는 형용사/부사	good/well – **best** bad – **worst**	many/much – **most** little – **least**	

대표 기출 문제

🔒 우리말과 같은 뜻이 되도록 주어진 단어들을 이용하여 문장을 완성하시오.

그는 한국에서 가장 인기 있는 가수이다.
(popular, singer)

→ ___________________________ in Korea.

CLUE 1
'가장 ~한'이라는 의미를 나타낼 때는 최상급을 사용해요.

CLUE 2
형용사 popular의 최상급은?
— the most popular

정답: He is[He's] the most popular singer

✅ **함정 피하기** 최상급 뒤에 '~ 중에서'라는 의미로 장소나 특정 집단을 쓸 때는 주로 「in+단수명사」를 쓰고, 기간을 나타내는 말이나 복수명사와 쓰일 때는 「of+기간」 또는 「of+복수명사」를 써요.
in the world / in Korea / in the class / in my family
of my life / of us / of all the people[students]

Point Exercise

[1-4] 우리말과 일치하도록 주어진 단어를 올바르게 배열하세요.

1
> 그 산은 우리나라에서 가장 아름답다.
> (most / in my country / is / beautiful / the)

→ The mountain ________________________

________________________ .

2
> Johnny는 우리 학교에서 춤을 가장 잘 춘다.
> (best / in our school / dances / the)

→ Johnny ________________________

________________________ .

3
> 수미는 우리 반에서 가장 긴 머리카락을 가지고 있다.
> (has / longest / in my class / the / hair)

→ Sumi ________________________

________________________ .

4
> 봄은 일 년 중 가장 멋진 시기이다.
> (wonderful / most / of the year / is / time / the)

→ Spring ________________________

________________________ .

[5-9] 우리말과 일치하도록 주어진 단어를 사용하여 문장을 완성하세요. (필요시 형태를 바꿀 것)

5
> 나는 세상에서 가장 행복한 사람이다.
> (happy, be, in the world, person)

→ ________________________

____

6
> 이 식당은 우리 마을에서 가장 좋다.
> (nice, restaurant, be, this, in my town)

→ ________________________

____

7
> 오늘은 올해 중 가장 더운 날이었다.
> (be, of this year, hot, today, day)

→ ________________________

____

8
> 과학은 나에게 가장 어려운 과목이다.
> (be, subject, science, difficult)

→ ________________________

________________________ for me.

9
> 판다는 그 동물원에서 가장 인기 있는 동물이다.
> (the panda, popular, be, in the zoo, animal)

→ ________________________

____

10 다음 표를 보고 주어진 단어를 사용하여 문장을 완성하세요. (단, 현재시제를 사용할 것)

	Cheetah	Lion	Rabbit
Speed	120 km/h	80 km/h	40 km/h

(1) ________________________
of the three. (fast)

(2) ________________________
of the three. (slow)

person 사람 subject 과목; 주제 cheetah 치타

Chapter Test *

STAGE 1) Go for it!

자신 있게 풀어보는 기초 문제!

빈칸 완성

[1-5] 우리말과 일치하도록 주어진 단어를 사용하여 빈칸에 알맞은 말을 쓰세요.

1
> 그녀는 화창한 날과 맑은 하늘을 아주 좋아한다.
> (day, clear, a, sky, sunny)

→ She loves ＿＿＿＿＿＿ ＿＿＿＿＿＿
＿＿＿＿＿＿ and ＿＿＿＿＿＿
＿＿＿＿＿＿ ＿＿＿＿＿＿.

2
> 이 거리에는 식당이 몇 개 있다.
> (restaurant, few)

→ There are ＿＿＿＿＿＿ ＿＿＿＿＿＿
＿＿＿＿＿＿ in this street.

3
> 내 컴퓨터는 네 것보다 더 느리다. (slow)

→ My computer is ＿＿＿＿＿＿
＿＿＿＿＿＿ yours.

4
> Kate의 방은 항상 깨끗하다.
> (clean, always, be)

→ Kate's room ＿＿＿＿＿＿ ＿＿＿＿＿＿
＿＿＿＿＿＿.

5
> 오늘은 내 인생에서 최악의 날이었다.
> (bad, day)

→ Today was ＿＿＿＿＿＿
＿＿＿＿＿＿ of my life.

배열 영작

[6-8] 우리말과 일치하도록 주어진 단어를 배열하여 문장을 완성하세요. (필요시 형태를 바꿀 것)

6
> Jake는 보통 저녁 식사 후에 설거지를 한다.
> (usually / the dishes / wash / dinner / after)

→ Jake ＿＿＿＿＿＿＿＿＿＿＿＿＿＿＿＿
＿＿＿＿＿＿＿＿＿＿＿＿＿＿＿＿＿.

7
> 냉장고에 시원한 거라도 있니?
> (cold / there / anything / is)

→ ＿＿＿＿＿＿＿＿＿＿＿＿＿＿＿＿＿
in the refrigerator?

8
> 어떤 동물들은 인간보다 더 오래 살 수 있다.
> (than / live / humans / can / long)

→ Some animals ＿＿＿＿＿＿＿＿＿＿＿
＿＿＿＿＿＿＿＿＿＿＿＿＿＿＿＿＿.

최신 기출

9 우리말과 일치하도록 주어진 단어를 배열하여 다음의 글을 완성하세요. (필요시 형태를 바꿀 것)

> My friend's name is Danny. He might not be the funniest person, (1) 하지만 그는 아주 잘 들어주는 사람이다. (2) 그는 항상 그의 친구들의 얘기를 주의 깊게 들어준다. He is a good friend.

(1) but ＿＿＿＿＿＿＿＿＿＿＿＿＿＿.
(be / great / a / he / listener)

(2) ＿＿＿＿＿＿＿＿＿＿＿＿＿＿＿＿＿
＿＿＿＿＿＿＿＿＿＿＿＿＿＿＿ carefully.
(always / his friends / listen to / he)

◦ 보기에서 골라 영작

[10-14] 다음 대화의 빈칸에 들어갈 알맞은 말을 〈보기〉에서 골라 쓰세요. (단, 한 번씩만 쓸 것)

〈보기〉
many　　much　　few　　little　　a little

10

A: Why is Ms. Kelly so angry?

B: _______________ students did their homework.

11

A: John, let's study at my house together.

B: I'm sorry. I don't have _______________ time. I should go home in an hour.

12

A: What did you eat for breakfast?

B: I ate _______________ bread for breakfast

13

A: Did you do well on the test?

B: No, I made _______________ mistakes on the test.

14

A: Where are you going?

B: I'm going to the supermarket. There's _______________ milk in the refrigerator.

◦ 그림 영작

15 다음 그림을 보고 〈조건〉에 맞게 키를 비교하는 문장을 완성하세요.

Maria　Sandra　Nick

〈조건〉
• be동사와 현재시제를 사용할 것
• tall과 short 중 하나를 사용할 것

(1) Sandra _______________ than Nick.

(2) Maria _______________ than Nick.

(3) Maria _______________ of the three.

(4) Sandra _______________ of the three.

최신 기출

16 다음 표를 보고 〈조건〉에 맞게 문장을 완성하세요.

	Phone A	Phone B	Phone C
가격	$750	$900	$1200
무게	150 g	170 g	160 g
인기	★	★★★	★★★★

〈조건〉
• 현재시제를 사용할 것
• 주어진 단어를 사용할 것

(1) Phone A _______________ Phone B. (cheap, be)

(2) Phone B _______________ of the three. (heavy, be)

(3) Phone C _______________ of the three. (popular, be)

[17-24] 다음 각 문장에서 어법상 <u>틀린</u> 부분을 찾아 바르게 고쳐 쓰세요.

17 Sad, Tim lost his wallet at the park.

_______________ → _______________

18 Did you buy special something for Jenny?

_______________ → _______________

19 There were a lot of child in the theater.

_______________ → _______________

20 These clothes are expensive than those shoes.

_______________ → _______________

21 This is the most big church in Paris.

_______________ → _______________

22 The streets are quiet today. There are not much people.

_______________ → _______________

23 This house is oldest in our village.

_______________ → _______________

24 My dad drives his car careful at night.

_______________ → _______________

[25-28] 괄호 안의 단어를 비교급과 최상급 중 알맞은 형태로 바꿔 문장 전체를 다시 쓰세요.

25 Jacob is (young) member in our book club.

→ _______________

____

26 I got up (early) than my brother this morning.

→ _______________

____

27 She answered the question (quickly) than me.

→ _______________

____

28 This is (interesting) book in the series.

→ _______________

____

29 다음 글을 읽고 우리말과 일치하도록 〈조건〉에 맞게 영작하세요.

Hello. I'm Kelly from Australia. The sunlight is very strong in my country. The strong sunlight isn't good for the skin. So our school has a special rule in summer. <u>우리는 밖에서 항상 모자를 써야 해요.</u> The hat is part of our school uniform.

〈조건〉
- wear, always, should, outside, a hat을 사용할 것
- 7 단어로 쓸 것

→ _______________

____

◦⟨ 문맥에 맞게 영작 ⟩

30 다음은 Henry의 여행 기록입니다. ⟨보기⟩에서 알맞은 말을 골라 many 또는 much와 함께 빈칸을 완성하세요. (필요시 형태를 바꿀 것)

⟨보기⟩
bear	information	fun
big fish	old tree	

Friday, July 20

   We arrived at Yosemite in the afternoon. We walked around Yosemite Valley and saw (1) ＿＿＿＿＿＿＿＿＿＿ and wild animals. We didn't have (2) ＿＿＿＿＿＿＿＿＿＿ about Yosemite. A park ranger told us, "There are (3) ＿＿＿＿＿＿＿＿＿＿ here. They love the honey inside the trees." Tomorrow, we're going to go fishing. I can't wait!

Saturday, July 21

   After breakfast, we went to Mirror Lake. Noah's father caught (4) ＿＿＿＿＿＿＿＿＿＿. We had so (5) ＿＿＿＿＿＿＿＿＿＿ all day. At night, Noah and I heard strange sounds. We looked outside and saw a big shadow. It wasn't a bear. It was Noah's father!

◦⟨ 도표 영작 ⟩

31 다음 민수의 일과표를 보고 ⟨보기⟩에서 알맞은 말을 골라 문장을 완성하세요.

Routine	Mon	Tue	Wed	Thur	Fri
(1) exercise in the morning			○		○
(2) be late to class					
(3) have dinner with his friends	○	○		○	○

⟨보기⟩
sometimes	often	never	always

(1) Minsu ＿＿＿＿＿＿＿＿＿＿＿＿＿＿＿＿

＿＿＿＿＿＿＿＿＿＿＿＿＿＿＿＿.

(2) Minsu ＿＿＿＿＿＿＿＿＿＿＿＿＿＿＿＿

＿＿＿＿＿＿＿＿＿＿＿＿＿＿＿＿.

(3) Minsu ＿＿＿＿＿＿＿＿＿＿＿＿＿＿＿＿

＿＿＿＿＿＿＿＿＿＿＿＿＿＿＿＿.

⌖ Challenge!   누적 문제 Ch 03-05

32 다음 중 어법상 틀린 문장 두 개를 찾아 그 기호를 쓰고, 문장 전체를 바르게 고쳐 쓰세요.

ⓐ Three knives and two fish are on the table.
ⓑ You should be not rude to others.
ⓒ There is two mouses on the farm.
ⓓ She didn't eat anything, but she drank a lot of water.
ⓔ My uncle never loses this board game.

＿＿＿＿＿ → ＿＿＿＿＿＿＿＿＿＿＿＿

＿＿＿＿＿＿＿＿＿＿＿＿＿＿＿＿＿＿

＿＿＿＿＿ → ＿＿＿＿＿＿＿＿＿＿＿＿

＿＿＿＿＿＿＿＿＿＿＿＿＿＿＿＿＿＿

여러 가지 문장 종류

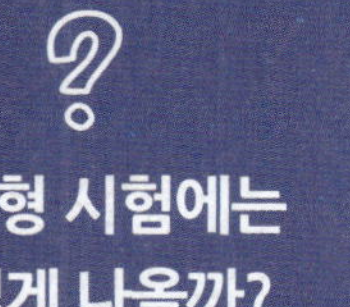

☑ Before You Write

- ☑ 명령문/제안문/감탄문/의문사 의문문/부가의문문의 각 쓰임을 구분할 수 있나요?
- ☑ 명령문과 제안문: 동사의 형태를 어떻게 써야 할까요?
- ☑ 감탄문과 의문사 의문문: 알맞은 어순으로 쓸 수 있나요?
- ☑ 부가의문문: 긍정문/부정문을 구분해서 그 뒤에 오는 부가의문문의 형태를 알맞게 쓸 수 있나요?

내신 기출 다음 우리말을 보고 머릿속으로 한번 영어 문장을 떠올려 보세요.

1 (A) 오랫동안 목을 굽히지 마라.
부정 명령문 → 일반동사(bend) → Don't+동사원형 → **Don't bend** `POINT 1`

2 내일 쇼핑하러 가는 것이 어때? (How, tomorrow)
제안문 → How about -ing ~? → **How about going ~?** `POINT 2`

3 참 아름다운 날이구나!
= __________ __________ __________ __________! (day)
감탄문 → 명사(day) 강조 → What 감탄문 → **What a beautiful day!** `POINT 3`

4 Dorothy: (B) 네가 가장 좋아하는 음식은 무엇이니?
What 의문문 → be동사 현재형 → 3인칭 단수 주어 → **What is ~?** `POINT4`

5 M: Jaden. (A) 안경 쓴 여자는 누구니?
Who 의문문 → be동사 현재형 → 3인칭 단수 주어 → **Who is ~?** `POINT 5`

6 (A) 동물들은 어떻게 세상을 보는가?
How 의문문 → 일반동사 현재형 → 3인칭 복수 주어 → **How do animals see ~?** `POINT 6`

7 The girl broke the flower pot, 그렇지 않니?
부가의문문 → 긍정문 → 일반동사 과거형 → 인칭대명사 주어 → **didn't she?** `POINT 7`

정답: **1** Don't[Do not] bend your neck for a long time. **2** How about going shopping tomorrow? **3** What a beautiful day **4** What is[What's] your favorite food? **5** Who is[Who's] the woman with the glasses? **6** How do animals see the world? **7** didn't she?

명령문, 제안문, 감탄문

POINT 1 | ~해라/~하지 마라: 명령문

창문을 열어라.
열어라 / 창문을.
동사원형

→ **Open** / the window.

도서관에서 조용히 해라.
조용히 **해라** / 도서관에서.
동사원형

→ **Be** quiet / in the library.

- 긍정 명령문은 상대방에게 무언가를 명령, 지시, 요청, 충고, 경고 등을 할 때 사용해요.
- '~해라, ~하세요'로 해석하며, **동사원형**으로 문장을 시작해요.
- 이때 명령문의 맨 앞이나 뒤에 please를 붙이면 좀 더 공손한 표현이 돼요.

도서관에서 뛰지 마라.
뛰지 마라 / 도서관에서.
Don't+동사원형

→ **Don't run** / in the library.

- '~하지 마라, ~하지 마세요'라는 의미의 금지, 경고, 주의 사항 등을 말할 때는 부정 명령문인 「Don't[Do not]+동사원형」으로 나타내요.
- Do not은 Don't보다 더 엄격하고 강한 어조로 느껴질 수 있으며, 표지판이나 안전 지침 등에 자주 쓰여요.
  Do not enter. 들어가지 마시오. (= 출입 금지)

대표 기출 문제

🔒 괄호 안의 동사와 주어진 조건을 이용하여 교실에서 지켜야 할 규칙을 완성하시오.

<조건> 명령문으로 문장을 완성할 것

(1) _________________ late for class. (be)
(2) _______________ to your teacher. (listen)

🔍 **CLUE 1**

'~해라'라는 긍정 명령문은 동사원형으로 문장을 시작하고, '~하지 마라'라는 부정 명령문은 「Don't[Do not]+동사원형」으로 문장을 시작해요.

🔍 **CLUE 2**

(1)은 지각은 하지 말아야 하는 것이므로 부정 명령문으로, (2)는 선생님 말씀을 듣는 것은 지켜야 하는 규칙이므로 긍정 명령문으로 써야 해요.

정답: (1) Don't[Do not] be, (2) Listen

✅ **함정 피하기**

1 형용사 앞에 be동사의 원형인 be를 빠뜨리거나 do를 쓰지 않도록 주의하세요.
Nice to your friends. (×) **Do nice** to your friends. (×) → **Be nice** to your friends. (네 친구들에게 친절해라.)
Don't late for classes. (×) → **Don't be late** for classes. (수업에 지각하지 마라.)

2 be동사로 시작하는 명령문의 부정은 Not be/Be not이 아니라 Don't be ~이므로 주의하세요.
Not be angry with me. (×) **Be not** angry with me. (×) → **Don't be** angry with me. (나한테 화내지 마.)

Point Exercise

[1-4] 우리말과 일치하도록 주어진 단어를 올바르게 배열하세요.

1
> 그 접시를 탁자 위에 놓아라.
> (the plate / on the table / put)

→ _______________________________ .

2
> 건강을 위해 물을 많이 마셔라.
> (water / drink / a lot of)

→ _______________________________
for your health.

3
> 시험에 대해서 너무 많이 걱정하지 마라.
> (worry / too much / don't)

→ _______________________________
_______________________ about the test.

4
> 그 결과에 대해 슬퍼하지 마.
> (be / the results / don't / about / sad)

→ _______________________________
_______________________________ .

[5-9] 우리말과 일치하도록 〈보기〉에서 알맞은 단어를 골라 주어진 단어를 사용하여 명령문을 완성하세요. (필요시 단어를 추가할 것)

> 〈보기〉
> open   take   be   speak

5
> 교과서 90페이지를 펴라. (your textbook)

→ _______________________________
to page 90.

6
> 지하철에서 크게 말하지 마라. (loudly)

→ _______________________________
in the subway.

7
> 이곳에서 사진을 찍지 마라. (pictures)

→ _______________________________
here.

8
> 네 자신에게 솔직해라. (with, yourself, honest)

→ _______________________________

9
> 다른 사람들에게 무례하게 굴지 마라.
> (to others, rude)

→ _______________________________

10 다음 그림을 보고 주어진 단어를 사용하여 금지하는 내용의 부정 명령문을 완성하세요.

(1)   (2)

(1) _______________ _______________
_______________ _______________ in the
movie theater. (your phone, use)

(2) _______________ _______________
_______________ in the classroom.
(play, soccer)

---

plate 접시 health 건강 loudly 큰 소리로 honest 솔직한, 정직한 rude 무례한, 버릇없는

~하자/~하는 게 어때?: 제안문

집에 일찍 가자.
집에 가자 / 일찍.

→ **Let's go** home / early.

우리 다음 주에 함께 노는 게 어때?
우리 (~하는 게) 어때 / 함께 노는 게 / 다음 주에?

→ **Why don't we** / **hang out** together / next week?

다음 주에 함께 노는 게 어때?
(~하는 게) 어때 / 함께 노는 게 / 다음 주에?

→ **How about** / **hanging out** together / next week?

• 상대방에게 제안이나 권유를 할 때 다음과 같은 표현을 쓸 수 있어요.

📢 제안이나 권유를 나타내는 표현

Let's+동사원형 ~.	~하자. *Let's not+동사원형 ~.: ~하지 말자.
Why don't you[we]+동사원형 ~?	너는[우리] ~하는 게 어때?
How about -ing ~?	~하는 게 어때?

대표 기출 문제

다음 대화에서 밑줄 친 우리말을 영작할 때, ( ) 안에
주어진 단어를 이용하여 문장을 완성하시오.

> A: It's very hot today.
> B: Yeah, it really is.
> A: 우리 오늘 오후에 수영하러 가는 것이 어때?
>   (why / go / this afternoon)
> B: Sounds great!

→ ______________________________________

CLUE 1
'우리 ~하는 게 어때?', '(우리) ~하자'라고 제안할
때는 Let's ~./Why don't we ~?/How about ~ing?
중 하나를 쓸 수 있어요.

CLUE 2
제안을 나타내는 표현 중 why가 들어가는 것은
「Why don't we+동사원형 ~?」이에요.

정답: Why don't we go swimming this afternoon?

✓ 함정 피하기

1 Let's나 Why don't you[we] 뒤에는 동사원형이 와요.
　 Let's **sit** on the bench over there. (저기 있는 벤치에 앉자.)

2 How about 뒤에는 동사의 -ing형이 와요.
　 How about **sitting** on the bench over there? (저기 있는 벤치에 앉는 게 어때?)

Point Exercise

정답 및 해설 p.15

배열 영작

[1-5] 우리말과 일치하도록 주어진 단어를 올바르게 배열하세요.

1
저녁으로 외식하는 게 어때?
(for dinner / how / going out / about)

→ ________________________________

________________________________ ?

2
같이 점심 먹자.
(together / lunch / let's / have)

→ ________________________________

________________________________ .

3
너는 병원에 가보는 게 어때?
(don't / why / see a doctor / you)

→ ________________________________

________________________________ ?

4
너는 나에게 사실을 말하는 게 어때?
(you / me / don't / tell / why)

→ ________________________________

________________________ the truth?

5
함께 음악을 듣는 게 어때?
(how / listening to / together / music / about)

→ ________________________________

________________________________ ?

주어진 단어로 영작

[6-8] 우리말과 일치하도록 주어진 단어를 사용하여 문장을 완성하세요. (필요시 단어를 추가하거나 형태를 바꿀 것)

6
우리 영화 보러 가는 건 어때?
(a movie, why, go to, we)

→ ________________________________

____

7
네 남동생과 놀아주는 것이 어때?
(how, play, your brother, with, about)

→ ________________________________

____

8
이 상자들을 재활용하자.
(recycle, let, these boxes)

→ ________________________________

____

기출: 조건 영작

9 다음 대화를 읽고 〈조건〉에 맞게 우리말을 영작하세요.

A: We should walk to school for our health.
우리 내일부터 시작하는 게 어때?
B: That sounds great.

〈조건〉
• from, why, tomorrow, start를 사용할 것
• 필요한 경우 단어를 추가하거나 형태를 바꿀 것

→ ________________________________

____

truth 사실, 진실 recycle 재활용하다

  정말 ~하구나!: 감탄문

> (그것은) 정말 좋은 생각이구나!
> 정말 좋은 생각이구나 / (그것은)!
>
> → **What** *a good idea* / (it is)!

> 햄버거가 정말 크구나!
> 정말 크구나 / 햄버거가!
>
> → **How** *big* / (the hamburger is)!

- 감탄문은 '정말 ~하구나!'라는 의미로 놀라움, 기쁨, 슬픔 등의 감정을 표현하는 문장이에요.
- **What**이나 **How로 시작**하는데, What을 쓰느냐, How를 쓰느냐는 감정을 나타내는 부분에 명사가 있느냐 없느냐로 결정이 됩니다. 각 감탄문의 어순을 잘 알아두세요.

📢 **감탄문의 어순**

명사가 포함된 어구나 형용사를 강조할 때는 주어와 동사를 생략해도 의미가 통해요.

명사가 포함된 어구 강조	**What+a/an+형용사+명사(+주어+동사)!**
형용사 강조	**How+형용사(+주어+동사)!**
부사 강조	**How+부사+주어+동사!**

대표 기출 문제

🔒 다음 대화를 읽고 밑줄 친 우리말을 영어 감탄문으로 쓰시오.

> A: Look at the picture.
> ① 이 신발들은 정말 예쁘구나!
> B: Yes. I think so. Look at another one.
> A: ② 정말 낡은 기타로구나!

① How __________ __________ __________ are!
　(3 단어)

② What __________ __________ __________ it is!
　(3 단어)

CLUE 1

우리말 '정말 ~하구나!'에서 형용사 '예쁜'을 강조하고 있으므로 How로 시작하는 감탄문으로 나타내요. 이때 어순은?
— 「How+형용사+주어+동사!」

CLUE 2

우리말 '정말 ~하구나!'에서 명사인 '기타'를 포함한 어구를 강조하고 있어요. 이때 사용하는 What 감탄문의 어순은?
— 「What+a/an+형용사+명사+주어+동사!」

정답: ① pretty[beautiful] these shoes
　　② an old guitar

✓ **함정 피하기**

1 What으로 시작하는 감탄문에서 셀 수 있는 명사의 단수형이 쓰이면 형용사 앞에 반드시 a나 an을 붙여요. 명사가 복수형이거나 셀 수 없는 경우 a나 an을 붙이지 않습니다.
What **a cute baby** she is! (그녀는 정말 귀여운 아기이구나!)
What **perfect weather** it is! (정말 완벽한 날씨구나!)

2 의문사 의문문에서의 주어, 동사 어순과 혼동하지 않도록 주의하세요.
How delicious **the cake is**! (그 케이크는 정말 맛있구나!) <감탄문>
How delicious **is the cake**? (그 케이크는 얼마나 맛있나요?) <의문사 의문문>

Point Exercise

[1-5] 우리말과 일치하도록 주어진 단어를 올바르게 배열하세요.

1
> 기차가 정말 빠르게 달리는구나!
> (runs / fast / the train / how)

→ ______________________________

______________________________ !

2
> 그는 정말 훌륭한 작가구나!
> (is / writer / what / he / great / a)

→ ______________________________

______________________________ !

3
> 이 파이는 정말 달콤하구나!
> (sweet / this / is / how / pie)

→ ______________________________

______________________________ !

4
> 그것은 정말 놀라운 이야기로구나!
> (amazing / it / an / story / what / is)

→ ______________________________

______________________________ !

5
> 그녀는 정말 좋은 친구구나!
> (is / good / a / she / what / friend)

→ ______________________________

______________________________ !

[6-9] 〈보기〉와 같이 빈칸에 알맞은 말을 넣어 감탄문을 완성하세요.

> 〈보기〉
> He was a very brave soldier.
> → What a brave soldier he was!

6
> He is very lazy.

→ How ______________________ !

7
> Henry is a very smart boy.

→ What ______________________ !

8
> The puppy is very cute.

→ How ______________________ !

9
> These shoes are very expensive.

→ How ______________________ !

10 다음 밑줄 친 ⓐ를 〈조건〉에 맞게 감탄문으로 바꿔 쓰세요.

> A: Did you visit Halla Mountain?
> B: Yes, I did. ⓐ It was so beautiful.
> A: I think so. I want to visit there again!

> 〈조건〉
> • How로 시작할 것
> • 주어와 동사를 모두 쓸 것

→ ______________________________

____

amazing 놀라운, 굉장한 soldier 군인 expensive 비싼

02 의문사 의문문

POINT 4　　what 의문문

A: 네가 가장 좋아하는 동물은 무엇이니?
무엇이니 / 네가 가장 좋아하는 동물은?

→ A: **What is** / your favorite animal?　　B: I like cats.

B: 나는 고양이를 좋아해.

응답에서 '무엇'에 해당하는 말이에요.

A: 너는 어제 무엇을 했니?
무엇을 / 너는 했니 / 어제?

→ A: **What** / **did** you **do** / yesterday?　　B: I watched a movie.

B: 나는 영화를 봤어.

- what은 '무엇, 무엇이, 무엇을'이라는 의미로 주로 '사물'을 나타내요.
- what 의문문의 응답에서는 주어, 시제, 응답 내용에 따라 동사를 적절하게 써야 하며, 응답을 보고 알맞은 의문문을 만드는 문제들도 자주 출제되므로 what 의문문을 언제 사용하는지 잘 알아두어야 합니다.

📢 **what으로 시작하는 의문문의 형태**

What+	be동사+	주어 ~?
	be동사+	주어+동사의 -ing형 ~?
	조동사+	주어+동사원형 ~?
	do/does/did+	주어+동사원형 ~?

- what은 '무슨 ~, 어떤 ~'이라는 의미로, 명사 앞에서 형용사처럼 쓰이기도 해요.
  A: **What kind** of food do you like? 너는 어떤 종류의 음식을 좋아하니?
  B: I like noodles. 나는 면을 좋아해.

대표 기출 문제

🔒 빈칸에 두 단어를 써서 다음 대화를 완성하시오.

A: ＿＿＿＿＿ ＿＿＿＿＿ Mrs. Parker play?
B: She plays the guitar.

CLUE 1
물음표로 끝나는 의문문으로 3인칭 단수 주어 다음에 동사원형이 쓰였으니, 두 번째 빈칸에 알맞은 말은 does/did, 조동사 중 하나예요! 대답의 동사가 현재형 plays이므로 does가 와야 해요.

CLUE 2
Yes, No로 대답하지 않는 의문사 의문문의 응답이에요. the guitar는 의문사 '무엇, 누구, 어디, 왜, 어떻게' 중 '무엇'에 해당하므로 알맞은 의문사는 What!

정답: What does

✅ **함정 피하기**　일반동사가 쓰인 의문사 의문문은 응답의 시제와 수에 유의하여 do/does/did를 적절하게 써야 해요.
A: What ＿＿＿＿＿ yesterday? (→ **did** you eat) (너는 어제 무엇을 먹었니?)　　B: I **ate** pizza. (나는 피자를 먹었어.)

Point Exercise

배열 영작

[1-5] 우리말과 일치하도록 주어진 단어를 올바르게 배열하세요.

1
> 그는 무엇을 가르치나요?
> (he / does / teach / what)

→ ______________________________
______________________________ ?

2
> 나는 무엇을 가져와야 하니?
> (what / I / should / bring)

→ ______________________________
______________________________ ?

3
> 지금이 몇 시인가요?
> (time / it / what / is / now)

→ ______________________________
______________________________ ?

4
> 네 강아지의 이름은 뭐니?
> (your puppy / what / the name / is / of)

→ ______________________________
______________________________ ?

5
> Dana와 Jenny는 무슨 이야기를 하는 중이니?
> (talking about / Dana / are / what / and Jenny)

→ ______________________________
______________________________ ?

대화문 완성

[6-8] 주어진 단어를 사용하여 다음 대화의 질문을 완성하세요.

6
> A: ______________ ______________ ______________
> ______________ ______________ ______________ ?
> (get up, time, Jay)
> B: He gets up at 7 o'clock every morning.

7
> A: ______________ ______________ ______________
> ______________ for your birthday present?
> (get)
> B: I got new shoes for my birthday present.

8
> A: ______________ ______________ ______________
> ______________ ______________ ______________
> ______________ ______________ ?
> (in your free time, do)
> B: I usually play computer games.

기출: 대화문 완성

9 주어진 단어를 사용하여 다음 대화의 질문을 완성하세요.

> A: (1) ______________________________
> ______________________________
> (do, last weekend)
> B: I went skiing with my family.
> A: Sounds interesting. I like winter sports, too.
> B: (2) ______________________________
> ______________________________
> (your, favorite winter sport)
> A: My favorite winter sport is snowboarding.

who/which/whose/when/where/why 의문문

A: Emma는 어디에 사니?
어디에 / Emma는 사니?

B: 그녀는 시카고에 살아.

→ A: **Where** / **does** Emma **live**?　　B: She lives in Chicago.

응답에서 '어디'에 해당하는 말이에요.

A: 너는 왜 그 가수를 좋아하니?
왜 / 너는 좋아하니 / 그 가수를?

B: 그가 놀라운 목소리를 가졌기 때문이야.

→ A: **Why** / **do** you **like** / the singer?
B: (Because) he has an amazing voice.

why 의문문에는 because를 이용해서 대답하는데, 생략할 수도 있어요.

- 다음과 같이 여러 의문사를 사용해서 의문문을 만들 수 있어요.
- 의문사가 있는 의문문의 어순은 앞에서 배운 what 의문문의 어순과 같아요.

여러 의문사의 의미와 쓰임

who	누구, 누가, 누구를	사람에 대해 물을 때
which	어느 것[쪽], 어느[어떤]	두 가지 이상의 정해진 것들 중 어느 하나를 선택하도록 물을 때 *which+명사: 어느 ~
whose	누구의 것, 누구의	물건의 소유에 대해 물을 때 *whose+명사: 누구의 ~
when	언제	시간이나 날짜 등을 물을 때
where	어디에, 어디서	위치나 장소 등을 물을 때
why	왜	이유나 원인에 대해 물을 때

주의 「what+명사 ~」 vs. 「which+명사 ~」

「what+명사 ~」는 주로 선택의 범위가 제한되지 않았을 때, 「which+명사 ~」는 제한된 선택지 중 하나를 고를 때 사용해요.
A: **What color** is your favorite shirt? (네가 가장 좋아하는 셔츠는 어떤 색이니?)
B: My favorite shirt is blue. (내가 가장 좋아하는 셔츠는 파란색이야.)

A: **Which color** do you prefer, blue or yellow? (너는 어떤 색을 더 좋아하니, 파란색 아니면 노란색?)
B: I prefer yellow. (나는 노란색을 더 좋아해.)

대표 기출 문제

괄호 안의 주어진 단어를 사용하여 A와 B의 대화가
자연스럽도록 문장을 완성하시오.

A: ________________? (the party)
B: The party starts at 7 p.m.

CLUE 1
의문문에 대한 대답이 '오후 7시에 시작한다(starts
at 7 p.m.)'이므로 시간이나 날짜 등을 물을 때 쓰는
의문사 When 또는 What time(몇 시에)을 사용해요.

CLUE 2
starts는 일반동사 현재형이고 주어가 3인칭 단수이
므로 의문문에는 does를 써서 「의문사+does+주어+
동사원형 ~?」으로 나타내요.

정답: When[What time] does the party start

Point Exercise

정답 및 해설 p.15

[1-6] 우리말과 일치하도록 주어진 단어를 올바르게 배열하세요.

1

저 키 큰 소년은 누구니?
(that / who / tall / is / boy)

→ ________________________________

________________________________ ?

2

너는 언제 Tom을 만났니?
(meet / did / Tom / you / when)

→ ________________________________

________________________________ ?

3

Brody 씨는 어디 출신인가요?
(is / from / where / Mr. Brody)

→ ________________________________

________________________________ ?

4

너는 어떤 가수를 좋아하니?
(singer / like / do / which / you)

→ ________________________________

________________________________ ?

5

너는 왜 그렇게 일찍 일어났니?
(why / you / did / wake up)

→ ________________________________

________________________________ so early?

6

탁자 위의 이것은 누구의 안경이니?
(are / whose / these / glasses)

→ ________________________________

________________________________ on the table?

[7-10] 주어진 단어를 사용하여 다음 대화의 질문을 완성하세요.

7

A: __________ __________ __________

__________ to the park last night?
   (you, go)
B: Because I wanted to ride a bike.

8

A: __________ __________ __________

__________ ? (Robert, work)
B: He works at a bank.

9

A: __________ __________ __________

__________ ? (your cousin)
B : The girl over there is my cousin.

10

A: __________ __________ __________

__________ , red or blue? (yours, T-shirt)
B: The red one is mine.

11 다음 대화의 질문을 〈조건〉에 맞게 완성하세요.

〈조건〉
• 주어진 단어를 사용할 것
• 6 단어로 쓸 것

A: ________________________________

____

(last Saturday, go)
B: I went to my grandma's house.

A: 너는 학교에 어떻게 가니?　　　　　　B: 버스를 타고 가.
어떻게 / 너는 가니 / 학교에?

→ A: **How** / **do** you **go** / to school?　　B: By bus.

응답에서 '어떻게(수단, 방법)'에 해당하는 말이에요.

- how는 '어떻게, 어떤'의 의미로 수단, 상태, 방법 등을 물을 때 사용해요.

A: **How** was the movie? 그 영화는 어땠니?　　B: It was great. 아주 좋았어.

A: **How** can I get to the bookstore? 서점에는 어떻게 갈 수 있나요?
B: Go straight two blocks. 곧장 두 블록을 가세요.

A: 너는 오늘 얼마나 많은 수업이 있니?　　　　B: 나는 오늘 수업이 여섯 개 있어.
얼마나 많은 수업이 / 너는 있니 / 오늘?

→ A: **How many *classes*** / **do** you **have** / today?
B: I have six classes today.

- how는 뒤에 형용사나 부사가 쓰여 '얼마나 ～한[하게]'의 의미로도 쓰여요.

📢 자주 쓰이는 「How + 형용사/부사」 표현

How many	얼마나 많은 (수의) ～? (수량)	How old	몇 살인 ～? (나이)
How much	얼마나 많은 (양의)/많이 ～? (양, 가격)	How big	얼마나 큰 ～? (크기)
How long	얼마나 긴/오래 ～? (길이, 시간)	How often	얼마나 자주 ～? (빈도)
How tall	얼마나 키가 큰/높은 ～? (키, 높이)	How far	얼마나 먼 ～? (거리)

주의! How many[much]+명사 ~?

「How many+복수명사 ～」, 「How much+셀 수 없는 명사 ～」의 형태로 쓰이는 것에 주의하세요.
How many **students** are in the class? (반에 얼마나 많은 학생이 있나요?)
How much **homework** do you have? (너는 숙제가 얼마나 많이 있어?)

대표 기출 문제

🔒 다음 상황에 적절한 표현을 괄호 안의 주어진 단어를 사용하여 문장을 완성하시오.

A: How do you go to school?
B: I usually go to school by bus.
A: Really? __________ __________
__________ __________? (long, take)
B: It takes about twenty minutes.

🔍 **CLUE 1**
B가 시간이 얼마나 걸리는지 대답한 것으로 보아 A의 질문에는 '얼마나 오래'라는 의미의 How long을 쓸 수 있어요.

🔍 **CLUE 2**
응답의 주어로는 '시간'을 나타낼 때 쓰는 비인칭 주어 it이 쓰였고 takes는 일반동사 현재형이므로, 의문문에는 does를 써서 「How long does+주어+동사원형 ~?」으로 나타내요.

정답: How long does it take

Point Exercise

정답 및 해설 p.16

[1-4] 우리말과 일치하도록 주어진 단어를 올바르게 배열하세요.

1
> 너는 오늘 기분이 어떠니?
> (feel / you / how / do / today)

→ ____
____ ?

2
> 공항에는 어떻게 갈 수 있나요?
> (the airport / can / get to / how / I)

→ ____
____ ?

3
> 거북이는 얼마나 오래 사니?
> (turtles / how / live / long / do)

→ ____
____ ?

4
> 너는 작년에 얼마나 많은 책을 읽었니?
> (books / how / you / read / did / many)

→ ____
______________________________________ last year?

[5-8] 주어진 단어를 사용하여 다음 대화의 질문을 완성하세요.

5
> A: ______________________________________ ?
> (you, tall)
> B: I'm 160 cm.

6
> A: ______________________________________
> ______________________________________ ?
> (last, long, the movie)
> B: It lasts about two hours.

7
> A: ______________________________________
> ______________________________________ ?
> (many, an octopus, have, legs)
> B: It has 8 legs.

8
> A: ______________________________________
> ______________________________ your grandmother?
> (often, call, you)
> B: I call her once a week.

9 다음 일정표를 보고 〈조건〉에 맞게 두 사람의 대화를 완성하세요.

Kate's Schedule

MON	TUE	WED	THU	FRI	SAT	SUN
piano lesson		piano lesson		piano lesson		

〈조건〉
- 주어진 단어를 사용할 것
- 7 단어로 쓸 것

> A: Look at Kate's schedule. She practices the piano hard.
> B: ______________________________________
> ______________________________________
> (times, she, have, many, lessons)
> A: She has lessons three times a week.

airport 공항 get to ~에 도착하다 last 계속되다 octopus 문어 schedule 일정, 스케줄 practice 연습하다

부가의문문

 부가의문문

너는 피자를 좋아해, 그렇지 않니?
너는 / 좋아해 / 피자를, / 그렇지 않니?

→ You / like / pizza, / **don't you**?

- 부가의문문은 평서문 뒤에 덧붙이는 간단한 의문문이에요.
- '그렇지?' 또는 '그렇지 않니?'라는 의미로 상대방에게 어떤 사실을 확인하거나 동의를 구할 때 쓰여요.

📢 **부가의문문의 형태와 만드는 방법**

긍정문 뒤	동사와 **not**의 축약형＋주어? 〈부정의 부가의문문〉
부정문 뒤	동사＋주어? 〈긍정의 부가의문문〉

① 동사: be동사 → **be동사**, 조동사 → **조동사**, 일반동사 → 주어의 수와 시제에 맞춰 **do/does/did**를 써요.
② 주어: 알맞은 **인칭대명사**로 바꿔 써요.

- 긍정, 부정에 상관없이 명령문과 제안문의 부가의문문은 다음과 같이 써요.

명령문, **will you?**	Close the door, **will you**? 문을 닫아줄래요?
제안문, **shall we?**	Let's go to the movies, **shall we**? 영화관에 갈까?

- 부가의문문의 대답은 물어보는 내용과 상관없이 대답이 긍정이면 Yes, 부정이면 No로 답해요.
  A: You aren't hungry, **are you**? 너 배고프지 않지, 그렇지?
  B: **Yes**, I **am**. 아니, 배고파. / **No**, I'm **not**. 응, 배고프지 않아.

대표 기출 문제

🔒 부가의문문을 이용하여 대화를 완성하시오.

A: Mike doesn't know that, ___________?
B: No, he doesn't.

CLUE 1
부가의문문은 앞의 문장이 긍정이면 부정으로, 부정이면 긍정으로 나타내요. 이때 주어는 대명사로 받아 「동사＋주어(대명사)?」로 써야 해요.

CLUE 2
부정문(doesn't know)이 쓰였으므로, 부가의문문은 긍정으로 써야 해요. 문장의 동사가 일반동사의 현재형이므로 does와 주어(Mike)를 받는 대명사로는 he를 사용해요.

정답: does he

✅ **함정 피하기** 부가의문문에서 문장의 주어를 대명사로 바꿀 때, 주어의 수에 주의하세요. 주어가 단수이거나 날짜, 시간 등이면 it으로 써요.
Mike and Julie said the right answer, **didn't they**? (Mike와 Julie는 정답을 말했어, 그렇지 않니?)
Today is Wednesday, **isn't it**? (오늘은 수요일이야, 그렇지 않니?)

Point Exercise

[1-6] 우리말과 일치하도록 빈칸에 알맞은 말을 넣어 부가의문문을 완성하세요.

1

너 배고프구나, 그렇지 않니?

→ You are hungry, ________________?

2

그녀는 오늘 학교에 오지 않았어, 그렇지?

→ She didn't come to school today, ________________?

3

너희 삼촌은 중국어를 말할 수 있어, 그렇지 않니?

→ Your uncle can speak Chinese, ________________?

4

그 똑똑한 여자아이는 시험에 통과했어, 그렇지 않니?

→ The smart girl passed the test, ________________?

5

Smith 씨는 여기 근처에서 살지 않아, 그렇지?

→ Mr. Smith doesn't live near here, ________________?

6

Mike와 Jane은 사촌이야, 그렇지 않니?

→ Mike and Jane are cousins, ________________?

[7-10] 우리말과 일치하도록 주어진 단어를 사용하여 부가의문문이 있는 문장을 완성하세요.

7

오늘 날씨가 좋아, 그렇지 않니? (be)

→ The weather __________ nice today, __________ __________?

8

James는 이미 집에 갔어, 그렇지 않니? (go)

→ James __________ home already, __________ __________?

9

수진이는 매운 음식을 좋아하지 않아, 그렇지? (like)

→ Sujin __________ __________ spicy food, __________ __________?

10

피자를 시켜 먹자, 그럴 거지? (order)

→ Let's __________ a pizza, __________ __________?

11 부가의문문을 사용해 다음 대화의 빈칸을 완성하세요.

(1) A: The paintings were really beautiful, __________?
    B: Yes, I think so.

(2) A: Kate wasn't tired, __________?
    B: No, she felt fine.

order 주문하다; 주문

Chapter Test *

정답 및 해설 p.16

STAGE 1) Go for it!

자신 있게 풀어보는 기초 문제!

배열 영작

[1-5] 우리말과 일치하도록 주어진 단어를 배열하여 문장을 완성하세요.

1
> 보드게임 하는 게 어때?
> (about / a board game / how / playing)

→ ___________________________________
___________________________________ ?

2
> 길에 쓰레기를 버리지 마세요.
> (throw away / not / trash / do)

→ ___________________________________
___________________________________ on the street.

3
> 너는 언제 거기에 도착할 거니?
> (there / will / get / when / you)

→ ___________________________________
___________________________________ ?

4
> 그것은 정말 끔찍한 사고였구나!
> (accident / a / what / it / terrible / was)

→ ___________________________________
___________________________________ !

5
> 너는 어떤 계절을 가장 좋아하니?
> (like / you / season / do / what)

→ ___________________________________
___________________________________ the most?

주어진 단어로 영작

[6-8] 우리말과 일치하도록 주어진 단어를 사용하여 문장을 완성하세요.

6
> 오늘은 밖에 나가지 말자. 눈이 오고 있어.
> (go out, let's)

→ ___________________________________ today.
It's snowing.

7
> 그는 비밀을 지킬 수 있어, 그렇지 않니?
> (can, a secret, keep)

→ ___________________________________,
___________________________________ ?

8
> 너는 어젯밤에 얼마나 오래 잤니? (long, sleep)

→ ___________________________________
last night?

최신 기출

9 우리말과 일치하도록 주어진 단어를 배열하여 다음의 대화를 완성하세요.

> A: Grace, is that your new hat?
> B: Yes, I made it in our fashion club.
> A: (1) 그것은 정말 멋진 모자구나! I really like it.
> B: (2) Then, 우리 동아리에 들어오는 게 어때?
> We always have fun!

(1) ___________________________________ !
(an / hat / what / it / amazing / is)

(2) Then, ___________________________________
___________________________________ ?
(join / don't / club / you / our / why)

◯━ 대화문 완성

[10-13] 다음 〈보기〉의 대화를 읽고, 주어진 단어를 사용하여 이어지는 각 대화를 완성하세요.

〈보기〉
Daniel: Let's play a game. You need to guess an animal.
Janice: Okay, I like this game. I'll ask questions about the animal.

10
Janice: ______________________________
______________________? (tall)
Daniel: It is about 2 meters tall.

11
Janice: ______________________________
______________________? (weigh, much)
Daniel: It weighs about 200 kg.

12
Janice: ______________________________
______________________? (eat)
Daniel: It eats other animals.

13
Janice: ______________________________
______________________?
(nickname, have)
Daniel: People call it "the king of the jungle."
Janice: I got it! It's a lion!
Daniel: You are right.

◯━ 어법 오류 수정

[14-17] 다음 각 문장의 밑줄 친 부분을 어법상 바르게 고쳐 쓰세요.

14 Please <u>careful</u> with my glasses.

____

15 Emma wasn't late for school, <u>did she</u>?

____

16 <u>How</u> a cold day today is!

____

17 A: How many <u>book</u> do you have now?
B: I have two.

____

최신 기출

18 다음 글을 읽고 〈조건〉에 맞게 우리말을 영작하세요.

Dogs can see blue and yellow, but they can't see other colors well. For example, they can't see red. (1) So, <u>당신의 개에게 빨간 공을 사주지 마라.</u> Your dog won't see it well. (2) But <u>슬퍼하지 마라.</u> Dogs don't need great eyes. They have a great sense of smell.

〈조건〉
• 각각 주어진 단어를 사용할 것
• (1)은 5 단어, (2)는 3 단어로 쓸 것

(1) So, ______________________________
for your dog. (a red ball, buy)

(2) But ______________________. (sad)

19 다음 설문지를 보고 건강한 생활을 위한 조언을 〈조건〉에 맞게 쓰세요.

〈조건〉
- (1)은 첫 번째 질문에 대한 긍정 명령문으로, (2)는 두 번째 질문에 대한 부정 명령문으로 쓸 것
- 주어진 단어를 사용할 것

---

1. 당신은 매일 아침을 먹습니까?
   □ 예 ☑ 아니요
2. 당신은 야식을 얼마나 자주 먹습니까?
   □ 1주일에 2∼3회 ☑ 1주일에 4∼5회
   □ 거의 먹지 않는다.

---

(1) ______________ ______________

______________ ______________ .

(have, every day)

(2) ______________ ______________

______________ ______________ at night.

(eat, food, late)

20 다음 그림을 참고하여 A에게 제안하는 문장을 〈조건〉에 맞게 <u>두 가지</u>로 쓰세요.

A: I'm very tired.
B: ______________
A: OK. I will.

〈조건〉
- (1)에는 why, (2)에는 how를 사용할 것
- go, early, bed를 반드시 사용할 것
- 필요시 주어진 단어의 형태를 변형할 것

(1) ________________________________

____

(2) ________________________________

____

21 다음 Clara의 인터뷰를 읽고, 〈조건〉에 맞게 대화를 완성하세요.

Reporter: Hello, can I have a moment for an interview?
Clara: Sure.
Reporter: Thanks. Can I ask your name?
Clara: My name is Clara.
Reporter: (1) ______________ ______________

______________ ______________ ?

Clara: I'm from Boston.
Reporter: How was today's game?
Clara: It was great! It was really exciting.
Reporter: Who is your favorite player?
Clara: My favorite player is Megan.
Reporter: (2) ______________ ______________

______________ ______________

______________ ?

Clara: Because she's a great team leader!

〈조건〉
- 의문사를 반드시 사용할 것
- from, her, like를 사용할 것

22 다음 Sarah의 일과표를 보고, 주어진 단어를 사용하여 대화를 완성하세요.

Time	Schedule
8:00	go to school
15:30	come home
18:30	have dinner with her family
20:00	take a shower

(1) Q: ________________________________

________________________________ ? (Sarah, time)

A: She goes to school at 8:00.

(2) Q: ________________________________

at 18:30? (do, Sarah)

A: She has dinner with her family.

(3) Q: Sarah takes a shower at 20:00, doesn't she?

A: ________________________________ .

도표 영작

[23-26] 다음 각 장소에서 따라야 하는 지시 사항을 〈보기 A〉와 〈보기 B〉에서 알맞은 표현을 골라 영작하세요.

영화관	• 다른 사람의 좌석을 발로 차지 마시오. • 휴대 전화의 전원을 끄시오.
도서관	• 건물 안에서 조용히 하시오. • 음식을 가져오지 마시오.
학교	• 교실에서 뛰지 마시오. • 학교에 제시간에 도착하시오.
콘서트장	• 사진을 찍지 마시오. • 시끄럽게 이야기하지 마시오.

〈보기 A〉

arrive	kick	bring	be
take	turn off	talk	run

〈보기 B〉

at school on time	your cell phones
food	loudly
in the classroom	others' seats
pictures	quiet in the building

\<movie theater\>

23 • ______________________________

• ______________________________

\<library\>

24 • ______________________________

• ______________________________

\<school\>

25 • ______________________________

• ______________________________

\<concert hall\>

26 • ______________________________

• ______________________________

어법 오류 수정

27 다음 ⓐ~ⓓ 중 어법상 틀린 두 개를 찾아 그 기호를 쓰고, 바르게 고쳐 쓰세요.

Today, our teacher told us about a field trip. ⓐ How great news! I asked her, ⓑ "Where will we go?" She said, "We'll go to Jeonju." Then Jiho asked, ⓒ "What far is it from here?" She answered, "It takes 2 hours by bus." My classmates and I will visit a lot of interesting places in Jeonju, ⓓ won't we? I'm so excited.

______ → ______________________________

______ → ______________________________

Challenge!

누적 문제 Ch 04-06

28 다음 중 어법상 틀린 문장 두 개를 찾아 그 기호를 쓰고, 문장 전체를 바르게 고쳐 쓰세요.

ⓐ There was little water in the glass.
ⓑ I can swim more faster than you.
ⓒ I have lots of books on my bookshelf.
ⓓ What time are you usually go to school?
ⓔ Every country has its own traditional food.

______ → ______________________________

____

______ → ______________________________

____

Chapter 07

문장의 여러 형식

✓ Before You Write

- ☑ 우리말 뜻을 보고 영어로 알맞은 동사를 떠올릴 수 있나요?
- ☑ 동사가 주어지면, 그 동사로 만들 수 있는 다양한 문장 구조를 떠올릴 수 있나요?
- ☑ SVC, SVO, SVOO 중 어떤 문장 구조가 적절할지 파악할 수 있나요?
- ☑ 동사 뒤에 오는 문장 요소들을 알맞은 어순으로 배열할 수 있나요?

내신 기출 다음 우리말을 보고 머릿속으로 한번 영어 문장을 떠올려 보세요.

1 ⓐ 우리는 신이 났어요. (excite, get)
~해지다 → get+형용사 → **got excited** `POINT 1`

2 이 모래는 부드럽게 느껴진다. (feel, soft)
~하게 느껴지다 → feel+형용사 → **feels soft** `POINT 1`

3 The jungle 너에게 신나는 경험을 줄 것이다.
→ The jungle ___________ ___________ ___________
    an e___________ e___________.
~에게 …을 주다 → give A B → **will give you an exciting experience** `POINT 2`

4 (B) 이 이야기는 우리에게 중요한 교훈을 가르쳐준다.
(story, teaches, important, lesson, us)
~에게 …을 가르쳐주다 → teach A B → **teaches us an important lesson** `POINT 2`

5 Peter는 Sarah에게 빵을 가져다줬다. (get, some / 6 단어)
~에게 …을 가져다주다 → 6 단어 → get B for A → **got some bread for Sarah** `POINT 3`

6 ⓐ 레몬껍질은 더러운 셔츠를 하얗게 만들어 준단다.
(lemon peel, make)
~을 …하게 만들다 → make+목적어+형용사 → **makes a dirty shirt white** `POINT 4`

POINT 1 주어+동사+주격보어

그는 학생이다.
그는 / ~이다 / 학생.
주어　동사　보어(명사)

→ He / is / **a student**.

- 문장에서 be동사가 '(무엇)이다, (어떠)하다'의 의미인 경우, 뒤에 주어를 보충 설명해 주는 **명사**나 **형용사**가 오는데 이를 **주격보어**라고 합니다. 주격보어가 없으면 불완전한 문장이 돼요.
- 동사 become, get 등이 '~(이) 되다'의 의미로 쓰인 경우에도 뒤에 보어가 와요.

그녀는 행복해 보인다.
그녀는 / ~해 보인다 / 행복한.
주어　　동사　　보어(형용사)

→ She / **looks** / **happy**.

- 아래와 같이 감각을 표현하는 동사인 look, sound, taste, feel, smell 뒤에는 **형용사 보어**가 쓰입니다.

📣 **감각동사+형용사 보어**

look beautiful **taste** sweet **smell** good	아름다워 **보이다** 달콤한 맛이 **나다** 좋은 냄새가 **나다**	**sound** nice **feel** tired	멋지게 **들리다** 피곤하게 **느끼다**

주의

감각동사 다음에 전치사 like(~처럼, ~와 같은)를 붙여 명사와 함께 쓸 수 있어요.
That cloud **looks like** *a rabbit*. (저 구름은 토끼처럼 보인다.)

대표 기출 문제

🔒 Chuchu: I have a new master. She's very kind. (A) 그녀의 손은 아주 따뜻하게 느껴진다.

위 글의 밑줄 친 (A)의 우리말을 'feel'을 사용하여 5 단어로 영작하시오.

→ _______________________________

CLUE 1
동사 feel 뒤에는 명사나 형용사가 올 수 있어요.
명사가 오면 '~을 느끼다'라는 뜻이고, 형용사가 오면 '~하게 느끼다'라는 의미예요.

CLUE 2
주어 '그녀의 손(Her hands)'의 상태(따뜻한)를 설명해 주는 말은? — 형용사 warm!

정답: Her hands feel so[very] warm.

✅ **함정 피하기** 감각동사가 쓰인 문장의 우리말 해석이 '~하게 …하다'로 될 때, 보어 자리에 부사를 쓰지 않도록 주의하세요.
그녀는 **행복해** 보인다. → She *looked* happily. (✕) She *looked* **happy**. (○)

Point Exercise

정답 및 해설 p.18

배열 영작

[1-3] 우리말과 일치하도록 주어진 단어를 올바르게 배열하세요.

1

> 그는 새 컴퓨터에 신이 났다.
> (got / he / excited)

→ ______________________________________

about the new computer.

2

> 그 바지는 Kevin에게 작아 보인다.
> (small / the pants / look)

→ ______________________________________

on Kevin.

3

> 이 피자는 맛이 정말 좋다.
> (good / tastes / very / this pizza)

→ ______________________________________ .

주어진 단어로 영작

[4-6] 우리말과 일치하도록 주어진 단어를 사용하여 문장을 완성하세요. (필요시 형태를 바꿀 것)

4

> 너의 아이디어는 좋게 들린다.
> (sound, good, your idea)

→ ______________________________________
____

5

> 그 배우는 매우 유명해졌다.
> (become, famous, the actor, so)

→ ______________________________________
____

6

> Ashley는 매우 졸리게 느꼈다.
> (feel, sleepy, very)

→ ______________________________________

어법 오류 수정

[7-8] 다음 각 문장에서 어법상 **틀린** 부분을 찾아 바르게 고쳐 쓰세요.

7 The milk smells strangely.

______________ → ______________

8 That chair looks like comfortable.

______________ → ______________

기출: 그림 영작

9 〈보기 A〉와 〈보기 B〉에서 알맞은 단어를 하나씩 골라 각 그림을 설명하는 문장을 완성하세요.

(1) 　　　　(2) 

〈보기 A〉			
taste	feel	sound	smell

〈보기 B〉			
soft	sour	sharp	sweet

〈조건〉
- 필요시 동사의 형태를 바꿀 것
- 현재시제를 사용할 것
- 각 〈보기〉의 단어는 한 번씩만 사용할 것

(1) The flowers ________________________ .

(2) The sweater ________________________ .

---

excited 신이 난　strangely 이상하게　comfortable 편한, 편안한　sour (맛이) 신, 시큼한　sharp 날카로운, 뾰족한

SVOO(4형식)

POINT 2 주어+동사+간접목적어+직접목적어

나는 오빠에게 책 한 권을 주었다.
나는 / 주었다 / 나의 오빠에게 / 책 한 권을.
주어　　동사　　간접목적어　　직접목적어
→ **I / gave / my brother / a book.**

- **목적어**는 우리말 '~을, ~를, ~에게'에 해당하며, 동사 뒤에 와서 동사가 나타내는 동작의 대상이 됩니다.
- 어떤 동사들은 목적어를 두 개 취하는 경우도 있는데, 「주어+동사+**간접목적어(~에게)**+**직접목적어(…을)**」의 어순으로 쓰여요.

📢 목적어를 2개 갖는 동사

give A B	A에게 B를 주다	bring A B	A에게 B를 가져다주다
send A B	A에게 B를 보내다	get A B	A에게 B를 얻어주다[가져다주다]
show A B	A에게 B를 보여 주다	ask A B	A에게 B를 묻다
teach A B	A에게 B를 가르치다	lend A B	A에게 B를 빌려주다
tell A B	A에게 B를 말하다	find A B	A에게 B를 찾아주다
buy A B	A에게 B를 사 주다	pass A B	A에게 B를 건네주다
cook A B	A에게 B를 요리해 주다	build A B	A에게 B를 지어 주다
make A B	A에게 B를 만들어 주다	read A B	A에게 B를 읽어주다

대표 기출 문제

🔒 주어진 단어를 활용하여 다음 문장을 완성하시오.

그녀는 우리에게 그녀의 사진을 보여 주었다.
(show)

→ She ＿＿＿＿＿＿ ＿＿＿＿＿＿ her photo.

CLUE 1
동사 show는 주어진 우리말 '보여 주었다'에 맞게 과거형 showed로 써야 해요. show는 「주어+동사+목적어」 또는 「주어+동사+간접목적어(~에게)+직접목적어(…을)」의 형태로 쓸 수 있어요.

CLUE 2
문장 마지막에 직접목적어에 해당하는 '그녀의 사진을(her photo)'이 있으므로 동사 바로 뒤에는 '~에게'에 해당하는 간접목적어가 와야 해요.

정답: showed us

✅ **함정 피하기**

1 간접목적어와 직접목적어의 순서를 뒤바꿔 쓰지 않도록 주의하세요.
　She bought **some ice cream** **her sister**. (×)
　→ She bought **her sister** **some ice cream**. (○) (그녀는 자신의 여동생에게 아이스크림을 좀 사 주었다.)

2 간접목적어 자리에는 알맞은 목적격 대명사가 와야 해요.
　Samuel sent ~~she~~(→ her) some flowers. (Samuel은 그녀에게 꽃을 좀 보냈다.)

Point Exercise

배열 영작

[1-4] 우리말과 일치하도록 주어진 단어를 올바르게 배열하세요.

1
> 나의 아빠는 나에게 물 한 잔을 주셨다.
> (gave / a cup of water / me)

→ My father ________________________

________________________.

2
> Mia는 그녀의 여동생에게 간식을 좀 사 주었다.
> (some snacks / bought / her sister)

→ Mia ________________________

________________________.

3
> Ella는 그녀의 친구에게 목걸이를 만들어 주었다.
> (a necklace / made / her friend)

→ Ella ________________________

________________________.

4
> 나의 삼촌은 학생들에게 역사를 가르치신다.
> (students / history / teaches)

→ My uncle ________________________

________________________.

주어진 단어로 영작

[5-8] 우리말과 일치하도록 주어진 단어를 사용하여 문장을 완성하세요. (필요시 형태를 바꿀 것)

5
> Lucas는 그의 남동생에게 모형 비행기를 만들어 주었다.
> (make, a model airplane, his brother)

→ ________________________

________________________.

6
> 그는 내게 그가 가장 좋아하는 책을 보여 주었다.
> (show, his favorite book)

→ ________________________

________________________.

7
> 나는 내 친구에게 문자 메시지를 보냈다.
> (send, a text message, my friend)

→ ________________________

8
> 그 가게는 고객들에게 무료 샘플을 제공했다.
> (give, free samples, the shop, the customers)

→ ________________________

________________________.

기출: 그림 영작

9 다음 그림을 보고 〈조건〉에 맞게 문장을 완성하세요.

(1)  (2) 

〈조건〉
• 〈보기〉의 단어를 사용하여 (1)은 4 단어, (2)는 5 단어로 쓸 것
• 동사 give를 사용하고 과거시제를 사용할 것
• 누구에게 무엇을 주었는지 포함할 것

〈보기〉

flowers	a cookie
her friend	her grandmother

(1) Betty ________________________.

(2) Betty ________________________.

snack 간식 free 무료의 sample 샘플 customer 손님, 고객

POINT 3 · 주어+동사+직접목적어+to/for+간접목적어

나는 오빠에게 책 한 권을 주었다.
나는 / 주었다 / 나의 오빠에게 / 책 한 권을.

→ I / **gave** / my brother / a book.

나는 / 주었다 / 책 한 권을 / 나의 오빠에게.

→ I / **gave** / a book / **to** my brother.

- 문장에서 목적어 두 개(간접목적어+직접목적어)가 올 경우, '누구에게'에 해당하는 간접목적어는 **to**나 **for**를 이용해서 직접목적어 뒤에 쓸 수도 있어요.
- 「주어+동사+목적어+전치사구」로 쓰면 목적어가 하나인 SVO 문장이 됩니다. 전치사구는 문장 필수 성분에 들어가지 않기 때문이에요.
- 동사에 따라 사용하는 전치사가 달라지지만, 대부분의 동사는 전치사 to를 쓰므로, for를 쓰는 몇 개의 동사 위주로 암기하면 됩니다.

📢 간접목적어를 뒤로 보낼 때 to/for를 쓰는 동사

to	give, show, send, tell, teach, lend, bring, write, pass, read 등
for	make, cook, buy, get 등

주의

동사 ask는 간접목적어를 뒤로 보낼 때 전치사 of를 써요. 그러나 ask a question, ask a favor(부탁을 하다)와 같은 표현에 한해 쓰이며, 목적어 2개인 형태가 더 자주 쓰입니다.
She **asked** me a few questions. (그녀는 나에게 몇 가지 질문을 했다.)
→ She **asked** a few questions **of** me.

대표 기출 문제

다음 <보기>와 같은 뜻을 가진 문장으로 바꾸시오.

<보기>
Sora bought them ice cream.
→ Sora bought ice cream for them.

I will show you my garden.
→ ______________________________

CLUE 1

「주어+동사+간접목적어(them)+직접목적어(ice cream)」의 문장이 간접목적어 them을 뒤로 보내 전치사 for와 함께 쓰인 것을 알 수 있어요.

CLUE 2

동사 show는 간접목적어를 뒤로 보낼 때 전치사 to를 쓰므로, 동사 뒤에 「직접목적어+to+간접목적어」의 순서로 문장을 바꿔 쓰면 돼요.

정답: I will[I'll] show my garden to you.

Point Exercise

배열 영작

[1-3] 우리말과 일치하도록 주어진 단어를 올바르게 배열하세요.

1

> 나는 Wendy에게 내 카메라를 빌려주었다.
> (to / lent / Wendy / my camera)

→ I ______________________________
______________________________ .

2

> 그는 그의 엄마에게 차 한 잔을 만들어 드렸다.
> (his mother / made / a cup of tea / for)

→ He ______________________________
______________________________ .

3

> Taylor는 나에게 그녀의 강아지를 보여 주었다.
> (her puppy / to / showed / Taylor / me)

→ ______________________________
______________________________ .

문장 전환

[4-6] 주어진 문장을 같은 의미가 되도록 바꿔 쓰세요.

4

> I wrote Lisa a letter.

→ ______________________________

5

> Jerry told us a funny story.

→ ______________________________
____

6

> My dad bought me the computer.

→ ______________________________
____

주어진 단어로 영작

[7-9] 우리말과 일치하도록 주어진 단어와 전치사를 사용하여 문장을 완성하세요. (필요시 형태를 바꿀 것)

7

> 나는 선생님께 이메일을 보냈다.
> (send, my teacher, an email)

→ ______________________________

8

> 이모가 나에게 중국 음식을 요리해 주셨다.
> (cook, Chinese food, my aunt)

→ ______________________________
____

9

> 그 경찰관은 Noah에게 몇 가지 질문을 했다.
> (ask, the policeman, some questions)

→ ______________________________
____

기출 : 도표 영작

10 다음 표의 내용을 보고, 〈조건〉에 맞게 글을 완성하세요.

| me → Vicky | a pencil case |
| Vicky → me | a diary |

〈조건〉
- 주어진 단어를 사용할 것
- 전치사를 사용할 것

> Today was Christmas Eve. My friend Vicky and I prepared presents for each other.
> (1) I ______________________________
> ______________________________ , (give) and
> (2) Vicky ______________________________
> ______________________________ . (buy)
> We loved our gifts and were very happy.

---

lend 빌려주다 diary 일기장 prepare 준비하다 present 선물 (= gift) each other 서로

SVOC(5형식)

POINT 4 주어+동사+목적어+목적격보어

나는 내 강아지를 Max라고 부른다.
나는 / 부른다 / 내 강아지를 / Max라고.
주어   동사   목적어   목적격보어(명사)

→ I / **call** / **my puppy** / **Max**.

그는 항상 나를 행복하게 한다.
그는 / 항상 / ~하게 만든다 / 나를 / 행복하게.
주어   동사   목적어 목적격보어(형용사)

→ He / always / **makes** / **me** / **happy**.

• 주어와 동사, 목적어만으로 문장의 의미가 어색한 경우가 있어요. 이때는 목적어 뒤에 **목적어를 보충 설명해 주는 말**인 **형용사나 명사**가 필요한데, 이를 **목적격보어**라고 해요.

📢 **목적격보어로 명사를 쓰는 동사**

make+목적어+명사	~을 …로 만들다
call+목적어+명사	~을 …라고 부르다
name+목적어+명사	~을 …라고 이름 짓다

📢 **목적격보어로 형용사를 쓰는 동사**

make+목적어+형용사	~을 …하게 만들다	**find**+목적어+형용사	~가 …하다는 것을 알게 되다
keep+목적어+형용사	~을 …한 상태로 유지하다	**leave**+목적어+형용사	~을 …한 상태에 두다

대표 기출 문제

🔒 주어진 단어들을 모두 사용해 재배열하여 문장을 완성하시오.

색들은 우리의 세상을 매우 멋지게 만든다.
(world / wonderful / make / colors / our / so)

→ _________________________________ .

🔍 **CLUE 1**
make는 여러 가지 문장 형식에 쓰일 수 있으므로 뒤에 어떤 말이 오는지 잘 확인해야 해요.

🔍 **CLUE 2**
목적어 '우리의 세상(our world)'의 상태를 설명해주는 말인 '매우 멋지게(so wonderful)'가 쓰였으므로 「make+목적어+목적격보어」의 구조로 써야 해요.

정답: Colors make our world so wonderful

✅ **함정 피하기** 아래 문장처럼 '그녀는 나를 행복하게 만든다.'를 영작할 때 우리말 '행복하게'는 happily로 쓸 것 같지만, 목적격보어 자리에 부사는 올 수 없어요.
She makes me **happily**. (×) → She makes me **happy**. (○)

# Point Exercise

정답 및 해설 p.18

[1-4] 우리말과 일치하도록 주어진 단어를 올바르게 배열하세요.

1
> 그는 그의 기타를 '오랜 친구'라고 부른다.
> ('The Old Friend' / calls / his guitar / he)

→ ___________________________________

___________________________________ .

2
> 나는 그 상자가 비어 있다는 것을 알게 되었다.
> (empty / I / the box / found)

→ ___________________________________

___________________________________ .

3
> 그는 문을 열어둔 채로 두었다.
> (the door / he / open / left)

→ ___________________________________

___________________________________ .

4
> 깜짝 파티는 그녀를 행복하게 만들었다.
> (happy / the surprise party / made / her)

→ ___________________________________

___________________________________ .

[5-8] 우리말과 일치하도록 주어진 단어를 사용하여 문장을
완성하세요. (필요시 형태를 바꿀 것)

5
> 아빠가 내 여동생을 Julia라고 이름 지으셨다.
> (name, my dad, my sister)

→ ___________________________________

____

6
> 조깅은 우리를 건강하게 한다.
> (keep, healthy, jogging)

→ ___________________________________

____

7
> 너는 그 이야기가 흥미롭다는 것을 알게 될 것이다.
> (find, interesting, will, the story)

→ ___________________________________

____

8
> 그 경험은 그를 더 나은 사람으로 만들었다.
> (the experience, a better person, make)

→ ___________________________________

____

9 주어진 단어를 사용하여 다음 대화를 완성하세요.

> A: Did you hear about the new student?
> B: Yes, I did. (1) ___________________________________
> ___________________________ about her.
>   (made, curious, the news)
> A: Me, too. Do you know her name?
> B: Yeah, (2) you ___________________________________
> ___________________________________ .
>   (call, Emma, can) She's from Canada.
> A: I see.

empty 비어 있는 surprise party 깜짝 파티 experience 경험 curious 궁금한, 호기심이 많은

Chapter Test *

정답 및 해설 p.18

STAGE 1 Go for it!

자신 있게 풀어보는 기초 문제!

○━ 배열 영작

[1-5] 우리말과 일치하도록 주어진 단어를 배열하여 문장을 완성하세요.

1
> 그 수프는 짠맛이 났다.
> (tasted / the soup / salty)

→ ______________________________
______________________________.

2
> 나는 Bill에게 돈을 좀 빌려주었다.
> (lent / some money / Bill / I)

→ ______________________________
______________________________.

3
> 사람들은 그 마을이 아름답다는 것을 알게 되었다.
> (the village / people / beautiful / found)

→ ______________________________
______________________________.

4
> 엄마가 나에게 예쁜 스웨터를 만들어 주셨다.
> (a pretty sweater / Mom / me / made / for)

→ ______________________________
______________________________.

5
> Eric은 경찰에게 사실을 말했다.
> (told / Eric / the police / the truth / to)

→ ______________________________
______________________________.

○━ 빈칸 완성

[6-7] 우리말과 일치하도록 주어진 단어를 사용하여 빈칸에 알맞은 말을 쓰세요. (필요시 형태를 바꿀 것)

6
> Ron의 목소리가 졸리게 들렸다.
> (sound, sleepy, Ron's voice)

→ ______________ ______________ ______________
______________.

7
> 그는 아이들에게 축구를 가르친다.
> (children, teach, soccer)

→ ______________ ______________ ______________
______________ ______________.

최신 기출

8 우리말과 일치하도록 〈보기〉에서 알맞은 단어를 골라 주어진 단어를 사용하여 문장을 완성하세요.

> 〈보기〉
> feel   look   smell   taste

(1) 비가 온 후에, 하늘은 맑아 보였다. (clear)
→ After the rain, the sky
______________________________.

(2) 아침에 공기는 차갑게 느껴진다. (cold)
→ The air ______________________________
in the morning.

(3) 이 컵케이크는 꼭 초콜릿과 같은 냄새가 난다.
(chocolate, like)
→ This cupcake just ______________________________
______________________________.

◦ 대화문 완성

[9-14] 주어진 단어를 사용하여 각 대화를 완성하세요.

9
A: How was the science class?
B: ______________ ______________ ______________
during the class. (bored, feel, I)

10
A: What did Jason teach you?
B: ______________ ______________ ______________

______________ ______________ ______________.
(teach, he, some new words, me)

11
A: This sandwich is very delicious!
B: Thank you. ______________ ______________

______________ ______________ ______________

______________. (my mom, it, make, me)

12
A: What's that sound?
B: I don't know. ______________ ______________

______________ ______________ ______________.
(make, uncomfortable, the noise, me)

13
A: What do you think about my idea?
B: ______________ ______________ ______________

______________.
(wonderful, sound, your idea)

14
A: When will you send me the files?
B: ______________ ______________ ______________

______________ ______________ ______________
right away. (send, them, will, you)

◦ 어법 오류 수정

[15-18] 다음 각 문장에서 어법상 **틀린** 부분을 찾아 바르게 고쳐 쓰세요.

15 My grandma called a baby me.

______________ → ______________

16 I'll show my childhood picture you.

______________ → ______________

17 The new jacket kept me warmly.

______________ → ______________

18 I felt sleep after lunch time.

______________ → ______________

최신 기출

19 다음 글을 읽고 〈조건〉에 맞게 우리말을 영작하세요.

My favorite food is pasta. My sister loves it, too. 우리 아빠는 매주 일요일에 우리에게 파스타를 만들어 주신다. He isn't a great cook, but he tries hard. We can feel his love.

〈조건〉
• (1)은 전치사를 사용하고, (2)는 사용하지 말 것
• dad, cook, pasta를 사용할 것

(1) ______________________________________

______________________________ on Sundays.

(2) ______________________________________

______________________________ on Sundays.

20 다음 글을 읽고 질문에 대한 대답을 〈조건〉에 맞게 쓰세요.

> Today was my birthday. In the evening, my family had a birthday party for me at home. My mom made me a strawberry cake. It was really delicious. My dad gave me a book. I loved it. My brother wrote a birthday card to me. We had a wonderful night. My family always makes me happy.

> 〈조건〉
> • 대명사를 주어로 사용할 것
> • (1)은 전치사를 사용하고, (2), (3), (4)는 사용하지 말 것

(1) What did your mom make for you?

→ ________________________________

____

(2) How did the strawberry cake taste?

→ ________________________________

(3) What did your brother write to you?

→ ________________________________

(4) How did you feel?

→ ________________________________

[21-23] 우리말과 일치하도록 〈보기〉에서 알맞은 말을 골라 주어진 단어를 사용하여 문장을 완성하세요. (필요시 형태를 바꿀 것)

> 〈보기〉
> bring   make   look   find

21
> Children are running on the grass. 그들은 매우 신나 보인다.

→ ________________________________ .

(excited, so)

22
> There is a new park in my town. For resting, 사람들은 그 새로운 공원이 좋은 장소라는 것을 알게 되었다.

→ For resting, ________________________

________________________________ .

(a good place, people, the new park)

23
> I left my lunch box at home today. Fortunately, 내 남동생이 나에게 도시락을 가져다 주었다.

→ Fortunately, ________________________

________________________________ .

(the lunch box, my brother, to)

24 우리말과 일치하도록 〈조건〉에 맞게 문장을 완성하세요.

> Last Saturday, our volunteer club visited Blue Children's Home. We held a show for children. We sang and danced together. (1) 아이들의 웃음소리가 모두를 즐겁게 했다. (2) 우리도 신이 났다. It was a great day.

> 〈조건〉
> • 주어진 단어와 알맞은 동사를 사용할 것
> • (1)은 6 단어, (2)는 3 단어로 쓸 것

(1) ________________________________ .

(everyone, the children's laughs, joyful)

(2) ________________________ , too.
(excited)

● 도표 영작

25 로봇에 관한 다음 메모를 보고 〈조건〉에 맞게 문장을 완성하세요.

로봇 이름	로봇이 하는 일
Brown	1. 내가 슬플 때 나에게 따뜻한 포옹을 해 준다.
	2. 우리 집을 깨끗하게 해 준다.
	3. 우리 가족에게 요리를 해 준다.
	4. 우리의 삶을 쉽게 만든다.

〈조건〉
• 주어진 단어를 사용할 것
• 전치사를 사용하지 말 것

(1) I'm introducing my new robot friend.

_______________________________________.

(name, it, I)

(2) Brown is a robot, but it cares about our feelings.

When I feel bad, _______________________

_______________________________________.

(give, a warm hug, it)

(3) Brown _________________________________

_______________________________________.

(keep, clean, our house)

(4) Brown _________________________________

_______________________________________.

(cook, meals, my family)

(5) Brown _________________________________

_______________________________________.

(make, easy, our lives)

● 어법 오류 수정

26 다음 ⓐ~ⓓ 중 어법상 <u>틀린</u> **두 개**를 찾아 그 기호를 쓰고, 바르게 고쳐 쓰세요.

> Mike: Jane, can I ask a favor ⓐ for you?
> Jane: What is it, Mike?
> Mike: Can you lend that book ⓑ to me? I need that book for my homework.
> Jane: I'm sorry, I need it for my homework, too. I ⓒ feel badly.
> Mike: Oh, I see. It's okay.
> Jane: Why don't you ⓓ tell Jenny your problem? She has this book, too.
> Mike: OK. I will.

________ → ________________________

________ → ________________________

🎯 **Challenge!**　　　　누적 문제 Ch 05-07

27 다음 중 어법상 <u>틀린</u> 문장 **두 개**를 찾아 그 기호를 쓰고, 문장 전체를 바르게 고쳐 쓰세요.

> ⓐ What should I wear to the party?
> ⓑ You exercise regularly, aren't you?
> ⓒ I bought a few apples at the supermarket.
> ⓓ He reads a book to his son every evening.
> ⓔ Her story made all the students in the class happily.

________ → ________________________

　　　　________________________

________ → ________________________

Chapter 08
to부정사

✔ **Before You Write**

- ☑ to부정사의 올바른 형태는 무엇일까요?
- ☑ 문장에서 to부정사의 여러 역할을 어떻게 구분해야 할까요?
- ☑ to부정사를 목적어로 쓰는 동사들에는 어떤 것들이 있을까요?
- ☑ 우리말을 보고 to부정사를 써야 할 위치를 파악할 수 있나요?

내신 기출　다음 우리말을 보고 머릿속으로 한번 영어 문장을 떠올려 보세요.

1　아침에 일찍 일어나기는 어렵다.
(동사)하기 → 명사적 쓰임 → ~하는 것은 → 주어 → **To wake up early**　　POINT 1

2　나의 바람은 영어를 잘 말하는 것이다.
(동사)하는 것 → 명사적 쓰임 → ~하는 것이다 → 보어 → **is to speak English well**　　POINT 1

3　그는 사진 찍는 것을 원한다. (take)
(동사)하는 것 → 명사적 쓰임 → ~하는 것을 → 동사 want의 목적어 → **wants to take**　　POINT 2

4　그녀는 나의 책을 오늘 돌려주기로 약속했다.
(promise / return / my book / today)
(동사)하기 → 명사적 쓰임 → ~하기를 → 동사 promise의 목적어 → **promised to return**　　POINT 2

5　ⓐ 사람들은 장수하기 위해 국수를 먹어.
(동사)하기 위해 → 부사적 쓰임 → 목적 → **to live a long life**　　POINT 3

6　그 말을 들으니 기쁘구나.
(동사)하니 (감정이) ~하다 → 부사적 쓰임 → 감정의 원인 → **glad to hear**　　POINT 3

7　(2) 그는 읽을 많은 책을 가지고 있다.
(동사)하는, (동사)할 ~명사 → 형용사적 쓰임 → **many books to read**　　POINT 4

정답: **1** To wake up early in the morning is difficult. **2** My hope is to speak English well. **3** He wants to take pictures. **4** She promised to return my book today. **5** People eat noodles to live a long life. **6** I am[I'm] glad[happy, pleased] to hear that. **7** He has many[a lot of, lots of] books to read.

to부정사의 명사적 쓰임

POINT 1 to부정사 = ~하는 것은(주어) / ~하는 것이다(보어)

자전거를 타는 것은 재미있다.
자전거를 타는 것은 / ~하다 / 재미있는.
　　　　주어　　　　동사　　　보어

→ **To ride** a bicycle / is / fun.
　　to-v(~하는 것은)　　to부정사는 대부분 뒤에 여러 어구가 함께 쓰여요.

- to부정사(to-v)는 to 뒤에 동사원형을 붙여 쓴 것이에요.
  문장에서 시제나 주어의 수, 인칭에 따라 동사의 형태가 변하더라도 「to+동사원형」의 형태는 변하지 않아요.
- to부정사는 동사를 명사처럼 활용해 문장의 주어, 보어, 목적어 자리에 쓸 수 있어요.
- **주어** 자리에 to부정사를 쓰면 '**~하는 것은, ~하기는**'이라는 의미가 돼요.
- to부정사 주어는 단수 취급하여 뒤에 이어지는 동사는 항상 단수형을 씁니다.

> **MORE +** to부정사가 주어 역할을 할 때는 주로 주어 자리에 가짜 주어인 It을 사용하여 「It ~ to부정사 …」 형태로 써요.
> **To ride** a bicycle is fun. → **It** is fun **to ride** a bicycle.

내 직업은 영어를 가르치는 것이다.
내 직업은 / ~이다 / 영어를 가르치는 것.
　주어　　　동사　　　　보어

→ My job / is / **to teach** English.
　　　　　　　　to-v(~하는 것)

- to부정사를 be동사 뒤 **보어** 자리에 쓰면 '**~하는 것(이다), ~하기(이다)**'의 의미로, 주어가 무엇인지를 보충 설명할 수 있어요.

대표 기출 문제

🔒 다음 주어진 단어를 해석에 맞게 순서대로 나열하시오.
반드시 to부정사를 사용하여 문장을 완성하되, 필요시 단어를 추가하시오.

(other languages / learn / interesting)
해석: 다른 언어를 배우는 것은 흥미롭다.

→ _______________________________________

CLUE 1
to부정사를 주어진 우리말 중 어느 부분에 써야 할지 살펴보세요.

CLUE 2
'~하는 것은'의 뜻으로 문장의 주어 자리에 동사 '배우다(learn)'를 쓰려면 to부정사 형태로 써야 해요.

정답: To learn other languages is interesting.

Point Exercise

[1-5] 우리말과 일치하도록 주어진 단어를 올바르게 배열하세요.

1 채소를 먹는 것은 너의 건강에 좋다.
(is / eat / to / vegetables / good)

→ ___________________________________

___________________________ for your health.

2 우리의 계획은 Tyler를 위해 파티를 여는 것이다.
(throw / for Tyler / to / a party)

→ Our plan is ___________________________

___________________________.

3 수영하러 가는 것은 정말 신난다.
(swimming / go / really / is / to / exciting)

→ ___________________________________

___________________________.

4 내 소원은 전 세계를 여행하는 것이다.
(is / travel / to / around the world / my wish)

→ ___________________________________

___________________________.

5 규칙적으로 운동하는 것이 중요하다.
(exercise / important / regularly / to / is)

→ ___________________________________

___________________________.

[6-9] 우리말과 일치하도록 주어진 단어를 사용하여 문장을 완성하세요. (단, to부정사를 반드시 사용할 것)

6 악기를 연주하는 것은 재미있다.
(musical instruments, be, play)

→ ___________________________________

fun.

7 그의 직업은 아이들을 돌보는 것이다.
(children, take care of, his job, be)

→ ___________________________________

____

8 하루 종일 집에 머무르는 것은 지루하다.
(stay, be, all day, at home)

→ ___________________________ boring.

9 내 여동생의 꿈은 요리사가 되는 것이다.
(be, a cook, my sister's dream, become)

→ ___________________________________

____

10 다음 대화를 읽고 〈조건〉에 맞게 우리말을 영작하세요.

A: Do you have any plans for the weekend?
B: Yeah, 내 목표는 이 책을 끝내는 거야.

〈조건〉
· to부정사를 사용할 것
· finish, this book, goal을 사용할 것

→ Yeah, ___________________________

___________________________.

---

health 건강 throw a party 파티를 열다 important 중요한 regularly 규칙적으로 musical instrument 악기 take care of ~을 돌보다 all day 하루 종일

POINT 2 to부정사 = ~하는 것을(목적어)

나는 피자를 먹고 싶다.
나는 / 원한다 / 피자 먹는 것을.
주어   동사   목적어

→ I / *want* / **to eat** pizza.
to-v(~하는 것을)

- 동사 뒤 **목적어** 자리에 '**~하는 것을, ~하기를**'의 의미를 표현할 때 to부정사(to+동사원형)를 쓸 수 있어요.
- 이때 동명사(v-ing) 형태도 목적어 자리에 올 수 있는데 (☞ Ch 09 동명사), to부정사와 동명사 중 어느 것을 쓰는지는 **동사에 따라 결정**이 돼요. 따라서 다음과 같이 to부정사를 목적어로 쓰는 동사들을 잘 알아둬야 합니다.

to부정사를 목적어로 쓰는 동사들

want to do	~하는 것을 원하다, ~하고 싶다	**choose** to do	~하기로 선택하다
hope to do	~하는 것을 희망하다[바라다]	**need** to do	~할 필요가 있다, ~해야 한다
wish to do	~하는 것을 바라다	**promise** to do	~하기로 약속하다
plan to do	~하는 것을 계획하다	**learn** to do	~하는 것을 배우다
expect to do	~하는 것을 기대하다	**like[love]** to do	~하는 것을 (아주) 좋아하다
decide to do	~하기로 결정[결심]하다	**start[begin]** to do	~하는 것을 시작하다

*like, love, hate, start, begin 등은 목적어로 to부정사/동명사가 모두 가능한 동사예요.

대표 기출 문제

다음 조건과 우리말에 맞게 괄호 안에 주어진 단어를 활용하여 영작하시오.

<조건>
- to부정사 형태를 활용할 것
- 필요하면 제시된 단어의 형태를 바꿀 것
- 문장부호와 대소문자를 바르게 쓸 것
- 제시된 글자 수를 맞출 것

(1) Jane은 안경 쓰는 것을 싫어한다. (wear)

→ ___________ ___________ ___________

___________ ___________ .

(2) 그는 사진 찍는 것을 원한다. (take)

→ ___________ ___________ ___________

___________ ___________ .

CLUE 1
조건을 보고 주어진 우리말에서 to부정사를 활용할 수 있는 부분을 확인해요.

CLUE 2
'싫어하다(hate)'와 '원하다(want)' 모두 to부정사를 목적어로 취하는 동사이므로, '~하는 것을'은 to부정사로 나타내요.

정답: (1) Jane hates to wear glasses
(2) He wants to take pictures

함정 피하기 동사의 목적어가 to부정사일 때 to부정사의 형태는 변함없지만, 문장의 동사는 주어와 시제에 맞게 알맞은 형태로 써야 해요.
Jane은 안경 쓰는 것을 싫어한다. ▶ Jane ~~hate~~(→ hates) to wear glasses.
우리는 쇼핑하러 가기로 결심했다. ▶ We ~~decide~~(→ decided) to go shopping.

Point Exercise

정답 및 해설 p.20

배열 영작

[1-3] 우리말과 일치하도록 주어진 단어를 올바르게 배열하세요.

1

Jimmy는 새 신발을 사기로 결정했다.
(buy / decided / new / to / shoes)

→ Jimmy ________________________________

________________________________ .

2

나는 내 가족과 함께 시간을 보내는 것을 좋아한다.
(with / time / like / spend / to / family / my)

→ I ________________________________

________________________________ .

3

그 학생들은 오늘 그들의 숙제를 끝내야 한다.
(their / homework / need / finish / to)

→ The students ________________________

________________________________ today.

빈칸 완성

[4-5] 우리말과 일치하도록 주어진 단어를 사용하여 빈칸에 알맞은 말을 쓰세요. (필요시 단어를 추가하거나 형태를 바꿀 것)

4

나의 형은 여기에 7시까지 온다고 약속했다.
(promise, come)

→ My brother ____________ ____________

____________ here by 7 o'clock.

5

그녀는 주말에 일찍 일어나는 것을 싫어한다.
(wake up, hate)

→ She ____________ ____________

____________ ____________ early on

weekends.

주어진 단어로 영작

[6-8] 우리말과 일치하도록 주어진 단어를 사용하여 문장을 완성하세요.

6

나는 무대 위에서 노래하기를 바란다.
(hope, sing, I)

→ ________________________________

on the stage.

7

우리는 이번 주말에 역사 박물관에 방문할 계획이다.
(plan, the history museum, we, visit)

→ ________________________________

________________________________ this weekend.

8

Mia는 그녀의 엄마에게서 빵을 굽는 것을 배웠다.
(learn, bread, bake)

→ ________________________________

________________________________ from her mom.

기출: 조건 영작

9 다음 대화를 읽고 〈조건〉에 맞게 우리말을 영작하세요.

A: Where do you want to go for your next
vacation?
B: 나는 나의 친구들과 부산에 방문하고 싶어.

〈조건〉
• 8 단어로 쓸 것
• Busan, visit, want, with를 사용할 것

→ ________________________________

____

spend (시간을) 보내다, (돈을) 쓰다 stage 무대 museum 박물관, 미술관 vacation 방학, 휴가

to부정사의 부사적 쓰임

POINT 3   to부정사 = ~하기 위해, ~하려고(목적) / ~해서(감정의 원인)

> 나는 질문을 하기 위해 Linda에게 전화했다.
> 나는 Linda에게 전화했다 / 질문을 하기 위해.
> 　　　　　　　　　　　　　　행동의 목적
>
> → I called Linda / **to ask** questions.
> 　　완전한 문장　　　　　부사구 to-v(행동의 목적)
>
> 질문을 하기 위해, / 나는 Linda에게 전화했다.
> 행동의 목적
>
> → **To ask** questions, / I called Linda.
> 　부사구 to-v(행동의 목적)　　　완전한 문장

- 문장에서 어떤 동작이나 행동의 **목적(~하기 위해, ~하려고)**을 나타낼 때 to부정사를 많이 사용해요.
- 완전한 문장의 맨 앞이나 뒤에 to부정사구를 붙여 의미를 추가하는 식으로 쓰기 때문에 부사적 역할이라고 합니다.

> 나는 너를 만나서 매우 기쁘다.
> 나는 매우 기쁘다 / 너를 만나서.
> 　　　　　　　　　　감정의 원인
>
> → I'm *very glad* / **to meet** you.
> 　완전한 문장　　　　부사구 to-v(감정의 원인)

- to부정사는 감정을 나타내는 형용사(happy, glad, pleased, sad, excited 등) 뒤에 쓰여 그 감정을 느끼는 원인을 표현할 수도 있어요.
- 즉, '**~해서(원인) …한 감정을 느낀다**'라는 의미는 「**감정 형용사+to부정사**」의 형태로 씁니다.

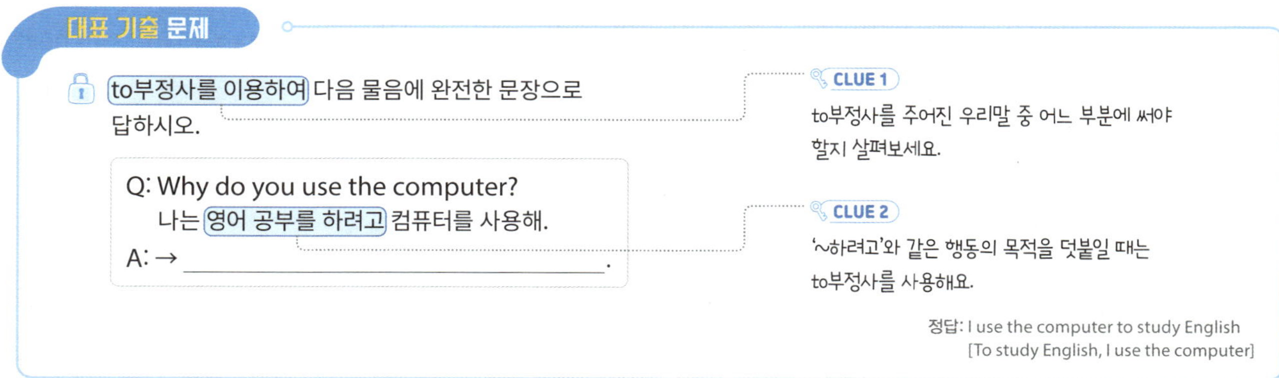

대표 기출 문제

to부정사를 이용하여 다음 물음에 완전한 문장으로 답하시오.

Q: Why do you use the computer?
　 나는 영어 공부를 하려고 컴퓨터를 사용해.
A: → ________________________________ .

CLUE 1
to부정사를 주어진 우리말 중 어느 부분에 써야 할지 살펴보세요.

CLUE 2
'~하려고'와 같은 행동의 목적을 덧붙일 때는 to부정사를 사용해요.

정답: I use the computer to study English
[To study English, I use the computer]

Point Exercise

배열 영작

[1-3] 우리말과 일치하도록 주어진 단어를 올바르게 배열하세요.

1
> 우리는 콘서트 표를 사기 위해 돈을 저축했다.
> (buy / money / to / concert tickets / saved)

→ We _________________________________

_________________________________ .

2
> 나는 질문하려고 내 손을 들었다.
> (ask / hand / my / to / a question / raised)

→ I _________________________________

_________________________________ .

3
> 그 학생들은 좋은 점수를 받게 되어 기뻤다.
> (happy / scores / to / good / were / get)

→ The students _________________________

_________________________________ .

주어진 단어로 영작

[4-7] 우리말과 일치하도록 주어진 단어를 사용하여 문장을 완성하세요. (필요시 형태를 바꿀 것)

4
> 당신의 글쓰기를 향상시키려면, 많은 책을 읽어라.
> (improve, writing)

→ _________________________________ ,

read a lot of books.

5
> 그 소녀는 연극을 보게 되어서 기뻤다.
> (see, glad, a play, be, the girl)

→ _________________________________

_________________________________ .

6
> 그들은 그 소식을 들어서 매우 슬펐다.
> (very sad, be, the news, hear)

→ _________________________________

_________________________________ .

7
> 그는 배드민턴을 치려고 운동장으로 갔다.
> (badminton, play, to the playground, go)

→ He _________________________________

_________________________________ .

기출 : 도표 영작

8 다음 학생들이 도서관에 간 목적을 나타내는 표를 보고 〈조건〉에 맞게 문장을 완성하세요.

학생	도서관에 간 목적
Joe	영어 공부를 하려고
Max	책을 한 권 빌리기 위해
Tim	숙제를 하려고

〈보기〉

study	do	borrow
his homework	English	a book

〈조건〉
- to부정사를 사용할 것
- 〈보기〉의 단어를 한 번씩만 사용할 것

(1) Joe went to the library ________________

_________________________________ .

(2) Max went to the library ________________

_________________________________ .

(3) Tim went to the library ________________

_________________________________ .

raise 올리다, 들어 올리다 improve 향상시키다 play 연극

to부정사의 형용사적 쓰임

POINT 4　(대)명사+to부정사: ~하는, ~할

영어를 배우는 좋은 방법들을 제게 말해주세요.
제게 말해주세요 / 좋은 방법들을 / 영어를 배우는.

→ Tell me / *good ways* / **to learn** English.

- 동사(~하다)가 명사나 대명사를 수식해 '**~하는, ~할 무엇**'이라는 의미를 나타내기 위해서는 동사를 to부정사 형태로 바꿔 써야 해요. 이때 to부정사는 (대)명사 뒤에 위치하며 즉, 「**(대)명사+to부정사(구)**」의 형태로 써야 해요.

나는 마실 것이 필요하다.
나는 필요하다 / 무언가가 / 마실.

→ I need / *something* / **to drink**.

- something, anyone, nobody 등과 같이 -thing, -one, -body로 끝나는 대명사는 to부정사가 뒤에서 수식하는 형태로 자주 써요.
  He has ***nothing* to eat** now. 그는 지금 먹을 것이 아무것도 없다.

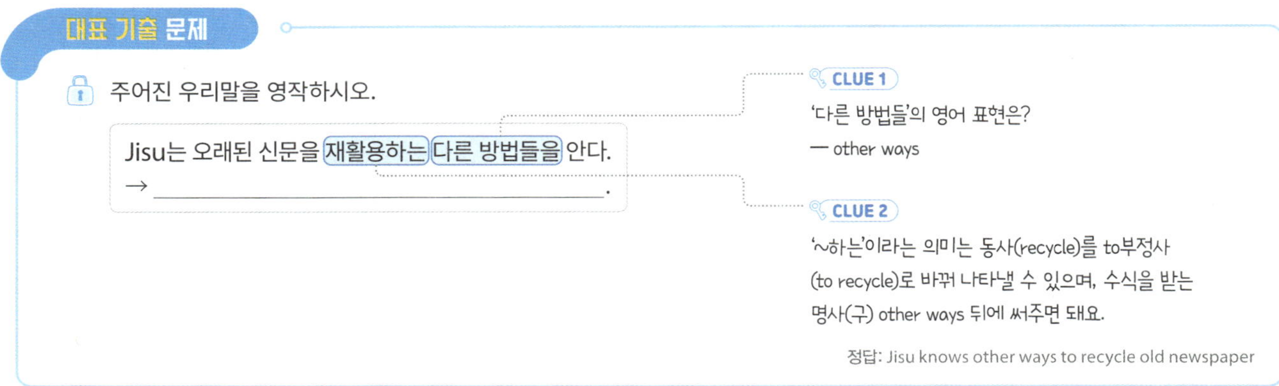

대표 기출 문제

🔒 주어진 우리말을 영작하시오.

Jisu는 오래된 신문을 재활용하는 다른 방법들을 안다.
→ _______________________________________.

CLUE 1
'다른 방법들'의 영어 표현은?
— other ways

CLUE 2
'~하는'이라는 의미는 동사(recycle)를 to부정사 (to recycle)로 바꿔 나타낼 수 있으며, 수식을 받는 명사(구) other ways 뒤에 써주면 돼요.

정답: Jisu knows other ways to recycle old newspaper

✔ **함정 피하기**　일반적으로 형용사는 (대)명사를 앞에서 수식하지만, to부정사는 (대)명사를 뒤에서 수식하도록 써야 함을 꼭 기억하세요.
There are **to visit** *many places* in this city. (✕)
→ There are *many places* **to visit** in this city. (○) (이 도시에는 방문할 곳이 많이 있다.)

Point Exercise

배열 영작

[1-5] 우리말과 일치하도록 주어진 단어를 올바르게 배열하세요.

1
나는 입을 코트가 없다.
(to / don't / a coat / wear / have / I)

→ ____________________

____________________ .

2
그는 출장 기간 동안 머물 장소를 찾았다.
(stay / found / he / to / a place)

→ ____________________

during his business trip.

3
그들은 같이 볼 영화를 골랐다.
(a movie / they / together / watch / picked / to)

→ ____________________

____________________ .

4
우리는 우리를 도와줄 누군가가 필요하다.
(someone / need / help / us / we / to)

→ ____________________

____________________ .

5
뉴욕의 브로드웨이에는 감상할 많은 뮤지컬들이 있다.
(to / are / there / many musicals / watch)

→ ____________________

____________________ on Broadway in New York.

주어진 단어로 영작

[6-9] 우리말과 일치하도록 주어진 단어를 사용하여 문장을 완성하세요. (필요시 형태를 바꿀 것)

6
나는 휴식을 취할 시간이 필요하다.
(take a rest, time, need)

→ ____________________

7
Justin은 파리를 여행할 기회를 얻었다.
(travel, get, Paris, a chance)

→ ____________________

8
나의 부모님은 운전할 차 한 대를 사셨다.
(parents, buy, drive, a car)

→ ____________________

____

9
수미는 친구들에게 줄 몇 장의 편지를 썼다.
(Sumi, write, give, some letters)

→ ____________________

____________________ to her friends.

기출·조건 영작

10 다음 글을 읽고 〈조건〉에 맞게 우리말을 영작하세요.

John found a book to read on vacation. He finished it in two days. 그것은 휴식을 취하는 완벽한 방법이었다.

〈조건〉
- 7 단어로 쓸 것
- relax, perfect, way, be, it을 사용할 것

→ ____________________

---

business trip 출장 pick 고르다, 선택하다 take a rest 휴식을 취하다 perfect 완벽한 way 방법; 길

Chapter Test *

정답 및 해설 p.21

STAGE 1 Go for it!

자신 있게 풀어보는 기초 문제!

빈칸 완성

[1-4] 우리말과 일치하도록 주어진 단어를 사용하여 빈칸에 알맞은 말을 쓰세요.

1
> 나는 새 모자를 하나 사고 싶다.
> (a new cap, buy, want)

→ I ___________ ___________

___________ ___________ ___________ .

2
> Becky의 꿈은 영국에서 사는 것이다.
> (in England, live, be)

→ Becky's dream ___________ ___________

___________ ___________ ___________ .

3
> Luke는 그 시험을 끝마친 첫 번째 학생이었다.
> (finish, student, the exam)

→ Luke was the first ___________

___________ ___________ ___________

___________ .

4
> 우리는 놀이공원에 가서 행복했다.
> (happy, go, the amusement park, to)

→ We were ___________ ___________

___________ ___________

___________ ___________ .

배열 영작

[5-7] 우리말과 일치하도록 주어진 단어를 배열하여 문장을 완성하세요.

5
> 친구들과 노는 것은 즐겁다.
> (fun / with / friends / play / is / to)

→ ___________

___________ .

6
> 나의 엄마는 다음 달에 새로운 일을 시작하는 것을 계획 중이시다.
> (a new job / to / is / my mom / start / planning)

→ ___________

___________ next month.

7
> 마실 것 좀 주시겠어요?
> (you / me / something / give / drink / to / can)

→ ___________

___________ ?

최신 기출

8 다음 글을 읽고, (A)의 주어진 단어를 배열하여 문장을 완성하세요.

> Ruby likes to bake. (A) (makes / give / to her friends / she / cookies / to). They always enjoy these gifts.

→ ___________

___________ .

● 단어 수 대로 영작

[9-14] 우리말과 일치하도록 주어진 단어 수에 맞게 문장을 완성하세요.

9
> 나는 수업 시간 동안 안경을 써야 한다. (3 단어)

→ I need ________________________
during class.

10
> 수미는 그녀의 책을 잃어버려서 슬펐다. (4 단어)

→ Sumi was sad ________________________
________________________.

11
> 우리는 그 문을 열 열쇠가 없다. (4 단어)

→ We don't have a key ________________________
________________________.

12
> 나는 내 친구를 만나기 위해 밖에 나갔다. (4 단어)

→ I went out ________________________
________________________.

13
> 나의 오빠는 배우가 되기를 원한다. (4 단어)

→ My older brother wishes ________________________
________________________.

14
> 축구 경기를 보는 것은 재미있다. (5 단어)

→ ________________________
________________________ is fun.

● 문맥에 맞게 영작

[15-16] 다음 대화를 읽고 to부정사를 사용하여 각 질문에 대한 대답을 완성하세요.

15
> A: Clara, where were you this morning?
> B: I was at the park. I jogged around the lake.

Q: Why did Clara go to the park?
A: She went to the park ________________________
________________________.

16
> A: Why are you late, Jinho?
> B: I stopped by the supermarket on my way. I bought some eggs.

Q: Why was Jinho late?
A: He stopped by the supermarket ________________________
________________________.

최신 기출

17 우리말과 일치하도록 〈조건〉에 맞게 문장을 완성하세요.

> 〈조건〉
> • to부정사를 사용할 것
> • 각각 5 단어로 쓸 것
> • 주어진 단어를 사용할 것

(1) Lena는 새 자전거를 위해 돈을 모으기 시작했다.
(save, begin)

→ ________________________
________________________ for a new bike.

(2) 그의 올해 목표는 열 권의 책을 읽는 것이다.
(read, be, ten)

→ His goal ________________________
________________________ this year.

[18-24] 다음 각 문장에서 어법상 <u>틀린</u> 부분을 찾아 바르게 고쳐 쓰세요.

18 Linda hopes to travels to Asia next year.

______________ → ______________

19 We chose visit an apple farm in our town.

______________ → ______________

20 They were sad to missing the concert.

______________ → ______________

21 The boy learned use a washing machine.

______________ → ______________

22 To solve this question were difficult.

______________ → ______________

23 She promised stayed at home after school today.

______________ → ______________

24 Do you have a pencil lend me?

______________ → ______________

[25-26] 우리말과 일치하도록 괄호 안에 주어진 조건에 맞게 영작하세요.

25

> Today, I'll talk about my future goal. (1) <u>나는 미래에 아픈 사람들을 돕길 원한다.</u> One day, I read about Florence Nightingale, and she became my role model. (2) So, <u>나는 간호사가 되기로 결심했다.</u>

(1) ______________________________
in the future. (want, people을 사용할 것)

(2) So, ______________________________.
(decide를 사용할 것)

26

> Homin is 13 years old. (1) <u>그는 새로운 언어들을 배우기를 좋아한다.</u> (2) <u>그의 목표는 많은 나라에서 이 언어들을 사용하는 것이다.</u> To get ready, he watches movies in different languages every day.

(1) ______________________________
(like, to부정사를 사용할 것)

(2) ______________________________
______________________ in many countries.
(goal, these, to부정사를 사용할 것)

27 다음 Liam의 주말 계획표를 보고, Liam이 주말에 하고 싶어하는 활동에 대해 완전한 영어 문장으로 영작하세요.

Want to Do	on Saturday	on Sunday
play board games with his friends	○	×
go skating	×	○

(1) Liam ______________________________

______________________________.

(2) Liam ______________________________

______________________________.

o— 도표 영작

28 다음은 Jina의 생일 파티를 위한 메모입니다. 〈보기〉에서 알맞은 말을 골라 to부정사를 사용하여 글을 완성하세요.

Plan for Jina's Birthday Party	
Jina's favorite Cake	cheesecake
Things to Buy	some roses
Friends to Invite	five

〈보기〉

buy	happy	invite
like	receive	eat

Jina is my best friend, and tomorrow is her birthday. My friends and I are going to hold a birthday party.

Jina (1) ___________________ cheesecake. So, we got one from the famous bakery. Then, I went to the flower shop (2) ___________________ some roses. Jina will be (3) ___________________ them. We also made invitations for the party. There are five friends (4) ___________________. Jina will have a fantastic birthday.

o— 조건 영작

29 Nate가 여행 후 쓴 글을 읽고, 〈조건〉에 맞게 문장을 완성하세요.

I went to New York with my family last summer. We went to the airport and took a plane. I traveled abroad for the first time, and I was very excited.

I visited many galleries and museums. New Yorkers speak very fast, and I couldn't understand them well. Everything was a challenge, but it was an exciting one. I really want to visit the city again next year.

〈조건〉
• to부정사를 사용할 것
• 글에 나온 단어를 활용할 것

(1) _______________________________, we went to the airport.

(2) I was very excited _______________________________.

(3) There are many galleries and museums _______________________________ in New York.

(4) Next year, I _______________________________ the city again.

🎯 **Challenge!**

누적 문제 Ch 06-08

30 다음 중 어법상 틀린 문장 <u>두 개</u>를 찾아 그 기호를 쓰고, 문장 전체를 바르게 고쳐 쓰세요.

ⓐ Ted made dinner for his mom.
ⓑ I didn't expect seeing you here.
ⓒ The chocolate cake tasted sweetly.
ⓓ Don't listen to music too loudly.
ⓔ People use a smartphone to check the weather.

_______ → _______________________
____

_______ → _______________________
____

✅ Before You Write

- ☑ 동명사의 올바른 형태는 무엇일까요?
- ☑ 문장에서 동명사의 여러 역할을 어떻게 구분해야 할까요?
- ☑ 동명사와 to부정사를 목적어로 쓰는 동사들을 구분해서 쓸 수 있나요?
- ☑ 우리말을 보고 동명사를 써야 할 위치를 파악할 수 있나요?

내신 기출 다음 우리말을 보고 머릿속으로 한번 영어 문장을 떠올려 보세요.

1 (2) 자전거를 타는 것은 그가 매우 좋아하는 활동이다.
(ride, a, bike, be)
(동사)하는 것은 → 주어 → **Riding a bike is**   `POINT 1`

2 그녀의 취미는 등산을 하는 것이다.
(is / the / hobby / climbing / her / mountains)
(동사)하는 것이다 → 보어 → **is climbing the mountains**   `POINT 1`

3 Jenny는 한국 음식 만드는 것을 즐긴다.
(enjoy / make / Korean food)
(동사)하는 것을 → 동사 enjoy의 목적어 → **enjoys making**   `POINT 2`

4 (B) 나는 매일 노래하는 것을 연습한다.
(every day / I / sing / practice)
(동사)하는 것을 → 동사 practice의 목적어 → **practice singing**   `POINT 2`

5 나는 그림 그리는 것을 잘한다. (paint, good)
~하는 것을 잘하다 → be good at → 전치사+동명사 → **am good at painting**   `POINT 3`

6 Tom은 아픈 사람들을 돕는 것에 관심(흥미)이 있다.
~하는 것에 관심이 있다 → be interested in → 전치사+동명사 → **is interested in helping**   `POINT 3`

정답: **1** Riding a bike is his favorite activity. **2** Her hobby is climbing the mountains. **3** Jenny enjoys making Korean food. **4** I practice singing every day. **5** I am[I'm] good at painting. **6** Tom is interested in helping sick people.

명사로 쓰이는 동명사

POINT 1 동명사 = ~하는 것은(주어) / ~하는 것이다(보어)

잘 자는 것은 건강에 좋다.
잘 자는 것은 / ~하다 / 좋은 / 건강에.
　　주어　　　　　동사　　보어

→ **Sleeping** well / *is* / good / for health.
　　v-ing(~하는 것은)

- 동명사란 동사원형 뒤에 -ing를 붙여 명사처럼 쓰는 것을 말해요. 동사의 -ing형은 진행형의 -ing형을 만드는 방법과 같고, to부정사와 마찬가지로 뒤에 여러 어구가 오기도 해요. (☞ p.172 동사 변화형)
- 동명사는 문장에서 '~하는 것은, ~하기는'이라는 의미로 **주어** 자리에 쓰일 수 있어요. 뒤에 이어지는 동사는 항상 단수형을 써요.

그의 직업은 학생들을 가르치는 것이다.
그의 직업은 / ~이다 / 학생들을 가르치는 것.
　　주어　　　　동사　　　　　보어

→ His job / is / **teaching** students.
　　　　　　　　v-ing(~하는 것)

- 동명사는 문장에서 be동사 뒤의 **보어** 자리에 '~하는 것(이다), ~하기(이다)'의 의미로도 쓰일 수 있어요.

대표 기출 문제

🔒 다음 <보기>에서 우리말 (A)와 같은 뜻이 되도록 (B)에 주어진 단어를 모두 포함하며, 동명사를 사용하여 영작하시오. (단, 필요시 단어의 형태를 변형시킬 것)

<보기>
(A) 거짓말을 하는 것은 나쁘다.
(B) lie, bad

→ _______________________

🔍 **CLUE 1**
동명사를 주어진 우리말 중 어느 부분에 써야 할지 살펴보세요.

🔍 **CLUE 2**
'~하는 것은'이라는 뜻의 동명사는 문장의 주어 자리에 쓰여요. 따라서 '거짓말하다'라는 뜻의 동사 lie를 「동사원형+-ing」으로 주어 자리에 쓰면 돼요.

정답: Lying is bad.

✅ **함정 피하기** 동명사 주어는 항상 단수 취급하므로, 동사 바로 앞에 복수명사가 있을 때 동사를 잘못 쓰지 않도록 주의하세요.

Visiting different places ~~are~~(→ is) interesting. (다양한 장소를 방문하는 것은 흥미롭다.)
　　주어

Point Exercise

배열 영작

[1-4] 우리말과 일치하도록 주어진 단어를 올바르게 배열하세요.

1
> 기차로 여행하는 것은 매우 신난다.
> (by train / is / a trip / taking)

→ _______________________________ very exciting.

2
> 손톱을 물어뜯는 것은 좋은 습관이 아니다.
> (is / your nails / biting)

→ _______________________________ not a good habit.

3
> 나의 도전 과제는 내 요리 실력을 향상시키는 것이다.
> (cooking skills / improving / is / my)

→ My challenge _______________________________
_______________________________ .

4
> 과일과 채소를 먹는 것은 건강을 유지하는 데 중요하다.
> (vegetables / is / and / eating / fruits)

→ _______________________________
_______________ important for staying healthy.

주어진 단어로 영작

[5-8] 우리말과 일치하도록 주어진 단어를 사용하여 문장을 완성하세요. (단, 동명사 형태로 쓸 것)

5
> 줄을 서서 기다리는 것은 대부분의 사람들에게 지루하다.
> (boring, in line, wait, be)

→ _______________________________ for most people.

6
> 시간을 지키는 것은 중요하다.
> (important, on time, be)

→ _______________________________

7
> 외국어를 배우는 것은 쉽지 않다.
> (be, foreign languages, learn, easy)

→ _______________________________
____

8
> 책을 읽는 것은 네 어휘력을 길러준다.
> (your vocabulary, a book, build, read)

→ _______________________________
____

기출: 조건 영작

9 다음 글을 읽고 질문에 대한 대답을 〈조건〉에 맞게 쓰세요.

> Olivia takes care of pets in the animal hospital. It's her job. In her free time, she likes to play the piano. It's her hobby.

〈조건〉
- 각 문장에 동명사를 반드시 사용할 것
- (1)은 7 단어, (2)는 6 단어로 쓸 것

(1) What is Olivia's job?

→ _______________________________
____

(2) What is Olivia's hobby?

→ _______________________________
____

---

bite 물어뜯다, 물다 skill 기술, 솜씨 improve 향상시키다 challenge 도전 important 중요한 on time 정시에, 제시간에 foreign 외국의 vocabulary 어휘력; 어휘

POINT 2   동명사 = ~하는 것을(목적어)

그들은 과학 실험하는 것을 끝냈다.
그들은 / 끝냈다 / 과학 실험하는 것을.
　주어　　동사　　　　목적어

→ They / **finished** / **doing** a science experiment.
　　　　　　　　　　　v-ing(~하는 것을)

나는 창문을 여는 것을 꺼리지 않아.
나는 / 꺼리지 않아 / 창문을 여는 것을.
　주어　　동사　　　　목적어

→ I / **don't mind** / **opening** the window.
　　　　　　　　　v-ing(~하는 것을)

- 동명사도 to부정사와 마찬가지로 동사 뒤 **목적어** 자리에 쓰여 '**~하는 것을, ~하기를**'이라는 의미를 나타냅니다.
- 다음 동사들은 동명사를 목적어로 취하는 동사들이며, to부정사를 목적어로 쓰는 동사들과 구별하여 꼭 알아두어야 합니다.

📢 동명사를 목적어로 쓰는 동사들

enjoy -ing	~하는 것을 즐기다	**give up** -ing	~하는 것을 포기하다
finish -ing	~하는 것을 끝내다	**mind** -ing	~하는 것을 꺼리다
keep -ing	~하는 것을 계속하다	**stop[quit]** -ing	~하는 것을 멈추다
practice -ing	~하는 것을 연습하다	**suggest** -ing	~하는 것을 제안하다
avoid -ing	~하는 것을 피하다	**consider** -ing	~하는 것을 고려하다

*to부정사/동명사 목적어가 모두 가능한 동사: like, love, hate, start, begin 등

대표 기출 문제

🔒 다음 주어진 조건에 맞게 영어로 문장을 쓰시오.

Mike는 다른 나라들을 여행하는 것을 즐긴다.
(travel, enjoy, other countries)

<조건>
1. 주어, 동사가 있는 완전한 문장으로 쓰기
2. 주어진 단어를 활용할 것

→ ________ ________ ________ ________
　 ________ ________.

CLUE 1
우리말의 '~하는 것을'에 해당하는 목적어 자리에는 동사원형에 -ing를 붙인 동명사나 to부정사를 쓸 수 있어요.

CLUE 2
enjoy는 동명사를 목적어로 취하는 동사예요.
— enjoys traveling

정답: Mike enjoys traveling to other countries

Point Exercise

[1-3] 우리말과 일치하도록 주어진 단어를 올바르게 배열하세요.

1
> Anna는 그녀의 시계를 찾는 것을 포기했다.
> (finding / gave up / her watch / Anna)

→ ____

____ .

2
> 우리는 해변에서 모래성을 짓는 것을 끝냈다.
> (finished / a sandcastle / we / building)

→ ____

________________________________ at the beach.

3
> Erica는 교통이 혼잡할 때 버스를 타는 것을 피한다.
> (a bus / avoids / taking / Erica)

→ ____

in heavy traffic.

[4-6] 우리말과 일치하도록 주어진 단어를 사용하여 문장을
완성하세요. (필요시 형태를 바꿀 것)

4
> Archie는 오늘 밤 영화 볼 것을 제안했다.
> (a movie, watch, suggest)

→ Archie ________________________________

________________________________ tonight.

5
> 나는 매일 영어를 말하는 것을 연습한다.
> (practice, English, speak)

→ I ________________________________

________________________________ every day.

6
> 당신은 에어컨을 켜는 것을 꺼리시나요?
> (mind, the air conditioner, turn on)

→ Do you ________________________________

________________________________ ?

[7-8] 우리말과 일치하도록 〈보기〉에서 알맞은 단어를 골라
주어진 단어를 사용하여 문장을 완성하세요.

> 〈보기〉 stop   keep   love

7
> 그 축구팀은 계속 이기고 있다.
> (the soccer team, win)

→ ____

8
> 나는 새로운 것들을 시도하는 것을 아주 좋아한다.
> (new things, try out)

→ ____

9 다음 표를 보고 〈조건〉에 맞게 두 사람의 대화를 완성하
세요.

	Brother	Sister
ride a bike		○
sing songs	○	

> 〈조건〉
> • 질문에 있는 동사를 사용할 것

A: What does your brother enjoy in his free
   time?
B: (1) ________________________________
A : What does your sister practice?
B: (2) ________________________________

sandcastle 모래성 heavy traffic 교통 혼잡 turn on 켜다

자주 쓰이는 동명사 표현

POINT 3 전치사+동명사

> 그는 우리에게 질문을 함으로써 시작했다.
> 그는 / 시작했다 / 우리에게 질문을 함으로써.
>
> → He / started / ***by*** **asking** us a question.

- at, by, about, for, without 등과 같은 전치사 뒤에 동사를 쓸 경우에는 동명사의 형태로 씁니다.
- 「전치사+명사」가 기본 형태이지만, 동명사도 명사의 역할을 하므로 전치사 뒤에 동명사가 올 수 있어요.

> 그들은 노래 부르는 것을 잘해.
> 그들은 / 잘해 / 노래 부르는 것을.
>
> → They / **are good** / **at singing** songs.

- 또한, 동명사가 숙어처럼 사용되는 자주 쓰이는 표현들은 잘 기억해 두세요.

📢 **동명사를 포함한 주요 표현**

go -ing	~하러 가다	**be afraid of -ing**	~하는 것을 무서워하다
be good at -ing	~하는 것을 잘하다	**be interested in -ing**	~에 관심[흥미]이 있다
How about -ing ~?	~하는 게 어때?	**thank you for -ing**	~해줘서 고맙다

대표 기출 문제

🔒 다음의 대화를 보고 밑줄 친 부분을 영작하시오.
(good을 사용하시오.)

> Sujin: You play the violin so beautifully!
> Brian: Thanks. Can you play the violin, Sujin?
> Sujin: No, I can't. But 나는 피아노 치는 것을 잘해.

→ ____________________________________ .

CLUE 1
우리말의 '치는 것을'은 '치다'라는 동사를 명사처럼 나타낸 것이에요. 이렇게 쓰일 수 있는 것은?
— 동명사, to부정사!

CLUE 2
'~을 잘하다'라는 의미이면서 good이 들어가는 표현은? — be good at!
전치사 at 뒤에 목적어로 쓰일 수 있는 것은 to부정사가 아니라 동명사예요.

정답: I am[I'm] good at playing the piano

✓ **함정 피하기** 동명사를 포함한 주요 표현을 사용하여 영작할 때, 전치사 뒤에 동사원형을 쓰지 않도록 유의하세요.
Don't **be afraid of** ~~swim~~(→ swimming) in the sea. (바다에서 수영하는 걸 무서워하지 마.)

Point Exercise

○ **배열 영작**

[1-4] 우리말과 일치하도록 주어진 단어를 올바르게 배열하세요.

1
> Maria는 지난 주말에 스키를 타러 갔다.
> (skiing / last weekend / went)

→ Maria ________________________

________________________ .

2
> 박쥐는 어둠 속에서 보는 것을 잘한다.
> (seeing / good / are / at)

→ Bats ________________________

in the dark.

3
> 나에게 책을 빌려줘서 고마워.
> (me / lending / you / thank / for / a book)

→ ________________________

________________________ .

4
> 나는 휴가 가는 것에 신이 나.
> (going on / excited / about / vacation / am)

→ I ________________________

________________________ .

○ **주어진 단어로 영작**

[5-9] 우리말과 일치하도록 주어진 단어를 사용하여 문장을 완성하세요. (필요시 형태를 바꿀 것)

5
> 토요일에 박물관에 방문하는 게 어때?
> (how, the museum, visit)

→ ________________________

________________________ on Saturday?

6
> 우리는 송편을 먹음으로써 추석을 기념한다.
> (have, Chuseok, by, celebrate)

→ ________________________

________________________ Songpyeon.

7
> 그는 롤러코스터 타는 것을 두려워해.
> (ride, afraid, roller coasters, of)

→ ________________________

____

8
> Andy는 세계사를 공부하는 것에 흥미가 있다.
> (in, study, interested)

→ ________________________

________________________ world history.

9
> 민지는 작별 인사 없이 그 파티를 떠났다.
> (the party, say goodbye, without, leave)

→ Minji ________________________

________________________ .

○ **기출: 문맥에 맞게 영작**

10 다음 글을 읽고 주어진 단어를 사용하여 Bella가 잘하는 것을 나타내는 문장을 완성하세요.

> I am Bella. I don't sing well, but I can play basketball very well. I score the most points in every game, and my team always wins the basketball games.

→ She ________________________

________________________ .

(good, play)

lend 빌려주다 celebrate 기념하다, 축하하다 roller coaster 롤러코스터 say goodbye 작별 인사를 하다 score (골·득점 등을) 하다; 득점, 스코어

Chapter Test *

STAGE 1 Go for it!

자신 있게 풀어보는 기초 문제!

배열 영작

[1-3] 우리말과 일치하도록 주어진 단어를 올바르게 배열하여 문장을 완성하세요.

1
> 내 취미는 패션 잡지를 읽는 것이다.
> (is / fashion magazines / reading)

→ My hobby ___________________
___________________ .

2
> Ethan은 탄산음료를 마시는 것을 멈췄다.
> (stopped / drinking / Ethan / soda)

→ ___________________
___________________ .

3
> 친구들과 쿠키를 만드는 것은 즐겁다.
> (friends / enjoyable / making / is / cookies / with)

→ ___________________
___________________ .

주어진 단어로 영작

[4-7] 우리말과 일치하도록 주어진 단어를 사용하여 문장을 완성하세요. (필요시 형태를 바꿀 것)

4
> 그는 밤에 너무 늦게 먹는 것을 피한다.
> (eat, too late, avoid)

→ ___________________
___________________ at night.

5
> 새로운 곳을 여행하는 것은 흥미진진하다.
> (be, to, interesting, new places, travel)

→ ___________________
____

6
> 엄마는 요즘 자동차를 운전하는 것을 연습하신다.
> (practice, Mom, her car, drive)

→ ___________________
___________________ these days.

7
> 나에게 그 정보를 알려줘서 고마워.
> (thank, tell, for)

→ ___________________
___________________ the information.

최신 기출

8 다음 글을 읽고 〈보기〉에서 알맞은 단어를 골라 빈칸을 완성하세요.

> 〈보기〉
> dance　　　watch　　　take　　　play

> The school festival is next week. I enjoy ___________________ the piano, so I will perform my favorite song. Jacob is good at ___________________, so he will perform with his friends. Emily's hobby is ___________________ pictures, so she will bring a camera to the festival.

[어법 오류 수정]

[9-17] 다음 각 문장에서 어법상 **틀린** 부분을 찾아 바르게 고쳐 쓰세요.

9 Do you mind to take a walk later?

________________ → ________________

10 Reading comic books aren't fun for me.

________________ → ________________

11 My brother kept to ask questions about nature.

________________ → ________________

12 My cousin enjoys to take trips to other countries.

________________ → ________________

13 Watch scary movies is exciting.

________________ → ________________

14 Jim avoided break school rules.

________________ → ________________

15 Jessica finished to bake an apple pie.

________________ → ________________

16 I entered the library by show my student ID card.

________________ → ________________

17 Sue gave up to put the puzzle together.

________________ → ________________

[도표 영작]

[18-19] 다음 표를 보고 주어진 단어를 사용하여 각 대화를 완성하세요.

	Dean	Alex	Judy
play soccer		○	
learn Spanish			○
cook dinner	○		

18

A: What is Dean thinking?

B: __________________________

____

for his family. (consider)

19

A: What did Judy give up?

B: __________________________

________________________. (give up)

[최신 기출]

20 우리말과 일치하도록 〈조건〉에 맞게 문장을 완성하세요.

〈조건〉
- 주어진 단어를 사용하되 필요시 형태를 바꿀 것
- (1)은 7 단어, (2)는 6 단어로 쓸 것

(1) 그는 그의 손으로 물건 만드는 것을 좋아한다.
  (hands, make, things, like, with)

  → __________________________

  ____

(2) 그녀는 도예를 배우는 것에 관심이 있다.
  (in, learn, interested, pottery, be)

  → __________________________

  ____

[21-25] 주어진 단어를 사용하여 각 대화를 완성하세요.

21
A: What's your brother's plan after high
   school?
B: _______________________________
   his next step. (be, college, go, to)

22
A: Are you done with your book report?
B: Yes, _______________________________
   yesterday. (write, finish, I, it)

23
A: I'm worried about camping for the first
   time.
B: Don't _______________________________
   _______________________________.
   (of, new things, afraid, try, be)

24
A: Wow, you really fixed my bike fast!
B: It was no big deal.
A: _______________________________
   _______________________________.
   (thank, it, for, fix, you)
   I can ride to school now!

25
A: What do you want to do this weekend?
B: _______________________________?
   (go, how, fish)
   There's a quiet spot by the river.

26 다음은 Serena가 친구에게 보내는 편지입니다. 글을 읽고
〈조건〉에 맞게 영작하세요.

Dear Leo,
    Hello, Leo. Long time no chat! How's
your new school?
    These days, (1) 나는 강아지를 키우는 것을 고려
하고 있어. But my parents didn't allow it at
first. (2) 나는 그분들을 설득하는 것을 계속했어.
And they finally agreed! I'll send you a
picture of the puppy when I bring him
home.
    I hope to see you soon!

Take care,
Serena

〈조건〉
• 주어진 단어와 동명사를 사용할 것

(1) These days, _______________________________

_______________________________.
  (a puppy, consider, get, be)

(2) _______________________________
  (persuade, keep)

27 다음 중 어법상 틀린 문장 **두 개**를 찾아 그 기호를 쓰고,
문장 전체를 바르게 고쳐 쓰세요.

ⓐ Did you finish cleaning the house?
ⓑ Mom suggested going for a picnic.
ⓒ Watching sports are fun and exciting.
ⓓ Noah always avoids making a decision.
ⓔ I love walk my dog on the weekend.

_______ → _______________________________

____

_______ → _______________________________

____

○ 도표 영작

28 다음 표를 보고 Amelia를 소개하는 글을 〈조건〉에 맞게 완성하세요.

즐기는 것	공원에서 산책하기
피하는 것	학교에 지각하기
연습하는 것	바이올린 연주하기
잘하는 것	춤추기
꺼리는 것	무서운 영화들을 보기

〈조건〉
• 〈보기〉에서 알맞은 말을 골라 주어진 단어와 함께 사용할 것
• 필요시 단어를 추가할 것
• 주어로 대명사를 사용할 것

〈보기〉

dance	watch	play	take
scary	late	a walk	to school

I'm introducing my friend, Amelia. She's from the United States.

(1) _______________________________________
_______________________ at the park. (enjoy)

(2) _______________________________________
_______________________________. (avoid)

(3) _______________________________________
_______________________________. (practice)

(4) _______________________________________
_______________________________. (good)

(5) _______________________________________
_______________________________. (mind)

○ 어법 오류 수정

29 다음 중 어법상 틀린 문장 **두 개**를 찾아 그 기호를 쓰고, 문장 전체를 바르게 고쳐 쓰세요.

ⓐ My brother wanted to have a special vacation last summer. ⓑ He enjoys to help other people. ⓒ So he started doing volunteer work at the hospital. ⓓ He loves making people happy. He told interesting stories to sick people. They felt thankful to him. ⓔ When he finished to volunteer, he was very proud of himself.

______ → _______________________________

______ → _______________________________

🎯 **Challenge!**   누적 문제 Ch 07-09

30 다음 중 어법상 틀린 문장 **두 개**를 찾아 그 기호를 쓰고, 문장 전체를 바르게 고쳐 쓰세요.

ⓐ The bread in the bakery smelled good.
ⓑ He hopes going to England next year.
ⓒ Can you teach French for me after school?
ⓓ To build muscle, he exercises every day.
ⓔ She didn't give up memorizing the lines for a play.

______ → _______________________________

______ → _______________________________

Chapter 10

전치사와 접속사

✅ Before You Write

서술형 시험에는 어떻게 나올까?

- [✓] 여러 전치사와 접속사의 의미를 파악하고 있나요?
- [✓] 전치사와 접속사를 문장에서 필요한 곳에 쓸 수 있나요?
- [✓] 우리말로는 의미가 같아도 쓰임이 다른 전치사/접속사를 구분할 수 있나요?
- [✓] and, but, or는 어떤 형태끼리 연결해야 할까요?
- [✓] 목적어 자리에 「주어+동사 ~」의 형태가 올 때는 어떻게 연결할까요?

내신 기출 다음 우리말을 보고 머릿속으로 한번 영어 문장을 떠올려 보세요.

1 (B) 그것은 테이블 위에 있어.
~ 위에 → 장소 → **on the table**   POINT 1

2 아빠는 (A) 일요일마다 우리를 위해 그것을 요리하신다.
~마다 → 요일 → **on Sundays**   POINT 2

3 나는 아침부터 저녁까지 춤을 춘다.
A부터 B까지 → 시간 → **from morning to evening**   POINT 3

4 나는 스키를 탈 수 있지만, 스노보드는 탈 수 없어.
절과 절 연결 → 서로 반대되는 내용 → **I can ~, but I cannot ...**   POINT 4

5 (1) 나는 비가 올 때, 우산이 필요하다.
절과 절 연결 → 시간(~할 때) → **when it rains**   POINT 5

6 (A) 나는 우주여행에 관심이 있기 때문에 우주선 조종사가 되고 싶어.
(space travel / because / a spaceship pilot)
절과 절 연결 → 이유(~하기 때문에) → **because I am interested in space travel**   POINT 5

7 놀부는 자신도 부자가 될 것이라고 생각한다.
절과 절 연결 → 목적어 자리에 절 → **Nolbu thinks that he will**   POINT 6

정답: **1** It is[It's] on the table. **2** Dad cooks it for us on Sundays. **3** I dance from morning to evening. **4** I can ski, but I cannot[can't] snowboard. **5** I need an umbrella when it rains. **6** I want to be a spaceship pilot because I am[I'm] interested in space travel. **7** Nolbu thinks (that) he will[he'll] become[be] rich, too.

Unit 01 전치사

 장소, 위치, 방향을 나타내는 전치사

내 고양이는 소파 위에서 자고 있다.
내 고양이는 / 자고 있다 / 소파 위에서.
　　주어　　　　동사　　　　부사구

→ My cat / is sleeping / **on** the sofa.
　　　　　　　　　　　　　전치사+명사

> 고양이가 "어디에서" 자고 있는지 더 구체적으로 나타낼 수 있어요

- 전치사는 **명사나 대명사 앞**에 쓰여서 장소나 시간 등과 같은 더 자세한 정보를 전달할 수 있습니다.
- 장소의 크기나 어디에 위치하는지에 따라 다음 중 알맞은 전치사를 사용해야 해요.

📢 **장소, 위치, 방향을 나타내는 주요 전치사**

at(~에)+비교적 좁은 장소나 특정한 지점	**at** the bus stop, **at** the corner, **at** home, **at** school, **at** the airport
on(~ 위에, ~에)+접촉해 있는 장소나 표면	**on** the table, **on** the wall, **on** the floor
in(~에, ~ 안에)+비교적 넓은 장소나 공간의 내부	**in** Korea, **in** the room, **in** a house

in front of(~ 앞에)	**in front of** my house	**behind**(~ 뒤에)	**behind** my house
over(~ (바로) 위에[위로], ~ 너머로)	**over** the hill	**under**(~ (바로) 아래에)	**under** the tree
next to[by, beside](~ 옆[곁]에)	**next to** my house	**between**(~ 사이에)	**between** two trees
around(~ 주위에)	**around** the park	**across**(~을 가로질러)	**across** the street
into(~ 안으로)	**into** the room	**out of**(~ 밖으로)	**out of** the room
above(~보다 위에)	**above** the clouds	**below**(~보다 아래에)	**below** sea level

주의

전치사 뒤에 오는 대명사는 목적격의 형태로 써야 해요.
An old woman was sitting *behind* **me**. (할머니 한 분이 내 뒤에 앉아계셨다.)

대표 기출 문제

🔒 그림을 보고 다음 질문에 답하시오.

A: [Where] are my glasses?
B: ＿＿＿＿＿＿＿＿＿＿＿ .

🔎 **CLUE 1**
안경이 어디에 있는지 '위치'를 묻고 있어요.

🔎 **CLUE 2**
안경은 책상 '바로 아래에' 있으므로
전치사 under를 사용해서 나타낼 수 있어요.

정답: They are[They're] under the desk

Point Exercise

정답 및 해설 p.24

[1-4] 우리말과 일치하도록 주어진 단어를 올바르게 배열하세요.

1
> 과학실은 도서실 옆에 있다.
> (is / the library / next to)

→ The science room ＿＿＿＿＿＿＿＿＿＿＿

＿＿＿＿＿＿＿＿＿＿＿＿＿＿＿＿ .

2
> 새들이 하늘에서 노래하고 있다.
> (the sky / singing / are / in)

→ The birds ＿＿＿＿＿＿＿＿＿＿＿

＿＿＿＿＿＿＿＿＿＿＿＿＿＿＿＿ .

3
> 벽에 많은 사진이 있었다.
> (many / on / were / the wall / pictures)

→ There ＿＿＿＿＿＿＿＿＿＿＿＿

＿＿＿＿＿＿＿＿＿＿＿＿＿＿＿＿ .

4
> 나는 내 지갑을 버스 정류장에서 찾았다.
> (the bus stop / found / my wallet / at)

→ I ＿＿＿＿＿＿＿＿＿＿＿＿＿＿

＿＿＿＿＿＿＿＿＿＿＿＿＿＿＿＿ .

[5-8] 우리말과 일치하도록 주어진 단어와 알맞은 전치사를
사용하여 문장을 완성하세요. (필요시 형태를 바꿀 것)

5
> 지구는 태양 주위를 돈다.
> (the Earth, the Sun, go)

→ ＿＿＿＿＿＿＿＿＿＿＿＿＿＿＿

＿＿＿＿＿＿＿＿＿＿＿＿＿＿＿＿

6
> 나비 한 마리가 그의 방 안으로 날아 들어왔다.
> (his room, a butterfly, fly)

→ ＿＿＿＿＿＿＿＿＿＿＿＿＿＿＿

＿＿＿＿＿＿＿＿＿＿＿＿＿＿＿＿

7
> 내가 정문에서 너를 기다릴게.
> (the main gate, wait for, will)

→ ＿＿＿＿＿＿＿＿＿＿＿＿＿＿＿

＿＿＿＿＿＿＿＿＿＿＿＿＿＿＿＿

8
> 우리 집 뒤에는 커다란 뜰이 있다.
> (a big yard, our house, be)

→ There ＿＿＿＿＿＿＿＿＿＿＿＿

＿＿＿＿＿＿＿＿＿＿＿＿＿＿＿＿ .

9 다음 그림을 보고 〈조건〉에 맞게 문장을 완성하세요.

> 〈조건〉
> • be동사 현재형을 사용할 것
> • 〈보기〉의 단어들을 한 번씩만 쓸 것

> 〈보기〉
> | in | between | on |
> |---|---|---|
> | two chairs | the vase | the table |

(1) A table ＿＿＿＿＿＿＿＿＿＿＿＿ .

(2) A vase ＿＿＿＿＿＿＿＿＿＿＿＿ .

(3) Some flowers ＿＿＿＿＿＿＿＿＿ .

---

wallet 지갑 main gate 정문 yard 뜰, 마당

시간을 나타내는 전치사

기차는 12시 30분에 떠난다.
기차는 / 떠난다 / 12시 30분에.
　주어　　　동사　　　부사구

→ The train / leaves / **at** twelve thirty.

너는 이 케이크를 40분 동안 구워야 한다.
너는 / 구워야 한다 / 이 케이크를 / 40분 동안.
주어　　　동사　　　　목적어　　　부사구

→ You / should bake / this cake / **for** 40 minutes.

가족들은 크리스마스 동안 시간을 같이 보낸다.
가족들은 / 보낸다 / 시간을 / 같이 / 크리스마스 동안.
　주어　　　동사　　목적어　부사　　　부사구

→ Families / spend / time / together / **during** Christmas.

- 어떤 일이 언제 일어나고 얼마나 지속되는지를 나타낼 때, 시간을 나타내는 전치사를 사용할 수 있어요.
- 시간의 범위나 기간, 시점에 따라 알맞은 전치사를 사용해야 합니다. 자주 사용되는 표현은 익히고 연습하는 것이 좋아요.

📢 시간을 나타내는 주요 전치사

at(~에)+시각, 하루 중[주중]의 특정한 때	**at** five, **at** noon, **at** lunchtime
on(~에)+요일, 날짜, 특별한 날	**on** Monday, **on** May 5th, **on** my birthday ***on** Sundays (일요일마다), **on** weekends (주말마다)
in(~에)+하루를 이루는 부분, 월, 연도, 계절, 긴 기간	**in** the morning, **in** May, **in** 2010, **in** winter
before(~ 전에) **after**(~ 후에)	**before** breakfast **after** breakfast
by(~까지)+'일회성'의 동작이나 상태가 완료되는 기한 **until[till]** (~까지 (쭉))+'계속'되던 동작이나 상태가 끝난 시점	Finish your homework **by** tomorrow. It will rain **until** tomorrow.
for(~ 동안)+숫자를 포함한 구체적인 기간 **during**(~ 동안)+특정한 때	**for** an hour, **for** five months, **for** two years **during** the vacation, **during** holidays

대표 기출 문제

🔒 주어진 표현을 사용하여 다음 문장을 완성하시오.

Hyejin은 월요일에 수업이 있다. (Monday)

→ Hyejin ＿＿＿＿＿＿＿＿＿＿＿＿＿＿＿＿ .

🔖 **CLUE 1**
'~에'라는 의미의 시간을 나타내는 전치사가 필요해요.

🔖 **CLUE 2**
요일(Monday) 앞에서 '~에'라는 의미로 쓰이는 전치사는? — on

정답: has classes on Monday

Point Exercise

보기에서 골라 영작

[1-3] 우리말과 일치하도록 〈보기〉에서 알맞은 전치사를 골라 주어진 단어와 함께 빈칸을 완성하세요.

〈보기〉
for   in   on

1 나는 화요일에 테니스를 쳤다. (Tuesday)

→ I played tennis _______________________ .

2 그 콘서트는 2023년에 열렸다. (2023)

→ The concert took place _______________ .

3 우리는 그 도시에서 5년 동안 살았다. (five years)

→ We lived in the city _______________ .

배열 영작

[4-6] 우리말과 일치하도록 주어진 단어를 올바르게 배열하세요.

4 Susan은 저녁 식사 전에 나에게 전화를 했다.
(dinner / before / called / me / Susan)

→ _______________________________
_______________________________ .

5 호주 사람들은 여름에 크리스마스를 즐긴다.
(Christmas / in / the Australians / enjoy / summer)

→ _______________________________
_______________________________ .

6 그녀는 휴가 동안 그녀의 고향을 방문했다.
(hometown / during / her / visited / she / the vacation)

→ _______________________________
_______________________________ .

주어진 단어로 영작

[7-9] 우리말과 일치하도록 주어진 단어와 알맞은 전치사를 사용하여 문장을 완성하세요.

7 우리 가족은 토요일마다 영화를 본다.
(Saturday, a movie, watch)

→ My family _______________________
_______________________________ .

8 민호는 7월에 부산으로 이사했다.
(July, move, to Busan)

→ Minho _______________________ .

9 우리는 추석날 밤에 보름달을 보았다.
(night, see, the full moon)

→ We _______________________
on Chuseok.

기출: 조건 영작

10 우리말과 일치하도록 〈조건〉에 맞게 문장을 완성하세요.

〈조건〉
• 전치사 2개를 추가하고 7 단어로 쓸 것
• get up, seven, always를 사용할 것

Greg은 항상 아침 7시에 일어난다.

→ _______________________
the morning.

take place 열리다, 개최되다 hometown 고향 full moon 보름달

POINT 3 · 여러 가지 전치사

할머니는 나를 아기처럼 대하신다.
나의 할머니는 / 대하신다 / 나를 / 아기처럼.
　　주어　　　　동사　　목적어　　부사구

→ My grandma / treats / me / **like** a baby.

• 장소와 시간 외에도 다음과 같이 다양한 의미를 가지는 전치사들이 있어요.

with	~와 함께	have pizza **with** soda 탄산음료와 함께 피자를 먹다
	~을 가지고, ~을 사용해	write a letter **with** a pen 펜으로 편지를 쓰다
	~을 가진, ~이 있는	a laptop **with** a large screen 큰 화면이 있는 노트북 컴퓨터
without	~ 없이	go out **without** an umbrella 우산 없이 외출하다
by	~로, ~를 타고 (수단)	go to school **by** bus 버스를 타고 학교에 가다
for	~을 위해	get a present **for** her 그녀를 위해 선물을 사다
from	~로부터, ~에서	the train **from** Busan 부산에서 오는 기차
to	~로 (방향)	walk **to** the window 창문 쪽으로 걸어가다
	~에게	send presents **to** children 아이들에게 선물을 보내다
about	~에 관해, ~에 관한	talk **about** our plan 우리의 계획에 관해 이야기하다
like	~처럼, ~같이	run **like** the wind 바람처럼 달리다
as	~로(서) (자격, 기능)	**as** a leader 리더로서

• 다음과 같이 전치사는 형용사와 함께 하나의 표현처럼 잘 쓰여요.

be good at	~을 잘하다	from A to B	A부터 B까지 (시간/장소)
be interested in	~에 관심[흥미]이 있다	thanks to	~ 덕분에
be different from	~와 다르다	be happy[pleased] with	~을 기뻐하다
be famous for	~로 유명하다	be proud of	~을 자랑스러워하다
be ready for	~에 준비가 되다	be full of	~으로 가득 차 있다

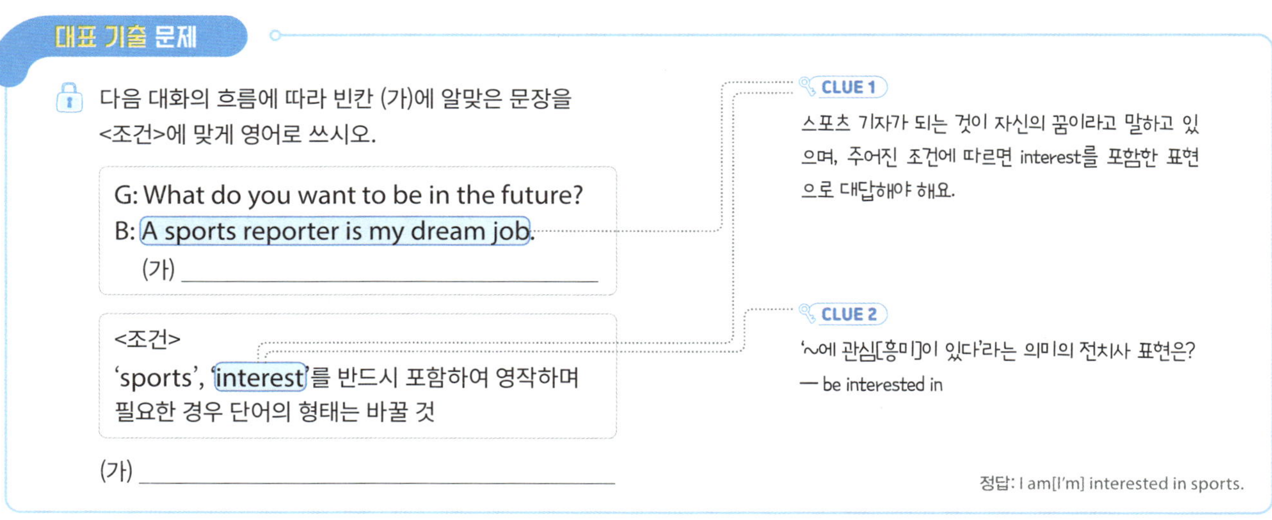

대표 기출 문제

다음 대화의 흐름에 따라 빈칸 (가)에 알맞은 문장을 <조건>에 맞게 영어로 쓰시오.

G: What do you want to be in the future?
B: A sports reporter is my dream job.
(가) ________________________

<조건>
'sports', 'interest'를 반드시 포함하여 영작하며
필요한 경우 단어의 형태는 바꿀 것

(가) ________________________

CLUE 1

스포츠 기자가 되는 것이 자신의 꿈이라고 말하고 있으며, 주어진 조건에 따르면 interest를 포함한 표현으로 대답해야 해요.

CLUE 2

'~에 관심[흥미]이 있다'라는 의미의 전치사 표현은?
— be interested in

정답: I am[I'm] interested in sports.

Point Exercise

빈칸 완성

[1-5] 우리말과 일치하도록 주어진 단어와 알맞은 전치사를 사용하여 빈칸을 완성하세요.

1

그 아기는 천사처럼 잠을 잔다. (an angel)

→ The baby sleeps ________________________.

2

나는 많은 주머니가 있는 가방을 샀다. (many pockets)

→ I bought a bag ________________________.

3

그녀는 잡지의 사진작가로서 일한다. (a photographer)

→ She works ________________________ for a magazine.

4

너는 그곳에 지하철을 타고 쉽게 갈 수 있다. (subway)

→ You can get there ________________________ easily.

5

그는 식당에서 서비스에 대해 불평했다. (the service)

→ He complained ________________________ at the restaurant.

배열 영작

[6-7] 우리말과 일치하도록 주어진 단어를 올바르게 배열하세요.

6

프랑스는 에펠탑으로 유명하다.
(is / France / for / the Eiffel Tower / famous)

→ ________________________.

7

Henry는 그의 시험 결과에 기뻐했다.
(results / was / Henry / his / happy / exam / with)

→ ________________________

________________________.

주어진 단어로 영작

[8-9] 우리말과 일치하도록 주어진 단어와 알맞은 전치사를 사용하여 문장을 완성하세요.

8

그는 어제 아침부터 저녁까지 수학 공부를 했다.
(math, evening, study, morning)

→ ________________________

________________________ yesterday.

9

그녀의 이야기는 진실과 다르다.
(be, the truth, different, story)

→ ________________________

기출: 조건 영작

10 다음 글을 읽고 우리말과 일치하도록 〈조건〉에 맞게 문장을 완성하세요.

Hans lives in Greenland. Dog-sledding is part of his daily life. In winter, his dogs deliver many things to people. Hans 덕분에, 사람들은 물건들을 쉽게 받을 수 있다.

*dog-sledding 개썰매

〈조건〉
• 알맞은 전치사를 사용할 것
• 주어진 단어를 사용하되 필요시 형태를 바꿀 것

→ ________________________, ________________________

________________________ easily.

(things, can, thank, get, people)

angel 천사 pocket 주머니 photographer 사진작가 magazine 잡지 complain 불평하다 result 결과 truth 진실, 사실 deliver 배달하다

접속사

POINT 4 and/but/or

우리는 여행을 계획했지만, 종일 비가 왔다.
우리는 / 여행을 계획했다, // 하지만 비가 왔다 / 종일.

→ We / planned a trip, // **but** it rained / all day.
   절   절

- 단어와 단어, 구와 구, 절과 절을 연결할 때는 **and(~과[와], 그리고), but(그러나, 하지만), or(또는, 아니면)**와 같은 접속사를 사용할 수 있어요.
- 이때 and/but/or는 형용사와 형용사, 동사와 동사, 부정사와 부정사 등 **문법적인 성격이 같은 것끼리 연결**해야 해요. 특히, 동사를 연결할 때는 동사의 수와 시제를 일치시켜야 합니다.

동사 – 동사	We usually *ride* bikes or *play* soccer at the park. 우리는 공원에서 주로 자전거를 타거나 축구를 한다. *Turn off* the lights and *close* the door. 불을 끄고 문을 닫아라. You *can read* books and *(can) watch* movies here. 너는 여기에서 책을 읽을 수 있고 영화를 볼 수 있다. *접속사 뒤에 반복되는 조동사는 보통 생략돼요.
동명사 – 동명사	*Running* and *hiking* are good for health. 달리는 것과 하이킹을 하는 것은 건강에 좋다.
to부정사 – to부정사	I love *to meet* her and *(to) have* fun. 나는 그녀를 만나서 재미있게 노는 것을 아주 좋아한다. *접속사 뒤에 오는 to부정사의 to는 자주 생략돼요.

주의

접속사 and/but/or를 사용할 때, 문맥상 어느 어구와 연결되는지를 잘 파악해서 올바른 형태로 써야 해요.
He **finished** doing his homework and **go**(→ **went**) out to eat. (그는 숙제를 끝내고 식사하러 나갔다.)

대표 기출 문제

밑줄 친 부분 ⓐ를 영어로 쓰시오.
(9 단어 / put, and를 사용하여 과거형 문장을 쓸 것.)

A few days later, Ms. Park ⓐ 벤치를 두 개 사서 그것들을 정원에 두었다.

→ ___________________________ .

CLUE 1

우리말에서 and가 연결하는 어구는?
— '벤치를 두 개 사다(buy two benches)'와
'그것들을 정원에 두다(put them in the garden)'

CLUE 2

and로 연결되는 두 어구의 성격이 같도록 동사의 과거형으로 써야 해요.

정답: bought two benches and put them in the garden

Point Exercise

정답 및 해설 p.24

[1-3] 우리말과 일치하도록 주어진 단어를 올바르게 배열하세요.

1

그는 축구하고 옷을 갈아입었다.
(clothes / and / soccer / changed / played)

→ He ________________________

________________________ .

2

내 친구들은 보드게임을 하고 점심을 먹을 계획이다.
(board games / lunch / play / and / plan / have / to)

→ My friends ________________________

________________________ .

3

너는 학교까지 버스를 타거나 걸어갈 수 있다.
(walk / to the school / you / take / can / the bus / or)

→ ________________________

________________________ .

[4-8] 우리말과 일치하도록 주어진 단어와 알맞은 접속사를 사용하여 문장을 완성하세요. (필요시 형태를 바꿀 것)

4

너는 밖에서 노는 것을 좋아하니, 아니면 TV 보는 것을 좋아하니? (watch, outside, TV)

→ Do you like playing ________________________

________________________ ?

5

그 이야기는 재밌었지만 너무 길었다.
(long, interesting, be, too, the story)

→ ________________________

________________________ .

6

나의 누나는 어제 공원에 가서 자전거를 탔다.
(go, ride, my sister, to the park, a bike)

→ ________________________

________________________ yesterday.

7

토요일마다 그는 집을 청소하고 빨래를 한다.
(do, the house, laundry, clean)

→ On Saturdays, ________________________

________________________ .

8

그와 나는 이번 여름에 일본 또는 홍콩을 방문할 것이다.
(Japan, Hong Kong, visit, will)

→ ________________________

________________________ this summer.

9 다음 그림을 보고 〈조건〉에 맞게 문장을 완성하세요.

〈조건〉
- 6 단어로 쓸 것
- 접속사 and, but, or 중 하나를 사용할 것
- have, an umbrella, I를 사용할 것

→ It rained heavily after school, ________________

________________________ .

outside 밖에서; 밖   laundry 세탁; 세탁물

POINT 5 　시간, 이유, 조건 등을 나타내는 접속사

나는 영화를 볼 때, 팝콘을 먹는다.
나는 볼 때 / 영화를, // 나는 먹는다 / 팝콘을.
　　　부사절 (시간)

접속사가 이끄는 절을 문장 앞에 쓸 때, 부사절 뒤에 콤마(,)를 붙여요.

→ **When** I watch / movies, // I eat / popcorn.
　 접속사　주어　동사

나는 아침에 늦게 일어났기 때문에 아침 식사를 걸렀다.
나는 걸렀다 / 아침 식사를 // 나는 일어났기 때문에 / 늦게.
　　　　　　　　　　　　　　부사절 (이유)

→ I skipped / breakfast // **because** I got up / late.
　　　　　　　　　　　 접속사　주어　동사

- '∼할 때, ∼하기 때문에' 등 시간이나 이유 등을 나타내는 접속사는 문장 앞이나 뒤에 쓰여, **주어와 동사를 포함한 절을 연결**합니다. 이러한 절은 문장에서 부사와 같은 역할을 하므로 **부사절**이라 불러요.

시간	when(∼할 때), before(∼하기 전에), after(∼한 후에), until[till](∼할 때까지)
이유·원인	because(∼하기 때문에)
결과	so(그래서, ∼해서)
조건	if(만약 ∼하다면)

주의 because vs. because of

because는 접속사이므로, 뒤에 「주어+동사」 형태의 절을 써요. 반면, because of는 전치사이므로 뒤에 명사(구)나 대명사를 씁니다.
I like her **because** she is kind. (나는 그녀가 친절하기 때문에 그녀가 좋다.)
I like her **because of** her kindness. (나는 그녀의 친절함 때문에 그녀가 좋다.)

MORE＋ 시간이나 조건을 나타내는 접속사가 이끄는 절이 미래를 나타내더라도 현재시제를 사용해요.
She will wait **until** he ~~will arrive~~ (→ **arrives**). (그녀는 그가 도착할 때까지 기다릴 것이다.)
We will leave **if** you ~~will be~~ (→ **are**) ready. (우리는 네가 준비되면 출발할 거야.)

대표 기출 문제

우리말과 같은 뜻이 되도록 괄호 안의 단어를 사용하여 영어 문장을 만드시오. 더 필요한 단어는 추가하시오.

이 그림을 볼 때 어떤 기분이 드나요?

→ ________________________ ,
how do you feel? (look)

CLUE 1
'∼할 때'라는 의미의 시간을 나타내는 접속사는 when이에요. 접속사이므로 「When+주어(you)+동사」의 어순으로 써야 해요.

CLUE 2
현재형 동사 do가 쓰였고, when이 이끄는 절의 동사가 '볼 때'이므로 현재시제 look으로 나타내요.
'∼을 보다'라고 쓸 때는 look at으로 씁니다.

정답: When you look at this painting

Point Exercise

정답 및 해설 p.25

[1-5] 우리말과 일치하도록 주어진 단어를 올바르게 배열하세요.

1

> 자기 전에 이 약을 먹어라.
> (go to bed / before / you)

→ Take this medicine _________________

_________________________________ .

2

> 내일 날씨가 화창하면 우리는 바다에 갈 것이다.
> (it / if / sunny / is / tomorrow)

→ _________________________________

_________________________ , we'll go to the sea.

3

> 그 가게가 문을 닫아서 나는 다른 가게에 갔다.
> (went / store / so / I / to / another)

→ The shop was closed, _________________

_________________________________ .

4

> 내가 박물관에 갔을 때 사람이 거의 없었다.
> (I / to / when / went / the museum)

→ There were few people _________________

_________________________________ .

5

> 나의 아빠는 신문을 읽으신 후에 아침을 드셨다.
> (my dad / a newspaper / after / read)

→ _________________________________

_________________________ , he had breakfast.

[6-8] 우리말과 일치하도록 주어진 단어와 when, if, because 중 하나를 사용하여 문장을 완성하세요. (필요시 형태를 바꿀 것)

6

> 만약 네가 답을 알고 있다면 손을 들어라.
> (the answer, know)

→ _________________________________ ,

raise your hand.

7

> 그는 이탈리아에 갈 때 그의 삼촌을 방문할 것이다.
> (go, Italy, to)

→ He will visit his uncle _________________

_________________________________ .

8

> Julia는 그녀의 휴대 전화를 잃어버렸기 때문에 그에게 전화할 수 없었다. (lose, cell phone)

→ _________________________________

_________________________ , she couldn't call him.

9 다음 그림을 보고 〈보기〉에서 알맞은 말을 골라 〈조건〉에 맞게 문장을 완성하세요.

> 〈조건〉
> • 과거시제로 쓸 것
> • happy, my team, win the game을 사용할 것

> 〈보기〉
> because of   before   because   if

→ I _________________________________ .

---

medicine 약 raise 들어 올리다; 올리다

나는 그가 현명하다고 생각한다.

나는 생각한다 // 그가 현명**하다고**.
주어   동사   목적어(명사절)

→ I think // **(that)** he is wise.
      접속사   주어   동사

- 문장에서 동사의 목적어 자리에 「주어+동사 ~」 형태의 절이 올 때는 **접속사 that**을 써서 연결할 수 있으며, '~이라는[~하다는] 것을'이라는 의미를 나타내요.
- 이때 접속사 that이 이끄는 절이 명사와 같은 역할을 하므로 **명사절**이라고 불러요.
- 접속사 that이 이끄는 절이 문장에서 목적어로 쓰였을 때 that은 생략할 수 있어요.

📢 **that절을 목적어로 취하는 동사**

I **think** that ~	나는 ~하다고 생각하다
I **believe** that ~	나는 ~하다고 믿다
I **hope** that ~	나는 ~하길 바라다
I **know** that ~	나는 ~하다는 것을 알고 있다
I **say** that ~	나는 ~하다고 말하다
I **learn** that ~	나는 ~하다는 것을 배우다[알게 되다]
I **remember** that ~	나는 ~하다는 것을 기억하다
I **guess** that ~	나는 ~하다고 추측하다
It **means** that ~	그것은 ~하다는 것을 의미하다

MORE + 주절에 쓰인 동사의 시제와 that절의 시제가 항상 같은 것은 아니에요.
We **thought** that it **was** a great idea. (우리는 그것이 아주 좋은 아이디어라고 생각했다.)
I **think** that I **ate** too much yesterday. (나는 어제 내가 너무 많이 먹었다고 생각한다.)
We **learned** that the park **has** a new playground. (우리는 그 공원에 새로운 놀이터가 있다는 것을 알게 되었다.)

대표 기출 문제

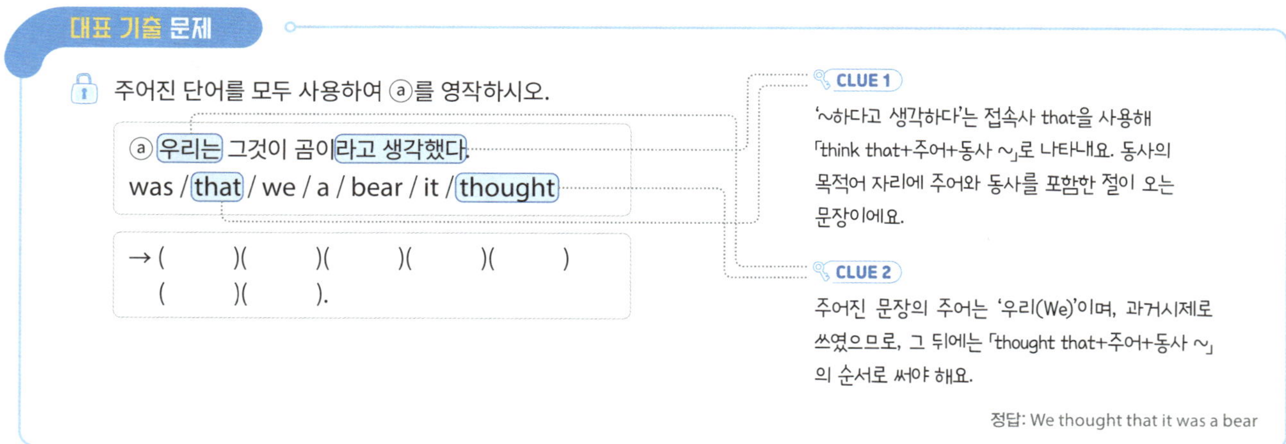

🔒 주어진 단어를 모두 사용하여 ⓐ를 영작하시오.

ⓐ 우리는 그것이 곰이라고 생각했다.
was / that / we / a / bear / it / thought

→ ( )( )( )( )( )
  ( )( ).

CLUE 1
'~하다고 생각하다'는 접속사 that을 사용해 「think that+주어+동사 ~」로 나타내요. 동사의 목적어 자리에 주어와 동사를 포함한 절이 오는 문장이에요.

CLUE 2
주어진 문장의 주어는 '우리(We)'이며, 과거시제로 쓰였으므로, 그 뒤에는 「thought that+주어+동사 ~」의 순서로 써야 해요.

정답: We thought that it was a bear

Point Exercise

정답 및 해설 p.25

[1-5] 우리말과 일치하도록 주어진 단어를 올바르게 배열하세요.

1

> 우리는 그것이 정답이라고 생각했다.
> (it / that / the answer / was / thought)

→ We ________________________________

________________________________ .

2

> 나는 Victor가 나를 도와줄 것이라고 믿는다.
> (that / me / Victor / will / believe / help)

→ I ________________________________

________________________________ .

3

> 우리 부모님은 내가 좋은 학생이 되길 바라신다.
> (a good student / that / become / hope / I)

→ My parents ____________________________

________________________________ .

4

> 그녀는 Tim이 매우 정직하다는 것을 알고 있다.
> (honest / is / that / knows / very / Tim)

→ She ________________________________

________________________________ .

5

> 나의 선생님은 우리가 내일 교실을 청소해야 한다고
> 말씀하셨다.
> (must / the classroom / said / we / clean)

→ My teacher ____________________________

________________________________ tomorrow.

[6-8] 우리말과 일치하도록 주어진 단어를 사용하여 문장을 완성하세요. (필요시 형태를 바꿀 것)

6

> 나는 그가 오래전에 가수였던 것을 기억한다.
> (remember, a singer, was)

→ ________________________________

________________________________ a long time ago.

7

> Emily는 그 뮤지컬이 재밌었다고 말했다.
> (said, interesting, the musical, was)

→ ________________________________

________________________________ .

8

> 사람들은 우리 마을에서 그 식당이 최고라고 생각한다.
> (the restaurant, the best, people, is, think)

→ ________________________________

________________________________ in our town.

9 다음 글을 읽고 우리말과 일치하도록 〈조건〉에 맞게 영작하세요.

> Adam is always nice to everyone in school.
> He is polite and listens carefully to others.
> Adam will run for school president next
> month. 나는 그가 학생회장이 될 거라고 믿는다.

> 〈조건〉
> • 생각이나 믿음을 나타내는 동사와 주어진 단어를
>   사용할 것
> • 9 단어로 쓸 것

→ ________________________________

____

(be, will, that, the school president)

polite 예의 바른 run (선거에) 출마하다 school president 학생회장

Chapter Test *

정답 및 해설 p.25

STAGE 1) Go for it!

자신 있게 풀어보는 기초 문제!

○ 배열 영작

[1-4] 우리말과 일치하도록 주어진 단어를 배열하여 문장을 완성하세요.

1
> 내일 비가 온다면 우리는 경기를 취소할 것이다.
> (it / if / tomorrow / rains)

→ ________________________________,

we will cancel the game.

2
> 나는 Mike가 여동생이 있다는 것을 기억한다.
> (a younger sister / that / has / Mike / remember)

→ I ________________________________

________________________________.

3
> 아빠가 호텔에 도착하실 때 너에게 전화하실 거야.
> (the hotel / arrives / he / when / at)

→ Dad will call you ________________

________________________________.

4
> Kate는 졸렸지만, 숙제를 마쳤다.
> (finished / she / her homework / but)

→ Kate was sleepy, ________________

________________________________.

○ 빈칸 완성

[5-7] 우리말과 일치하도록 주어진 단어를 사용하여 빈칸에 알맞은 말을 쓰세요. (필요시 단어를 추가할 것)

5
> 그녀는 책상 위에 장갑을 올려 두었다. (the desk)

→ She put her gloves ________________

________________ ________________.

6
> 내일은 춥거나 눈이 올 것이다. (cold, snowy)

→ Tomorrow will be ________________

________________ ________________.

7
> 그 마을은 7월과 8월에 여름 축제를 연다.
> (July, August)

→ The town holds summer festivals

________________ ________________

________________ ________________.

최신 기출

8 다음 대화를 읽고, 주어진 단어를 배열하여 빈칸에 들어갈 문장을 완성하세요.

> A: Can you solve this math problem for me?
> B: Sorry, I can't. Why don't you ask Mike?
> A: Is he good at math?
> B: Yes, he is.
> ________________________________.

→ ________________________________

________________________________.

(think / he / solve / can / I / it / that)

보기에서 골라 영작

[9-16] 다음 빈칸에 들어갈 말을 〈보기〉에서 골라 쓰세요.
(단, 한 번씩만 사용할 것)

〈보기〉
| for | by | in |
| during | until | |

9 We waited in line ＿＿＿＿＿ two hours.

10 The movie came out ＿＿＿＿＿ 2024.

11 Fred fell asleep ＿＿＿＿＿ the classical music concert.

12 You should return the books to the library ＿＿＿＿＿ next Friday.

13 My dad won't come home ＿＿＿＿＿ tomorrow. He's on a business trip now.

〈보기〉
| because | so | when |

14 ＿＿＿＿＿ it rains, I usually stay at home.

15 I don't like that restaurant ＿＿＿＿＿ it's too noisy.

16 We missed the bus, ＿＿＿＿＿ we had to walk to school.

그림 영작

17 다음 그림을 보고 〈보기〉에서 알맞은 전치사를 골라 주어진 단어와 함께 문장을 완성하세요.

〈보기〉
| under | on | behind | beside |

(1) A girl ＿＿＿＿＿＿＿＿＿＿＿
＿＿＿＿＿＿＿＿＿. (lying, the bed, is)

(2) A table ＿＿＿＿＿＿＿＿＿＿＿
＿＿＿＿＿＿＿＿＿. (the bed, is)

(3) A dog ＿＿＿＿＿＿＿＿＿＿＿
＿＿＿＿＿＿＿＿. (sitting, the table, is)

(4) A box ＿＿＿＿＿＿＿＿＿＿＿
＿＿＿＿＿＿＿＿＿. (is, the dog)

최신 기출

18 다음 글을 읽고 우리말과 일치하도록 〈조건〉에 맞게 영작하세요.

There is a library near my house. (1) 그 도서관은 오전 8시부터 오후 5시까지 문을 연다. (2) 그곳은 최신 책들로 유명하다, so I love going there.

〈조건〉
• 각각 알맞은 전치사를 사용할 것
• 주어진 단어를 사용하되 필요시 형태를 바꿀 것

(1) ＿＿＿＿＿＿＿＿＿＿＿＿＿＿＿
(open, 5 p.m., the library, 8 a.m.)

(2) It ＿＿＿＿＿＿＿＿＿＿＿＿＿
＿＿＿＿＿＿＿＿＿, so I love going there.
(newest books, famous, its)

[19-23] 우리말과 일치하도록 〈보기 A〉와 〈보기 B〉에서 각각 알맞은 말을 골라 문장을 완성하세요. (단, 〈보기 A〉는 중복해서 사용 가능)

〈보기 A〉
when   because   after

〈보기 B〉
wait for the bus   get home
miss the subway   have a cold
sleep well

19 나는 감기에 걸릴 때 물을 많이 마신다.

→ I drink a lot of water ________________

________________________________ .

20 나는 어젯밤에 잠을 잘 자지 못해서 매우 피곤하다.

→ I feel so tired ________________________

________________________________ last night.

21 그녀는 버스를 기다릴 때 음악을 듣는다.

→ ________________________________

________________________ , she listens to music.

22 Andrew는 집에 도착한 후에 항상 책을 읽는다.

→ Andrew always reads a book ____________

________________________________ .

23 나는 지하철을 놓쳤기 때문에, 제시간에 도착할 수 없었다.

→ ________________________________

________________________ , I couldn't arrive on time.

[24-28] 다음 각 문장에서 어법상 <u>틀린</u> 부분을 찾아 바르게 고쳐 쓰세요.

24 There will be a baseball match at Friday.

________________ → ________________

25 I'm tired now because of I stayed up late last night.

________________ → ________________

26 It rained heavily during an hour.

________________ → ________________

27 She hung the calendar in the wall.

________________ → ________________

28 I met my friend and go to a movie a week ago.

________________ → ________________

29 〈보기〉에서 알맞은 접속사를 골라 주어진 두 문장을 한 문장으로 완성하세요.

〈보기〉
because   until   before

(1) · I always wash my hands.
   · I eat dinner.

→ I ________________________________

________________________________ .

(2) · We waited.
   · The rain stopped.

→ We ________________________________

________________________________ .

○━ 보기에서 골라 영작

30 다음 컵케이크 만드는 방법을 보고 빈칸에 들어갈 알맞은 접속사를 〈보기〉에서 골라 글을 완성하세요. (단, 한 번씩만 쓸 것)

How to Make Cupcakes

1. Put the butter and sugar in a bowl and beat them.
2. Add flour, eggs, baking powder, and salt, and stir well.
3. Put the mix into the baking cups.
4. Bake the cupcakes in the oven for ten minutes.
5. Wait for another ten minutes until the cupcakes get cool. Now enjoy your cupcakes!

〈보기〉

before   because   if   after

---

(1) ________________ you like sweets, how about making cupcakes?

First, you put the butter and sugar in a bowl and beat them! And then stir well (2) ________________ you add flour, eggs, baking powder, and salt in the bowl.

When you bake the mix, you need some baking cups. (3) ________________ you enjoy your cupcakes, you have to wait for ten minutes (4) ________________ they will be too hot.

○━ 조건 영작

31 다음 글을 읽고 〈조건〉에 맞게 문장을 완성하세요.

My best friend, Suho, wants to be a soccer player. When he was ten years old, he watched a soccer game at the stadium. Since then, he started to dream of becoming a soccer player. After school, he always practices hard. So, I ________________________________ in the future.

〈조건〉
- 8 단어로 쓸 것
- will, believe, the best player, be를 사용할 것

→ So, I ________________________________

________________________________ in the future.

🎯 **Challenge!**

누적 문제 Ch 08-10

32 다음 중 어법상 틀린 문장 **두 개**를 찾아 그 기호를 쓰고, 문장 전체를 바르게 고쳐 쓰세요.

ⓐ I exercise regularly to lose weight.
ⓑ My mom and I are good at sing songs.
ⓒ I think you should be proud of yourself.
ⓓ He travels a lot and meet many people.
ⓔ She screamed when she saw the snake.

________ → ________________________________

____

________ → ________________________________

____

동사 변화형

✳ A-B-B형

동사원형	과거형	과거분사형 (p.p.)	현재분사형 (-ing)
bleed (피를 흘리다)	bled	bled	bleeding
bring (가져오다)	brought	brought	bringing
build (짓다)	built	built	building
buy (사다)	bought	bought	buying
catch (잡다)	caught	caught	catching
feed (먹이를 주다)	fed	fed	feeding
feel (느끼다)	felt	felt	feeling
fight (싸우다)	fought	fought	fighting
find (찾다)	found	found	finding
flee (도망치다)	fled	fled	fleeing
get (얻다)	got	got/gotten	getting
have (가지다)	had	had	having
hang (걸다)	hung	hung	hanging
hear (듣다)	heard	heard	hearing
hold (잡다)	held	held	holding
keep (유지하다)	kept	kept	keeping
kneel (무릎을 꿇다)	knelt	knelt	kneeling
lay (눕히다, 놓다)	laid	laid	laying
lead (인도하다)	led	led	leading
learn (배우다)	learned/ learnt	learned/ learnt	learning
leave (떠나다)	left	left	leaving
lose (잃다)	lost	lost	losing
lend (빌려주다)	lent	lent	lending
make (만들다)	made	made	making
mean (의미하다)	meant	meant	meaning
meet (만나다)	met	met	meeting
pay (지불하다)	paid	paid	paying
say (말하다)	said	said	saying

동사원형	과거형	과거분사형 (p.p.)	현재분사형 (-ing)
seek (찾다)	sought	sought	seeking
sell (팔다)	sold	sold	selling
send (보내다)	sent	sent	sending
sleep (잠자다)	slept	slept	sleeping
smell (냄새 맡다)	smelled/ smelt	smelled/ smelt	smelling
shine (빛나다)	shone	shone	shining
shoot (쏘다)	shot	shot	shooting
sit (앉다)	sat	sat	sitting
spend (소비하다)	spent	spent	spending
spill (엎지르다)	spilled/ spilt	spilled/ spilt	spilling
stand (서다, 서 있다)	stood	stood	standing
sweep (청소하다)	swept	swept	sweeping
teach (가르치다)	taught	taught	teaching
tell (말하다)	told	told	telling
think (생각하다)	thought	thought	thinking
win (이기다)	won	won	winning

✳ A-B-A형

동사원형	과거형	과거분사형 (p.p.)	현재분사형 (-ing)
become (되다)	became	become	becoming
come (오다)	came	come	coming
run (달리다)	ran	run	running

✳ A-B-C형

동사원형	과거형	과거분사형 (p.p.)	현재분사형 (-ing)
bite (물다)	bit	bitten	biting
blow (불다)	blew	blown	blowing

break (깨뜨리다)	broke	broken	breaking
choose (고르다)	chose	chosen	choosing
do (하다)	did	done	doing
draw (그리다)	drew	drawn	drawing
drink (마시다)	drank	drunk	drinking
drive (운전하다)	drove	driven	driving
eat (먹다)	ate	eaten	eating
fall (떨어지다)	fell	fallen	falling
fly (날다)	flew	flown	flying
forget (잊다)	forgot	forgotten	forgetting
forgive (용서하다)	forgave	forgiven	forgiving
freeze (얼다)	froze	frozen	freezing
give (주다)	gave	given	giving
go (가다)	went	gone	going
grow (자라다)	grew	grown	growing
hide (숨다)	hid	hidden	hiding
know (알다)	knew	known	knowing
lie (눕다)	lay	lain	lying
ride (타다)	rode	ridden	riding
ring (울리다)	rang	rung	ringing
rise (오르다)	rose	risen	rising
see (보다)	saw	seen	seeing
shake (흔들다)	shook	shaken	shaking
show (보여주다)	showed	shown/ showed	showing
sing (노래하다)	sang	sung	singing
speak (말하다)	spoke	spoken	speaking
steal (훔치다)	stole	stolen	stealing
swell (부풀다)	swelled	swollen/ swelled	swelling
swim (수영하다)	swam	swum	swimming

take (잡다)	took	taken	taking
throw (던지다)	threw	thrown	throwing
wake (잠이 깨다)	woke	woken	waking
wear (입다)	wore	worn	wearing
write (쓰다)	wrote	written	writing

✳ A-A-A형

동사원형	과거형	과거분사형 (p.p.)	현재분사형 (-ing)
cast (던지다)	cast	cast	casting
cost (비용이 들다)	cost	cost	costing
cut (베다)	cut	cut	cutting
hit (치다, 때리다)	hit	hit	hitting
hurt (다치다)	hurt	hurt	hurting
let (~하게 하다)	let	let	letting
put (놓다)	put	put	putting
set (놓다)	set	set	setting
shut (닫다)	shut	shut	shutting
spread (퍼지다)	spread	spread	spreading
read[riːd] (읽다)	read [red]	read [red]	reading
upset (화나게 하다)	upset	upset	upsetting

✳ A-A-B형

동사원형	과거형	과거분사형 (p.p.)	현재분사형 (-ing)
beat (치다, 때리다)	beat	beaten	beating

논술형 *
수행평가

평가 개요	
주제	나의 장래 희망 소개하기
세부 내용	① 장래 희망 ② 장래 계획 (2가지 이상) ③ 꿈을 이루기 위해 노력하고 있는 일 (3가지 이상)
언어 형식	① 현재진행형 ② 미래 표현 will

Step 1 | 예시 글 분석하기

➕ 형광펜 친 부분에 유의하여 예시 글을 읽은 후, 각 질문에 답해보세요.

My Future Dream

장래 희망	→	I want to be a scientist in the future.
장래 계획	→	I will study medicine and develop new medicines.
현재의 활동	→	For my dream, I am doing many things.
노력하는 일 ①	→	First, I am studying hard in my science classes.
노력하는 일 ②	→	Second, I am participating in the science club.
노력하는 일 ③	→	And, I am reading many science books.

1   **What does the writer want to be in the future?**

→ He[She] wants to be a ________________________ in the future.

2   **What will the writer plan to do?**

→ He[She] will ________________________ and ________________________ .

3   **What is the writer doing for his[her] dream?**

→ First, he[she] is ________________________ .

→ Second, he[she] is ________________________ .

→ And, he[she] is ________________________ .

1 scientist 2 study medicine, develop new medicines 3 studying hard in his[her] science classes, participating in the science club, reading many science books

Step 2 | 글의 뼈대 만들기

✚ 나의 장래 희망을 떠올리며, 다음 표의 빈칸을 완성해 보세요.

My Future Dream

장래 희망	I want to be a(n) ________________________________ in the future.
장래 계획	I will ________________________ and ________________________ .
현재의 활동	For my dream, I am doing many things.
노력하는 일 ①	First, I am ________________________________ .
노력하는 일 ②	Second, I am ________________________________ .
노력하는 일 ③	And, I am ________________________________ .

Useful Words & Expressions

장래 희망	계획	노력하는 일
scientist 과학자	study 연구하다 develop 개발하다	participate in the science club 과학 동아리에 참여하다 read many science books 과학책을 많이 읽다
zookeeper 사육사	take care of ~을 돌보다 train 훈련시키다	read books about ~에 관한 책들을 읽다 volunteer at ~에서 봉사활동하다
game developer 게임 개발자	create 만들다 share 공유하다	learn game design 게임 디자인을 배우다 practice programming skills 프로그래밍 기술을 연습하다
soccer player 축구 선수	win first place 우승하다 become famous 유명해지다	exercise daily 매일 운동하다 join a soccer team 축구팀에 가입하다
firefighter 소방관	put out a fire 불을 끄다 save lives 생명을 구하다	study fire safety rules 화재 안전 규칙을 공부하다 practice teamwork 팀워크를 연습하다
chef 요리사(특히 주방장)	open my own restaurant 내 소유의 식당을 열다	take cooking classes 요리 수업을 듣다 try new recipes 새로운 조리법을 시도해보다

✚ 앞에서 작성한 내용을 바탕으로 다음 〈조건〉에 맞게 글을 완성해 보세요.

〈조건〉
① 5문장 이상 작성할 것
② 다음 언어 형식을 사용해 작성할 것
  • 현재진행형
  • 미래 표현 will

My Future Dream

I want to be a(n) ____.

I will ____

and ____.

For my dream, I am doing many things.

First, ____.

Second, ____.

And, ____.

논술형 수행평가 2회

Chapter 01~03

○ 예시 답안 p.206

평가 개요	
주제	나의 스트레스 해소 방법 소개하기
세부 내용	① 스트레스 해소 방법 (3가지 이상) ② 각 방법의 효과 (3가지 이상)
언어 형식	① 일반동사의 현재형 ② 미래 표현 will ③ 조동사 can

Step 1 | 예시 글 분석하기

➕ 형광펜 친 부분에 유의하여 예시 글을 읽은 후, 표의 빈칸을 완성해 보세요.

Tips for Reducing Stress

도입부	→	Here are my tips for reducing stress.
방법 ①	→	First, I listen to my favorite music.
효과	→	I can calm down with its nice sounds.
방법 ②	→	Second, I play with my puppy.
효과	→	I can forget my worries for a while.
방법 ③	→	Finally, I go for a walk outside.
효과	→	I can feel the cool breeze and see beautiful flowers.
맺음말	→	Follow my tips, and you will feel better.

방법 ①	1	I __________________.
효과	2	I can __________________.
방법 ②	3	I __________________.
효과	4	I can __________________.
방법 ③	5	I __________________.
효과	6	I can __________________.

1 listen to my favorite music **2** calm down with its nice sounds **3** play with my puppy **4** forget my worries for a while **5** go for a walk outside **6** feel the cool breeze and see beautiful flowers

✚ 나의 스트레스 해소 방법을 떠올리며, 다음 표의 빈칸을 완성해 보세요.

Tips for Reducing Stress

도입부	Here are my tips for reducing stress.
방법 ①	First, I _______________________________________.
효과	I can _______________________________________.
방법 ②	Second, I _______________________________________.
효과	I can _______________________________________.
방법 ③	Finally, I _______________________________________.
효과	I can _______________________________________.
맺음말	Follow my tips, and you will feel better.

Useful Words & Expressions

방법	listen to music 음악을 듣다 read books 책을 읽다 draw pictures 그림을 그리다 eat delicious food 맛있는 음식을 먹다 play computer games 컴퓨터 게임을 하다	go for a walk 산책하러 가다 sing a song 노래를 부르다 spend time with ~와 시간을 보내다 watch fun movies 재미있는 영화를 보다 take a short nap 잠깐 낮잠을 자다
효과	calm down 진정하다 laugh a lot 많이 웃다 get advice 조언을 얻다 express emotion 감정을 표현하다 gain positive energy 긍정적인 에너지를 얻다	forget my worries 내 걱정을 잊다 share feelings 감정을 공유하다 clear my head 머리를 비우다 talk about my worries 내 걱정에 관해 이야기하다 relax my mind and body 내 마음과 몸을 편안하게 하다

✚ 앞에서 작성한 내용을 바탕으로 다음 〈조건〉에 맞게 글을 완성해 보세요.

〈조건〉
① 6문장 이상 작성할 것
② 다음 언어 형식을 사용해 작성할 것
   • 일반동사의 현재형
   • 미래 표현 will
   • 조동사 can

Tips for Reducing Stress

Here are my tips for reducing stress.

First, ____.

____.

Second, ____.

____.

Finally, ____.

____.

Follow my tips, and you will feel better.

평가 개요	
주제	지난 여름방학 때 있었던 일 일기 쓰기
세부 내용	① 다녀온 곳 ② 한 일 (3가지 이상) ③ 먹은 것과 맛 표현 ④ 느낀 점
언어 형식	① be동사의 과거형 ② 일반동사의 과거형

Step 1 | 예시 글 분석하기

➕ 형광펜 친 부분에 유의하여 예시 글을 읽은 후, 표의 빈칸을 완성해 보세요.

Diary of My Last Summer Vacation

날짜	➜	Date: July 21st
다녀온 곳	➜	I went to the swimming pool with my family.
한 일 ①	➜	We played water volleyball.
한 일 ②	➜	I rode a water slide.
한 일 ③	➜	I also made a new friend.
먹은 것, 맛	➜	I ate chocolate ice cream, and it was very sweet.
느낀 점	➜	Overall, it was a wonderful experience.
맺음말	➜	I want to go to the swimming pool again.

다녀온 곳	**1**	I went to ________________ with my family.
한 일 ①	**2**	We ________________.
한 일 ②	**3**	I ________________.
한 일 ③	**4**	I also ________________.
먹은 것, 맛	**5**	I ate ________________, and it was ________________.
느낀 점	**6**	Overall, it was a ________________ experience.

1 the swimming pool　**2** played water volleyball　**3** rode a water slide　**4** made a new friend　**5** chocolate ice cream, very sweet　**6** wonderful

Step 2 | 글의 뼈대 만들기

➕ 지난 여름방학 때 있었던 일을 떠올리며, 다음 표의 빈칸을 완성해 보세요.

Diary of My Last Summer Vacation

다녀온 곳	I went to ______________________________________.
한 일 ①	I/We ______________________________________.
한 일 ②	I/We ______________________________________.
한 일 ③	I/We also ______________________________________.
먹은 것, 맛	I/We ate ____________________________, and it was/they were ____________________________.
느낀 점	Overall, it was a(n) ____________________ experience.
맺음말	I want to go to ____________________ again.

Useful Words & Expressions

장소	beach 해변 museum 박물관 my friend's house 내 친구 집		library 도서관 aquarium 수족관 amusement park 놀이동산
활동	watch a movie 영화를 보다 feed fish 물고기에게 먹이를 주다 take pictures 사진을 찍다 play board games 보드게임을 하다		sing along 노래를 따라 부르다 read books 책을 읽다 ride a bike 자전거를 타다 go on the rides 놀이기구를 타다
음식	pizza 피자 spaghetti 스파게티	hamburger 햄버거 ice cream 아이스크림	fried chicken 프라이드치킨 tteokbokki 떡볶이
맛	sweet 달콤한 spicy 매운	sour 신 salty 짭짤한	tasty/yummy/delicious 맛있는 bitter 맛이 쓴
느낌	fun 재미있는 memorable 기억에 남는	great 멋진 amazing 놀라운	exciting 신나는 interesting 즐거운

✚ 앞에서 작성한 내용을 바탕으로 다음 〈조건〉에 맞게 글을 완성해 보세요.

〈조건〉
① 7문장 이상 작성할 것
② 다음 언어 형식을 사용해 작성할 것
  · be동사의 과거형
  · 일반동사의 과거형

Diary of My Last Summer Vacation

Date: ________________

I went to ____.

____.

____.

____.

____.

Overall, it was a(n) ____________________________ experience.

I want to go to ________________________________ again.

평가 개요	
주제	내년에 입학할 신입생에게 우리 학교 소개하기
세부 내용	① 학교의 특징 (3가지 이상) ② 제안하고 싶은 것
언어 형식	① There is/are ② many/much/(a) few/(a) little ③ 형용사 ④ Why don't you ~?

Step 1 | 예시 글 분석하기

✚ 형광펜 친 부분에 유의하여 예시 글을 읽은 후, 각 질문에 답해보세요.

Our School

환영 인사	➡	Welcome to our school!
도입부	➡	Here are some of the good things about our school.
특징 ①	➡	First, there are many books in the school library.
특징 ②	➡	Second, there is a beautiful garden. Many students relax in the garden during breaks.
특징 ③	➡	Third, we have a few school events. They are really fun.
제안하고 싶은 것	➡	Why don't you participate in the events later?
맺음말	➡	Have a great time at our school!

1 **What are the good things about the writer's school? Write down 3 sentences.**

→ There are ______________________ in his[her] school library.

→ There is ______________________ at his[her] school.

→ There are ______________________ at his[her] school.

2 **What do the students at the writer's school do in the garden?**

→ Many students ______________ there ______________.

3 **How are the writer's school events?**

→ They are ______________.

4 **What is the writer's suggestion?**

→ The writer said, "Why don't you ______________ later?"

---

1 many books, a beautiful garden, a few school events **2** relax, during breaks **3** really fun **4** participate in the events

✚ 우리 학교의 여러 특징을 떠올리며, 다음 표의 빈칸을 완성해 보세요.

Our School

환영 인사	Welcome to our school!
도입부	Here are some of the good things about our school.
특징 ①	First, there is/are _______________ .
특징 ②	Second, there is/are _______________ .
특징 ③	Third, we have _______________ .
제안하고 싶은 것	Why don't you _______________ later?
맺음말	Have a great time at our school!

Useful Words & Expressions

학교 시설	school hall 학교 강당 nurse's office 양호실 cafeteria 급식실	music room 음악실 school gym 학교 체육관 art room 미술실	science lab 과학 실험실 teacher's room 교무실 computer room 컴퓨터실
특징	good 좋은 friendly 친절한 clean 깨끗한 bright 밝은 modern 현대적인	great 훌륭한 comfortable 편안한 safe 안전한 interesting 흥미로운 colorful (색이) 다채로운	nice 멋진, 좋은 helpful 도움이 되는 fun 재미있는 big 큰 delicious 맛있는
제안하고 싶은 것	participate in school events 학교 행사에 참여하다 join the club 동아리에 가입하다	make new friends 새로운 친구들을 사귀다 enjoy the school festival 학교 축제를 즐기다	

✚ 앞에서 작성한 내용을 바탕으로 다음 〈조건〉에 맞게 글을 완성해 보세요.

〈조건〉
① 4문장 이상 작성할 것
② 다음 언어 형식을 사용해 작성할 것
- There is/are
- many/much/(a) few/(a) little
- 형용사
- Why don't you ~?

Our School

Welcome to our school! Here are some of the good things about our school.

First, ____

____ .

Second, ____

____ .

Third, ____ .

Why don't you ____

____ later?

Have a great time at our school!

평가 개요	
주제	내가 가장 좋아하는 계절 소개하기
세부 내용	① 가장 좋아하는 계절 ② 그 계절을 좋아하는 이유 (3가지 이상) ③ 그 계절에 주로 하는 활동
언어 형식	① 형용사 ② 빈도부사 always/often/usually ③ 비교급 또는 최상급

Step 1 | 예시 글 분석하기 ···○

➕ 형광펜 친 부분에 유의하여 예시 글을 읽은 후, 각 질문에 답해보세요.

My Favorite Season

가장 좋아하는 계절	→	My favorite season is autumn for these reasons.
이유 ①	→	First, the weather is cooler than summer. The weather is perfect for outdoor activities.
이유 ②	→	Second, the trees have many colorful leaves. This beautiful scenery is the best thing about autumn.
이유 ③	→	Finally, autumn has the freshest air of all the seasons.
주로 하는 활동	→	For these reasons, I often go for walks during this season.

1　What is the writer's favorite season?

→ The writer's favorite season is ______________________________.

2　Why does the writer like autumn? Write down 3 sentences.

→ First, the weather is ______________________ summer.

→ Second, the trees have ____.

→ Finally, autumn has ____.

3　For these reasons, what does the writer often do during autumn?

→ The writer often ____________________________________ during autumn.

---

1 autumn　2 cooler than, many colorful leaves, the freshest air of all the seasons　3 goes for walks

Step 2 | 글의 뼈대 만들기 ⦁⦁⦁⦁⦁⦁⦁⦁⦁⦁⦁⦁⦁⦁⦁⦁⦁⦁⦁⦁⦁⦁⦁

✚ 내가 가장 좋아하는 계절을 떠올리며, 다음 표의 빈칸을 완성해 보세요.

My Favorite Season

가장 좋아하는 계절	My favorite season is ________________________ for these reasons.
이유 ①	First, ________________________ ________________________ .
이유 ②	Second, ________________________ ________________________ .
이유 ③	Finally, ________________________ ________________________ .
주로 하는 활동	For these reasons, I often[usually, always] ________________________ ________________________ during this season.

Useful Words & Expressions

이유	weather 날씨 perfect 완벽한 scenery 풍경 snow a lot 눈이 많이 오다 have snowball fights 눈싸움을 하다 decorate a Christmas tree 크리스마스트리를 장식하다	temperature 온도, 기온 cozy 아늑한 outdoor activities 야외활동 watch fireworks 불꽃놀이를 보다	fresh 신선한 cherry blossoms 벚꽃 colorful leaves 다채로운 낙엽 build a snowman 눈사람을 만들다
활동	봄	go flower viewing 꽃놀이를 가다 go on a picnic 소풍을 가다	go hiking 하이킹을 가다 climb the mountain 등산하다
	여름	go to the swimming pool 수영장에 가다 swim in the river 강에서 수영하다	go to the beach 해변에 가다 enjoy a summer festival 여름 축제를 즐기다
	가을	have a barbecue 바비큐를 하다 go camping 캠핑하러 가다	go for a walk 산책하러 가다 ride a bicycle 자전거를 타다
	겨울	go skiing 스키를 타러 가다 go snowboarding 스노보드를 타러 가다	go skating 스케이트를 타러 가다

✚ 앞에서 작성한 내용을 바탕으로 다음 〈조건〉에 맞게 글을 완성해 보세요.

〈조건〉
① 5문장 이상 작성할 것
② 다음 언어 형식을 사용해 작성할 것
 • 형용사
 • 빈도부사 always/often/usually
 • 비교급 또는 최상급

My Favorite Season

My favorite season is ＿＿＿＿＿＿＿＿＿＿＿＿＿＿ for these reasons.

First, ＿＿＿＿＿＿＿＿＿＿＿＿＿＿＿＿＿＿＿＿＿＿＿＿＿＿＿＿

＿＿＿＿＿＿＿＿＿＿＿＿＿＿＿＿＿＿＿＿＿＿＿＿＿＿＿＿＿＿＿.

Second, ＿＿＿＿＿＿＿＿＿＿＿＿＿＿＿＿＿＿＿＿＿＿＿＿＿＿＿

＿＿＿＿＿＿＿＿＿＿＿＿＿＿＿＿＿＿＿＿＿＿＿＿＿＿＿＿＿＿＿.

Finally, ＿＿＿＿＿＿＿＿＿＿＿＿＿＿＿＿＿＿＿＿＿＿＿＿＿＿＿＿

＿＿＿＿＿＿＿＿＿＿＿＿＿＿＿＿＿＿＿＿＿＿＿＿＿＿＿＿＿＿＿.

For these reasons, I ＿＿＿＿＿＿＿＿＿＿＿＿＿＿＿＿＿＿＿＿＿

＿＿＿＿＿＿＿＿＿＿＿＿＿＿＿＿＿＿＿＿＿＿ during this season.

평가 개요	
주제	나의 comfort food(기분을 좋게 해 주는 음식) 소개하기
세부 내용	① 나의 comfort food ② 그 음식을 고른 이유 (3가지 이상) ③ 그 음식을 먹는 빈도 ④ 제안하는 내용
언어 형식	① 형용사 ② 빈도부사 usually ③ How about ~?

Step 1 | 예시 글 분석하기

✚ 형광펜 친 부분에 유의하여 예시 글을 읽은 후, 표의 빈칸을 완성해 보세요.

My Comfort Food

도입부	→	What is your favorite comfort food?
나의 comfort food	→	My comfort food is Korean ramen.
이유 ①	→	I like it because it's spicy.
이유 ②	→	Also, there are many different flavors.
이유 ③	→	Finally, the recipe is very simple, and it only takes less than 10 minutes to cook.
먹는 빈도	→	I usually eat ramen once a week.
제안	→	How about adding some toppings like vegetables next time?

comfort food	**1**	My comfort food is ________________________.
이유 ①	**2**	I like it because ________________________.
이유 ②	**3**	Also, ________________________.
이유 ③	**4**	Finally, the recipe is ________________, and it only takes less than 10 minutes to cook.
먹는 빈도	**5**	I ________________ ramen ________________.
제안	**6**	How about ________________ like vegetables next time?

---

1 Korean ramen **2** it's spicy **3** there are many different flavors **4** very simple **5** usually eat, once a week **6** adding some toppings

✚ 나의 **comfort food**를 떠올리며, 다음 표의 빈칸을 완성해 보세요.

My Comfort Food

도입부	What is your favorite comfort food?
comfort food	My comfort food is _______________________________________ .
이유 ①	I like it because _______________________________________ .
이유 ②	Also, _______________________________________ .
이유 ③	Finally, _______________________________________ .
먹는 빈도	I _______________________________________ .
제안	How about _______________________________________ ?

Useful Words & Expressions

음식	ramen 라면 sushi 초밥 pizza 피자 mala soup 마라탕 grilled pork belly 삼겹살 hamburger 햄버거	pasta 파스타 tteokbokki 떡볶이 fried chicken 프라이드 치킨 tanghulu 탕후루 bulgogi 불고기 macaron 마카롱	bibimbap 비빔밥 dumpling 만두 gimbap 김밥 steak 스테이크 pork cutlet 돈가스 chocolate cake 초콜릿 케이크
이유	flavor 맛 healthy 건강에 좋은 convenient 간편한 various options 다양한 선택권	recipe 레시피, 요리법 cheap 값이 싼 easy to make 만들기 쉬운 various kinds of 다양한 종류의	ingredient 재료 light 기름지지 않은, 담백한 a clean taste 깔끔한 맛 topping (음식 위에 얹는) 토핑, 고명
빈도	once a week 일주일에 한 번 every day 매일 every weekend 매주 주말	twice a week 일주일에 두 번 every other day 이틀에 한 번 every morning 매일 아침	three times a week 일주일에 세 번

✚ 앞에서 작성한 내용을 바탕으로 다음 〈조건〉에 맞게 글을 완성해 보세요.

〈조건〉
① 6문장 이상 작성할 것
② 다음 언어 형식을 사용해 작성할 것
  • 형용사
  • 빈도부사 usually
  • How about ~?

My Comfort Food

What is your favorite comfort food? My comfort food is ______________________.

I like it because ____________________________________

____.

Also, ____

____.

Finally, ____

____.

I ____

____.

How about ____

____ ?

평가 개요	
주제	가장 기억에 남는 여행지 소개하기
세부 내용	① 여행 장소 ② 여행 시기 및 함께한 사람 ③ 여행지에서 한 활동 (4가지 이상) ④ 여행 소감
언어 형식	① 접속사 when ② 접속사 and ③ 접속사 that (I think[believe, hope] that ~)

Step 1 | 예시 글 분석하기

✚ 형광펜 친 부분에 유의하여 예시 글을 읽은 후, 각 질문에 답해보세요.

My Most Memorable Trip

여행 장소	→	My most memorable trip was to Nami Island.
여행 시기 및 함께 간 사람	→	I went there with my family when I was in the 5th grade.
활동 ① and ②	→	On Nami Island, we walked along beautiful paths and saw many colorful flowers.
활동 ③ and ④	→	We also rented bikes and rode around the island.
여행 소감	→	The trip was fun and relaxing.
맺음말	→	I think that Nami Island is a great place for families.

1 Where was the writer's memorable trip?

→ The writer's memorable trip was to ___________________________ .

2 Who did the writer visit Nami Island with, and when?

→ He[She] visited Nami Island with ___________________ when ___________________________ .

3 What did the writer do on Nami Island? Write down 2 sentences.

→ He[She] ___________________________ and ___________________________ .

→ He[She] also ___________________ and ___________________________ with his[her] family.

4 How did the writer feel about the trip?

→ The trip was ___________________ and ___________________ .

1 Nami Island **2** his[her] family, he[she] was in the 5th grade **3** walked along beautiful paths, saw many colorful flowers, rented bikes, rode around the island
4 fun, relaxing

Step 2 | 글의 뼈대 만들기

➕ 가장 기억에 남는 여행지를 떠올리며, 다음 표의 빈칸을 완성해 보세요.

My Most Memorable Trip

여행 장소	My most memorable trip was to ________________________ .
여행 시기 및 함께 간 사람	I went there with ________________________ when ________________________ .
활동 ① and ②	I/We ________________________ and ________________________ .
활동 ③ and ④	I/We also ________________________ and ________________________ .
여행 소감	The trip was ________________ and ________________ .
맺음말	I ________________________ .

Useful Words & Expressions

장소	camping site 캠핑장 Jeju Island 제주도	amusement park 놀이공원 Nami Island 남이섬	water park 워터파크 Gyeongju 경주
활동	roast marshmallows 마시멜로를 굽다 make a campfire 캠프파이어를 만들다 taste traditional food 전통 음식을 맛보다 shop at the gift shop 기념품 가게에서 쇼핑하다 go on a safari tour 사파리 투어를 하다 watch a parade 퍼레이드를 보다		ride a bike 자전거를 타다 swim in the swimming pool 수영장에서 수영하다 visit museums 박물관을 방문하다 relax at a beach 해변에서 휴식을 취하다 feed the wild animals 야생 동물에게 먹이를 주다
감정	exciting 신나는 satisfying 만족스러운	enjoyable 즐거운 peaceful 평화로운	thrilling 아주 신나는, 흥분되는 comfortable 편안한

✚ 앞에서 작성한 내용을 바탕으로 다음 〈조건〉에 맞게 글을 완성해 보세요.

〈조건〉
① 6문장 이상 작성할 것
② 다음 언어 형식을 사용해 작성할 것
  · 접속사 when
  · 접속사 and
  · 접속사 that (I think[believe, hope] that ~)

My Most Memorable Trip

My most memorable trip was to ____ .

____ .

____ .

____ .

____ .

The trip was ____ .

I ____ .

○ 예시 답안 p.212

평가 개요	
주제	여가 시간에 즐기는 활동 소개하기
세부 내용	① 여가 시간에 즐기는 활동 ② 활동을 할 때 느끼는 감정 ③ 활동을 좋아하는 이유 ④ 활동을 통해 배우는 것
언어 형식	① 감각동사 feel ② teach A B ③ 동명사 (주어, 목적어)

Step 1 | 예시 글 분석하기

✚ 형광펜 친 부분에 유의하여 예시 글을 읽은 후, 각 질문에 답해보세요.

My Leisure Activity

즐기는 활동	→	In my free time, I enjoy playing soccer with my friends.
느끼는 감정	→	When I play soccer, I feel happy and energetic.
구체적인 이유	→	Scoring a goal gives me a lot of joy.
배우는 것	→	Soccer also teaches me important skills like teamwork.
맺음말	→	I hope to keep playing soccer for a long time.

1   **What leisure activity does the writer enjoy?**

→ The writer enjoys ________________________ with his[her] friends.

2   **How does the writer feel when he[she] plays soccer?**

→ He[She] ________________________.

3   **What brings the writer a lot of joy?**

→ ________________________ gives him[her] a lot of joy.

4   **What does the activity teach the writer?**

→ It teaches him[her] ________________________.

---

1 playing soccer   **2** feels happy and energetic   **3** Scoring a goal   **4** important skills like teamwork

✚ 여가 시간에 즐겨 하는 활동을 떠올리며, 다음 표의 빈칸을 완성해 보세요.

My Leisure Activity

즐기는 활동	In my free time, I enjoy ______________________________.
느끼는 감정	When I ______________________________, I feel ______________________________.
구체적인 이유	______________________________ gives me a lot of joy.
배우는 것	______________________ also teaches me important skills like ______________ ______________________________.
맺음말	I hope to ______________________________.

Useful Words & Expressions

즐기는 활동	watch a movie 영화를 보다 bake cookies 쿠키를 굽다 listen to music 음악을 듣다 go for a walk 산책하러 가다		watch a baseball game 야구 경기를 보다 play a musical instrument 악기를 연주하다 hang out with friends 친구들과 어울리다 play computer games 컴퓨터 게임하다
감정	excited 신나는 comfortable 편안한 focused 집중한	relaxed 느긋한 satisfied 만족스러운 energetic 활기에 찬	thrilled 아주 신이 난 calm 침착한
구체적인 이유	cheer loudly 큰 목소리로 응원하다 win a game 게임에서 이기다 perform on stage 무대에서 공연하다		make different cookies 다양한 쿠키를 만들다 try out a new recipe 새로운 레시피를 시도하다 play one's favorite song 가장 좋아하는 곡을 연주하다
배우는 것	creativity 창의력 confidence 자신감 strategy 전략 problem-solving skills 문제 해결 능력		imagination 상상력 patience 인내심 communication skills 의사소통 능력 teamwork 팀워크, 협동 작업

✚ 앞에서 작성한 내용을 바탕으로 다음 〈조건〉에 맞게 글을 완성해 보세요.

〈조건〉
① 5문장 이상 작성할 것
② 다음 언어 형식을 사용해 작성할 것
  • 감각동사 feel
  • teach A B
  • 동명사 (주어, 목적어)

My Leisure Activity

In my free time, ____ .

____ .

____ .

____ .

____ .

____ .

I hope to ____ .

○ 예시 답안 p.213

평가 개요	
주제	나의 바쁜 하루
세부 내용	① 하루 동안 한 일 (5가지 이상) ② 한 일의 목적 (1가지 이상)
언어 형식	① to부정사의 부사적 쓰임 (목적) ② 시간을 나타내는 접속사 when ③ 시간을 나타내는 접속사 before 또는 after

Step 1 │ 예시 글 분석하기

➕ 형광펜 친 부분에 유의하여 예시 글을 읽은 후, 각 질문에 답해보세요.

My Busy Day

도입부	➔	Today was a busy day.
한 일 ①	➔	I woke up early to get ready for school.
한 일 ②	➔	After school, I did my homework first.
한 일 ③	➔	After I finished, I went outside to play with my friends.
한 일 ④	➔	When I got home, I helped my mom with dinner.
한 일 ⑤	➔	Before I went to bed, I read a book to relax.
맺음말	➔	It was a tiring but happy day!

1 Why did the writer wake up early?

→ He[She] woke up early ___________________________________.

2 When and why did the writer go out?

→ He[She] went out after _____________________________ to play
   with his[her] friends.

3 What did the writer do after he[she] got home?

→ He[She] _____________________________________ with dinner.

4 When did the writer read a book?

→ He[She] read a book before _____________________________ to relax.

---

1 to get ready for school 2 he[she] finished his[her] homework 3 helped his[her] mom 4 he[she] went to bed

Step 2 | 글의 뼈대 만들기 ···○

✚ 나의 바빴던 하루를 떠올리며, 다음 표의 빈칸을 완성해 보세요.

My Busy Day

도입부	Today was a busy day.
한 일 ①	____________________________ .
한 일 ②	_______________________________________ .
한 일 ③	_______________________________________ .
한 일 ④	_______________________________________ .
한 일 ⑤	Before I went to bed, ________________________ .
맺음말	It was a tiring but happy day!

Useful Words & Expressions

하루 일과	**wake up early** 일찍 일어나다 / **get ready for school** 학교 갈 준비를 하다 **have breakfast** 아침을 먹다 / **go to school** 학교에 가다 **eat lunch** 점심을 먹다 / **play outside** 밖에서 놀다 **do homework** 숙제를 하다 / **play games** 게임을 하다 **read a book** 책을 읽다 / **spend time with family** 가족과 시간을 보내다 **study for a test** 시험공부를 하다 / **hang out with friends** 친구들과 어울리다 **join a club activity** 동아리 활동에 참여하다 / **help with household chores** 집안일을 돕다 **go to bed early** 일찍 잠자리에 들다 **prepare my school bag for the next day** 다음 날을 위해 내 학교 가방을 준비하다

✚ 앞에서 작성한 내용을 바탕으로 다음 〈조건〉에 맞게 글을 완성해 보세요.

〈조건〉
① 5문장 이상 작성할 것
② 다음 언어 형식을 사용해 작성할 것
  · to부정사의 부사적 쓰임 (목적)
  · 시간을 나타내는 접속사 when
  · 시간을 나타내는 접속사 before 또는 after

My Busy Day

Today was a busy day. ____ .

____ .

____ .

____ .

____ .

____ .

Before I went to bed, ____ .

It was a tiring but happy day!

평가 개요	
주제	나의 올해 목표 소개하기
세부 내용	① 한 해 동안 이루고 싶은 목표 ② 세부 계획 (3가지 이상) ③ 목표에 대한 생각이나 바람
언어 형식	① to부정사의 명사적 쓰임 (want to+동사원형) ② to부정사의 부사적 쓰임 (목적) ③ I believe that ~.

Step 1 | 예시 글 분석하기

➕ 형광펜 친 부분에 유의하여 예시 글을 읽은 후, 각 질문에 답해보세요.

My Goals for This Year

목표	→	This year, I want to improve my grades in school.
세부 계획	→	I set three goals to achieve this.
계획 ①	→	First, I'll join a study group to learn from others.
계획 ②	→	Second, I'll take notes during class to remember important things.
계획 ③	→	Lastly, I'll make a study schedule to manage my time.
맺음말	→	I believe that I'll be able to get better grades.

1 What does the writer want to do this year?

→ The writer ____________________________________.

2 Why will the writer join a study group?

→ He[She] will join a study group ____________________________________.

3 Why will the writer take notes during class?

→ He[She] will take notes during class ____________________________________.

4 Why will the writer make a study schedule?

→ He[She] will make a study schedule ____________________________________.

---

1 wants to improve his[her] grades in school **2** to learn from others **3** to remember important things **4** to manage his[her] time

✚ 올해 이루고 싶은 목표를 떠올리며, 다음 표의 빈칸을 완성해 보세요.

My Goals for This Year

목표	This year, I want to ____ .
세부 계획	I set three goals to achieve this.
계획 ①	First, I'll ________________________________ to ____ .
계획 ②	Second, I'll ________________________________ to ____ .
계획 ③	Lastly, I'll ________________________________ to ____ .
맺음말	I believe that ____ .

Useful Words & Expressions

| 목표 & 계획 | **manage my time** 내 시간을 관리하다
improve my grades 내 성적을 올리다
improve soccer/drawing/writing skills 축구/그림/글쓰기 실력을 키우다
learn Japanese/Chinese/Spanish/French 일본어/중국어/스페인어/프랑스어를 배우다
join a soccer team/book club 축구팀/독서 모임에 가입하다
reduce screen time (휴대전화 등 전자기기의) 화면을 보는 시간을 줄이다
listen to music/radio/courses 음악/라디오/강의를 듣다
make many friends 많은 친구를 사귀다
walk/jog/run every morning 매일 아침 걷다/조깅하다/달리다
practice shooting/passing 슈팅/패스를 연습하다
watch a movie/drama/cartoon 영화/드라마/만화를 보다
save my time/money 내 시간/돈을 절약하다
read one book every month 매달 책 한 권을 읽다 |

✚ 앞에서 작성한 내용을 바탕으로 다음 〈조건〉에 맞게 글을 완성해 보세요.

〈조건〉
① 6문장 이상 작성할 것
② 다음 언어 형식을 사용해 작성할 것
  • to부정사의 명사적 쓰임 (want to+동사원형)
  • to부정사의 부사적 쓰임 (목적)
  • I believe that ~.

My Goals for This Year

This year, ____ .

____ .

First, ____ .

Second, ____ .

Lastly, ____ .

____ .

I believe that ____ .

 논술형 수행평가 1회

평가 기준			배점
내용 **(6점)**	**<내용> 채점 조건** ① 장래 희망　② 장래 계획 (2가지 이상)　③ 꿈을 이루기 위해 노력하고 있는 일 (3가지 이상)		
	내용 조건 (3점)	<내용 조건> 중 3가지 모두 만족한 경우	3
		<내용 조건> 중 2가지를 만족한 경우	2
		<내용 조건> 중 1가지를 만족한 경우	1
	문장 개수 (3점)	5문장 이상 작성한 경우	3
		4문장 이상 작성한 경우	2
		3문장 이하로 작성한 경우	1
언어 형식 **(5점)**	**<언어 형식> 채점 조건** ① 현재진행형　② 미래 표현 will		
	언어 형식 사용 (2점)	제시된 <언어 형식 조건> 2가지를 목적에 맞게 사용한 경우	2
		제시된 <언어 형식 조건> 2가지 중 1가지를 목적에 맞게 사용한 경우	1
	정확한 언어 사용 (3점)	문법적 오류가 3개 이하인 경우	3
		문법적 오류가 4개 이상 6개 이하 포함되었으나 내용 전달에 무리가 없는 경우	2
		문법적 오류가 7개 이상 있고, 내용이 제대로 전달되지 않는 경우	1
총점 **(11점)**			

예시 답안 1

I want to be a zookeeper in the future. I will take care of animals and train them.
For my dream, I am doing many things.
First, I am reading books about animals. Second, I am volunteering at an animal shelter.
And, I am joining an animal protection campaign.

저는 장래에 사육사가 되고 싶습니다. 저는 동물들을 돌보고 훈련시킬 것입니다.
제 꿈을 위해, 저는 많은 것을 하고 있습니다. 첫째, 저는 동물에 관한 책들을 읽고 있습니다. 둘째, 저는 동물 보호소에서 자원봉사하고 있습니다.
그리고 저는 동물 보호 캠페인에 참여하고 있습니다.

예시 답안 2

I want to be a game developer in the future. I will create games and share them with others.
For my dream, I am doing many things.
First, I am learning game design. Second, I am practicing programming skills.
And, I am playing and reviewing games.

저는 장래에 게임 개발자가 되고 싶습니다. 저는 게임을 만들고 다른 사람들과 공유할 것입니다.
제 꿈을 위해, 저는 많은 것을 하고 있습니다. 첫째, 저는 게임 디자인을 배우고 있습니다. 둘째, 저는 프로그래밍 기술을 연습하고 있습니다.
그리고 저는 게임을 하고 리뷰하고 있습니다.

평가 기준			배점
내용 (5점)	**<내용> 채점 조건** ① 스트레스 해소 방법 (3가지 이상) ② 각 방법의 효과 (3가지 이상)		
	내용 조건 (2점)	<내용 조건> 중 2가지 모두 만족한 경우	2
		<내용 조건> 중 1가지를 만족한 경우	1
	문장 개수 (3점)	6문장 이상 작성한 경우	3
		5문장 이상 작성한 경우	2
		4문장 이하로 작성한 경우	1
언어 형식 (6점)	**<언어 형식> 채점 조건** ① 일반동사의 현재형 ② 미래 표현 will ③ 조동사 can		
	언어 형식 사용 (3점)	제시된 <언어 형식 조건> 3가지를 목적에 맞게 사용한 경우	3
		제시된 <언어 형식 조건> 3가지 중 2가지를 목적에 맞게 사용한 경우	2
		제시된 <언어 형식 조건> 3가지 중 1가지를 목적에 맞게 사용한 경우	1
	정확한 언어 사용 (3점)	문법적 오류가 3개 이하인 경우	3
		문법적 오류가 4개 이상 6개 이하 포함되었으나 내용 전달에 무리가 없는 경우	2
		문법적 오류가 7개 이상 있고, 내용이 제대로 전달되지 않는 경우	1
총점 (11점)			

예시 답안 1

Here are my tips for reducing stress.
First, I draw pictures. I can express my emotion through my drawings.
Second, I spend time with my friends. I can talk about my worries with them.
Finally, I read a lot of books. I can gain positive energy from them.
Follow my tips, and you will feel better.

여기 제 스트레스 해소 방법이 있습니다.
첫째, 저는 그림을 그립니다. 그림을 통해 제 감정을 표현할 수 있습니다.
둘째, 저는 제 친구들과 시간을 보냅니다. 친구들과 제 걱정에 대해 이야기할 수 있습니다.
마지막으로, 저는 책을 많이 읽습니다. 저는 책에서 긍정적인 에너지를 얻을 수 있습니다.
제 방법을 따라 해 보세요, 그러면 기분이 나아질 거예요.

예시 답안 2

Here are my tips for reducing stress.
First, I watch fun movies and entertainment shows. I can laugh a lot.
Second, I play my favorite computer games. I can clear my head.
Finally, I talk with my mom. I can get advice.
Follow my tips, and you will feel better.

여기 제 스트레스 해소 방법이 있습니다.
첫째, 저는 재미있는 영화와 예능 프로그램을 봅니다. 많이 웃을 수 있습니다.
둘째, 저는 제가 좋아하는 컴퓨터 게임을 합니다. 머리를 맑게 할 수 있습니다.
마지막으로, 저는 엄마와 대화를 나눕니다. 조언을 얻을 수 있습니다.
제 방법을 따라 해 보세요, 그러면 기분이 나아질 거예요.

논술형 수행평가 3회

평가 기준			배점
내용 (6점)	**<내용> 채점 조건** ① 다녀온 곳 ② 한 일 (3가지 이상) ③ 먹은 것과 맛 표현 ④ 느낀 점		
	내용 조건 (3점)	<내용 조건> 중 4가지 모두 만족한 경우	3
		<내용 조건> 중 3가지를 만족한 경우	2
		<내용 조건> 중 2가지를 만족한 경우	1
	문장 개수 (3점)	7문장 이상 작성한 경우	3
		6문장 이상 작성한 경우	2
		5문장 이하로 작성한 경우	1
언어 형식 (5점)	**<언어 형식> 채점 조건** ① be동사의 과거형 ② 일반동사의 과거형		
	언어 형식 사용 (2점)	제시된 <언어 형식 조건> 2가지를 목적에 맞게 사용한 경우	2
		제시된 <언어 형식 조건> 2가지 중 1가지를 목적에 맞게 사용한 경우	1
	정확한 언어 사용 (3점)	문법적 오류가 3개 이하인 경우	3
		문법적 오류가 4개 이상 6개 이하 포함되었으나 내용 전달에 무리가 없는 경우	2
		문법적 오류가 7개 이상 있고, 내용이 제대로 전달되지 않는 경우	1
총점 (11점)			

예시 답안 1

Date: July 25th
I went to my best friend's house.
We watched a movie. We listened to music and sang along.
We also played board games. We ate cheese tteokbokki, and it was really yummy.
Overall, it was a fun experience. I want to go to my friend's house again.

날짜: 7월 25일
나는 내 가장 친한 친구 집에 갔다.
우리는 영화를 봤다. 우리는 음악을 듣고 함께 따라 불렀다. 우리는 또한 보드게임도 했다. 우리는 치즈 떡볶이를 먹었는데, 정말 맛있었다.
전체적으로 즐거운 경험이었다. 나는 내 친구 집에 또 가고 싶다.

예시 답안 2

Date: August 2nd
I went to the aquarium with my parents.
I took pictures of a big shark. I fed cute penguins and fish. I also watched the Little Mermaid show.
I ate some snacks and popcorn, and they were very tasty.
Overall, it was an exciting experience. I want to go to the aquarium again.

날짜: 8월 2일
나는 부모님과 함께 수족관에 갔다.
나는 큰 상어의 사진을 찍었다. 나는 귀여운 펭귄과 물고기에게 먹이를 주었다. 나는 인어공주 쇼도 관람했다.
나는 간식과 팝콘을 먹었는데, 아주 맛있었다.
전체적으로 신나는 경험이었다. 나는 수족관에 또 가고 싶다.

평가 기준			배점
내용 **(5점)**	**<내용> 채점 조건** ① 학교의 특징 (3가지 이상) ② 제안하고 싶은 것		
	내용 조건 (2점)	<내용 조건> 중 2가지 모두 만족한 경우	2
		<내용 조건> 중 1가지를 만족한 경우	1
	문장 개수 (3점)	4문장 이상 작성한 경우	3
		3문장 이상 작성한 경우	2
		2문장 이하로 작성한 경우	1
언어 형식 **(6점)**	**<언어 형식> 채점 조건** ① There is/are ② many/much/(a) few/(a) little ③ 형용사 ④ Why don't you ~?		
	언어 형식 사용 (3점)	제시된 <언어 형식 조건> 4가지를 목적에 맞게 사용한 경우	3
		제시된 <언어 형식 조건> 4가지 중 3가지를 목적에 맞게 사용한 경우	2
		제시된 <언어 형식 조건> 4가지 중 2가지를 목적에 맞게 사용한 경우	1
	정확한 언어 사용 (3점)	문법적 오류가 3개 이하인 경우	3
		문법적 오류가 4개 이상 6개 이하 포함되었으나 내용 전달에 무리가 없는 경우	2
		문법적 오류가 7개 이상 있고, 내용이 제대로 전달되지 않는 경우	1
총점 **(11점)**			

예시 답안 1

Welcome to our school! Here are some of the good things about our school.
First, there is a large school gym. We can play badminton or volleyball there. Second, we have many friendly teachers. Third, there is a modern science lab. We can do interesting experiments there. Why don't you join us for fun science experiments later? Have a great time at our school!

우리 학교에 온 것을 환영해! 여기 우리 학교의 몇 가지 좋은 점을 소개할게.
첫째, 우리 학교에는 큰 체육관이 있어. 거기서 배드민턴이나 배구를 할 수 있어. 둘째, 우리는 친절한 선생님들이 많아. 셋째, 현대적인 과학 실험실이 있어. 거기서 재미있는 실험을 할 수 있어. 나중에 재미있는 과학 실험에 참여해 보는 게 어때? 우리 학교에서 즐거운 시간 보내!

예시 답안 2

Welcome to our school! Here are some of the good things about our school.
First, there are a few comfortable computer rooms. Second, there are colorful classrooms for each grade. Third, there are delicious meals in the cafeteria. Everyone waits for lunchtime. Why don't you try the meals later? Have a great time at our school!

우리 학교에 온 것을 환영해! 여기 우리 학교의 몇 가지 좋은 점을 소개할게.
첫째, 몇 개의 편안한 컴퓨터실이 있어. 둘째, 학년마다 다양한 색깔의 교실이 있어. 셋째, 급식실에는 맛있는 식사가 준비되어 있어. 모두가 점심시간을 기다려. 나중에 한 번 식사해 보는 게 어때? 우리 학교에서 즐거운 시간 보내!

평가 기준			배점
내용 (6점)	**<내용> 채점 조건** ① 가장 좋아하는 계절 ② 그 계절을 좋아하는 이유 (3가지 이상) ③ 그 계절에 주로 하는 활동		
	내용 조건 (3점)	<내용 조건> 중 3가지 모두 만족한 경우	3
		<내용 조건> 중 2가지를 만족한 경우	2
		<내용 조건> 중 1가지를 만족한 경우	1
	문장 개수 (3점)	5문장 이상 작성한 경우	3
		4문장 이상 작성한 경우	2
		3문장 이하로 작성한 경우	1
언어 형식 (6점)	**<언어 형식> 채점 조건** ① 형용사 ② 빈도부사 always/often/usually ③ 비교급 또는 최상급		
	언어 형식 사용 (3점)	제시된 <언어 형식 조건> 3가지를 목적에 맞게 사용한 경우	3
		제시된 <언어 형식 조건> 3가지 중 2가지를 목적에 맞게 사용한 경우	2
		제시된 <언어 형식 조건> 3가지 중 1가지를 목적에 맞게 사용한 경우	1
	정확한 언어 사용 (3점)	문법적 오류가 3개 이하인 경우	3
		문법적 오류가 4개 이상 6개 이하 포함되었으나 내용 전달에 무리가 없는 경우	2
		문법적 오류가 7개 이상 있고, 내용이 제대로 전달되지 않는 경우	1
총점 (12점)			

예시 답안 1

My favorite season is spring for these reasons. First, I can see lots of cherry blossoms. Beautiful flowers are blooming in spring. Second, spring has the best weather. Finally, I can enjoy picnics with my family. We usually go to the park for a picnic. For these reasons, I often go out and take many pictures during this season.

제가 가장 좋아하는 계절은 봄입니다. 첫째, 벚꽃을 많이 볼 수 있습니다. 봄에는 예쁜 꽃들이 피어 있습니다. 둘째, 봄은 날씨가 제일 좋습니다. 마지막으로, 가족과 함께 소풍을 즐길 수 있습니다. 우리는 보통 소풍을 가기 위해 공원에 갑니다. 이런 이유들로 저는 이 계절에 자주 밖에 나가서 사진을 많이 찍습니다.

예시 답안 2

My favorite season is summer for these reasons. First, I can enjoy fun festivals. Second, I can go to the beach and swim. Finally, I can go camping with my family. During summer vacation, my family usually goes camping. Summer is the hottest season, but it's the most exciting season to me. For these reasons, I often enjoy outdoor activities during this season.

제가 가장 좋아하는 계절은 여름입니다. 첫째, 재미있는 축제들을 즐길 수 있습니다. 둘째, 해변에 가서 수영을 할 수 있습니다. 마지막으로, 가족과 함께 캠핑을 갈 수 있습니다. 여름방학 동안 우리 가족은 보통 캠핑을 갑니다. 여름은 가장 더운 계절이지만, 저에게는 가장 신나는 계절입니다. 이런 이유들로 저는 이 계절에 야외 활동을 자주 즐깁니다.

 ## 논술형 수행평가 6회

평가 기준			배점
내용 (6점)	**<내용> 채점 조건** ① 나의 comfort food ② 그 음식을 고른 이유 (3가지 이상) ③ 그 음식을 먹는 빈도 ④ 제안하는 내용		
	내용 조건 (3점)	<내용 조건> 중 4가지 모두 만족한 경우	3
		<내용 조건> 중 3가지를 만족한 경우	2
		<내용 조건> 중 2가지를 만족한 경우	1
	문장 개수 (3점)	6문장 이상 작성한 경우	3
		5문장 이상 작성한 경우	2
		4문장 이하로 작성한 경우	1
언어 형식 (6점)	**<언어 형식> 채점 조건** ① 형용사 ② 빈도부사 usually ③ How about ~?		
	언어 형식 사용 (3점)	제시된 <언어 형식 조건> 3가지를 목적에 맞게 사용한 경우	3
		제시된 <언어 형식 조건> 3가지 중 2가지를 목적에 맞게 사용한 경우	2
		제시된 <언어 형식 조건> 3가지 중 1가지를 목적에 맞게 사용한 경우	1
	정확한 언어 사용 (3점)	문법적 오류가 3개 이하인 경우	3
		문법적 오류가 4개 이상 6개 이하 포함되었으나 내용 전달에 무리가 없는 경우	2
		문법적 오류가 7개 이상 있고, 내용이 제대로 전달되지 않는 경우	1
총점 (12점)			

예시 답안 1

What is your favorite comfort food? My comfort food is tteokbokki. I like it because I can add special ingredients like noodles and sausages. Also, I love its spicy sauce. The spicy sauce can reduce my stress. Finally, there are many different kinds of tteokbokki. I usually order it once a week. How about trying the spicy tteokbokki next time?

가장 좋아하는 기분을 좋게 해 주는 음식이 무엇인가요? 제가 가장 좋아하는 기분을 좋게 해 주는 음식은 떡볶이예요. 떡볶이는 면이나 소시지 같은 특별한 재료를 넣을 수 있어서 좋아해요. 그리고 저는 매운 소스를 정말 좋아해요. 매운 소스는 제 스트레스를 줄여 줄 수 있거든요. 마지막으로, 떡볶이에는 정말 다양한 종류가 있어요. 저는 보통 일주일에 한 번 떡볶이를 시켜 먹어요. 다음에는 매운 떡볶이를 한번 먹어 보는 게 어때요?

예시 답안 2

What is your favorite comfort food? My comfort food is gimbap. I like it because it is very convenient. I can take it anywhere and enjoy it anytime. Also, gimbap has healthy ingredients like vegetables, meat, and eggs. Finally, there are various options like cheese gimbap and tuna gimbap. I usually eat gimbap three times a week. How about trying this healthy and delicious food?

가장 좋아하는 기분을 좋게 해 주는 음식이 무엇인가요? 제가 가장 좋아하는 기분을 좋게 해 주는 음식은 김밥이에요. 김밥은 매우 간편해서 좋아해요. 어디든 가지고 갈 수 있고, 언제든 즐길 수 있어요. 그리고 김밥에는 채소, 고기, 달걀과 같은 건강에 좋은 재료들이 들어 있어요. 마지막으로, 치즈김밥이나 참치김밥처럼 다양한 선택지가 많아요. 저는 보통 일주일에 세 번 김밥을 먹어요. 건강하고 맛있는 이 음식을 한번 먹어 보는 게 어때요?

논술형 수행평가 7회

평가 기준			배점
내용 (6점)	**<내용> 채점 조건** ① 여행 장소 ② 여행 시기 및 함께한 사람 ③ 여행지에서 한 활동 (4가지 이상) ④ 여행 소감		
	내용 조건 (3점)	<내용 조건> 중 4가지 모두 만족한 경우	3
		<내용 조건> 중 3가지를 만족한 경우	2
		<내용 조건> 중 2가지를 만족한 경우	1
	문장 개수 (3점)	6문장 이상 작성한 경우	3
		5문장 이상 작성한 경우	2
		4문장 이하로 작성한 경우	1
언어 형식 (6점)	**<언어 형식> 채점 조건** ① 접속사 when ② 접속사 and ③ 접속사 that (I think[believe, hope] that ~)		
	언어 형식 사용 (3점)	제시된 <언어 형식 조건> 3가지를 목적에 맞게 사용한 경우	3
		제시된 <언어 형식 조건> 3가지 중 2가지를 목적에 맞게 사용한 경우	2
		제시된 <언어 형식 조건> 3가지 중 1가지를 목적에 맞게 사용한 경우	1
	정확한 언어 사용 (3점)	문법적 오류가 3개 이하인 경우	3
		문법적 오류가 4개 이상 6개 이하 포함되었으나 내용 전달에 무리가 없는 경우	2
		문법적 오류가 7개 이상 있고, 내용이 제대로 전달되지 않는 경우	1
총점 (12점)			

예시 답안 1

My most memorable trip was to Nanji camping site.
I went there with my family when I was 10 years old.
We swam in the swimming pool and played badminton.
We also made a campfire and roasted marshmallows over the fire.
The trip was exciting and enjoyable. I hope that I can go back to Nanji camping site again.

가장 기억에 남는 여행은 난지 캠핑장이에요. 제가 10살 때 가족과 함께 그곳에 갔어요. 우리는 수영장에서 수영을 하고 배드민턴을 쳤어요. 또한 캠프파이어를 하고 불 위에서 마시멜로를 구워 먹었어요. 그 여행은 정말 신나고 즐거웠어요. 난지 캠핑장에 다시 갈 수 있기를 바라요.

예시 답안 2

My most memorable trip was to Lotte World.
I went there with my friends when I was in the 6th grade.
We rode a pirate ship ride and watched a parade.
We also went on a safari tour and fed the wild animals.
The trip was thrilling and exciting. I think that this trip will always be a happy memory for me.

가장 기억에 남는 여행은 롯데월드에 갔던 거예요. 제가 6학년 때 제 친구들과 함께 갔어요. 우리는 해적선 놀이기구를 타고 퍼레이드를 구경했어요. 또한 사파리 투어를 하면서 야생 동물에게 먹이도 주었어요. 그 여행은 아주 짜릿하고 신나는 경험이었어요. 이 여행은 항상 행복한 추억으로 남을 것 같아요.

논술형 수행평가 8회

평가 기준			배점
내용 (6점)	**<내용> 채점 조건** ① 여가 시간에 즐기는 활동 ② 활동을 할 때 느끼는 감정 ③ 활동을 좋아하는 이유 ④ 활동을 통해 배우는 것		
	내용 조건 (3점)	<내용 조건> 중 4가지 모두 만족한 경우	3
		<내용 조건> 중 3가지를 만족한 경우	2
		<내용 조건> 중 2가지를 만족한 경우	1
	문장 개수 (3점)	5문장 이상 작성한 경우	3
		4문장 이상 작성한 경우	2
		3문장 이하로 작성한 경우	1
언어 형식 (6점)	**<언어 형식> 채점 조건** ① 감각동사 feel ② teach A B ③ 동명사 (주어, 목적어)		
	언어 형식 사용 (3점)	제시된 <언어 형식 조건> 3가지를 목적에 맞게 사용한 경우	3
		제시된 <언어 형식 조건> 3가지 중 2가지를 목적에 맞게 사용한 경우	2
		제시된 <언어 형식 조건> 3가지 중 1가지를 목적에 맞게 사용한 경우	1
	정확한 언어 사용 (3점)	문법적 오류가 3개 이하인 경우	3
		문법적 오류가 4개 이상 6개 이하 포함되었으나 내용 전달에 무리가 없는 경우	2
		문법적 오류가 7개 이상 있고, 내용이 제대로 전달되지 않는 경우	1
총점 (12점)			

예시 답안 1

In my free time, I enjoy playing board games with my sister.
When I play board games, I feel happy and excited.
Winning a game gives me a lot of joy.
Board games also teach me important skills like strategy and problem-solving.
I hope to play more new board games in the future.

여가 시간에 저는 동생과 함께 보드게임을 하는 것을 즐겨요. 보드게임을 할 때 저는 행복하고 신이 나요.
게임에서 이기는 것은 제게 큰 기쁨을 줘요. 보드게임은 전략과 문제 해결 같은 중요한 기술도 제게 가르쳐 줘요.
저는 앞으로 더 많은 새로운 보드게임을 해보고 싶어요.

예시 답안 2

In my free time, I enjoy playing musical instruments in a band.
When I play the guitar, I feel focused.
Performing new songs with friends gives me a lot of joy.
Playing music also teaches me important skills like teamwork and creativity.
I hope to perform on stage one day.

여가 시간에 저는 밴드에서 악기를 연주하는 것을 즐겨요. 기타를 칠 때 저는 집중이 잘 돼요.
친구들과 함께 새로운 곡을 연주하는 것은 제게 큰 기쁨을 줘요. 음악을 연주하는 것은 또한 팀워크와 창의력 같은 중요한 기술도 제게 가르쳐 줘요.
저는 언젠가 무대에서 공연할 수 있기를 바랍니다.

평가 기준			배점
내용 (5점)	**<내용> 채점 조건** ① 하루 동안 한 일 (5가지 이상) ② 한 일의 목적 (1가지 이상)		
	내용 조건 (2점)	<내용 조건> 중 2가지 모두 만족한 경우	2
		<내용 조건> 중 1가지를 만족한 경우	1
	문장 개수 (3점)	5문장 이상 작성한 경우	3
		4문장 이상 작성한 경우	2
		3문장 이하로 작성한 경우	1
언어 형식 (6점)	**<언어 형식> 채점 조건** ① to부정사의 부사적 쓰임 (목적) ② 시간을 나타내는 접속사 when ③ 시간을 나타내는 접속사 before 또는 after		
	언어 형식 사용 (3점)	제시된 <언어 형식 조건> 3가지를 목적에 맞게 사용한 경우	3
		제시된 <언어 형식 조건> 3가지 중 2가지를 목적에 맞게 사용한 경우	2
		제시된 <언어 형식 조건> 3가지 중 1가지를 목적에 맞게 사용한 경우	1
	정확한 언어 사용 (3점)	문법적 오류가 3개 이하인 경우	3
		문법적 오류가 4개 이상 6개 이하 포함되었으나 내용 전달에 무리가 없는 경우	2
		문법적 오류가 7개 이상 있고, 내용이 제대로 전달되지 않는 경우	1
총점 (11점)			

예시 답안 1

Today was a busy day. I went to the park in the morning to exercise.
When I got home, I cleaned my house. In the afternoon, I spent time with my family.
After I had dinner, I helped my sister with her homework. Before I went to bed, I wrote my diary.
It was a tiring but happy day!

오늘은 바쁜 하루였다. 나는 아침에 운동하기 위해 공원에 갔다. 집에 도착했을 때 집을 청소했다. 오후에는 가족과 시간을 보냈다.
저녁을 먹은 후, 여동생의 숙제를 도와주었다. 자기 전에 일기를 썼다. 힘들었지만 행복한 하루였다!

예시 답안 2

Today was a busy day. I went to the library to borrow some books.
When I got home, I studied math to prepare for the test. After I finished my studies, I watched a movie.
In the evening, I hung out with my friends. Before I went to bed, I packed my bag to get ready for tomorrow.
It was a tiring but happy day!

오늘은 바쁜 하루였다. 나는 책을 빌리기 위해 도서관에 갔다. 집에 도착했을 때 시험 준비를 위해 수학 공부를 했다.
공부를 마친 후, 영화를 보았다. 저녁에는 친구들과 함께 시간을 보냈다. 자기 전에 내일을 준비하기 위해 가방을 챙겼다.
힘들었지만 행복한 하루였다!

평가 기준			배점
내용 (6점)	<내용> 채점 조건 ① 한 해 동안 이루고 싶은 목표　② 세부 계획 (3가지 이상)　③ 목표에 대한 생각이나 바람		
	내용 조건 (3점)	<내용 조건> 중 3가지 모두 만족한 경우	3
		<내용 조건> 중 2가지를 만족한 경우	2
		<내용 조건> 중 1가지를 만족한 경우	1
	문장 개수 (3점)	6문장 이상 작성한 경우	3
		5문장 이상 작성한 경우	2
		4문장 이하로 작성한 경우	1
언어 형식 (6점)	<언어 형식> 채점 조건 ① to부정사의 명사적 쓰임 (want to+동사원형)　② to부정사의 부사적 쓰임 (목적)　③ I believe that ~.		
	언어 형식 사용 (3점)	제시된 <언어 형식 조건> 3가지를 목적에 맞게 사용한 경우	3
		제시된 <언어 형식 조건> 3가지 중 2가지를 목적에 맞게 사용한 경우	2
		제시된 <언어 형식 조건> 3가지 중 1가지를 목적에 맞게 사용한 경우	1
	정확한 언어 사용 (3점)	문법적 오류가 3개 이하인 경우	3
		문법적 오류가 4개 이상 6개 이하 포함되었으나 내용 전달에 무리가 없는 경우	2
		문법적 오류가 7개 이상 있고, 내용이 제대로 전달되지 않는 경우	1
총점 (12점)			

예시 답안 1

This year, I want to improve my soccer skills. I set three goals to achieve this.
First, I'll join a soccer team to learn and play more. Second, I'll run every morning to increase my speed.
Lastly, I'll practice shooting to get better at the game. I believe that I'll become a good soccer player someday.

올해 나는 축구 실력을 향상시키고 싶다. 나는 이것을 이루기 위해 세 가지 목표를 세웠다.
첫째, 더 많이 배우고 경기에 참여하기 위해 축구팀에 들어갈 것이다. 둘째, 속도를 높이기 위해 매일 아침 달리기를 할 것이다.
마지막으로, 경기에서 더 잘하기 위해 슈팅 연습을 할 것이다. 나는 언젠가 좋은 축구 선수가 될 것이라고 믿는다.

예시 답안 2

This year, I want to learn Japanese. I set three goals to achieve this.
First, I'll take notes to practice Japanese characters. Second, I'll watch Japanese movies to learn useful expressions.
Lastly, I'll join a Japanese club to practice speaking. I believe that I'll be able to speak Japanese well someday.

올해 나는 일본어를 배우고 싶다. 나는 이것을 이루기 위해 세 가지 목표를 세웠다.
첫째, 일본어 문자를 연습하기 위해 필기할 것이다. 둘째, 유용한 표현을 배우기 위해 일본 영화를 볼 것이다.
마지막으로, 말하기를 연습하기 위해 일본어 동아리에 가입할 것이다. 나는 언젠가 일본어를 잘하게 될 것이라고 믿는다.

1001개 문장으로 완성하는 중등 필수 영단어

천일문 VOCA

중등 교과서 및 교육부 지정
필수 어휘 반영

주제별 중등 단어
및 빈출 표현 수록

문장을 통한
자연스러운 누적 학습

영단어에 대한 이해를 높이는
쉬운 우리말 풀이와 단어 Tip

쎄듀런 P보카
온라인 연계 어휘 확장·반복 학습

쎄듀 VOCA TEST
무료 시험지 제작 및 인쇄

쎄듀북닷컴(www.cedubook.com)에서 부가 자료를 무료로 다운로드할 수 있습니다.

CEDU쎄듀

1. '나'에게 딱! 맞는 암기&문제모드만 골라서 학습!

5가지 암기모드

8가지 문제모드

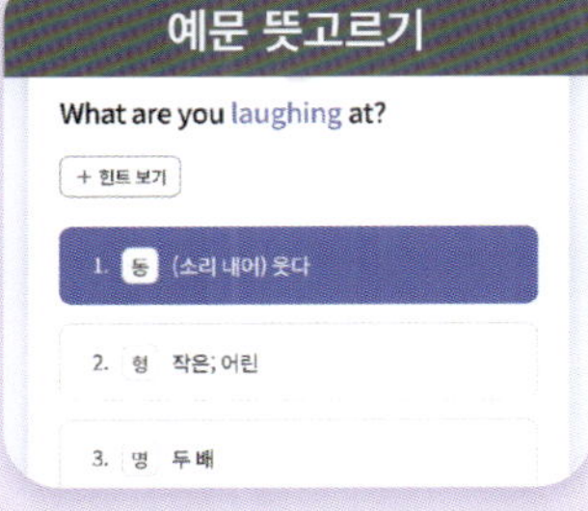

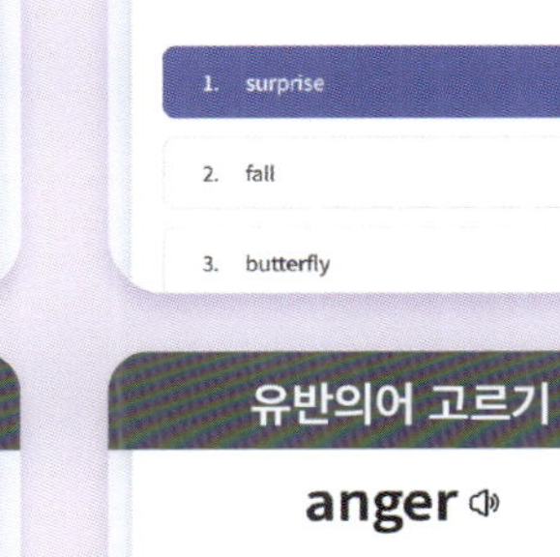

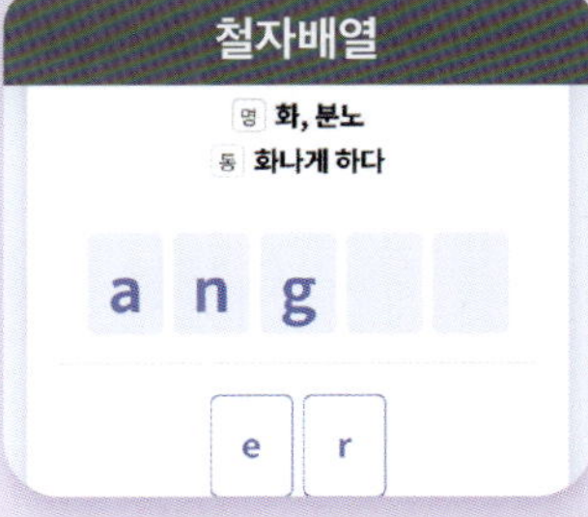

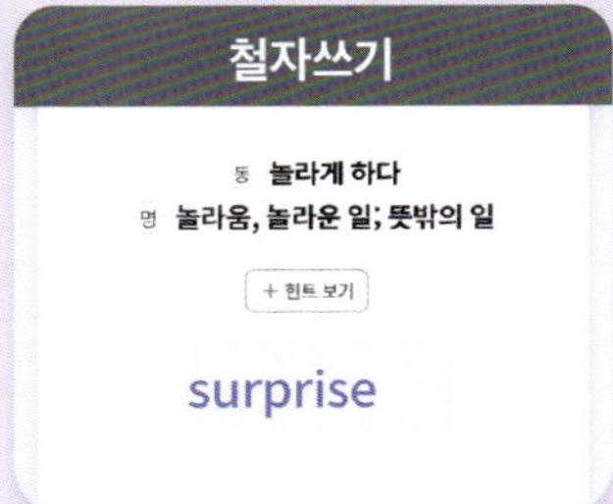

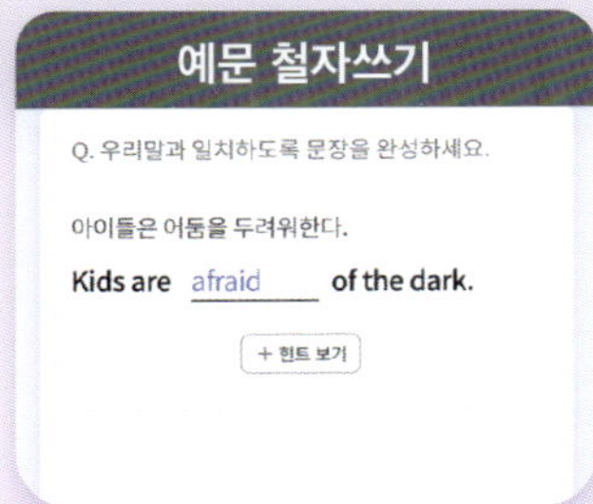

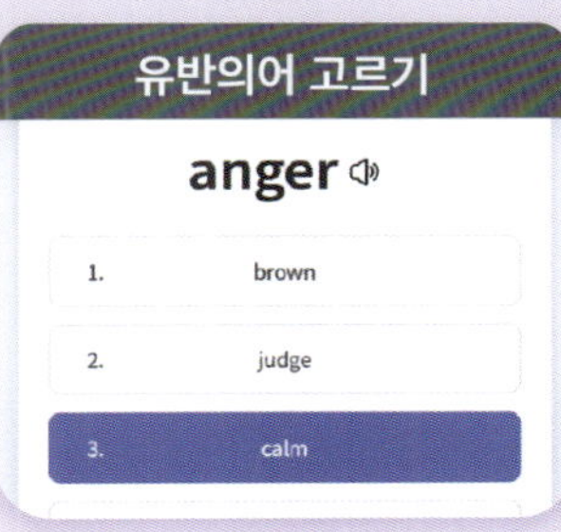

 암기모드를 선택하면, 최적의 문제 모드를 자동 추천!

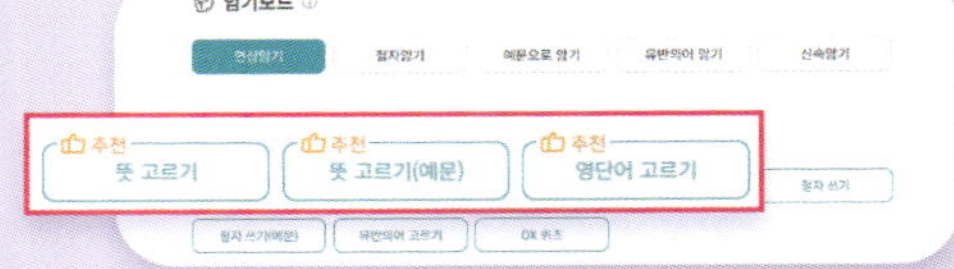

2. 자동 생성 단어장! 단어장만 복습하는 다양한 액티비티!

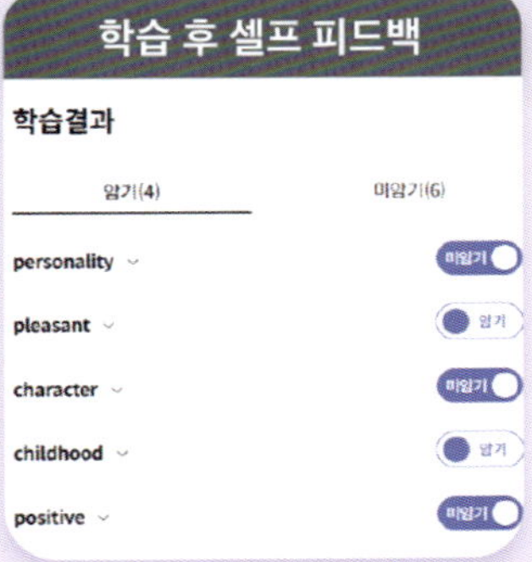

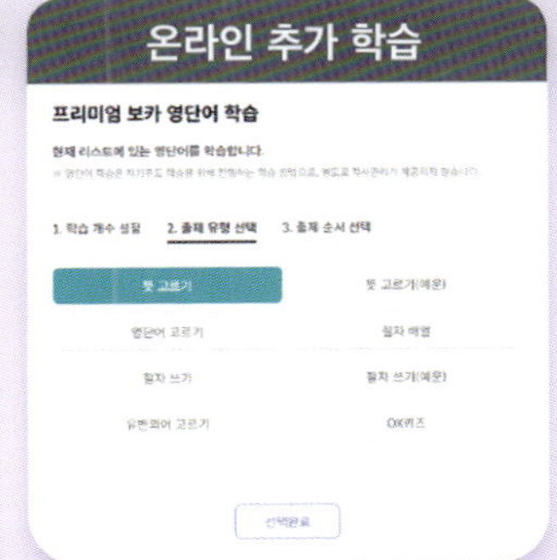

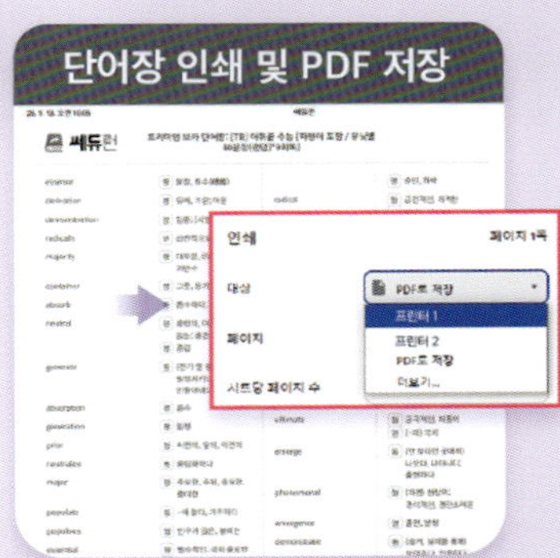

EGU 서술형 기초 세우기

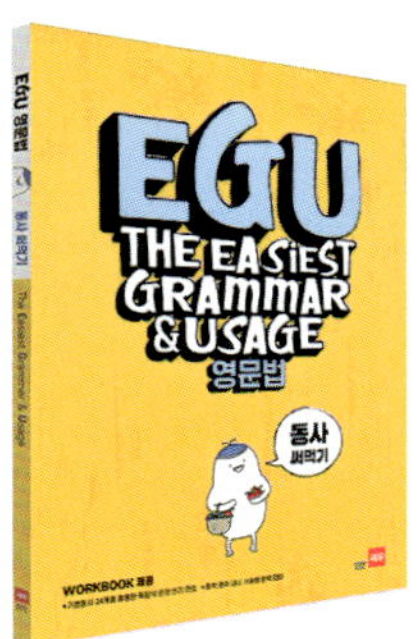

영단어&품사

서술형·문법의 기초가 되는
영단어와 품사 결합 학습

문장 형식

기본 동사 32개를 활용한
문장 형식별 학습

동사 써먹기

기본 동사 24개를 활용한
확장식 문장 쓰기 연습

EGU 서술형·문법 다지기

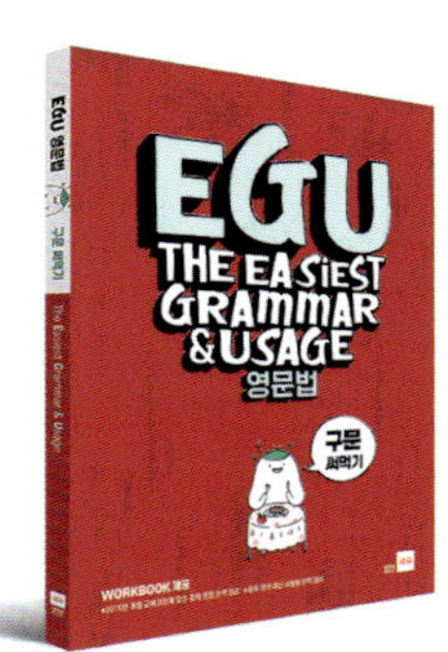

문법 써먹기

개정 교육 과정
중1 서술형·문법 완성

구문 써먹기

개정 교육 과정
중2, 중3 서술형·문법 완성

쎄듀북닷컴(www.cedubook.com)에서 부가 자료를 무료로 다운로드할 수 있습니다.

CEDU쎄듀

천일문

LEVEL 1

WORKBOOK

중등

WRITING

천일문

중등

WRiTiNG

Unit 01

be동사

배열 영작

[1-3] 우리말과 일치하도록 주어진 단어를 올바르게 배열하세요.

1
> 그는 타고난 가수이다.
> (is / a talented singer / he)

→ ____ .

2
> Brian과 나는 같은 축구팀에 있다.
> (and I / the same soccer team / are / on / Brian)

→ ____
____ .

3
> 그녀는 그 결과에 행복하지 않았다.
> (was / not / with the result / she / happy)

→ ____
____ .

대화문 완성

[4-6] 다음 대화의 빈칸에 알맞은 말을 쓰세요.
(부정형은 줄임말로 쓸 것)

4
> A: ____________ ____________ tired after
>   your long trip?
> B: Yes, I was. I was at home all day.

5
> A: Are you sleepy now?
> B: ____________, ____________ ____________ .
>   I want to take a rest.

6
> A: Is your cell phone in your pocket?
> B: ____________, ____________ ____________ .
>   It is on my desk.

주어진 단어로 영작

[7-9] 우리말과 일치하도록 주어진 단어를 사용하여 문장을 완성하세요. (필요시 단어를 추가하거나 형태를 바꿀 것)

7
> 이 장갑은 매우 따뜻하다.
> (be, these gloves, warm, very)

→ ____
____

8
> 걱정하지 마. 우리는 영화에 늦지 않았어.
> (be, for the movie, we, late)

→ Don't worry. ____________________________
____

9
> 그녀는 어제 나에게 화가 났니?
> (with me, she, be, angry)

→ ____
yesterday?

기출: 조건 영작

10 다음 대화를 읽고 〈조건〉에 맞게 우리말을 영작하세요.

> A: Were you in England two years ago?
> B: (1) 아니, 그렇지 않아. (no)
>   (2) 나는 한국에 있었어. (in Korea)

〈조건〉
· (1)은 3 단어, (2)는 4 단어로 쓸 것
· 각각 be동사와 주어진 단어를 사용할 것

(1) ____

(2) ____

---

talented 재능이 있는 result 결과 tired 피곤한, 지친 all day 하루 종일 take a rest 쉬다 pocket 주머니

Unit 02⁺

일반동사의 현재형과 과거형

빈칸 완성

[1-4] 우리말과 일치하도록 주어진 단어를 알맞은 형태로 고쳐 쓰세요.

1 그는 학교에서 수학을 가르친다. (teach)

→ He _____________ math at school.

2 나의 누나는 그녀의 도시락을 작은 가방에 가지고 다닌다. (carry)

→ My sister _____________ her lunchbox in a small bag.

3 나는 이번 주말에 가족 소풍을 계획했다. (plan)

→ I _____________ a family picnic this weekend.

4 그녀는 그녀의 반지를 안전한 곳에 보관했다. (keep)

→ She _____________ her ring in a safe place.

배열 영작

[5-7] 우리말과 일치하도록 주어진 단어를 올바르게 배열하세요. (필요시 형태를 바꿀 것)

5 Carol은 3개 국어를 한다.
(three languages / Carol / speak)

→ ____.

6 우리는 밖에서 이상한 소리를 들었다.
(a strange noise / hear / we)

→ ____
_________________________________ outside.

7 내 친구들과 나는 금요일 밤에 영화를 봤다.
(a movie / and / watch / I / my friends)

→ ____
_________________________ on Friday night.

주어진 단어로 영작

[8-10] 우리말과 일치하도록 주어진 단어를 사용하여 문장을 완성하세요. (필요시 형태를 바꿀 것)

8
그는 그의 예전 학교 친구들을 그리워한다.
(his friends, he, miss)

→ ____
_________________________ from his old school.

9
나는 지난주에 감기에 걸렸다.
(I, a cold, catch)

→ ____
last week.

10
Jamie와 나는 항상 다른 생각을 가지고 있다.
(ideas, I, have, different, and)

→ ____
all the time.

기출:보기에서 골라 영작

11 빈칸에 들어갈 말을 〈보기〉에서 골라 알맞은 형태로 쓰세요. (단, 현재시제로 쓸 것)

〈보기〉
wash   set   have   make

In our house, we all ⓐ _____________ our own jobs. Every morning, my dad ⓑ _____________ breakfast for everyone. My little sister ⓒ _____________ the table. My mom ⓓ _____________ the dishes. I take out the trash. We clean our home together.

---

lunchbox 도시락 language 언어, 말 strange 이상한, 낯선 catch a cold 감기에 걸리다 different 다른 take out (쓰레기를) 내놓다, 버리다

Unit 03 

정답 및 해설 p.28

일반동사의 부정문과 의문문

문장 전환

[1-3] 다음 각 문장을 괄호 안의 지시대로 바꿔 빈칸에 알맞은 말을 쓰세요.

1

He spends much time on his smartphone.
(부정문으로)

→ He ______________________
much time on his smartphone.

2

Last year, we went on a trip to Singapore.
(부정문으로)

→ Last year, we ______________________
on a trip to Singapore.

3

Sally's mom reads the newspaper daily.
(의문문으로)

→ ______________________
the newspaper daily?

주어진 단어로 영작

[4-6] 우리말과 일치하도록 주어진 단어를 사용하여 문장을 완성하세요.

4

나는 평일에는 컴퓨터 게임을 하지 않는다.
(computer games, play, I)

→ ______________________
______________________ on weekdays.

5

이 책은 내 소유가 아니다.
(belong, this book)

→ ______________________
______________________ to me.

6

그녀는 내 조언을 듣지 않았다.
(listen to, my advice, she)

→ ______________________

____

대화문 완성

[7-8] 주어진 단어를 사용하여 각 대화를 완성하세요.

7

A: ______________________ ______________________ ______________________
______________________ ? (broccoli, like)
B: No, I don't. I hate vegetables.

8

A: Did the students arrive at the bus
terminal on time?
B: ______________________, ______________________ ______________________.
(no) They missed the bus.

기출: 대화문 완성

9 우리말과 일치하도록 주어진 단어를 사용하여 다음의 대화를 완성하세요.

A: Let's get a birthday gift for Samuel.
B: That's a great idea.
A: (1) 그는 공상 과학 소설책을 좋아하니?
B: (2) 응, 맞아. He loves space stories.
A: Then, let's buy him a new sci-fi book!

(1) ______________________

____
(like, science fiction books)

(2) ______________________

spend (돈·시간을) 쓰다 daily 매일 weekday 평일 belong (to) ~의 소유이다 advice 조언, 충고 terminal (버스 등의) 터미널 on time 제때에
sci-fi (= science fiction) 공상 과학 소설

Unit 01 

현재진행형

[1-4] 우리말과 일치하도록 주어진 단어를 사용하여 문장을 완성하세요.

1

나는 내일 학교에 갈 가방을 싸고 있다.
(pack, my bag, I)

→ ______________________________________

______________________ for school tomorrow.

2

그녀는 그녀의 가족 그림을 그리고 있다.
(draw, she, a picture)

→ ______________________________________

______________________ of her family.

3

언덕 위로 해가 떠오르고 있다.
(rise, the Sun)

→ ______________________________________

over the hills.

4

그 학생들은 동물원으로의 현장 학습을 계획하고 있다.
(the students, a field trip, plan)

→ ______________________________________

______________________ to the zoo.

[5-8] 다음 주어진 단어를 사용해 괄호 안의 지시대로 문장을 완성하세요.

5

he, ride, his bike, be
(현재진행형 부정문으로)

→ ______________________________________

______________________ now.

6

on the phone, be, you, talk
(현재진행형 의문문으로)

→ ______________________________________

______________________ now?

7

stop, the cars, be
(현재진행형 부정문으로)

→ ______________________________________

______________________ at the red light.

8

our team, win, be, the game
(현재진행형 의문문으로)

→ ______________________________________

____

9 다음 그림을 보고 주어진 단어를 사용하여 현재진행형으로 문장을 완성하세요.

(1)   (2)

(1) The cats ______________________________

______________________________________.

(on the sofa, sleep)

(2) She ______________________________

______________________________________.

(for lunch, a sandwich, make)

pack (짐을) 싸다, 꾸리다 rise (해, 달이) 뜨다 field trip 현장 학습

Unit 02 

미래 표현

○ 배열 영작

[1-5] 우리말과 일치하도록 주어진 단어를 올바르게 배열하세요.

1
> 나는 이번 주말에 내 방을 청소할 것이다.
> (clean / will / I / my room)

→ __________________________

__________________________ this weekend.

2
> 그녀는 오늘 학교에 버스를 타고 가지 않을 것이다.
> (not / the bus / will / take / she)

→ __________________________

__________________________ to school today.

3
> 너는 오늘 학급 회의에 올 거니?
> (to / will / the class meeting / you / come)

→ __________________________

__________________________ today?

4
> 우리는 내일 우리 이모를 찾아뵐 것이다.
> (to / we / our aunt / going / visit / are)

→ __________________________

__________________________ tomorrow.

5
> 시에서 이곳에 도서관을 지을 예정인가요?
> (a library / going / is / build / the city / to)

→ __________________________

__________________________ here?

○ 주어진 단어로 영작

[6-9] 우리말과 일치하도록 주어진 단어를 사용하여 문장을 완성하세요. (필요시 단어를 추가하거나 형태를 바꿀 것)

6
> Taylor는 저녁 식사로 피자를 주문할 것이다.
> (will, pizza, order)

→ __________________________ for dinner.

7
> 나는 파티에 그 드레스를 입지 않을 것이다.
> (the dress, will, wear, I)

→ __________________________

__________________________ to the party.

8
> 그들은 내일 일정을 바꾸지 않을 것이다.
> (going, they, change)

→ __________________________

__________________________ tomorrow's schedule.

9
> 그는 곧 새로운 일을 시작할 예정이니?
> (a new job, he, going, start)

→ __________________________

__________________________ soon?

기출: 조건 영작

10 다음 대화를 읽고 〈조건〉에 맞게 우리말을 영작하세요.

> A: What will you do at the school festival?
> B: 나는 한국의 전통 간식을 만들 거야.
>   Then, I'll sell them to introduce our culture.
> A: That's a great idea!

> 〈조건〉
> • 6 단어로 쓸 것
> • Korean traditional snacks, make를 사용할 것

→ __________________________

order 주문하다 schedule 일정, 스케줄 introduce 소개하다 traditional 전통의, 전통적인

can, may

◉ 배열 영작

[1-3] 우리말과 일치하도록 주어진 단어를 올바르게 배열하세요.

1

> 그는 복잡한 퍼즐을 빨리 풀 수 있다.
> (solve / can / complex puzzles / he)

→ ______________________________________

______________________________ quickly.

2

> 볼륨을 줄여주시겠어요?
> (the volume / you / turn down / can)

→ ______________________________________

______________________________ ?

3

> 너는 도서관에서 전화통화를 하면 안 된다.
> (talk / not / may / on the phone / you)

→ ______________________________________

______________________________ in the library.

◉ 보기에서 골라 영작

[4-6] 우리말과 일치하도록 〈보기〉에서 알맞은 단어를 골라 can 또는 may와 함께 문장을 완성하세요.

> 〈보기〉
> close   swim   borrow

4 나는 바다에서 수영할 수 있다.

→ I ______________ ______________ in the ocean.

5 당신의 펜을 잠깐 빌려도 될까요?

→ ______________ I ______________ your pen for a moment?

6 그 가게는 오늘 일찍 문을 닫을지도 모른다.

→ The store ______________ ______________ early today.

◉ 주어진 단어로 영작

[7-9] 우리말과 일치하도록 주어진 단어와 can 또는 may를 사용하여 문장을 완성하세요.
(필요시 단어를 추가하거나 형태를 바꿀 것)

7

> Tom에 대한 그 소문은 사실이 아닐지도 모른다.
> (true, be)

→ The rumor about Tom ______________

______________________________ .

8

> 제가 메뉴 좀 봐도 될까요?
> (the menu, take a look at)

→ ______________________________________

____

9

> 나는 그녀의 이름을 기억할 수 없다.
> (her name, remember)

→ ______________________________________

____

기출: 문맥에 맞게 영작

10 우리말과 일치하도록 주어진 단어와 알맞은 조동사를 사용하여 문장을 완성하세요.

> My favorite animals are cheetahs. They have beautiful spots on their bodies. (1) 그것들은 매우 빠르게 달릴 수 있다. (2) But 그것들은 장거리를 빨리 달리지 못한다.

(1) ______________________________________

(very fast, run)

(2) But ______________________________________

for long distances. (run, fast)

---

complex 복잡한   volume 음량   turn down (소리 등을) 낮추다   for a moment 잠시   rumor 소문   take a look (at) (~을) 한번 보다, 살펴보다   spot 점, 반점   distance 거리

Unit 02+

정답 및 해설 p.29

must, have to, should

[1-5] 우리말과 일치하도록 〈보기〉에서 알맞은 단어를 골라 주어진 조동사와 함께 문장을 완성하세요. (필요시 형태를 바꿀 것)

〈보기〉

wear	arrive	buy	wait	lie

1 우리는 공항에 오전 10시까지 도착해야 한다. (must)

→ We ________ ________ at the airport by 10 a.m.

2 너는 안전을 위해 헬멧을 써야 한다. (have to)

→ You ________ ________ ________ a helmet for safety.

3 너는 네 부모님께 거짓말을 해서는 안 된다. (must)

→ You ________ ________ ________ to your parents.

4 그녀는 그녀의 차례를 기다려야 한다. (have to)

→ She ________ ________ ________ her turn.

5 너는 새 책을 살 필요 없어. 내 것을 빌려줄게. (have to)

→ You ________ ________ ________ ________ a new book. I'll lend you mine.

[6-9] 우리말과 일치하도록 주어진 단어를 사용하여 문장을 완성하세요. (필요시 형태를 바꿀 것)

6 당신은 당신의 신분증을 보여주셔야 합니다.
(must, your ID card, show, you)

→ ________

7 우리는 음식을 낭비해서는 안 된다.
(should, food, we, waste)

→ ________

8 나의 가족은 아버지의 일 때문에 새로운 도시로 이사를 가야 했다.
(to a new city, move, my family, have)

→ ________ for my father's job.

9 나의 엄마는 오늘 저녁 식사를 요리할 필요가 없으시다.
(dinner, my mom, have, cook)

→ ________ today.

10 다음 대화를 읽고 〈조건〉에 맞게 우리말을 영작하세요.

A: What should I wear for the field trip tomorrow?
B: (1) 너는 내일 교복을 입을 필요가 없어.
   (2) 너는 편안한 옷을 입어야 해. We're going to have sports activities.

〈조건〉
- must not, must, don't have to 중 하나를 사용할 것
- 주어진 단어를 사용할 것

(1) ________ tomorrow.
(your school uniforms, wear)

(2) ________. (comfortable clothes, wear)

airport 공항 safety 안전 turn 차례 lend 빌려주다 ID (= identification) card 신분증 waste 낭비하다 school uniform 교복 comfortable 편안한

[1-3] 우리말과 일치하도록 주어진 단어를 올바르게 배열하세요.

1

나는 높은 산들을 오를 수 있다.
(climb / can / mountains / I / tall)

→ ___________________________________.

___________________________________.

2

너는 여기서 사진을 찍어선 안 된다.
(not / a picture / you / take / must / here)

→ ___________________________________

___________________________________.

3

소라는 방과 후에 피아노를 연습해야 한다.
(practice / has / the piano / Sora / to)

→ ___________________________________

___________________________________ after school.

[4-7] 우리말과 일치하도록 주어진 단어를 사용하여 빈칸에 알맞은 말을 쓰세요. (필요시 형태를 바꿀 것)

4

내 남동생과 나는 심한 감기로 아팠다.
(be, sick)

→ My brother and I ___________
___________ with bad colds.

5

Jim은 누나와 함께 학교에 간다.
(go to school)

→ Jim ___________ ___________
___________ with his sister.

6

우리 아빠는 오늘 아침 9시에 집을 나가셨다.
(leave, home)

→ Our dad ___________ ___________
at 9 a.m. this morning.

7

그들은 방과 후에 자전거를 탈 예정이다. (ride)

→ They ___________ ___________
___________ ___________ bikes
after school.

[8-10] 우리말과 일치하도록 주어진 단어를 사용하여 문장을 완성하세요. (필요시 단어를 추가하거나 형태를 바꿀 것)

8

그녀는 주말마다 그녀의 개를 씻긴다.
(her dog, wash)

→ ___________________________________

___________________________________ every weekend.

9

Aaron과 나는 지금 그림을 그리고 있다.
(a picture, draw, and)

→ ___________________________________

___________________________________ now.

10

나는 오늘 밤에 TV를 보지 않을 것이다.
(will, TV, watch)

→ ___________________________________

___________________________________ tonight.

[11-14] 다음 각 문장을 괄호 안의 지시대로 바꿔 쓰세요.

11

Mr. Kim is a firefighter. (의문문으로)

→ _________________________________

____

12

He takes a nap in his room. (현재진행형으로)

→ _________________________________

____

13

I eat breakfast at eight-thirty. (부정문으로)

→ _________________________________

____

14

She went to the jazz concert. (의문문으로)

→ _________________________________

____

[15-18] 주어진 단어를 사용하여 각 대화를 완성하세요.
(단, 완전한 문장으로 쓸 것)

15

A: _________________________________
your homework? (finish)
B: Yes, I did. Can I go out and play now?

16

A: Lily, is your favorite dessert cheesecake?
B: _________________________________. (no)
My favorite dessert is pudding.

17

A: What is Sujin doing in the garden now?
B: She _________________________________

_________________________________.

(pick, some vegetables)

18

A: What are you and Tom going to do this
weekend?
B: We _________________________________

_________________________________.

(go shopping)

[19-21] 다음 대화의 빈칸에 들어갈 알맞은 말을 〈보기〉에서
골라 쓰세요. (단, 한 번씩만 사용할 것)

〈보기〉
should   can   may

19

A: _________________ you pass me some salt?
B: Sure. Here you are. Do you need anything
else?

20

A: I accidentally broke Minho's cell phone.
He's really mad at me.
B: Oh no, that's too bad.
You _____________ apologize to him.

21

A: _____________ I play computer games
for an hour?
B: No, you must clean your room first.

[22-25] 다음 각 문장에서 어법상 **틀린** 부분을 찾아 바르게
고쳐 쓰세요.

22 My parents doesn't drive a car.

_______________ → _______________

23 I see my friend at the park last night.

_______________ → _______________

24 A bird is fly in the sky right now.

_______________ → _______________

25 Will the weather is fine soon?

_______________ → _______________

고난도

26 이번 주 일정표를 보고, 〈보기〉와 같이 문장을
완성하세요.

This Week's Schedule	
Monday	visit the art museum
(1) Tuesday	make a cake for Mom
(2) Wednesday (Today)	swim in the pool
(3) Thursday	be in the movie theater

〈보기〉
I visited the art museum on Monday.

(1) I _______________
_______________ on Tuesday.

(2) I _______________
_______________ now.

(3) I _______________
_______________ on Thursday.

27 다음 표를 보고 미나와 태민이의 어머니가 남긴 메모를
〈조건〉에 맞게 완성하세요.

Things to do	Mina	Taemin
해야 할 일	(1) 영어 공부하기	(2) 고양이 씻기기
할 필요가 없는 일	(3) 거실 청소하기	(4) 시장 가기
해서는 안 되는 일	(5) 컴퓨터 게임하기	

〈조건〉
• 〈보기〉에서 알맞은 말을 골라 사용할 것
• 주어진 조동사를 사용할 것

〈보기〉
play computer games　　study English
wash the cat　　go to the market
clean the living room

　　Sorry, kids.
I'm out for a meeting, and I'll be back by
10 p.m.

　　Mina, you (1) _______________
_______________. (should)

Taemin, you (2) _______________
_______________. (have to)

Mina, you (3) _______________
_______________. (have to)

Taemin, you (4) _______________
_______________. (have to)

　　And remember, you two (5) _______________
_______________. (must)

Unit 01 + 명사

정답 및 해설 p.30

배열 영작

[1-5] 우리말과 일치하도록 주어진 단어를 올바르게 배열하세요.
(필요시 형태를 바꿀 것)

1
> 나는 오래된 상자에서 손목시계 두 개를 발견했다.
> (watch / found / two / I)

→ ____________________________________

____________________________ in an old box.

2
> 그녀는 그녀의 아이들을 위해 세 편의 이야기를 읽어 주었다.
> (story / read / three / she)

→ ____________________________________

____________________________ for her children.

3
> 그는 그의 SNS에 다섯 장의 사진을 올렸다.
> (photo / posted / he / five)

→ ____________________________________

____________________________ on his social media.

4
> 오늘 하늘에 구름이 없다.
> (isn't / there / cloud / in the sky / a)

→ ____________________________________

____________________________ today.

5
> Wi-Fi에 문제가 있나요?
> (problem / with the Wi-Fi / there / is / a)

→ ____________________________________

____________________________ ?

보기에서 골라 영작

[6-8] 우리말과 일치하도록 〈보기〉에서 알맞은 말을 골라 주어진 단어를 사용하여 문장을 완성하세요.
(단, 수를 나타내는 말은 영문으로 쓸 것)

> 〈보기〉
> piece of   loaf of   bottle of

6
> 그녀는 냉장고에서 주스 한 병을 꺼냈다.
> (take, juice, she)

→ ____________________________________

from the refrigerator.

7
> 엄마는 바나나 빵 세 덩이를 구우셨다.
> (banana bread, Mom, bake)

→ ____________________________________

____________________________ .

8
> 책상 위에 다섯 장의 종이가 있다. (there, paper, five)

→ ____________________________________

____________________________ on the desk.

기출: 그림 영작

9 다음 그림을 보고 주어진 단어를 사용하여 문장을 완성하세요. (단, 현재시제로 쓸 것)

(1) ____________________________________
(picture, a, there, the wall, on)

(2) ____________________________________
(under, mouse, there, two, the table)

post 올리다, 게시하다; 우편물 social media 소셜 미디어, SNS Wi-Fi 와이파이 refrigerator 냉장고

Unit 02

인칭대명사와 재귀대명사

빈칸 완성

[1-3] 우리말과 일치하도록 빈칸에 들어갈 알맞은 말을 쓰세요.

1
> 그는 어제 내 영어 교과서를 빌렸다.

→ ______________ borrowed ______________
English textbook yesterday.

2
> 그들은 경기 중에 우리를 응원했다.

→ ______________ cheered for ______________
during the game.

3
> 이것은 내 코트가 아니다. 그것은 그의 것이다.

→ This isn't ______________ coat.
It's ______________.

배열 영작

[4-5] 우리말과 일치하도록 주어진 단어를 올바르게 배열하세요.

4
> 사람들은 자기 자신에 대해 잘 알지 못한다.
> (know / people / don't / about / themselves)

→ ______________________________________
______________________________ very well.

5
> 우리는 스트레스로부터 우리 자신을 보호해야 한다.
> (from stress / protect / we / ourselves /
> should)

→ ______________________________________
______________________________.

주어진 단어로 영작

[6-8] 우리말과 일치하도록 주어진 단어를 사용하여 문장을
완성하세요. (필요시 형태를 바꿀 것)

6
> 그의 강아지는 그를 어디든 따라다닌다.
> (follow, puppy, everywhere)

→ ______________________________________
____

7
> 너는 네 자신을 잘 대해 주어야 한다.
> (well, treat, should)

→ ______________________________________
____

8
> 매년 그녀는 새로운 목표로 자기 자신에게 도전한다.
> (a new goal, challenge, with)

→ Every year, ____________________________
____

기출: 문맥에 맞게 영작

9 우리말과 일치하도록 주어진 단어를 사용해 다음 대화를
완성하세요.

> A: Did you take this photo yourself?
> B: Yes, I did. 나는 사진을 통해 나 자신을 표현해
>   보았어.
> A: It's really beautiful!
> B: Thank you.

→ ______________________________________
through the photo. (express)

---

textbook 교과서 cheer for ∼을 응원하다 stress 스트레스 protect 보호하다 follow 따라가다[오다] everywhere 어디에나 treat 대하다 challenge ∼에게 도전하다
oneself 직접 through ∼을 통해 express 표현하다

Unit 03

지시대명사와 부정대명사

배열 영작

[1-3] 우리말과 일치하도록 주어진 단어를 올바르게 배열하세요.

1
> 나는 어제 이 운동화를 샀다.
> (bought / sneakers / I / these)

→ _______________________________________

   yesterday.

2
> 해변까지 차로 30분 걸린다.
> (to the beach / it / thirty minutes / takes)

→ _______________________________________

_______________________________________ by car.

3
> 나는 나의 오래된 코트에서 돈을 좀 찾았다.
> (my old coat / money / in / found / I / some)

→ _______________________________________

_______________________________________ .

어법 오류 수정

[4-6] 다음 각 문장에서 어법상 틀린 부분을 찾아 바르게 고쳐 쓰세요.

4 Look! That mountains are beautiful.

_______________ → _______________

5 Kate, someone are looking for you.

_______________ → _______________

6 There aren't some cookies in the jar.

_______________ → _______________

주어진 단어로 영작

[7-9] 우리말과 일치하도록 주어진 단어를 사용하여 문장을 완성하세요. (필요시 형태를 바꿀 것)

7
> 한국에서는 8월에 매우 더워진다.
> (really hot, get)

→ _______________________________________

_______________________ in August in Korea.

8
> 아무도 그의 이야기를 믿지 않는다.
> (believe, his story, nobody)

→ _______________________________________

____

9
> 근처에 괜찮은 식당이 있나요?
> (good restaurants, any, there)

→ _______________________________________

_______________________________ nearby?

기출: 문맥에 맞게 영작

10 다음 글을 읽고 우리말과 일치하도록 주어진 단어를 사용해 문장을 완성하세요.

> (1) <u>밖에 비가 와요.</u> I like rainy days. I usually read books on rainy days. I like the sound of raindrops, too. (2) <u>여러분은 비 오는 날에 가장 좋아하는 활동이 있나요?</u>

(1) _______________________________________

   (outside, rainy)

(2) _______________________________________

_______________________ for rainy days?

   (favorite activities, have, any)

---

sneakers 운동화 look for ~을 찾다 jar (잼 등을 담아 두는) 병 get (어떤 상태가) 되다 nearby 근처에 raindrop 빗방울 activity 활동

Unit 01 형용사

○─ 배열 영작

[1-3] 우리말과 일치하도록 주어진 단어를 올바르게 배열하세요.

1
그녀는 시장에서 신선한 야채들을 좀 샀다.
(bought / vegetables / fresh / she / some)

→ ____________________________________

____________________________ from the market.

2
Aiden은 매일 그의 책상을 깨끗하게 유지한다.
(keeps / desk / Aiden / clean / his)

→ ____________________________________

____________________________ every day.

3
그는 디저트로 달콤한 무언가를 원했다.
(for dessert / sweet / he / something / wanted)

→ ____________________________________

____________________________________ .

○─ 보기에서 골라 영작

[4-7] 우리말과 일치하도록 〈보기〉에서 알맞은 말을 골라 주어진 단어를 사용하여 문장을 완성하세요. (단, 한 번씩만 쓸 것)

〈보기〉
a few   much   few   little

4
그 병에는 물이 거의 없다.
(be, water, there)

→ ____________________________________

____________________________ in the bottle.

5
Jay는 새 신발을 사는 데 많은 돈을 썼다.
(money, spend)

→ ____________________________________

____________________________ on the new shoes.

6
White 씨는 오늘 아침에 몇 통의 이메일을 받았다.
(get, email, Mr. White)

→ ____________________________________

____________________________ this morning.

7
오늘 수업을 이해한 학생이 거의 없었다.
(understand, student, today's lesson)

→ ____________________________________

____

기출: 보기에서 골라 영작

8 우리말과 일치하도록 〈보기〉에서 알맞은 말을 골라 주어진 단어를 사용하여 대화를 완성하세요.
(필요시 형태를 바꿀 것)

A: Mom, I invited my friends to today's party.
B: (1) <u>너는 파티에 많은 손님들을 초대했니?</u>
A: No. (2) <u>몇 명의 친구들만 올 거예요.</u>
B: OK. I'll prepare some delicious food for them.
A: Thank you, Mom.

〈보기〉
many   much   a few   a little

(1) ____________________________________

____________________________ to the party?
(do, guest, invite)

(2) Just ____________________________________ .
(come, friend, will)

dessert 디저트, 후식 sweet 달콤한 lesson 수업; 과 prepare 준비하다 guest 손님, 하객

Unit 02 + 부사

[1-3] 우리말과 일치하도록 주어진 단어를 올바르게 배열하세요.

1
해변에서의 일몰은 너무 아름다웠다.
(so / was / the sunset / beautiful)

→ ______________________________
______________________________ at the beach.

2
어젯밤에 눈이 아주 많이 내렸다.
(heavily / fell / very / the snow)

→ ______________________________
______________________________ last night.

3
놀랍게도, 아기는 오늘 빨리 잠이 들었다.
(fell / quickly / the baby / asleep / surprisingly)

→ ______________, ______________
______________________________ today.

[4-7] 우리말과 일치하도록 〈보기〉에서 알맞은 말을 골라 주어진 단어를 사용하여 문장을 완성하세요.
(단, 한 번씩만 쓸 것)

〈보기〉
always   usually   often   never

4
Jake는 수업 중에 선생님께 자주 질문을 한다.
(questions, ask)

→ ______________________________
______________________________ of teachers in class.

5
대부분의 학생들은 보통 오전 9시까지 학교에 온다.
(come, most students, to school)

→ ______________________________
______________________________ by 9 a.m.

6
나의 여동생은 항상 모든 것에 대해 궁금해한다.
(my little sister, curious, be)

→ ______________________________
______________________________ about everything.

7
너는 네 여권을 절대 잃어버려서는 안 된다.
(lose, must, your passport)

→ ______________________________
____

8   다음 글을 읽고 〈조건〉에 맞게 우리말을 영작하세요.

On weekends, Minho wakes up at 8 in the morning. (1) 아침 식사 후, 그는 때때로 그의 강아지 Molly와 공원에 간다. In the afternoon, he usually helps his mom or dad with chores. (2) 그는 그의 주말을 바쁘게 보낸다.

〈조건〉
• 주어진 단어를 사용할 것
• 필요시 단어의 형태를 바꿀 것

(1) After breakfast, ______________________________
______________________________ with his puppy, Molly.
(to the park, go, sometimes)

(2) ______________________________
____
(busy, weekends, spend)

---

sunset 일몰 heavily 아주 많이 fall asleep 잠들다 be curious about ~에 대해 궁금해하다 lose 잃어버리다 passport 여권 chores 집안일, 잡일

Unit 03 비교급과 최상급

◦ **배열 영작**

[1-3] 우리말과 일치하도록 주어진 단어를 올바르게 배열하세요.

1
빨간색 사과들이 초록색 사과들보다 더 달다.
(sweeter / the green ones / are / than)

→ The red apples _______________________

_______________________ .

2
Noah는 그의 남동생보다 피아노를 더 잘 친다.
(his / the piano / than / plays / brother / better)

→ Noah _______________________

_______________________ .

3
이것이 그 가게에 있는 가장 최신 헤드폰이다.
(headphones / in the shop / the / are / newest)

→ These _______________________

_______________________ .

◦ **주어진 단어로 영작**

[4-7] 우리말과 일치하도록 주어진 단어를 사용하여 문장을 완성하세요. (필요시 형태를 바꿀 것)

4
Tony의 책가방은 내 것보다 더 무겁다.
(be, mine, heavy, Tony's backpack)

→ _______________________

____

5
오늘 날씨가 어제보다 더 덥다.
(yesterday's, today's weather, hot, be)

→ _______________________

____

6
이 산은 동아시아에서 가장 높다.
(high, this, in East Asia, mountain, be)

→ _______________________

____

7
Tim은 그의 팀 동료들 중 가장 열심히 훈련한다.
(hard, train, of his teammates)

→ _______________________

____

◦ **기출: 도표 영작**

8 다음 표를 보고 우리말과 일치하도록 〈조건〉에 맞게 문장을 완성하세요.

<Jack's Bakery>

	Chocolate Cake	Mango Cake	Cheese-cake
인기	★★★	★★	★
가격	$27	$30	$24

〈조건〉
• 현재시제를 사용할 것
• 주어진 단어를 사용할 것

(1) Chocolate cake _______________________

_______________________ of the three.

(popular, be)

(2) Mango cake _______________________

cheesecake. (be, popular)

(3) Cheesecake _______________________

chocolate cake. (be, cheap)

headphones (복수형) 헤드폰 Asia 아시아 (대륙) train 훈련하다 teammate 팀 동료

명령문, 제안문, 감탄문

○● 배열 영작

[1-6] 우리말과 일치하도록 주어진 단어를 올바르게 배열하세요.

1
> 내일 수업에 네 공책을 가져와라.
> (your / to class / bring / notebook)

→ _______________________________________

    tomorrow.

2
> 박물관에 있는 예술품들을 만지지 마라.
> (in the museum / touch / the artworks / don't)

→ _______________________________________

_______________________________________ .

3
> 뒷마당에서 바비큐 파티를 하자.
> (a barbecue party / have / let's)

→ _______________________________________

    in the backyard.

4
> 우리 독서 동아리를 시작해 보는 건 어때?
> (start / why / a book club / we / don't)

→ _______________________________________

_______________________________________ ?

5
> 그 소파는 정말 편안하구나!
> (the sofa / how / is / comfortable)

→ _______________________________________

_______________________________________ !

6
> 그는 정말 재능 있는 가수구나!
> (a / singer / is / what / he / talented)

→ _______________________________________

_______________________________________ !

○● 주어진 단어로 영작

[7-9] 우리말과 일치하도록 주어진 단어를 사용하여 문장을 완성하세요. (필요시 단어를 추가하거나 형태를 바꿀 것)

7
> 그것은 정말 귀여운 강아지이구나!
> (be, cute puppy, what, it)

→ _______________________________________

8
> 시간이 정말 빨리 지나가는구나!
> (the time, quickly, how, fly)

→ _______________________________________

9
> 우리와 함께 콘서트에 가는 게 어때?
> (how, go, to the concert, about)

→ _______________________________________

_______________________________________ with us?

기출: 조건 영작

10 다음 대화를 읽고 〈조건〉에 맞게 우리말을 영작하세요.

> A: (1) 외출할 때는 네 방의 불을 끄렴.
> B: Okay, Mom.
> A: (2) And 오늘 가족 모임을 잊지 마렴.
> B: Sure, I won't forget.

> 〈조건〉
> • 주어진 단어를 사용할 것
> • 필요한 경우 단어를 추가할 것

(1) _______________________________________

_______________________________________ when you go out.

    (the light, in your room, turn off)

(2) And _______________________________________

_______________________________________ today.

    (the family gathering, forget)

museum 박물관, 미술관 artwork 예술품, 미술품 barbecue 바비큐(파티) backyard 뒷마당 go out 외출하다, (놀러) 나가다 turn off (불 등을) 끄다 gathering 모임

Unit 02+

의문사 의문문

◯━ 배열 영작

[1-5] 우리말과 일치하도록 주어진 단어를 올바르게 배열하세요.

1

> 네 롤 모델은 누구니?
> (role model / is / your / who)

→ ____________________________________

____________________________________ ?

2

> 그녀는 크리스마스 선물로 무엇을 원하니?
> (want / does / what / she)

→ ____________________________________

____________________ for her Christmas gift?

3

> 너는 일주일에 얼마나 자주 운동을 하니?
> (you / how / exercise / do / often)

→ ____________________________________

____________________________ in a week?

4

> 너는 어떤 종류의 영화를 좋아하니?
> (kind / like / do / what / you / movie / of)

→ ____________________________________

____________________________________ ?

5

> 우리는 가장 가까운 버스 정류장을 어디에서 찾을 수 있을까요?
> (bus stop / can / find / the nearest / we / where)

→ ____________________________________

____________________________________ ?

◯━ 대화문 완성

[6-8] 주어진 단어를 사용하여 각 대화의 질문을 완성하세요. (필요시 형태를 바꿀 것)

6

> A: ____________ ____________ ____________
> ____________ ____________ hard?
> (English, study, Jim)
> B: Because he plans to study abroad.

7

> A: ____________ ____________ ____________
> ____________ ____________ ?
> (finish, the fireworks)
> B: They just finished five minutes ago.

8

> A: ____________ ____________ ____________
> ____________ on the chair?
> (be, it, jacket)
> B: It's Elly's. She left it there this morning.

기출: 대화문 완성

9 우리말과 일치하도록 주어진 단어를 사용하여 다음의 대화를 완성하세요. (필요시 단어를 추가할 것)

> A: (1) 네 휴가 계획은 무엇이니?
> B: I'll go to Jeju Island. It's my favorite place.
> A: (2) 너는 그 섬을 왜 좋아하니?
> B: Because it has beautiful beaches and mountains.

(1) ____________________________________

____

(for the vacation, plan)

(2) ____________________________________

(that island, like)

---

role model 롤 모델, 본보기 near (거리상으로) 가까운 study abroad 유학 가다 fireworks (복수형) 불꽃놀이 leave ~을 두고 오다, 남기다; 떠나다 island 섬

Unit 03 

부가의문문

[1-5] 우리말과 일치하도록 빈칸에 알맞은 말을 넣어 부가의문문을 완성하세요.

1

너 지금 졸리구나, 그렇지 않니?

→ You are sleepy now, ________________?

2

뮤지컬은 저녁 7시에 시작해, 그렇지 않니?

→ The musical starts at 7 in the evening, ________________?

3

Emily는 오늘 점심을 먹지 않았어, 그렇지?

→ Emily didn't have lunch today, ________________?

4

너희 형은 아직 차를 운전할 수 없어, 그렇지?

→ Your brother can't drive a car yet, ________________?

5

새로운 일식당에 가 보자, 그럴 거지?

→ Let's try the new Japanese restaurant, ________________?

[6-10] 우리말과 일치하도록 주어진 단어를 사용하여 부가의문문이 있는 문장을 완성하세요.

6

Anna는 너에게 화가 나 있어, 그렇지 않니? (be)

→ Anna ____________ angry with you, ____________ ____________?

7

우리는 오늘 숙제가 전혀 없어, 그렇지? (have)

→ We ____________ ____________ any homework today, ____________ ____________?

8

Ethan과 Lucas는 형제가 아니야, 그렇지? (be)

→ Ethan and Lucas ____________ brothers, ____________ ____________?

9

Davis 씨는 그의 집에 학생들을 초대했어, 그렇지 않니? (invite)

→ Mr. Davis ____________ the students to his house, ____________ ____________?

10

소금을 나에게 건네줘, 그럴 거지? (pass)

→ ____________ me the salt, ____________ ____________?

11 다음 대화를 읽고 〈조건〉에 맞게 우리말을 영작하세요.

A: Did you enjoy the comedy movie yesterday?
B: Yes, it was really fun.
  넌 그 영화를 보지 않았지, 그렇지?
A: Yes, I did. I laughed a lot, too.

〈조건〉
• 주어진 단어를 사용할 것
• 7 단어로 쓸 것

→ ________________________________,
________________________? (that movie, watch)

musical 뮤지컬 Japanese 일본의 be angry with ~에게 화나다 pass 건네주다; 지나가다, 통과하다 comedy movie 코미디 영화

○ 정답 및 해설 p.32

[1-3] 우리말과 일치하도록 주어진 단어를 올바르게 배열하세요.

1

공원에 이상한 누군가가 있었다.
(strange / there / someone / was)

→ _______________________________

_______________________________ at the park.

2

그녀는 매일 아침 커피 한 잔과 사과 한 개를 먹는다.
(apple / a / has / of / coffee / she / cup / an / and)

→ _______________________________

_______________________________ every morning.

3

정말 커다란 호수로구나!
(it / huge / is / what / a / lake)

→ _______________________________

_______________________________ !

[4-7] 우리말과 일치하도록 주어진 단어를 사용하여 빈칸에 알맞은 말을 쓰세요. (필요시 단어를 추가할 것)

4

기차에 많은 승객들이 있다. (passengers)

→ There are ___________ ___________
on the train.

5

Janet은 하루에 물을 거의 마시지 않는다. (water)

→ Janet drinks ___________ ___________
in a day.

6

우리는 겨울 방학에 특별한 계획이 하나도 없다.
(special plans)

→ We don't have ___________

___________ ___________ for winter
vacation.

7

우리는 우리 자신을 사랑해야 한다.
(love, should)

→ We ___________ ___________

___________ .

[8-10] 우리말과 일치하도록 주어진 단어를 사용하여 문장을 완성하세요. (필요시 단어를 추가할 것)

8

너의 충고는 나에게 항상 도움이 된다.
(helpful, your advice, always, be)

→ _______________________________

_______________________________ to me.

9

수업 중에 휴대 전화를 사용하지 마라.
(use, in class, your cell phone)

→ _______________________________

____

10

우리 함께 수학을 공부하는 게 어때?
(we, why, study, together, math)

→ _______________________________

____

[11-13] 다음 대화의 빈칸에 들어갈 알맞은 말을 〈보기〉에서 골라 쓰세요. (단, 한 번씩만 사용할 것)

〈보기〉
few   little   a few

11
A: Do you have many books in your room?
B: I have _______________ books,
   but not many.

12
A: Brian, you came early today!
B: Yes, there were _______________ cars
   on the road.

13
A: Can you help me with my science
   project?
B: Sorry, I have _______________ time
   today.

14 다음 그림을 보고 주어진 단어를 사용하여 〈보기〉와 같이 문장을 완성하세요.

〈보기〉
There is a box next to the bed. (box)

(1) _______________________________________
   in the box. (baseball)

(2) _______________________________________
   next to the desk. (two, chair)

(3) _______________________________________
   on the desk. (paper, sheet, three)

[15-18] 주어진 단어를 사용하여 각 대화를 완성하세요.

15
A: Which one is my gift?
B: The red box is _______________ (you),
   and the blue one is _______________. (I)

16
A: Do you play sports often?
B: I __________ _____________ __________,
   but not every week.
   (tennis, sometimes, play)

17
A: __________ __________ __________
   __________ the key? (leave)
   I can't find it.
B: I put it on the table.

18
A: __________ __________ __________
   __________ __________ __________
   __________? (kind, food, want)
B: Umm, spaghetti. It's my favorite.

19 다음 표를 보고 각 도시의 날짜와 그날의 날씨를 순서대로 쓰세요.

	Seoul	London
Date	November 17th	November 16th
Weather	rainy and cold	sunny and clear

(1) Seoul
   → _______________________________________.
   → _______________________________ today.

(2) London
   → _______________________________________.
   → _______________________________ today.

[20-24] 다음 각 문장에서 어법상 <u>틀린</u> 부분을 찾아 바르게 고쳐 쓰세요.

20 Nick talked to his friend quiet.

____________________ → ____________________

21 My brother and I drink never soda.

____________________ → ____________________

22 How cute is the baby!

____________________ → ____________________

23 Tom and Brian are brothers, don't they?

____________________ → ____________________

24 Is there wrong anything with your bicycle?

____________________ → ____________________

25 다음 표를 보고 〈조건〉에 맞게 문장을 완성하세요.

	Horse	Elephant	Bear	Giraffe
Height (m)	1.6	3	2	5
Weight (kg)	600	5,000	800	1,300

〈조건〉
• 주어진 단어를 사용해 현재시제로 쓸 것
• 비교급 또는 최상급을 사용할 것

(1) The horse ____________________

____________________ the bear. (light, be)

(2) The elephant ____________________

____________________ animal of all. (heavy, be)

(3) The bear ____________________

____________________ the giraffe. (short, be)

26 다음 대화의 흐름이 자연스럽도록 〈조건〉에 맞게 (1)~(4)에 알맞은 의문사 의문문을 쓰세요.

〈조건〉
• 각 단어 수에 맞게 쓸 것
• 의문사 what, how, why, where를 한 번씩만 쓸 것
• travel, do, visit, choose를 반드시 사용할 것

A: What is your hobby?
B: I like traveling!
A: (1) ____________________

____
(5 단어)
B: I usually travel every month.
A: Cool! (2) ____________________

____________________ last month?
(4 단어)
B: I visited Busan with my family.
A: (3) ____________________

____________________ for your trip?
(5 단어)
B: Because it has nice beaches.
A: I see. (4) ____________________

____________________ there?
(4 단어)
B: I swam in the sea and enjoyed fireworks at night.

Unit 01

SVC(2형식)

배열 영작

[1-4] 우리말과 일치하도록 주어진 단어를 올바르게 배열하세요.

1 날씨가 추워졌다.
(cold / got / the weather)

→ ____________________

____________________ .

2 네 목소리는 전화기에서 낮게 들린다.
(low / your voice / sounds)

→ ____________________

on the phone.

3 바닥이 매우 미끄럽게 느껴진다.
(very / the floor / slippery / feels)

→ ____________________

____________________ .

4 그의 얼굴은 나에게 상당히 낯익어 보인다.
(familiar / his face / quite / looks)

→ ____________________

____________________ to me.

주어진 단어로 영작

[5-8] 우리말과 일치하도록 주어진 단어를 사용하여 문장을 완성하세요. (필요시 형태를 바꿀 것)

5 이 쿠키들은 달콤한 냄새가 난다.
(smell, sweet, these cookies)

→ ____________________

____

6 나는 그 시험 전에 매우 긴장되었다.
(very, become, nervous)

→ ____________________

before the test.

7 레모네이드는 너무 신맛이 났다.
(the lemonade, sour, taste, too)

→ ____________________

____

8 그 담요는 부드럽고 따뜻하게 느껴진다.
(feel, and, warm, the blanket, soft)

→ ____________________

____

기출: 대화문 완성

9 우리말과 일치하도록 주어진 단어를 사용하여 각 대화를 완성하세요.

(1)

A: How does my new shirt look?
B: <u>그것은 너에게 잘 어울려 보여!</u>

→ ____________________

(on you, look, great)

(2)

A: How does the tea taste?
B: <u>그것은 쓴맛이 나.</u>
A: You can add some honey, then.

→ ____________________

(bitter, taste)

floor 바닥; 층 slippery 미끄러운 familiar 익숙한 quite 꽤, 상당히 nervous 긴장한 lemonade 레모네이드 sour (맛이) 신 blanket 이불, 담요 add 더하다 bitter (맛이) 쓴

Unit 02

SVOO (4형식)

◦ 배열 영작

[1-3] 우리말과 일치하도록 주어진 단어를 올바르게 배열하세요.

1
> Nate는 나에게 그의 사진첩을 보여주었다.
> (me / showed / his photo album)

→ Nate ____________________

____________________ .

2
> 그녀는 그녀의 개에게 묘기들을 좀 가르쳤다.
> (some tricks / her dog / taught)

→ She ____________________

____________________ .

3
> 그 사서가 네게 베스트셀러를 가져다 줄 것이다.
> (you / bring / to / the bestseller / will)

→ The librarian ____________________

____________________ .

◦ 문장 전환

[4-6] 주어진 문장을 같은 의미가 되도록 바꿔 쓰세요.

4
> He will buy his wife a new watch.

→ ____________________ .

5
> Ann asked her neighbor a favor.

→ ____________________ .

6
> Joseph sent me a package of snacks last weekend.

→ ____________________

____________________ last weekend.

◦ 빈칸 완성

[7-8] 우리말과 일치하도록 주어진 단어를 사용하여 빈칸에 알맞은 말을 쓰세요. (필요시 형태를 바꿀 것)

7
> Emma는 남동생의 생일에 그에게 편지를 써 주었다.
> (her brother, a letter, write)

→ ____________________ ____________________ ____________________

____________________ ____________________ ____________________

on his birthday.

8
> Jim은 수업 중에 선생님께 그의 의견을 말했다.
> (his opinion, tell, the teacher)

→ ____________________ ____________________ ____________________

____________________ ____________________ ____________________

____________________ during class.

기출: 조건 영작

9 다음 대화를 읽고 〈조건〉에 맞게 우리말을 영작하세요.

> A: (1) 난 어제 David에게 내 그림을 보여주었어.
> B: Oh, did you? What did he say?
> A: He said he loved it! (2) So 난 그에게 그 그림을 선물로 주었어.
> B: He'll thank you for sure.

> 〈조건〉
> • 주어진 단어를 사용할 것
> • (1)은 전치사를 사용하지 말 것
> • (2)는 전치사를 사용할 것

(1) ____________________

yesterday. (show, my painting)

(2) So ____________________

as a present. (the painting, give)

trick 묘기; 재주, 기술 bestseller 베스트셀러 librarian (도서관) 사서 package 소포, 꾸러미 opinion 의견 for sure 확실히 as ~로서

Unit 03+

SVOC(5형식)

배열 영작

[1-3] 우리말과 일치하도록 주어진 단어를 올바르게 배열하세요.

1
> 우리는 Ben의 아이디어가 창의적이라는 것을 알게 되었다.
> (found / creative / we / Ben's idea)

→ __________________________

__________________________ .

2
> 내 친구들과 나는 그를 슈퍼히어로라고 부른다.
> (him / my friends / a superhero / call / and I)

→ __________________________

__________________________ .

3
> 우리는 우리의 환경을 깨끗하게 유지해야 한다.
> (should / our environment / clean / keep / we)

→ __________________________

__________________________ .

주어진 단어로 영작

[4-8] 우리말과 일치하도록 주어진 단어를 사용하여 문장을 완성하세요. (필요시 형태를 바꿀 것)

4
> 나는 상쾌한 공기를 위해 문을 열어두었다.
> (leave, open, the window)

→ __________________________

__________________________ for fresh air.

5
> 그 부모들은 그들의 아기를 Oliver라고 이름 지었다.
> (the parents, their baby, name)

→ __________________________

____

6
> Jane의 미소는 모두를 행복하게 만든다.
> (make, Jane's smile, everyone, happy)

→ __________________________

____

7
> 운동은 근육을 튼튼하게 유지시켜 준다.
> (strong, keep, muscles, exercise)

→ __________________________

8
> 그녀는 항상 그녀의 침대를 지저분한 상태로 둔다.
> (her bed, leave, messy)

→ __________________________

all the time.

기출: 문맥에 맞게 영작

9 다음 글을 읽고 우리말과 일치하도록 주어진 단어를 사용하여 문장을 완성하세요.

> I will introduce my favorite singer to you. Charlie is a singer and also a songwriter. He has a nice voice and plays the guitar very well. His first song is my favorite.
> <u>그 노래가 그를 유명한 가수로 만들었습니다.</u>

→ __________________________

____

(a famous singer, the song, make)

---

creative 창의적인 environment 환경 muscle 근육 messy 지저분한, 엉망진창의 all the time 항상, 줄곧, 내내 songwriter 작곡가 famous 유명한

Unit 01

to부정사의 명사적 쓰임

○── 배열 영작

[1-3] 우리말과 일치하도록 주어진 단어를 올바르게 배열하세요.

1
> 내 목표는 내년에 마라톤을 뛰는 것이다.
> (next year / to / a marathon / run / is)

→ My goal ________________________________

____ .

2
> 나는 동물 보호소에서 강아지를 입양하기를 원한다.
> (a puppy / I / to / want / adopt)

→ ________________________________

from the animal shelter.

3
> 아침 식사를 매일 하는 것은 중요하다.
> (is / to / breakfast / important / have / daily)

→ ________________________________

____ .

○── 빈칸 완성

[4-7] 우리말과 일치하도록 주어진 단어를 사용하여 빈칸에 알맞은 말을 쓰세요.

4
> 나의 소원은 조종사가 되는 것이다.
> (become, be, a pilot)

→ My wish ________________________________

________________________________ .

5
> Chris는 모형 비행기를 만드는 것을 좋아한다.
> (make, model airplanes, like)

→ ________________________________

________________________________ .

6
> Lily는 오늘 그 파일들을 보내주기로 약속했다.
> (the files, send, promise)

→ ________________________________

____

today.

7
> 우리는 정원에 장미를 몇 송이 심기로 결정했다.
> (decide, some roses, plant)

→ ________________________________

____

in our garden.

○── 기출: 우리말에 맞게 영작

8 우리말과 일치하도록 주어진 단어를 사용하여 빈칸에 알맞은 말을 쓰세요.

> My cousin, Tommy, visited Korea last week.
> He loves Korean barbecue. (1) So, 나의 부모님
> 은 캠핑장에서 바비큐 파티를 열기로 계획하셨다.
> Tommy and I really like to go camping.
> (2) 캠핑을 가는 것은 우리에게 매우 즐겁다.

(1) So, my parents ________________________________

____

________________ in the campsite.

(a barbecue party, have, plan)

(2) ________________________________

____

for us.

(be, enjoyable, very, go camping)

---

adopt 입양하다 animal shelter 동물 보호소 daily 매일, 날마다 plant 심다; 식물 barbecue 바비큐 go camping 캠핑하러 가다 campsite 캠핑장 enjoyable 즐거운

Unit 02

to부정사의 부사적 쓰임

[1-4] 우리말과 일치하도록 주어진 단어를 올바르게 배열하세요.

1
나는 작별 인사를 하게 되어 슬펐다.
(sad / say goodbye / was / to)

→ I ______________________________ .

2
Anna는 스트레스를 줄이려고 요가를 연습한다.
(reduce / practices / to / yoga / stress)

→ Anna ______________________________

______________________________ .

3
그는 시험을 통과하기 위해 열심히 공부하고 있다.
(the exam / to / is / hard / pass / studying)

→ He ______________________________

______________________________ .

4
방문객들은 오로라를 보게 되어 매우 신났다.
(to / very / see / were / the aurora / excited)

→ Visitors ______________________________

______________________________ .

[5-8] 우리말과 일치하도록 주어진 단어를 사용하여 문장을
완성하세요. (필요시 형태를 바꿀 것)

5
밤에 잠을 잘 자기 위해서는, 너는 커피를 마시면 안 된다.
(at night, well, sleep)

→ ______________________________ ,

you shouldn't drink coffee.

6
그녀는 반 친구들 앞에서 발표하게 되어 긴장되었다.
(a presentation, nervous, give, be)

→ ______________________________

______________________________ in front of her classmates.

7
그는 중요한 것들을 기억하기 위해 메모를 한다.
(things, remember, important, take notes)

→ He ______________________________

____

8
나는 댄스 동아리에 가입하게 되어 기쁘다.
(join, be, the dance club, pleased)

→ ______________________________

____

9
우리말과 일치하도록 주어진 단어를 사용하여 다음의
대화를 완성하세요.

A: Why did you start to draw a picture?
B: (1) 난 내 감정을 표현하려고 그것을 시작했어.
A: How do you like your new hobby?
B: It's great! (2) 난 나만의 예술 작품을 만들게 돼서
행복해.

(1) ______________________________

____

(it, feelings, express, begin)

(2) ______________________________

____

(own artwork, be, make, happy)

---

say goodbye 작별 인사를 하다 reduce 줄이다 yoga 요가 aurora 오로라 excited 신이 난 give a presentation 발표하다 take notes 메모하다 pleased 기쁜
feelings (복수형) 감정 express 표현하다

Unit 03⁺

to부정사의 형용사적 쓰임

○─ 배열 영작

[1-4] 우리말과 일치하도록 주어진 단어를 올바르게 배열하세요.

1

나는 오늘 해야 할 많은 숙제가 있다.
(a lot of / to / have / I / do / homework)

→ ___________________________________

________________________________ today.

2

그들은 저녁 식사에 초대할 몇 명의 손님들이 있다.
(some / have / to / they / invite / guests)

→ ___________________________________

___________________________ for dinner.

3

나의 부모님은 그들을 공항까지 태워다 줄 누군가가
필요하시다.
(someone / my parents / drive / them / need
/ to)

→ ___________________________________

___________________________ to the airport.

4

Lisa는 공부할 조용한 장소를 찾고 있다.
(a quiet place / is / Lisa / study / looking for
/ to)

→ ___________________________________

___________________________________ .

○─ 빈칸 완성

**[5-8] 우리말과 일치하도록 주어진 단어를 사용하여 빈칸에
알맞은 말을 쓰세요.**

5

잠자리에 들 시간이야. (go to bed, time)

→ It's ______________ ______________

______________ ______________ ______________ .

6

그는 서랍을 열 열쇠를 잃어버렸다.
(unlock, lose, the key)

→ He ______________ ______________

______________ ______________ ______________

the drawer.

7

너는 볼 만한 코미디 영화 아는 거 있니?
(any comedy movies, watch, know)

→ Do you ______________ ______________

______________ ______________ ______________

______________ ?

8

나는 너에게 물어볼 몇 가지 질문들이 있다.
(ask, some questions, you, have)

→ I ______________ ______________ ______________

______________ ______________ ______________ .

기출: 조건 영작

9 다음 대화를 읽고 〈조건〉에 맞게 우리말을 영작하세요.

A: 난 주말에 할 새로운 보드게임을 샀어.
B: Sounds fun! What is it?
A: It's "Monopoly." Will you play with me?
B: Of course, I'd love to!

〈조건〉
• 8 단어로 쓸 것
• play, buy, a new board game을 사용할 것

→ ___________________________________

_________________________ on the weekend.

guest 손님, 하객 look for ~을 찾다 unlock (열쇠로) 열다 lose 잃어버리다 drawer 서랍 Monopoly 모노폴리 ((주사위를 던져 나오는 숫자만큼 말을 옮겨 자산을 불려가는 보드게
임)) board game 보드게임

Chapter 09 동명사

정답 및 해설 p.34

명사로 쓰이는 동명사

○— 배열 영작

[1-3] 우리말과 일치하도록 주어진 단어를 올바르게 배열하세요.

1

그녀의 직업은 아픈 환자들을 돌보는 것이다.
(is / patients / taking care of / sick)

→ Her job _________________________

_________________________ .

2

Henry는 매일 기타를 연주하는 것을 연습한다.
(the guitar / practices / Henry / playing)

→ _________________________

_________________________ every day.

3

새로운 친구들을 사귀는 것은 나에게 쉽지 않다.
(new friends / not / is / easy / making)

→ _________________________

_________________________ for me.

○— 빈칸 완성

[4-5] 우리말과 일치하도록 주어진 단어를 사용하여 빈칸에 알맞은 말을 쓰세요.

4

내가 가장 좋아하는 겨울 활동은 스노보드를 타는 것이다. (snowboard, be)

→ My favorite winter activity _________________

_________________ .

5

하나의 언어를 완전히 익히는 것은 시간이 걸린다.
(a new language, master, take)

→ _________ _________ _________

_________ _________ time.

○— 보기에서 골라 영작

[6-8] 우리말과 일치하도록 〈보기〉에서 알맞은 단어를 골라 주어진 단어와 함께 문장을 완성하세요.

〈보기〉
give up　　　finish　　　keep

6

나는 학교 축제용 영상을 편집하는 것을 끝냈다.
(the video, edit)

→ _________________________

for the school festival.

7

그녀는 계속 그녀의 다리를 떨었다.
(her leg, shake)

→ _________________________

8

나의 오빠는 그의 자전거를 수리하는 것을 포기했다.
(fix, his bike, my brother)

→ _________________________

기출: 대화문 완성

9　우리말과 일치하도록 주어진 단어를 사용하여 다음의 대화를 완성하세요.

A: Playing video games is always fun.
B: I agree! Which game do you like the most?
A: 사실, 난 모험 게임을 하는 것을 즐겨.
B: Me too!

→ Actually, _________________________

_________________________ .

(adventure games, enjoy)

snowboard 스노보드를 타다; 스노보드　activity 활동　language 언어　master 완전히 익히다　edit 편집하다　shake 흔들다　adventure 모험

Unit 02

자주 쓰이는 동명사 표현

[1-4] 우리말과 일치하도록 주어진 단어를 올바르게 배열하세요.

1

내일 아침에 테니스를 치는 건 어때?
(playing / how / tennis / about)

→ _______________________________

_______ tomorrow morning?

2

내 생일 파티에 와줘서 고마워.
(for / you / coming / thank)

→ _______________________________

to my birthday party.

3

Emma는 사람들을 이끄는 것을 잘한다.
(people / good / is / leading / at / Emma)

→ _______________________________

_______________________________.

4

그는 집에서 요리함으로써 건강한 음식을 먹는다.
(healthy food / he / cooking / by / eats)

→ _______________________________

_______________________________ at home.

[5-8] 우리말과 일치하도록 주어진 단어를 사용하여 문장을 완성하세요. (필요시 형태를 바꿀 것)

5

나는 이번 여름에 해변에 서핑하러 갈 것이다.
(go, at the beach, surf, will)

→ _______________________________

_______________________________ this summer.

6

우리는 어떤 실수도 하지 않고 발표를 마쳤다.
(mistakes, make, without, any)

→ We finished the presentation _______

_______________________________.

7

우리는 더 적은 플라스틱을 사용함으로써 환경을 보호할 수 있다. (use, plastic, by, less)

→ We can protect the environment _______

_______________________________.

8

나의 엄마는 새로운 조리법을 시도하는 것에 관심이 있으시다.
(new recipes, interested, try, in)

→ My mom _______________________________

_______________________________.

9 다음 글을 읽고 질문에 대한 대답을 〈조건〉에 맞게 쓰세요.

Martin swims very well. He won the swimming competition last year. But, he doesn't like diving from high places. He feels scared of jumping from high places.

〈조건〉
• 각 문장에 반드시 동명사 표현을 사용할 것
• (1)은 5 단어, (2)는 8 단어로 쓸 것

(1) What is Martin good at?

→ _______________________________

(2) What is Martin afraid of?

→ _______________________________

---

lead 이끌다 surf 서핑을 하다 presentation 발표 protect 보호하다 recipe 조리법 competition 대회; 경쟁 dive 다이빙하다, 뛰어들다 scared 무서워하는

Unit 01 전치사

정답 및 해설 p.34

보기에서 골라 영작

[1-5] 우리말과 일치하도록 〈보기〉에서 알맞은 전치사를 골라 주어진 단어와 함께 빈칸을 완성하세요.

> 〈보기〉
> for   in   to   at   by

1
> 그 버스는 자정에 운행을 중단한다.
> (midnight)

→ The bus stops running ________________ .

2
> Chris는 런던으로 가는 항공편을 예약했다.
> (London)

→ Chris booked a flight ________________ .

3
> 그들은 기차를 타고 전국을 여행했다.
> (train)

→ They traveled across the country

________________ .

4
> 나의 반 친구들은 그 춤을 2주 동안 연습했다.
> (two weeks)

→ My classmates practiced the dance

________________ .

5
> 학교는 체육관에서 축제를 열 것이다.
> (the gym)

→ The school will hold a festival

________________ .

주어진 단어로 영작

[6-8] 우리말과 일치하도록 주어진 단어와 알맞은 전치사를 사용하여 문장을 완성하세요.

6
> 우리는 조명을 사용해 우리 텐트를 장식했다.
> (our tent, lights, decorate)

→ ________________

____

7
> 나는 관객들 앞에서 긴장했다.
> (the audience, nervous, feel)

→ ________________

____

8
> 그 기차는 서울에서 부산까지 3시간 만에 간다.
> (go, the train, Busan, Seoul)

→ ________________

________________ in 3 hours.

기출: 대화문 완성

9 우리말과 일치하도록 주어진 단어와 알맞은 전치사를 사용하여 다음의 대화를 완성하세요.
(필요시 형태를 바꿀 것)

> A: Can we live on Mars?
> B: Maybe not. There is not enough water on it. <u>우리는 물 없이 살 수 없어.</u>
> A: Right. But we may live on other planets someday.
> B: I agree with you.

→ ________________

____

(can, water, live)

---

midnight 자정 book 예약하다 flight 항공편; 비행 hold 열다, 개최하다 decorate 장식하다, 꾸미다 audience 관객 nervous 긴장한 Mars 화성 planet 행성

Unit 02 접속사

[1-3] 우리말과 일치하도록 주어진 단어를 올바르게 배열하세요.

1

당신은 차나 커피를 선택할 수 있습니다.
(or / can / coffee / you / choose / tea)

→ ____________________________ .

2

우리는 영화를 보고 외식하기로 정했다.
(decided / a movie / eat out / and / we / to / watch)

→ ____________________________
____________________________ .

3

Mark는 봄이 캠핑을 가기에 가장 좋은 계절이라고 생각한다.
(that / is / thinks / the best season / spring / Mark)

→ ____________________________
____________________________ to go camping.

[4-6] 우리말과 일치하도록 주어진 단어와 when, if, because 중 하나를 사용하여 문장을 완성하세요.
(필요시 형태를 바꿀 것)

4

날씨가 좋을 때 그녀는 산책하는 것을 즐긴다.
(nice, be, the weather)

→ She enjoys going for a walk ____________
____________________________ .

5

나는 몸이 좋지 않았기 때문에 집에 있었다.
(feel well)

→ I stayed home ____________________
____________________________ .

6

여러분이 더 많은 정보를 원한다면 우리 웹사이트에 방문해주세요.
(more information, want)

→ ____________________________ ,
visit our website.

[7-8] 우리말과 일치하도록 주어진 단어를 사용하여 문장을 완성하세요.

7

나는 네가 안전한 여행을 하길 바라.
(have, hope, a safe trip)

→ ____________________________

8

나는 돈이 행복을 살 수 없다고 믿는다.
(can't, believe, happiness, money, buy)

→ ____________________________
____

9 다음 글을 읽고 〈보기〉에서 알맞은 접속사를 골라 우리말과 일치하도록 문장을 완성하세요.

Jogging is Inho's hobby. (1) But 그는 오늘 아침에 달리고 난 후, 그는 다리에 통증을 느꼈다.
(2) So 그는 얼음을 좀 꺼내 그것을 다리에 두었다.

〈보기〉
before   after   and   or

(1) But ____________________________ ,
____________________________ in his leg.
(pain, this morning, feel, run)

(2) So ____________________________
on his leg. (put, take out, some ice)

---

eat out 외식하다 go for a walk 산책하러 가다 feel well 건강 상태가 좋다 information 정보 happiness 행복 pain 통증 take out 꺼내다

[1-3] 우리말과 일치하도록 주어진 단어를 올바르게 배열하세요.

1
> 저 튤립들은 근사한 향기가 난다.
> (wonderful / those / smell / tulips)

→ ____________________

____________________ .

2
> 우리는 그 강아지를 Coco라고 불렀다.
> (Coco / called / the puppy / we)

→ ____________________

____________________ .

3
> 나는 Han이 정직한 사람이라는 걸 안다.
> (know / I / Han / an / that / honest / is / person)

→ ____________________

____________________ .

[4-7] 우리말과 일치하도록 주어진 단어를 사용하여 빈칸에 알맞은 말을 쓰세요. (필요시 단어를 추가하거나 형태를 바꿀 것)

4
> 우리 걸어갈까 아니면 버스를 탈까?
> (take a bus, walk)

→ Shall we ____________ ____________

____________ ____________

____________ ?

5
> 나의 할머니는 우리에게 그녀의 정원을 보여주셨다.
> (her garden, show)

→ My grandmother ____________

____

____________ .

6
> 나의 엄마는 내게 문자 메시지를 보내셨다.
> (a text message, send)

→ My mom ____________ ____________

____________ ____________

____________ ____________ .

7
> Eric은 자기 전에 항상 책을 읽는다.
> (go to bed, he)

→ Eric always reads a book ____________

____________ ____________

____________ ____________ .

[8-10] 우리말과 일치하도록 주어진 단어를 사용하여 문장을 완성하세요. (필요시 단어를 추가하거나 형태를 바꿀 것)

8
> Mark는 한국에서 인기 있는 가수가 되고 싶다.
> (be, a popular singer, want)

→ Mark ____________

____________ in Korea.

9
> 우리는 파티를 위해 집을 꾸미는 것을 마쳤다.
> (decorate, finish, the house)

→ We ____________

____________ for the party.

10
> Alex는 이번 주말에 그의 사촌을 방문할 것을 고려하고 있다.
> (considering, his cousin, be, visit)

→ Alex ____________

____________ this weekend.

[11-15] 빈칸에 들어갈 말을 〈보기〉에서 골라 쓰세요.
(단, 한 번씩만 사용할 것)

〈보기〉
on　　by　　in　　during　　until

11 Mina wants to live _______________ a larger house.

12 Tom's family goes to an amusement park _______________ Christmas every year.

13 My cousin will stay at our home _______________ next month.

14 You should buy a ticket for the concert _______________ tomorrow.

15 Susan was wearing a witch costume _______________ the Halloween party.

[16-21] 우리말과 일치하도록 주어진 단어를 사용하여 단어 수에 맞게 영작하세요.

16 우리는 기다릴 시간이 없다. (3 단어)

→ We don't have _______________.
(wait, time)

17 일요일마다 등산을 가는 것은 나의 아버지의 취미이다. (3 단어)

→ _______________
is my father's hobby. (every Sunday, hike)

18 나에게 네 공책을 빌려줘서 고마워. (4 단어)

→ _______________
me your notebook. (lend, for, thank you)

19 Kate는 동아리에 가입함으로써 많은 친구들을 사귀었다. (4 단어)

→ Kate made many friends _______________
_______________. (join, a club, by)

20 나는 큰 소리를 듣고 깜짝 놀랐다. (5 단어)

→ I was surprised _______________
_______________. (the loud noise, hear)

21 나는 내 우산을 찾기 위해 주변을 둘러보았다. (4 단어)

→ I looked around _______________
_______________. (umbrella, find)

[22-25] 다음 각 문장에서 어법상 **틀린** 부분을 찾아 바르게 고쳐 쓰세요.

22 The peach pie tastes greatly.
_______________ → _______________

23 He promised to got a good grade this year.
_______________ → _______________

24 Do you mind to turn the volume up?
_______________ → _______________

25 Taking photos are a great way to remember things.
_______________ → _______________

[26-27] 우리말과 일치하도록 괄호 안에 주어진 조건에 맞게 영작하세요.

26

> Yesterday was Mother's Day, (1) <u>나는 선물을 하나 사야 했다.</u> So, I went to the shopping mall. After a few hours, (2) <u>나는 목걸이를 사는 것을 선택했다.</u> Mom loved my gift.

(1) so ___________________________

___________________________ .

(need를 사용할 것)

(2) ___________________________

___________________________ .

(choose, a necklace를 사용할 것)

27

> I am Hojin. I'm a middle school student. I hope to be a scientist. Today, I'll go to the library and borrow some books about science. (1) <u>내 여동생은 그리는 것을 아주 좋아한다.</u> She draws very well. (2) <u>그녀의 꿈은 예술가가 되는 것이다.</u>

(1) ___________________________

____

(love를 사용하되 4 단어로 쓸 것)

(2) ___________________________

____

(an artist, be를 사용하되 7 단어로 쓸 것)

28 각 문장의 의미가 통하도록 〈보기〉에서 알맞은 문장을 골라 〈조건〉에 맞게 문장을 완성하세요.

> 〈보기〉
> It rains.
> She was very tired.
> She had dinner.

> 〈조건〉
> · if, because, after 중 하나를 골라 사용할 것
>   (단, 한 번씩만 사용할 것)

(1) Lily went to bed early ________________

___________________________ .

(2) Lily brushed her teeth ________________

___________________________ .

(3) Lily won't go outside ________________

___________________________ .

29 다음 글을 읽고 ⓐ~ⓔ 중 어법상 틀린 **두 개**를 찾아 그 기호를 쓰고, 바르게 고쳐 쓰세요.

> Sue had a headache yesterday. She didn't ⓐ <u>feel good</u>, so she went to the school clinic before class. The school nurse ⓑ <u>gave some medicine to her.</u> It ⓒ <u>made her sleepily.</u>
> During science class, she couldn't focus on the class. The teacher ⓓ <u>found her behavior strange.</u> He ⓔ <u>asked a question her</u>, but she couldn't hear.

_________ → ___________________________

_________ → ___________________________

____

 학급 파티에 참가한 반 친구들이 한 일을 〈조건〉에 맞게 완성하세요.

Jay	선생님께 시를 써 드림
Kevin	우리에게 흥미로운 마술 묘기를 보여줌
Eric	모두에게 샌드위치를 좀 만들어 줌
Everyone	선생님을 행복하게 해 드림

〈조건〉
• 표 내용의 순서대로 쓸 것
• 주어진 단어를 사용할 것 (단, 과거시제로 쓸 것)
• (2), (3)은 전치사를 사용할 것

Today was Teachers' Day! Our class had a party for our teacher.
Every student prepared something for him.
(1) _______________________
(2) _______________________
(3) _______________________
(4) _______________________
He bought some ice cream for us. It was a great day!

(1) _______________________

____

(a poem, our teacher, write)

(2) _______________________

____

(show, magic tricks, interesting, us)

(3) _______________________

____

(some sandwiches, make, everyone)

(4) _______________________

____

(happy, make, our teacher)

 다음은 "토끼와 거북이"의 경주 이야기입니다. 글을 읽고 〈조건〉에 맞게 빈칸을 완성하세요.

〈조건〉
• 과거시제로 쓸 것
• 주어진 단어를 사용하되 필요시 형태를 바꿀 것

One day, Rabbit and Turtle had a race.
Rabbit (1) _______________________, but Turtle was not.
Rabbit expected to win the race, so she (2) _______________________ for a moment. Rabbit lay under the tree and (3) _______________________.
However, while Rabbit was sleeping, Turtle (4) _______________________.
He never stopped running until the finish line.
As a result, Turtle won the race.
He (5) _______________________ himself.

(1) _______________________
(good, run, at)

(2) _______________________
(decide, a rest, have)

(3) _______________________
(enjoy, a nap, take)

(4) _______________________
(go, keep)

(5) _______________________
(of, proud)

MEMO

천일문

LEVEL 1

| 정답 및 해설 |

중등

WRITiNG

Chapter 01 | be동사와 일반동사

Unit 01 be동사

POINT 1
p.11

1 Your book is on the table
2 I was late for school
3 Her room is clean and neat
4 These shoes are too small
5 You are very smart!
6 Justin was sick
7 Pasta is my favorite food.
8 Sam and Jane are from England.
9 His dog is so cute.
10 My classmates are friendly and funny.
11 Kate and I were best friends
12 Alex and I were in the park.

POINT 2
p.13

1 are not[aren't]
2 is not[isn't]
3 was not[wasn't]
4 Are
5 No, they aren't
6 No, she isn't
7 Yes, he is
8 Yes, they were
9 Are you free this afternoon?
10 Paul and Frank are not[aren't] my cousins.
11 (1) No, they aren't
   (2) They are happy
      happy 대신에 pleased, glad, joyful 등도 가능

5 A: 그들은 영어 선생님들이시니?
  B: 아니, 그렇지 않아. 그들은 수학 선생님들이셔.
6 A: Ellie는 지금 집에 있니?
  B: 아니, 그렇지 않아. 그녀는 지금 학교에 있어.
7 A: 그 남자는 가수니?
  B: 응, 맞아. 그는 내가 가장 좋아하는 가수야.
8 A: Ted와 Alice는 콘서트장에 있었니?
  B: 응, 그랬어. 그들은 콘서트를 즐겼어.
11 〈보기〉 A: Harrison 씨는 화가 나셨니?
         B: (1) 아니, 그렇지 않아.
            (2) 그는 놀라셨어.
   A: Bella와 그녀의 친구는 슬프니?
   B: (1) 아니, 그렇지 않아.
      (2) 그들은 행복해.

Unit 02 일반동사의 현재형과 과거형

POINT 3
p.15

1 takes
2 does
3 makes
4 cries
5 My mom and I cook dinner
6 The dog has long ears

7 She studies English
8 Many people wear sunglasses
9 Mr. Miller washes his car
10 Her sister teaches Korean
11 (1) She plays the piano
   (2) she goes to concerts with friends

11 나는 Emma이다. 나는 음악을 좋아한다. 나는 피아노를 연주한다. 가끔 나는 친구들과 함께 콘서트에 간다.
⬇
이 사람은 내 친구 Emma이다. 그녀는 음악을 좋아한다. 그녀는 피아노를 연주한다. 가끔 그녀는 친구들과 함께 콘서트에 간다.
해설 동사 play와 go의 3인칭 단수 현재형은 각각 plays와 goes이다.

POINT 4
p.17

1 studied
2 swam
3 went
4 wrote
5 My sister enjoyed her walk in the park.
6 Tom read a book before bedtime.
7 We ate some ice cream after lunch.
8 Tina took a picture
9 I left my umbrella
10 (1) had lunch
   (2) met his friends
11 ⓐ woke up ⓑ brushed ⓒ washed ⓓ ran

[5~7] 〈보기〉 나는 토요일에 영화를 본다.
       → 나는 토요일에 영화를 봤다.
5 나의 언니는 공원에서 산책을 즐긴다.
   → 나의 언니는 공원에서 산책을 즐겼다.
6 Tom은 자기 전에 책을 읽는다.
   → Tom은 자기 전에 책을 읽었다.
7 우리는 점심 식사 후에 아이스크림을 좀 먹는다.
   → 우리는 점심 식사 후에 아이스크림을 좀 먹었다.

10

시간	할 일
12:30	점심 식사하기
2:00	그의 친구들을 만나기

(1) Dan은 12시 30분에 점심 식사를 했다.
(2) Dan은 2시에 그의 친구들을 만났다.
11 나는 어제 늦게 일어났다. 나는 양치질을 하고 세수했다. 나는 학교로 달려갔다. 하지만 교실에는 아무도 없었다. 어제는 일요일이었던 것이다!
해설 동사 wake up과 run의 과거형은 각각 woke up과 ran이다.

Unit 03 일반동사의 부정문과 의문문

POINT 5
p.19

1 don't remember
2 doesn't like
3 doesn't have
4 don't live
5 doesn't get up
6 doesn't exercise

7 didn't clean   **8** didn't visit
9 didn't wear   **10** didn't go
11 Jack did not[didn't] call me
12 Kate does not[doesn't] watch TV
13 Dave and Jason did not[didn't] come to the party
14 (1) My mom and dad don't drink coffee.
     (2) The dog doesn't sleep in its bed.
     (3) I didn't buy a gift for my sister.

1 나는 그의 이름을 기억한다.
   → 나는 그의 이름을 기억하지 못한다.
2 그는 스테이크와 파스타를 좋아한다.
   → 그는 스테이크와 파스타를 좋아하지 않는다.
3 우리 학교에는 수영장이 있다.
   → 우리 학교에는 수영장이 없다.
4 Jenny와 Bill은 런던에 산다.
   → Jenny와 Bill은 런던에 살지 않는다.
5 나의 오빠는 일찍 일어난다.
   → 나의 오빠는 일찍 일어나지 않는다.
6 Brown 씨는 매일 운동을 하신다.
   → Brown 씨는 매일 운동을 하지 않으신다.
7 나는 오늘 오후에 내 방을 청소했다.
   → 나는 오늘 오후에 내 방을 청소하지 않았다.
8 지난주에 그녀는 박물관을 방문했다.
   → 지난주에 그녀는 박물관을 방문하지 않았다.
9 Liam은 오늘 검은색 코트를 입었다.
   → Liam은 오늘 검은색 코트를 입지 않았다.
10 Olivia와 나는 함께 학교에 갔다.
   → Olivia와 나는 함께 학교에 가지 않았다.
14 (1) 나의 엄마와 아빠는 커피를 마시지 않으신다.
     (2) 그 개는 자신의 침대에서 잠을 자지 않는다.
     (3) 나는 나의 여동생을 위한 선물을 사지 않았다.
   해설 (1) 주어 My mom and dad는 3인칭 복수 They로 받을 수 있으므로 doesn't가 아닌 don't를 써야 한다.
   (2) 주어 The dog는 3인칭 단수 It으로 받을 수 있으므로 doesn't가 쓰였다. 이때 doesn't 뒤에는 동사원형을 써야 한다.
   (3) didn't 뒤에는 항상 동사원형이 오므로 bought의 원형인 buy로 고쳐야 한다.

1 Do you need any help
2 Does she watch the news
3 Do you and Linda have plans
4 Did you go shopping
5 Does Bella worry about the history exam?
6 Did he get the tickets for the concert?
7 No, I don't   **8** Yes, she does
9 No, he doesn't   **10** No, they didn't
11 (1) Does she know my phone number?
     (2) Did you break the glass?

5 Bella는 역사 시험에 대해 걱정한다.
   → Bella는 역사 시험에 대해 걱정하니?
6 그는 콘서트 표를 얻었다.
   → 그는 콘서트 표를 얻었니?
7 A: 너는 선글라스가 있니?
   B: 아니, 그렇지 않아. 나는 사야 해.
8 A: 그녀는 다른 언어를 할 줄 아니?
   B: 응, 맞아. 그녀는 프랑스어도 해.
9 A: Charlie는 학교에 버스를 타고 가니?

B: 아니, 그렇지 않아. 그는 걸어서 학교에 가.
10 A: 학생들은 오늘 소풍을 갔니?
   B: 아니, 그렇지 않았어. 그들은 내일 갈 거야.
11 (1) A: 그녀는 내 전화번호를 알고 있니?
     B: 응, 알고 있어. 그녀가 너에게 전화할 거야.
   (2) A: 네가 유리잔을 깼니?
     B: 아니, 그렇지 않았어. 나의 남동생이 그랬어.
   해설 (1) B의 응답의 주어가 she이고 does로 답했으므로 A의 질문은 「Does she ~?」가 알맞다.
   (2) B의 응답의 주어가 I이고 didn't로 답했으므로 A의 질문은 「Did you ~?」가 알맞다.

Chapter Test

STAGE 1

1 My dad is a police officer
2 My aunt takes a yoga class
3 Mike was not late for school
4 Did you finish your homework
5 are in the same club
6 did not[didn't] have breakfast
7 Does the library close
8 I play computer games
9 (1) Is Ms. Smith a nurse
     (2) No, she isn't, She is a doctor

2 어휘 yoga 요가   take a class 수업을 듣다
3 어휘 be late for ~에 늦다
5 해설 주어 My friend and I는 복수이고 시제가 현재이므로 be동사는 are를 써야 한다.
   어휘 club 동아리, 클럽

STAGE 2

10 he is my friend
11 No, I'm not
12 she doesn't play the violin
13 Was your sister in Seoul
14 is in the living room
15 Did you see a movie
16 cleaned her room
17 broke the window
18 (1) played the guitar
     (2) did not[didn't] sing
     (3) swam
19 amn't → am not 또는 I amn't → I'm not
20 visits → visit   **21** washs → washes
22 don't wears → doesn't wear
23 am → are   **24** finded → found
25 Is → Does   **26** Do → Did
27 Is → Are 또는 the students → the student
28 Does John do the homework at home?
29 She does not[doesn't] grow flowers in the garden.
30 I did not[didn't] hear the news yesterday.
31 Were your friends in the mall?

32 (1) She is a middle school student.
(2) She likes art, but she doesn't like math.

10 A: James, 너는 저 남자아이를 아니?
B: 응, 그는 내 친구야. 우리는 같은 반이야.

11 A: 당신은 고등학생인가요?
B: 아니요, 그렇지 않아요. 저는 중학생이에요.
[어휘] **high school** 고등학교   **middle school** 중학교

12 A: Susan은 바이올린을 연주하니?
B: 아니, 그녀는 바이올린을 연주하지 않아. 그녀는 드럼을 연주해.

13 A: 너희 언니는 지난주에 서울에 있었니?
B: 아니, 그렇지 않았어. 그녀는 부산에 있었어.

14 A: Olivia는 욕실에 있니?
B: 아니, 그렇지 않아. 그녀는 거실에 있어.

15 A: 너는 어제 영화를 봤니?
B: 응, 그랬어. 나는 가족과 함께 봤어.
[어휘] **see a movie** 영화를 보다

16 Mia는 어제 그녀의 방을 청소했다.

17 민호는 일주일 전에 창문을 깼다.

18 지난주에 Andy의 가족은 캠핑을 갔다. Andy의 아빠는 기타를 연주하셨다. Emily는 그녀의 아빠와 함께 노래를 불렀다. 하지만 Andy는 그들과 함께 노래를 부르지 않았다. 그는 호수에서 수영을 했다.

19 나는 지금 피곤하지 않다.
[해설] am not은 amn't로 줄여 쓸 수 없다. 또는 주어와 be동사를 줄인 I'm not으로 고쳐 써야 한다.
[어휘] **tired** 피곤한, 지친

20 그녀는 주말마다 할머니 댁을 방문하니?

21 Kevin은 식사 전에 손을 씻는다.
[어휘] **meal** 식사, 끼니

22 나의 형은 겨울에 장갑을 끼지 않는다.
[어휘] **gloves** 장갑

23 Jane과 나는 지금 지하철 안에 있다.

24 나는 서랍에서 몇몇 오래된 사진들을 찾았다.
[어휘] **drawer** 서랍

25 네 아버지는 차를 타고 출근하시니?
[해설] 의문문의 동사가 일반동사인 drive이고 주어가 3인칭 단수인 your father이므로 Is를 Does로 고쳐 써야 한다.

26 너는 지난주에 책 한 권을 빌렸니?
[해설] 과거를 나타내는 last week이 있으므로 Do는 Did로 고쳐 써야 한다.

27 그 학생들은 시험 전에 긴장을 하니?
[해설] 주어 the students는 복수이므로 Is는 Are로 고쳐 써야 한다. 또는 주어를 복수(the students)가 아닌 단수(the student)로 고쳐 써야 한다.
[어휘] **nervous** 긴장한, 초조한

28 John은 집에서 숙제를 한다.
→ John은 집에서 숙제를 하니?

29 그녀는 정원에서 꽃을 기른다.
→ 그녀는 정원에서 꽃을 기르지 않는다.

30 나는 어제 그 소식을 들었다.
→ 나는 어제 그 소식을 듣지 못했다.

31 네 친구들은 쇼핑몰 안에 있었다.
→ 네 친구들은 쇼핑몰 안에 있었니?

32 Amy는 14살이다. 그녀는 중학생이다. 그녀는 그녀의 부모님과 그녀의 개 Molly와 함께 산다. 그녀는 미술을 좋아하지만 수학은 좋아하지 않는다. 그녀는 매일 그림을 그린다.
[해설] (1) 주어 She는 3인칭 단수이므로 are가 아닌 is를 써야 한다. (2) 주어 She는 3인칭 단수이므로 don't가 아닌 doesn't를 써야 한다. doesn't 뒤에는 동사원형이 와야 하므로 like로 고쳐야 한다.

33 (1) read, does not[doesn't] read
(2) do not[don't] study, studies
(3) do not[don't] watch, does not[doesn't] watch

34 ⓒ → we ate delicious seafood
ⓔ → Did you have a good time

33

일정	나	Janet
아침 요리하기	○	○
아침 식사 후에 신문 읽기	○	×
학교에서 중국어 공부하기	×	○
밤에 TV 보기	×	×

〈보기〉 나는 아침을 요리한다.
Janet은 아침을 요리한다.
(1) 나는 아침 식사 후에 신문을 읽는다.
Janet은 아침 식사 후에 신문을 읽지 않는다.
(2) 나는 학교에서 중국어를 공부하지 않는다.
Janet은 학교에서 중국어를 공부한다.
(3) 나는 밤에 TV를 보지 않는다.
Janet은 밤에 TV를 보지 않는다.
[어휘] **Chinese** 중국어

34 Cindy에게,
잘 지내니? 크리스마스카드 고마워. 정말 네가 그걸 만들었니? 나는 카드에 있는 네 그림이 마음에 들었어.
크리스마스에 나는 가족과 함께 디즈니랜드에 갔어. 그다음 날엔 해변에서 맛있는 해산물을 먹었어. 우리는 또 해변 근처에 있는 멋진 호텔에서 묵었어.
너도 크리스마스에 좋은 시간 보냈니? 나에게 말해줘! 네가 아주 그리워.
사랑을 담아.
Sara
[해설] ⓒ 동사 eat의 과거형은 eated가 아닌 ate이다.
ⓔ 일반동사 과거형의 의문문인 「Did+주어」 뒤에는 동사원형을 써야 하므로 had는 have로 고쳐 써야 한다.
[어휘] **drawing** 그림   **delicious** 맛있는   **seafood** 해산물
have a good time 좋은 시간을 보내다

Chapter 02 | 현재진행형과 미래 표현

Unit 01 현재진행형

9 (1) 그 남자아이는 TV를 보고 있다.
   (2) 수지와 그녀의 친구는 전화로 이야기하고 있다.

Unit 02 미래 표현

9 A: 상호야, 너는 이번 주말에 무엇을 할 예정이니?
   B: 나는 미술관에 갈 거야. 거기엔 많은 유명한 그림들이 있어.

Chapter Test   p.36

2 [어휘] take a shower 샤워하다
4 [어휘] go out 나가다, 외출하다
5 [어휘] gym 체육관
7 [어휘] move 이사하다
8 A: Claire는 지금 무엇을 하고 있니?
   B: 그녀는 그녀의 반 친구들을 위해 바닥을 청소하는 중이야.
   A: 오, 그녀는 정말 착하구나.
   [어휘] classmate 반 친구

19 I am[I'm] drinking a cup of tea after lunch.

20 Will the English class begin at 10 a.m.?

21 Is our school going to finish early today?

22 stand → standing　　　**23** is → are

24 come → coming

25 going not → not going 또는 He is going not → He isn't[He's not] going

26 goes → go

27 (1) I'm going to start exercising this summer.
(2) I won't eat junk food like hamburgers and coke.

9 A: John은 지금 그의 방에서 무엇을 하고 있니?
B: 그는 그림을 그리고 있어.

10 A: 지원이와 수지는 지금 무엇을 하니?
B: 그들은 축구공을 차고 있어.

11 A: 너는 방과 후에 무엇을 할 예정이니?
B: 나는 자전거를 탈 거야.

12 A: 수민이는 일요일에 무엇을 하니?
B: 그녀는 그녀의 엄마와 요리를 할 거야.

13 A: 너희 아빠는 내일 무엇을 할 예정이시니?
B: 그는 내 컴퓨터를 고쳐주실 거야.

14 A: 그녀는 지금 무엇을 하고 있니?
B: 그녀는 음악을[노래를] 듣고 있어.
〔해설〕 현재진행형 시제로 묻고 있으므로 대답도 현재진행형으로 한다.

15 A: 그들은 지금 무엇을 하고 있니?
B: 그들은 농구를 하고 있어.

16 콘서트는 학교 체육관에서 열릴 거예요. Nate와 Sam은 기타를 연주할 거예요. Jenny는 몇몇 인기 있는 노래들을 부를 거예요. 여러분은 지루하지 않을 거예요. 여러분은 아주 좋아할 거예요!
〔어휘〕 take place 열리다, 개최되다　popular 인기 있는, 대중적인　bored 지루한, 지루해하는

17 그는 크리스마스 파티를 위해 쿠키를 만든다.
→ 그는 크리스마스 파티를 위해 쿠키를 만들고 있다.

18 Jenny는 토요일에 내 책을 돌려줄 예정이다.
→ Jenny는 토요일에 내 책을 돌려주지 않을 예정이다.

19 나는 점심식사 후에 차 한 잔을 마신다.
→ 나는 점심식사 후에 차 한 잔을 마시고 있다.
〔어휘〕 tea 차

20 영어 수업은 오전 10시에 시작할 것이다.
→ 영어 수업은 오전 10시에 시작하니?

21 우리 학교는 오늘 일찍 끝날 예정이다.
→ 우리 학교는 오늘 일찍 끝날 예정이니?

22 Sally의 남동생은 지금 그녀 뒤에 서 있다.

23 나의 부모님은 새 차를 사실 예정이다.
〔해설〕 주어(My parents)가 3인칭 복수명사이므로 is를 are로 고쳐야 한다.

24 Janet은 지금 여기로 오고 있니?

25 그는 이번 주말에 그의 할머니 댁에 방문하지 않을 예정이다.
〔해설〕 be going to의 부정형은 be동사 뒤에 not을 붙인다.

26 네 여동생은 내년에 너희 학교에 다닐 거니?
〔해설〕 will 의문문은 「Will+주어+동사원형~?」으로 써야 한다.

27　지금, 나는 휴대전화로 게임을 하고 있다. 나는 사실 운동을 많이 하지 않아서, 체중이 늘고 있다. 나는 나의 생활 방식을 바꿀 것이다.
　먼저, 나는 이번 여름에 운동을 시작할 예정이다. 나는 햄버거와 콜라 같은 정크 푸드를 먹지 않을 것이다.
〔어휘〕 gain weight 체중이 늘다　lifestyle 생활 방식　junk food 정크 푸드　like (예를 들어) ~같은

28 (1) is going to travel
(2) Are you[Is your family] going to go
(3) aren't[are not]
(4) are going to go

29 (1) Is your dad taking care of
(2) are going to our uncle's house

28

여행 계획
✔ 일본으로 여행
✔ 8월에
✔ 배를 타고

Peter: 있잖아, Liam. 너는 올해 여름에 계획이 있니?
Liam: 물론이지. 나의 가족은 8월에 일본으로 여행을 갈 예정이야.
Peter: 멋지다! 너희 가족은 비행기를 타고 가니?
Liam: 아니, 그렇지 않아. 우리는 거기에 배를 타고 갈 예정이야.

29 (두 사람이 전화로 대화를 나누고 있는 중이다.)
A: 어디야, Sam? 너 오늘 밤에 영화를 보러갈 거니?
B: 아니, 그렇지 않아. 우리 엄마가 아프셔서 병원에 입원해 계셔.
A: 안됐구나. 너희 아빠가 엄마를 돌보고 계시니?
B: 응, 맞아. 아빠가 오늘 밤 엄마와 병원에 같이 계실 거야.
A: 그러면, 너와 네 여동생은?
B: 우리는 지금 삼촌 댁에 가고 있어. 우리는 오늘 밤 그곳에 머물 거야.
A: 아, 그렇구나.
〔해설〕 (1) B의 대답이 'Yes, he is.'인 것으로 보아 현재진행형 의문문이 가장 적절하다. (2) 뒤에 right now가 있으므로 현재진행형 are going을 써야 한다.
〔어휘〕 be in the hospital 입원하다　take care of ~을 돌보다, 보살피다

30 ⓓ → Do your friends have a pet dog?
ⓔ → My little brother is sleeping on the sofa now.

30 ⓐ 그 가게는 9시에 문을 연다.
ⓑ Leo와 나는 그 동아리의 멤버가 아니다.
ⓒ 영화는 10분 뒤에 시작할 것이다.
ⓓ 너의 친구들은 반려견을 키우니?
ⓔ 나의 남동생은 지금 소파에서 자고 있다.
〔해설〕 ⓓ 일반동사(have) 현재형의 의문문으로 주어(your friends)가 복수이므로 Are를 Do로 고쳐 써야 한다.
ⓔ 지금 일어나고 있는 일을 말할 때는 「am/are/is+동사의 -ing」로 써야 한다.

Chapter 03 | 조동사

Unit 01 can, may

POINT 1 p.43

1 can swim
2 can play
3 cannot[can't] run
4 Can, sing
5 We can go to the airport
6 She can speak Japanese very well
7 Can Nate come to the meeting
8 He can read this book in a day.
9 Can Mina solve the question?
10 I cannot[can't] find my cell phone.
11 (1) Can you play badminton?
   (2) I can't, I can play tennis

POINT 2 p.45

1 may take
2 cannot[can't] sit
3 may not swim
4 May, ask
5 Can, go
6 You may not make noise
7 you cannot bring your pet
8 You can call me
9 You may not leave during the class.
10 Can[May] I try on this T-shirt

10 이 티셔츠를 입어 봐도 되나요?
해설 '~해도 되나요?'라는 '허가'의 의미를 나타낼 수 있는 표현은 「Can[May]＋주어＋동사원형 ~?」이다.

POINT 3, 4 p.47

1 Can you help me
2 may be at home
3 Can you wait a moment
4 They may join the same club
5 Can you turn off the lights
6 The baby may not be hungry
7 You may need an umbrella
8 Lucas may be late for the science class
9 She may not come to school
10 Can you take me
11 can you return these books to the library

11 A: Fred, 날 위해 이 책들을 도서관에 반납해줄래?
B: 물론이지! 나는 지금 도서관에 가는 중이야.
해설 '~해줄래?'라는 '요청'의 의미를 나타낼 수 있는 표현은 「Can you＋동사원형 ~?」이다.

Unit 02 must, have to, should

POINT 5 p.49

1 must wear
2 have to do
3 must follow
4 have to study
5 must not miss
6 You have to drink enough water.
7 My sister has to save her pocket money.
8 I don't[do not] have to get up early
9 Tom had to study late
10 You must not be late
11 has to clean her room

11 나라는 그녀의 방을 청소해야 한다.
해설 방이 더러워 청소를 해야 하는 상황이므로 〈보기〉 중 have to(~해야 한다)를 사용해야 한다. 주어인 Nara가 3인칭 단수이므로, has to로 바꿔 쓰고 그 뒤에는 동사원형 clean을 쓴다.

POINT 6 p.51

1 should exercise
2 should buy
3 shouldn't watch
4 should go
5 shouldn't eat
6 I should keep my promise
7 You should not[shouldn't] waste money.
8 She should help her brother
9 We should not[shouldn't] bring food to the library.
10 People should not[shouldn't] talk loudly here.
11 (1) shouldn't run in the hallway
   (2) should wear a raincoat

11 (1) 복도가 매우 미끄럽다. 조심해라.
→ 너는 복도에서 뛰면 안 된다.
(2) 밖에 비가 아주 많이 내리고 있다.
→ 너는 우비를 입어야 한다.

Chapter Test p.52

STAGE 1

1 Can you hold the door
2 I should go to my uncle's house
3 Linda must not skip meals
4 He has to study math this afternoon
5 May I call you later?
6 We have to protect nature.
7 You must be careful on icy roads.
8 can play soccer, can't play baseball

1 어휘 hold 잡고 있다, 들다
3 어휘 skip 빼먹다, 거르다

5 어휘 later 나중에

6 어휘 protect 보호하다, 지키다

7 어휘 icy (도로 등이) 얼어붙은

8

	○	×
Chris	수영하기	스케이트 타기
Sophia	축구하기	야구하기

〈보기〉 Chris는 수영을 할 수 있지만, 스케이트는 탈 수 없다.
→ Sophia는 축구를 할 수 있지만, 야구는 할 수 없다.
어휘 ice-skate 스케이트를 타다

9 Can **10** May
11 have to **12** must not
13 must not throw trash
14 must wear a life jacket
15 (1) I may not come early
  (2) Can you send a message
16 Can Emily eat raw fish?
17 Jinsu had to wait for his friend for an hour.
18 You may not go into this room.
19 She should not[shouldn't] come here before 8 p.m.
20 Leo had to bring his textbook
21 should not[shouldn't] play computer games too much
22 should wash the dishes
23 should not[shouldn't] go to bed late at night
24 students don't have to carry heavy books

9 A: 나는 지금 정말 배가 고파. 날 위해 무언가 요리해 줄래?
  B: 물론이야. 무엇을 원해?
  해설 주어 you를 사용해 '~해 줄래요?'의 요청의 의미를 나타낼 때는 조동사 may가 아닌 can을 쓴다.
10 A: 내가 네 펜을 써도 되니?
  B: 물론이야. 어떤 게 필요해. 까만색 아니면 파란색?
11 A: Erica, 오늘 오후에 나랑 쇼핑 갈래?
  B: 미안해. 나는 병원에 가야 해.
  어휘 go see a doctor 병원에 가다, 진찰을 받다
12 A: 엄마, 저 햄버거 먹어도 돼요?
  B: Dan, 너는 패스트푸드를 먹어선 안 돼. 그건 네 건강에 좋지 않아.
  어휘 fast food 패스트푸드 health 건강
[13~14] 〈보기〉 당신은 상점 안으로 반려동물을 데리고 들어와서는 안 됩니다.
13 당신은 거리에 쓰레기를 버리면 안 됩니다.
  어휘 throw 던지다 trash 쓰레기
14 당신은 보트에서 구명조끼를 입어야 합니다.
  어휘 life jacket 구명조끼
15 A: 나는 네 생일 파티에 일찍 오지 못할지도 몰라.
  B: 괜찮아. 나중에 나에게 메시지를 보내줄래?
  A: 물론이지.
  해설 (1) '~하지 않을지도 모른다'라는 추측의 의미를 나타낼 때는 조동사 may not을 쓴다.
  (2) '~해 줄래요?'라는 요청의 의미를 나타낼 때는 조동사 can을 쓴다.
  어휘 message 메시지, 문자
16 Emily는 회를 먹을 수 있다.
  → Emily는 회를 먹을 수 있니?
  어휘 raw fish 날생선, 생선회
17 진수는 한 시간 동안 그의 친구를 기다려야 한다.

→ 진수는 한 시간 동안 그의 친구를 기다려야 했다.
  어휘 wait for ~을 기다리다
18 너는 이 방에 들어가도 된다.
  → 너는 이 방에 들어가선 안 된다.
19 그녀는 오후 8시 전에 여기에 와야 한다.
  → 그녀는 오후 8시 전에 여기에 오면 안 된다.
20 Leo는 내일 그의 교과서를 가져와야 한다.
  → Leo는 어제 그의 교과서를 가져와야 했다.
  해설 조동사 must는 과거형이 없기 때문에 had to로 쓰는 것에 유의한다.
[21~23] 〈보기〉 문제: Susan은 또 TV를 끄지 않았다.
     충고: 너는 TV를 꺼야 한다.
21 문제: Kate는 컴퓨터 게임을 너무 많이 한다.
  충고: 너는 컴퓨터 게임을 너무 많이 해서는 안 된다.
22 문제: Amy는 또 설거지를 하지 않았다.
  충고: 너는 설거지를 해야 한다.
  어휘 wash the dishes 설거지를 하다
23 문제: 수호는 밤늦게 자러 간다.
  충고: 너는 밤늦게 자러 가선 안 된다.
24 Jane: 모든 교실에 학생들을 위한 사물함이 있니?
  Nina: 응. 그들은 그것들 안에 많은 책을 보관할 수 있어. 그래서 학생들은 집에서 무거운 책들을 가지고 다닐 필요가 없어.
  어휘 locker 사물함

25 (1) should not[shouldn't] go shopping too often
  (2) have to study hard
  (3) should find another hobby
  (4) must not eat many sweets
26 ⓒ → don't[do not] have to bring

25

고민
(1) 나는 매달 쇼핑하는 데 너무 많은 돈을 쓴다.
(2) 나는 다음 주 금요일에 수학 시험이 있다.
(3) 나는 자유 시간에 항상 TV를 본다.
(4) 나는 체중이 너무 많이 늘었다.

(1) 너는 너무 자주 쇼핑하러 가지 말아야 한다.
(2) 너는 열심히 공부해야 한다.
(3) 너는 다른 취미를 찾아봐야 한다.
(4) 너는 단것을 많이 먹으면 안 된다.
  어휘 spend (돈·시간을) 쓰다, 소비하다 gain weight 체중이 늘다 sweets (복수형) 단 것
26   수지의 반은 다음 주에 경주로 현장학습을 갈 것이다. 그들은 현장학습 전에 신라에 대해 공부해야 한다.
  다음 주 수요일에 학생들은 오전 8시 전까지 학교에 와야 한다. 그들은 기차를 타고 경주를 방문할 것이다. 그들은 그들의 점심을 가져오지 않아도 된다. 왜냐하면, 그들은 경주에 있는 유명한 식당들 중 한 곳에서 먹을 것이기 때문이다. 그들은 혼자 여행할 수 없고 선생님을 따라가야만 한다. 학생들은 많은 멋진 곳들을 방문할 예정이다. 모두 함께 즐거울 것이다.
  해설 문맥상 점심을 가져올 필요가 없는 것이므로 have to를 don't[do not] have to로 고쳐 써야 한다.
  어휘 field trip 현장학습 kingdom 왕국 famous 유명한 tour 여행하다, 관광하다

Challenge!

27 ⓐ → We're making an English magazine
  ⓓ → Jenny can write it

27 A: Matt, 너희들은 지금 무엇을 하고 있니?

B: 안녕. Tom. 우리는 영어 잡지를 만들고 있고, 도움이 좀 필요해.
A: 물론이지. 내가 너를 위해 무엇을 할 수 있을까?
B: 너는 영어 시를 쓸 수 있니?
A: 아니, 할 수 없어. 하지만, Jenny는 그것을 쓸 수 있어.
　그녀가 너를 도와줄 거야.
B: 알겠어. 고마워.

해설 ⓐ 지금 일어나고 있는 일을 말할 때는 현재진행형인 「am/
are/is＋동사의 -ing형」으로 써야 한다.
ⓓ 조동사 뒤에는 반드시 동사원형을 써야 하므로 can writes는
can write로 고쳐 써야 한다.
어휘 magazine 잡지　poem (한 편의) 시

Chapter 04 | 명사와 대명사

Unit 01　명사

POINT 1　p.59

1	rabbits	2	buses
3	orange	4	children
5	hour	6	pencils
7	fish	8	feet
9	women	10	knives

11 We have three rooms
12 Wendy needs five potatoes.
13 He has a sister and two brothers.
14 The baby has four teeth.
15 She is[She's] carrying boxes.
16 (1) had an[one] egg and two bananas
　　(2) had two sandwiches

1 사진 속에 토끼 세 마리가 있다.
2 도로에 버스 두 대가 있다.
3 그 소녀는 그에게 오렌지 한 개를 가져다줬다.
4 그녀는 다섯 명의 아이들을 그녀의 집에 초대했다.
5 우리는 한 시간밖에 없다.
6 나의 오빠는 나에게 연필 여섯 자루를 줬다.
7 그는 물고기 열 마리를 살 것이다.
8 곰은 두 발로 설 수 있다.
9 네 명의 여성이 피자를 먹고 있다.
10 그들은 식사를 위해 칼 여덟 자루가 필요하다.
16 (1) Brandon은 아침 식사로 달걀 한 개와 바나나 두 개를 먹었다.
　　(2) Brandon은 점심 식사로 샌드위치 두 개를 먹었다.

POINT 2　p.61

1 four bowls of rice
2 three loaves of bread
3 ten bottles of juice
4 five slices[pieces] of cheese
5 two glasses[cups] of milk
6 two slices[pieces] of cake
7 a cup of tea
8 five pieces of paper
9 three bottles of water
10 a bar of soap
11 a bowl of salad
12 Can you give two glasses of water

12 정말 더운 날이다. 너와 네 친구는 매우 목이 마르다. 너는 집에 와
서 네 남동생이 부엌에 있는 것을 본다. 너는 그에게 뭐라고 말하
겠는가?
→ 우리에게 물 두 잔 좀 줄래?

POINT 3　p.63

1	There is	2	There was
3	There are	4	There were

5 There is soup in the pot.
6 Is there a ticket in your pocket?
7 There was a big spider in the bathroom.
8 There is not[isn't] a computer in my room.
9 Were there many animals in the zoo?
10 (1) There are two cups on the table.
　　(2) There is a bridge over the river.

10 (1) 테이블 위에 컵 두 개가 있다.
　(2) 강 위로 다리가 하나 있다.

Unit 02　인칭대명사와 재귀대명사

POINT 4　p.65

1	mine	2	We, our
3	He, us	4	their
5	me, his	6	them
7	your	8	my
9	her	10	them
11	hers		

12 (1) ⓑ → His (2) ⓓ → them

7 내가 너의 우산을 빌려도 될까?
해설 명사 umbrella의 소유를 나타내는 소유격 대명사로 쓴다.

8 그의 부모님은 나의 이름을 모르신다.

9 나의 언니는 나에게 그녀의 책들을 주었다.

10 나는 쿠키를 만들었다. 나는 그에게 그것들을 줄 것이다.
해설 동사의 목적어 자리이므로 목적격 대명사를 쓴다.

11 그 빨간 배낭은 그녀의 것이다. 그것은 내 것이 아니다.

12 (1) 나는 내 친구를 소개하고 싶다. 그의 이름은 Nate이다.
그는 캐나다에 산다. 나는 그를 5년 전에 서울에서 만났다.
해설 명사(name) 앞에 쓰여 '~의'라는 의미가 되어야 하므로 소유
격 대명사로 바꿔야 한다.
(2) 나의 이름은 Sara이다. 나는 가장 친한 친구가 있다. 그녀의 이
름은 Jenny이다. 하지만 우리는 매우 다르다. 나는 음악을 좋아하
지만, Jenny는 운동을 좋아한다. 나는 동물들을 좋아하지 않지만,
Jenny는 그것들을 아주 좋아한다.
해설 3인칭 복수명사 animals를 대신하는 목적격 대명사로는
them을 써야 한다.

1 I am proud of myself

2 You should focus on yourself

3 We have to believe in ourselves

4 Peter looked at himself in the mirror

5 She blamed herself for the mistake

6 They took a picture of themselves.

7 The boy hid himself

8 You should take care of yourselves.

9 I cut myself on the broken glass.

10 She drew herself on canvas.

10 Tina는 오늘 미술 수업을 들었다. 그녀는 캔버스에 자기 자신을 그
렸다. 그녀는 그녀의 그림을 반 친구들에게 보여 주었다. 모두가 그
녀의 그림에 대해 그녀를 칭찬했다. 그녀는 매우 행복했다.

Unit 03 지시대명사와 부정대명사

1 That   **2** This

3 These   **4** those

5 It is warm today

6 Are those your pens

7 These shoes are too tight

8 That is Richard over there

9 It takes an hour to the library

10 It is[It's] July 30th.

11 It is[It's] rainy.

12 (1) it is Thursday, it is Friday
(2) it is 11:00 p.m., it is 7:00 a.m.

10 A: 너의 생일은 언제니?
B: 7월 30일이야.

11 A: 오늘 날씨가 어때?
B: 비가 와.

12

도시	날짜	요일	시간
파리	3월 28일	목요일	오후 11:00
서울	3월 29일	금요일	오전 7:00

〈보기〉 날짜: 파리는 3월 28일이다.
　　　　서울은 3월 29일이다.

(1) 요일: 파리는 목요일이다.
　　　　서울은 금요일이다.
(2) 시간: 파리는 오후 11시이다.
　　　　서울은 오전 7시이다.

1 Do you want some cookies

2 Everyone in the theater laughed

3 I don't have any homework

4 There isn't anything on the table

5 any → some   **6** know → knows

7 some → any   **8** like → likes

9 Something smells

10 do not[don't] have any money

11 There was nothing

12 share → shares

5 제가 물 좀 마실 수 있을까요?

6 아무도 모든 것을 알지는 못한다.

7 나는 이번 주말에 아무 계획이 없다.

8 나의 반에 있는 모두가 그를 좋아한다.

12 우리는 오늘 우리가 가장 좋아하는 동물들에 대해 이야기하고 있
다. 모두가 그들의 가장 좋아하는 동물을 공유한다. 나의 가장 친한
친구인 민호는 그의 고양이 사진을 보여 준다. 그것은 정말 귀엽다!
해설 everyone이 주어로 쓰일 때는 항상 단수 취급하므로 동사도
3인칭 단수형 shares로 고쳐야 한다.

Chapter Test p.72

1 It was very cloudy

2 This movie is very interesting

3 My little sister bought three bottles of juice

4 There are five boys in the playground

5 two bowls of rice

6 Someone[Somebody] is knocking

7 doesn't have any coins

8 (1) we don't have any cookies
(2) there is some cake

2 어휘 interesting 흥미로운, 재미있는

5 해설 셀 수 없는 명사 rice의 양을 나타내는 단위 bowl에 s를 붙여
복수형을 만든다.

6 해설 someone[somebody]이 주어로 쓰일 때는 항상 3인칭 단수
취급한다.
어휘 knock (문을) 두드리다, 노크하다

7 해설 부정문에서 '전혀[하나도] ~없는'을 나타낼 때는 any를 쓴다.
어휘 coin 동전

8 Diana: 엄마, 쿠키가 좀 남아있나요?
엄마: 아니, 우리는 쿠키가 하나도 없단다. 하지만 케이크는 좀 있
어. 그건 어때?
어휘 be left (시간, 음식 등이) 남다

9 I bought five tomatoes

10 I introduced myself

11 Can I have a cup of green tea

12 It is[It's] ten o'clock

13 there aren't

14 (1) There is a[one] dog
  (2) There are two children
  (3) There is a[one] duck

15 (1) It is March 20th today
  (2) this is Tom
  (3) These socks don't match

16 loaves of   **17** glasses of

18 bar of   **19** pieces of

20 sheet of

21 (1) Is there any food in the fridge
  (2) There are two slices[pieces] of pizza and some juice

22 tooth → teeth

23 my → mine[my book]

24 piece → pieces 또는 two → a[one]

25 That → It

26 this → these 또는 math problems → math problem

27 some → any

28 Cats can clean themselves.

9 A: 너는 슈퍼마켓에서 무엇을 샀니?
   B: 나는 슈퍼마켓에서 토마토 다섯 개를 샀어.
   해설 다섯 개이므로 tomato의 복수형 tomatoes를 쓴다.

10 A: 민준아, 학교에서의 첫날은 어땠어?
   B: 좋았어. 모두 착했고, 나는 반 친구들에게 자기소개를 했어.

11 A: 오늘 정말 춥다. 차 좀 줄까?
   B: 네, 주세요. 녹차 한 잔 마실 수 있을까요?

12 A: 지금 몇 시니, Jane?
   B: 지금은 10시 정각이야.
   해설 시간을 나타낼 때는 비인칭 주어 It을 쓴다.

13 A: 너희 마을에는 많은 영화관이 있니?
   B: 아니, 그렇지 않아. 우리 마을에는 영화관이 딱 하나 있어.
   해설 「Are there ~?」 의문문에 대한 대답은 Yes, there are. 또는 No, there aren't.로 한다.

14 〈보기〉 돗자리 위에 세 명의 소녀들이 있다.
   (1) 나무 아래에 개 한 마리가 있다.
   (2) 벤치에 두 명의 아이들이 있다.
   (3) 연못에 오리 한 마리가 있다.
   해설 그림의 내용과 일치하도록 문장을 완성하되, 명사의 단수형 앞에는 There is를 쓰고, 명사의 복수형 앞에는 There are를 쓴다.
   어휘 mat 매트, 돗자리   bench 벤치   pond 연못

15 어휘 match 짝이 맞다, 어울리다

16 Joseph은 빵집에서 빵 다섯 덩이를 샀다.

17 나의 언니는 매일 우유 두 잔을 마신다.

18 나는 가게에서 초콜릿 바 한 개를 샀다.

19 그 레스토랑은 케이크 100조각을 준비했다.
   어휘 prepare 준비하다

20 너는 시험을 위해 연필 한 자루, 지우개 하나 그리고 종이 한 장이 필요하다.

21 A: 나는 정말 배가 고파. 냉장고에 음식이 좀 있니?
   B: 잠깐만. 내가 확인해 볼게. 음... 피자 두 조각이랑 주스가 좀 있어.
   A: 잘됐다! 나는 그것을 먹을 수 있어!
   해설 (1) '~이 있니?'라는 의미를 나타낼 때는 「Is[Are] there ~?」의 형태로 나타낼 수 있는데, 뒤에 오는 명사가 any food인 단수명사

이므로 Is를 쓴다.
   어휘 fridge (= refrigerator) 냉장고

22 달팽이는 천 개가 넘는 이빨을 가지고 있다.
   해설 앞에 over a thousand가 있으므로 tooth는 복수형 teeth로 써야 한다.

23 탁자 위에 있는 이 책은 내 것[내 책]이 아니다.
   해설 소유대명사인 mine으로 고쳐 쓰거나 소유격 my 뒤에는 명사 book을 써야 한다.

24 나는 오후에 피자를 두 조각[한 조각] 먹었다.
   해설 셀 수 없는 명사 pizza를 세는 단위인 piece를 pieces로 쓰거나 two를 a 또는 one으로 고쳐야 한다.

25 오늘은 8월 15일이다.
   해설 날짜를 나타내는 비인칭 주어 It이 와야 한다.

26 너는 이 수학 문제들을[수학 문제를] 풀 수 있니?
   해설 지시대명사(this) 뒤에 오는 명사가 math problems로 복수명사이므로 this를 these로 쓰거나, math problems를 math problem으로 고쳐야 한다.
   어휘 solve 풀다, 해결하다

27 A: Logan, 너 펜 있니?
   B: 미안, 하나도 없어.
   해설 부정문이므로 some을 any로 고쳐야 한다.

28 A: 우리 가족은 최근에 고양이를 데려왔어.
   B: 잘됐다! 나도 고양이 키워.
   A: 아, 나는 질문이 있어. 너는 네 고양이를 목욕시키니?
   B: 그렇지 않아. 고양이들은 그들 자신을 깨끗하게 할 수 있어.
   어휘 recently 최근에   give A a bath A를 목욕시키다   clean 깨끗하게 하다, 청소하다

29 (1) It is[It's] cloudy
  (2) It will[It'll] be rainy
  (3) It will[It'll] be windy
  (4) It will[It'll] be sunny
  (5) It will[It'll] be sunny

30 ⓐ → our club, ⓓ → This is

29 (1) 오늘은 월요일이다. 지금은 흐리다.
   (2) 화요일에는 비가 올 것이다.
   (3) 수요일에는 바람이 불 것이다.
   (4) 목요일에는 맑을 것이다.
   (5) 금요일에도 맑을 것이다.
   해설 모두 날씨를 나타내는 표현이므로 비인칭 주어 It으로 문장을 시작하여 쓴다.

30 내 친구들과 나는 학교 미술 동아리에 가입했다. 우리 동아리에서 우리는 사람, 장소 그리고 물건들의 그림을 그린다. 우리는 가끔 공원에 가서 나무, 꽃 그리고 동물들을 그린다. 그것은 정말 재미있다!
   우리는 매년 학교 축제에서 모두에게 우리의 그림을 보여 준다. 이것은 일 년 중에 우리가 가장 좋아하는 행사이다. 이것이 너에게 흥미롭게 들리니? 그럼 우리 동아리에 와서 우리와 함께 그림을 그리자.
   해설 ⓐ 명사 club 앞에는 소유격인 our를 써야 한다.
   ⓓ 앞에서 언급된 단수명사인 the school festival을 가리켜야 하므로 This is로 고쳐 써야 한다.
   어휘 event 행사, 사건

31 ⓐ → She doesn't have to come here.
   ⓓ → There isn't much milk in the refrigerator.

31 ⓐ 그녀는 이곳에 오지 않아도 된다.
   ⓑ 우리는 바다에서 많은 물고기를 잡았다.

ⓒ 이곳에서 역까지는 약 2킬로미터이다.
ⓓ 냉장고에 우유가 많이 없다.
ⓔ 우리는 집에서 쿠키를 좀 구울 예정이다.
해설 ⓐ 주어가 She로 3인칭 단수이기 때문에 doesn't have to로 고쳐 써야 한다.

ⓓ milk는 셀 수 없는 명사이므로 aren't를 isn't로 고쳐야 한다.
어휘 about 약, 대략; ~에 대해   kilometer 킬로미터

Chapter 05 | 형용사, 부사, 비교

Unit 01 형용사

POINT 1 p.79

1 She buys fresh bread every day.
2 A famous pianist visited Seoul.
3 Daniel gave a special present to me.
4 Jane should not drink anything cold.
5 Our new semester starts
6 The children ate delicious hamburgers
7 Cute boys are holding pretty flowers
8 His answer made her angry
9 (1) a strong boy   (2) a tall girl
   (3) a colorful umbrella (4) something heavy

1 그녀는 매일 갓 구운 빵을 산다.
2 한 유명한 피아니스트가 서울을 방문했다.
3 Daniel은 나에게 특별한 선물을 주었다.
4 Jane은 어떠한 차가운 것도 마시면 안 된다.
9 (1) 지호는 튼튼한 소년이다.
   (2) 유나는 키가 큰 소녀이다.
   (3) Peter는 다채로운 색의 우산을 들고 있다.
   (4) Leah는 무거운 무언가를 들고 있다.

POINT 2 p.81

1 There wasn't much rain
2 She has lots of snacks
3 I left a little food for my little brother
4 She will[She'll] buy a few flowers
5 It doesn't take much time
6 He has little interest in sports.
7 The bookstore sells many children's books.
8 (1) There were few students
   (2) There are many cats

8 해설 (1) '거의 없는'이라는 의미로 셀 수 있는 명사(student) 앞에 쓸 수 있는 말은 few이다. 이때 student는 복수형인 students로 써야 한다.
(2) '많은'이라는 의미로 셀 수 있는 명사(cat) 앞에 쓸 수 있는 말은 many이다. 이때 cat은 복수형인 cats로 써야 한다.

Unit 02 부사

POINT 3 p.83

1 You should speak clearly[clearly speak]
2 The writer's book is very difficult
3 My dog barked so loudly
4 Luckily, found an empty seat easily[easily found an empty seat]
5 We prepared for the performance really hard
6 The curtain matches perfectly[perfectly matches]
7 He played the guitar beautifully[beautifully played the guitar].
8 Paul answered my question very calmly.
9 Happily, I won first place in the race.
10 I can solve the questions very easily.

10 해설 동사를 수식하는 것은 형용사가 아닌 부사이므로 easy를 easily로 바꿔야 한다.

POINT 4 p.85

1 sometimes watches a movie
2 is usually at home
3 I will never skip breakfast
4 My parents are always proud of me
5 It doesn't usually rain
6 We always listen to our teacher
7 You can often see dolphins
8 My friends are never late for school.
9 (1) is always busy
   (2) never rides a bike
   (3) often play the violin

9

	항상	보통	자주	전혀 ~않다
일찍 일어나다		○		
(1) 바쁘다	○			
(2) 자전거를 타다				○
(3) 바이올린을 연주하다			○	

〈보기〉 그녀는 보통 일찍 일어난다.
(1) 나의 아빠는 항상 바쁘시다.
(2) Nick은 자전거를 전혀 타지 않는다.
(3) 그들은 바이올린을 자주 연주한다.

Unit 03 비교급과 최상급

1 runs faster than Paul
2 is more expensive than oil
3 can sing better than my sister
4 Susan gets up earlier than Jina.
5 The team did worse than last year.
6 The Eiffel Tower is more famous than the Louvre Museum.
7 high → higher
8 healthyer → healthier
9 (1) is bigger than Bag C
   (2) is heavier than Bag B
   (3) is more popular than Bag A

7 그 연은 나무들보다 더 높게 날아갔다.
8 집에서 만든 음식은 패스트푸드보다 더 건강하다.

9
	A 가방	B 가방	C 가방
크기	중간의	큰	작은
무게	1 kg	0.5 kg	0.7 kg
인기	★	★★★	★★★★

〈보기〉 A 가방은 B 가방보다 더 작다.
(1) A 가방은 C 가방보다 더 크다.
(2) C 가방은 B 가방보다 더 무겁다.
(3) B 가방은 A 가방보다 더 인기 있다.

1 is the most beautiful in my country
2 dances the best in our school
3 has the longest hair in my class
4 is the most wonderful time of the year
5 I am[I'm] the happiest person in the world.
6 This restaurant is the nicest in my town.
7 Today was the hottest day of this year.
8 Science is the most difficult subject
9 The panda is the most popular animal in the zoo.
10 (1) Cheetah is the fastest
   (2) Rabbit is the slowest

10
	치타	사자	토끼
속도	시속 120 km	시속 80 km	시속 40 km

(1) 치타는 셋 중에서 가장 빠르다.
(2) 토끼는 셋 중에서 가장 느리다.

Chapter Test

STAGE 1

1 a sunny day, a clear sky   2 a few restaurants
3 slower than   4 is always clean
5 the worst day
6 usually washes the dishes after dinner
7 Is there anything cold
8 can live longer than humans
9 (1) he is a great listener
   (2) He always listens to his friends

2 [해설] '약간의, 조금 있는'의 의미로 셀 수 있는 명사의 복수형을 꾸밀 때는 a few를 쓴다.
4 [해설] be동사가 있을 때 빈도부사는 be동사 뒤에 쓴다.
7 [해설] -thing으로 끝나는 대명사는 형용사가 뒤에서 꾸며 준다.
   [어휘] refrigerator 냉장고
8 [해설] long을 비교급 longer로 바꿔 써야 한다.
9 내 친구의 이름은 Danny이다. 그는 가장 재미있는 사람은 아닐 수 있다. 하지만 그는 아주 잘 들어주는 사람이다. 그는 항상 그의 친구들의 얘기를 주의 깊게 들어준다. 그는 좋은 친구이다.
   [해설] (2) 빈도부사 always는 일반동사 listen to 앞에 와야 하며, 주어가 3인칭 단수이므로 listens to로 써야 한다.

STAGE 2

10 Few   11 much
12 a little   13 many
14 little
15 (1) is taller   (2) is shorter
   (3) is the shortest   (4) is the tallest
16 (1) is cheaper than   (2) is the heaviest
   (3) is the most popular
17 Sad → Sadly
18 special something → something special
19 child → children
20 expensive → more expensive
21 most big → biggest
22 much → many[a lot of, lots of]
23 oldest → the oldest
24 careful → carefully
25 Jacob is the youngest member in our book club.
26 I got up earlier than my brother this morning.
27 She answered the question more quickly than me.
28 This is the most interesting book in the series.
29 We should always wear a hat outside.

10 A: Kelly 선생님은 왜 그렇게 화가 나셨니?
   B: 학생들이 거의 숙제를 해 오지 않았어.
11 A: John, 우리 집에서 같이 공부하자.
   B: 미안해. 난 시간이 많이 없어. 한 시간 안에 집에 가야 해.
12 A: 너는 아침 식사로 무엇을 먹었니?
   B: 나는 아침 식사로 빵을 조금 먹었어.
13 A: 너는 시험을 잘 봤니?
   B: 아니, 나는 시험에서 실수를 많이 했어.
   [어휘] mistake 실수, 잘못
14 A: 너는 지금 어디에 가는 중이니?
   B: 나는 슈퍼마켓에 가는 중이야. 냉장고에 우유가 거의 없어.

15 (1) Sandra는 Nick보다 키가 더 크다.
　(2) Maria는 Nick보다 키가 더 작다.
　(3) Maria는 셋 중에 가장 키가 작다.
　(4) Sandra는 셋 중에 가장 키가 크다.
16 (1) A 휴대 전화는 B 휴대 전화보다 더 싸다.
　(2) B 휴대 전화는 셋 중에 가장 무겁다.
　(3) C 휴대 전화는 셋 중에 가장 인기 있다.
17 슬프게도, Tim은 공원에서 그의 지갑을 잃어버렸다.
　어휘 **lose** 잃어버리다; 지다　**wallet** 지갑
18 너는 Jenny를 위해 무언가 특별한 것을 샀니?
　해설 something은 형용사가 뒤에서 꾸며 준다.
19 영화관에 많은 아이들이 있었다.
　해설 '많은'을 나타내는 a lot of가 쓰였으므로 child를 복수형인 children으로 고쳐야 한다.
　어휘 **theater** 영화관, 극장
20 이 옷은 저 신발보다 더 비싸다.
21 이것은 파리에서 가장 큰 교회이다.
22 오늘 거리가 조용하다. 사람들이 많이 없다.
　해설 셀 수 있는 명사의 복수형 people이 쓰였으므로 many 또는 a lot of[lots of]로 고쳐야 한다.
23 이 집은 우리 마을에서 가장 오래됐다.
　해설 최상급 앞에는 the를 쓴다.
　어휘 **village** 마을
24 우리 아빠는 밤에 조심해서 운전하신다.
25 Jacob은 우리 독서 동아리에서 가장 어린 회원이다.
26 나는 오늘 아침에 나의 형보다 더 일찍 일어났다.
27 그녀는 나보다 더 빨리 그 질문에 대답했다.
28 이것은 시리즈 중 가장 흥미로운 책이다.
　어휘 **series** (책 등의) 시리즈, 연속물
29 안녕하세요. 저는 호주에 사는 Kelly예요. 우리나라는 햇빛이 매우 강해요. 강한 햇빛은 피부에 좋지 않아요. 그래서 우리 학교에는 여름에 특별한 규칙이 있어요. 우리는 밖에서 항상 모자를 써야 해요. 모자는 우리 학교 교복의 일부예요.
　해설 빈도부사 always는 조동사 should 뒤에 온다.
　어휘 **sunlight** 햇빛　**rule** 규칙, 원칙

STAGE 3

30 (1) many old trees　　(2) much information
　(3) many bears　　(4) many big fish
　(5) much fun
31 (1) sometimes exercises in the morning
　(2) is never late to class
　(3) often has dinner with his friends

30 7월 20일 금요일
　우리는 오후에 요세미티에 도착했다. 우리는 요세미티 계곡을 걸어 다니면서 많은 오래된 나무들과 야생 동물들을 보았다. 우리는 요세미티에 대한 많은 정보가 없었다. 한 공원 관리인이 우리에게 말했다. "이곳에는 곰들이 많아요. 그것들은 나무 속에 있는 꿀을 아주 좋아하죠." 내일 우리는 낚시를 하러 갈 것이다. 얼른 가고 싶다!

7월 21일 토요일
　아침을 먹은 후, 우리는 미러 호수에 갔다. Noah의 아버지는 많은 큰 물고기들을 잡으셨다. 우리는 하루 종일 정말 많이 재미있었다. 밤에 Noah와 나는 이상한 소리를 들었다. 우리는 밖을 내다보았고 큰 그림자를 봤다. 그것은 곰이 아니었다. 그것은 Noah의 아버지였다!
　어휘 **information** 정보　**wild animal** 야생동물　**park ranger** 공원 관리인　**strange** 이상한, 낯선　**shadow** 그림자

31

일과	월	화	수	목	금
(1) 아침에 운동하다			○		○
(2) 수업에 늦다					
(3) 그의 친구들과 저녁을 먹다	○	○		○	○

(1) 민수는 가끔 아침에 운동한다.
(2) 민수는 절대 수업에 늦지 않는다.
(3) 민수는 자주 그의 친구들과 저녁을 먹는다.
해설 표에서 민수가 하는 일과 그 빈도를 찾아 연결하되, 일반동사 앞과 be동사 뒤에 빈도부사를 쓴다.
어휘 **routine** 일과, 일상

Challenge!

32 ⓑ →You should not[shouldn't] be rude to others.
　ⓒ →There are two mice on the farm.

32 ⓐ 칼 세 자루와 물고기 두 마리가 탁자 위에 있다.
　ⓑ 너는 다른 사람들에게 무례하게 굴면 안 된다.
　ⓒ 농장에 쥐 두 마리가 있다.
　ⓓ 그녀는 아무것도 먹지 않았지만, 물을 많이 마셨다.
　ⓔ 나의 삼촌은 이 보드게임에서 절대 지지 않으신다.
　해설 ⓑ 조동사 바로 뒤에 부정어 not이 와야 하므로 should not[shouldn't] be로 고쳐야 한다.
　ⓒ mouse의 복수형은 mice이며, 복수명사 two mice가 오므로 There is가 아닌 There are를 써야 한다.
　어휘 **rude** 무례한, 예의 없는

Chapter 06 | 여러 가지 문장 종류

Unit 01 명령문, 제안문, 감탄문

1 Put the plate on the table
2 Drink a lot of water
3 Don't worry too much
4 Don't be sad about the results
5 Open your textbook
6 Don't[Do not] speak loudly
7 Don't[Do not] take pictures
8 Be honest with yourself.
9 Don't[Do not] be rude to others.
10 (1) Don't use your phone
　 (2) Don't play soccer

10 (1) 영화관에서 네 휴대 전화를 사용하지 마라.
　 (2) 교실에서 축구를 하지 마라.

1 How about going out for dinner
2 Let's have lunch together
3 Why don't you see a doctor
4 Why don't you tell me
5 How about listening to music together
6 Why don't we go to a movie?
7 How about playing with your brother?
8 Let's recycle these boxes.
9 Why don't we start from tomorrow?

9 A: 우리는 건강을 위해 학교까지 걸어가야 해.
　　 우리 내일부터 시작하는 게 어때?
　 B: 좋은 의견이야.
　 해설 제안을 나타내는 표현 중 why가 들어가는 「Why don't we+
동사원형 ~?」을 쓴다.

1 How fast the train runs
2 What a great writer he is
3 How sweet this pie is
4 What an amazing story it is
5 What a good friend she is
6 lazy he is
7 a smart boy Henry is
8 cute the puppy is
9 expensive these shoes are
10 How beautiful it was!

[6~9] 〈보기〉 그는 정말 용감한 군인이었다.
　　　　 → 그는 정말 용감한 군인이었구나!

6 그는 정말 게으르다.
　 → 그는 정말 게으르구나!
7 Henry는 정말 영리한 소년이다.
　 → Henry는 정말 영리한 소년이구나!
8 그 강아지는 정말 귀엽다.
　 → 그 강아지는 정말 귀엽구나!
9 이 신발은 정말 비싸다.
　 → 이 신발은 정말 비싸구나!
10 A: 너는 한라산에 방문했니?
　 B: 응, 그랬어. 그것은 정말 아름다웠어.
　 A: 나도 그렇게 생각해. 나는 그곳에 다시 방문하고 싶어!
　 → 그것은 정말 아름답구나!
　 해설 How로 시작하는 감탄문은 「How+형용사(+주어+동사)」로
나타낸다. 밑줄 친 문장의 시제가 과거이므로 감탄문의 시제도 과
거인 was로 쓴다.

Unit 02 의문사 의문문

1 What does he teach
2 What should I bring
3 What time is it now
4 What is the name of your puppy
5 What are Dana and Jenny talking about
6 What time does Jay get up
7 What did you get
8 What do you do in your free time
9 (1) What did you do last weekend?
　 (2) What is[What's] your favorite winter sport?

6 A: Jay는 몇 시에 일어나니?
　 B: 그는 매일 아침 7시에 일어나.
7 A: 너는 네 생일 선물로 무엇을 받았니?
　 B: 나는 나의 생일 선물로 새 신발을 받았어.
8 A: 너는 여가 시간에 무엇을 하니?
　 B: 나는 주로 컴퓨터 게임을 해.
9 A: 너는 지난 주말에 무엇을 했니?
　 B: 나는 나의 가족들과 스키를 타러 갔어.
　 A: 재미있었겠다. 나도 겨울 스포츠를 좋아해.
　 B 네가 가장 좋아하는 겨울 스포츠는 뭐니?
　 A: 내가 가장 좋아하는 겨울 스포츠는 스노보드 타기야.
　 해설 (1) 일반동사가 쓰이는 what 의문문의 어순은 「What+do/
does/did+주어+동사원형 ~?」인데, 과거(last weekend)의 일에
관해 묻고 있으므로 과거형 did를 쓴다.
　 (2) 이어지는 대답을 통해 가장 좋아하는 겨울 스포츠가 무엇인지
묻는 질문임을 알 수 있다. what 의문문의 주어가 단수명사인
your favorite winter sport이므로 앞에 be동사 is를 쓴다.

1 Who is that tall boy
2 When did you meet Tom
3 Where is Mr. Brody from
4 Which singer do you like

5 Why did you wake up
6 Whose glasses are these
7 Why did you go
8 Where does Robert work
9 Who is your cousin
10 Which T-shirt is yours
11 Where did you go last Saturday?

7 A: 너는 어젯밤에 왜 공원에 갔니?
　 B: 나는 자전거를 타고 싶었기 때문이야.
8 A: Robert는 어디에서 일하나요?
　 B: 그는 은행에서 일해요.
9 A: 누가 너의 사촌이니?
　 B: 저기에 있는 여자아이가 내 사촌이야.
10 A: 어느 티셔츠가 너의 것이니, 빨강 아니면 파랑?
　 B: 빨간색이 나의 것이야.
11 A: 너는 지난 토요일에 어디에 갔니?
　 B: 나는 나의 할머니 댁에 갔어.

POINT 6　　p.107

1 How do you feel today
2 How can I get to the airport
3 How long do turtles live
4 How many books did you read
5 How tall are you
6 How long does the movie last
7 How many legs does an octopus have
8 How often do you call
9 How many times does she have lessons?

5 A: 너는 키가 얼마나 크니?
　 B: 나는 160 cm야.
6 A: 그 영화는 얼마 동안 계속되니?
　 B: 그것은 대략 2시간 정도 계속돼.
7 A: 문어는 얼마나 많은 다리를 가지고 있니?
　 B: 그것은 8개의 다리를 가지고 있어.
8 A: 너는 너의 할머니께 얼마나 자주 전화하니?
　 B: 나는 그녀에게 일주일에 한 번 전화해.
9

Kate의 일정표

월	화	수	목	금	토	일
피아노 레슨		피아노 레슨		피아노 레슨		

A: Kate의 일정표를 봐. 그녀는 피아노를 열심히 연습해.
B: 그녀는 몇 번이나 레슨을 받니?
A: 그녀는 일주일에 세 번 레슨을 받아.

Unit 03 부가의문문

POINT 7　　p.109

1 aren't you　　　2 did she
3 can't he　　　　4 didn't she
5 does he　　　　6 aren't they
7 is, isn't it　　　8 went, didn't he
9 doesn't like, does she　10 order, shall we
11 (1) weren't they　　(2) was she

11 (1) A: 그 그림들은 정말 아름다웠어, 그렇지 않니?
　　　B: 맞아, 나도 그렇게 생각해.
　 (2) A: Kate는 피곤하지 않았어, 그렇지?
　　　B: 응, 그녀는 괜찮았어.

Chapter Test　　p.110

STAGE 1

1 How about playing a board game
2 Do not throw away trash
3 When will you get there
4 What a terrible accident it was
5 What season do you like
6 Let's not go out
7 He can keep a secret, can't he
8 How long did you sleep
9 (1) What an amazing hat it is
　 (2) why don't you join our club

2 어휘 throw away ~을 버리다
4 어휘 accident 사고　terrible 끔찍한, 무서운
7 어휘 secret 비밀
9 A: Grace, 저것은 너의 새 모자니?
　 B: 응, 나는 그것을 우리 패션 동아리에서 만들었어.
　 A: 그것은 정말 멋진 모자구나! 나는 그것이 정말 마음에 들어.
　 B: 그러면, 우리 동아리에 들어오는 게 어때? 우리는 항상 재미있어!

STAGE 2

10 How tall is it
11 How much does it weigh
12 What does it eat
13 What nickname does it have
14 be careful　　　15 was she
16 What　　　　　17 books
18 (1) don't buy a red ball
　 (2) don't be sad
19 (1) Have breakfast every day
　 (2) Don't eat food late
20 (1) Why don't you go to bed early?
　 (2) How about going to bed early?
21 (1) Where are you from
　 (2) Why do you like her
22 (1) What time does Sarah go to school
　 (2) What does Sarah do
　 (3) Yes, she does

[10~13] 〈보기〉 Daniel: 게임을 해 보자. 너는 동물에 대해 추측을 해야 해.
　　　　Janice: 그래, 나 이 게임 좋아해. 내가 그 동물에 대해 질문을 할게.
10 Janice: 그것은 얼마나 키가 크니?
　 Daniel: 그것은 약 2m 정도야.
11 Janice: 그것은 얼마나 무게가 나가니?
　 Daniel: 그것은 약 200kg 정도야.
　 어휘 weigh 무게가 ~이다

12 Janice: 그것은 무엇을 먹니?

Daniel: 그것은 다른 동물들을 먹어.

13 Janice: 그것은 무슨 별명을 가지고 있니?

Daniel: 사람들은 그것을 '정글의 왕'이라 불러.

Janice: 알겠다! 그것은 사자야!

Daniel: 맞아.

[어휘] nickname 별명

14 제 안경을 조심해 주세요.

[해설] 명령문은 동사원형으로 시작해야 하므로, 형용사 careful 앞에 be동사가 필요하다.

[어휘] careful 조심하는

15 Emma는 학교에 늦지 않았어, 그렇지?

[해설] 문장의 동사로 일반동사가 아닌 be동사(wasn't)가 쓰였으므로, 부가의문문의 did she는 was she로 고쳐 써야 한다.

16 오늘은 정말 추운 날이구나!

[해설] 문장에 명사가 포함된 어구(a cold day)가 있으므로 How가 아닌 What 감탄문으로 써야 한다.

17 A: 너는 지금 얼마나 많은 책을 가지고 있니?

B: 나는 두 권을 가지고 있어.

[해설] 셀 수 있는 명사의 개수를 물을 때는 「How many+복수명사」의 형태를 사용한다.

18 개들은 파란색, 노란색을 볼 수 있지만 다른 색들은 잘 볼 수 없다. 예를 들어, 그들은 빨간색을 볼 수 없다. 그러니, 당신의 개에게 빨간 공을 사 주지 마라. 너의 개는 그것을 잘 볼 수 없을 것이다. 하지만 슬퍼하지 마라. 개들은 좋은 시력이 필요하지 않다. 그들은 좋은 후각을 가지고 있다.

[어휘] for example 예를 들어   eye 시력; 눈   sense of smell 후각

19 (1) 매일 아침 식사를 해라.

(2) 밤늦게 음식을 먹지 마라.

20 A: 나는 너무 피곤해.

B: ___________________________

A: 알겠어. 그렇게.

(1) 너는 일찍 자러 가는 게 어때?

(2) 일찍 자러 가는 게 어때?

[해설] why를 사용하는 제안문은 「Why don't you+동사원형 ~?」를, how를 사용하는 제안문은 「How about -ing ~?」를 쓴다.

21 기자: 안녕하세요, 제가 잠시 인터뷰를 할 수 있을까요?

Clara: 물론이죠.

기자: 감사합니다. 당신의 이름을 여쭤봐도 될까요?

Clara: 저의 이름은 Clara예요.

기자: 당신은 어디서 오셨나요?

Clara: 저는 보스턴에서 왔어요.

기자: 오늘의 경기는 어땠나요?

Clara: 멋졌어요! 그것은 정말 흥미로웠어요.

기자: 당신이 가장 좋아하는 선수는 누구인가요?

Clara: 제가 가장 좋아하는 선수는 Megan이에요.

기자: 당신은 왜 그녀를 좋아하나요?

Clara: 왜냐하면 그녀는 팀의 멋진 리더이기 때문이에요!

[어휘] reporter 기자   interview 인터뷰   leader 지도자, 리더

22

시간	일과
8:00	학교 가기
15:30	집에 오기
18:30	가족과 함께 저녁 식사하기
20:00	샤워 하기

(1) Q: Sarah는 몇 시에 학교에 가니?

A: 그녀는 8시에 학교에 가.

(2) Q: Sarah는 18:30시에 무엇을 하니?

A: 그녀는 그녀의 가족과 함께 저녁 식사를 해.

(3) Q: Sarah는 20:00시에 샤워를 해, 그렇지 않니?

A: 응, 맞아.

[어휘] take a shower 샤워를 하다

23 Don't[Do not] kick others' seats.

Turn off your cell phones.

24 Be quiet in the building.

Don't[Do not] bring food.

25 Don't[Do not] run in the classroom.

Arrive at school on time.

26 Don't[Do not] take pictures.

Don't[Do not] talk loudly.

27 ⓐ → What ⓒ → How far

[23~26] [어휘] turn off 끄다   on time 제시간에   seat 좌석, 자리

27 오늘, 선생님은 우리에게 현장 학습에 대해 말씀해 주셨다. 정말 좋은 소식이었다! 나는 그녀에게 질문했다. "우리는 어디로 가나요?" 그녀가 말했다. "우리는 전주로 갈 거란다." 그다음에 지호도 질문했다. "여기서 얼마나 먼가요?" 그녀는 대답했다. "버스로 두 시간이 걸린단다." 나의 반 친구들과 나는 전주에서 많은 흥미로운 장소를 방문할 것이다, 그렇지 않을까? 나는 매우 신난다.

[해설] ⓐ How 감탄문에서 How 바로 뒤에는 형용사나 부사가 오는데, great news가 쓰였으므로 What 감탄문으로 써야 한다.

ⓒ 거리를 물을 때는 How far(얼마나 먼 ~)를 사용한다.

[어휘] field trip 현장학습

28 ⓑ → I can swim faster than you.

ⓓ → What time do you usually go to school?

28 ⓐ 유리잔 안에 물이 거의 없었다.

ⓑ 나는 너보다 더 빠르게 수영할 수 있어.

ⓒ 나는 나의 책장에 많은 책을 가지고 있다.

ⓓ 너는 보통 몇 시에 학교를 가니?

ⓔ 모든 나라는 전통적인 음식을 갖고 있다.

[해설] ⓑ fast는 1음절의 형용사이므로 뒤에 -er를 붙여서 비교급을 만든다.

ⓓ 일반동사(go)가 쓰인 현재시제 의문사 의문문으로, 주어(you)가 2인칭 단수이므로 are를 do로 고쳐 써야 한다.

[어휘] bookshelf 책장, 책꽂이   traditional 전통적인

Chapter 07 | 문장의 여러 형식

Unit 01 SVC(2형식)

POINT 1   p.117

1 He got excited
2 The pants look small
3 This pizza tastes very good
4 Your idea sounds good.
5 The actor became so famous.
6 Ashley felt very sleepy.
7 strangely → strange
8 looks like → looks
9 (1) smell sweet   (2) feels soft

7 그 우유는 이상한 냄새가 난다.
8 저 의자는 편안해 보인다.
9 (1) 그 꽃들은 달콤한 향기가 난다.
   (2) 그 스웨터는 부드럽게 느껴진다.

Unit 02 SVOO(4형식)

POINT 2   p.119

1 gave me a cup of water
2 bought her sister some snacks
3 made her friend a necklace
4 teaches students history
5 Lucas made his brother a model airplane.
6 He showed me his favorite book.
7 I sent my friend a text message.
8 The shop gave the customers free samples.
9 (1) gave her grandmother flowers
   (2) gave her friend a cookie

9 (1) Betty는 그녀의 할머니께 꽃 여러 송이를 드렸다.
   (2) Betty는 그녀의 친구에게 쿠키 한 개를 주었다.

POINT 3   p.121

1 lent my camera to Wendy
2 made a cup of tea for his mother
3 Taylor showed her puppy to me
4 I wrote a letter to Lisa.
5 Jerry told a funny story to us.
6 My dad bought the computer for me.
7 I sent an email to my teacher.
8 My aunt cooked Chinese food for me.
9 The policeman asked some questions of Noah.
10 (1) gave a pencil case to Vicky
   (2) bought a diary for me

4 나는 Lisa에게 편지를 썼다.
5 Jerry는 우리에게 재미있는 이야기를 말해주었다.
6 나의 아빠는 나에게 컴퓨터를 사주셨다.

10

| 나 → Vicky | 필통 |
| Vicky → 나 | 일기장 |

오늘은 크리스마스이브였다. 내 친구 Vicky와 나는 서로를 위해 선물을 준비했다. 나는 Vicky에게 필통을 주었다. 그리고 Vicky는 나에게 일기장을 사 주었다. 우리는 우리의 선물이 아주 마음에 들었고 매우 행복했다.

Unit 03 SVOC(5형식)

POINT 4   p.123

1 He calls his guitar 'The Old Friend'
2 I found the box empty
3 He left the door open
4 The surprise party made her happy
5 My dad named my sister Julia.
6 Jogging keeps us healthy.
7 You will[You'll] find the story interesting.
8 The experience made him a better person.
9 (1) The news made me curious
   (2) can call her Emma

9 A: 너는 그 전학생에 관해 들었니?
   B: 응, 들었어. 그 소식은 나를 그녀에 대해 궁금하게 만들었어.
   A: 나도 그래. 너는 그녀의 이름을 아니?
   B: 응, 너는 그녀를 Emma라고 부르면 돼. 그녀는 캐나다에서 왔어.
   A: 그렇구나.

Chapter Test   p.124

STAGE 1

1 The soup tasted salty
2 I lent Bill some money
3 People found the village beautiful
4 Mom made a pretty sweater for me
5 Eric told the truth to the police
6 Ron's voice sounded sleepy
7 He teaches soccer to children
8 (1) looked clear   (2) feels cold
   (3) smells like chocolate

1 어휘 salty 짠, 짠맛이 나는
3 어휘 village 마을

9 I felt bored

10 He taught me some new words

11 My mom made it for me

12 The noise makes me uncomfortable

13 Your idea sounds wonderful

14 I will send them to you

15 a baby me → me a baby

16 my childhood picture you → you my childhood picture 또는 you → to you

17 warmly → warm

18 sleep → sleepy

19 (1) Our dad cooks pasta for us
(2) Our dad cooks us pasta

20 (1) She made a strawberry cake for me.
(2) It tasted really delicious.
(3) He wrote me a birthday card.
(4) I felt happy.

21 They look so excited

22 people found the new park a good place

23 my brother brought the lunch box to me

24 (1) The children's laughs made[kept] everyone joyful
(2) We were[got, became, felt] excited

9 A: 과학 수업은 어땠니?
B: 나는 수업 동안 지루했어.

10 A: Jason이 너에게 무엇을 가르쳐 주었니?
B: 그는 나에게 새로운 단어들을 좀 가르쳐 줬어.

11 A: 이 샌드위치는 정말 맛있구나!
B: 고마워. 엄마가 나에게 그것을 만들어 주셨어.

12 A: 저게 무슨 소리니?
B: 모르겠어. 그 소음은 나를 불편하게 만들어.
[어휘] uncomfortable 불편한   noise 소음

13 A: 너는 내 아이디어에 대해서 어떻게 생각하니?
B: 너의 아이디어는 훌륭하게 들려.

14 A: 너는 언제 나에게 그 파일들을 보내줄 거니?
B: 나는 네게 그것을 지금 바로 보내줄게.

15 나의 할머니는 나를 아기라고 부르셨다.
[해설] 동사 call은 '~을 …라고 부르다'라는 의미로 쓰일 때, 「call+목적어+명사」의 순서로 쓰여야 한다.

16 나는 네게 나의 어린 시절 사진을 보여줄게.
[해설] 동사 show는 「show+간접목적어+직접목적어」의 형태로 쓰거나, 또는 「show+직접목적어+to+간접목적어」로 써야 한다.
[어휘] childhood 어린 시절

17 그 새 재킷은 나를 따뜻하게 했다.
[해설] 「keep+목적어+목적격보어」의 SVOC 구조이므로 목적격보어로 형용사를 사용한다.

18 나는 점심시간 후에 졸렸다.
[해설] 감각동사는 형용사 보어를 쓴다.

19 내가 가장 좋아하는 음식은 파스타이다. 나의 여동생도 그것을 아주 좋아한다. 우리 아빠는 매주 일요일에 우리에게 파스타를 만들어 주신다. 그는 훌륭한 요리사는 아니지만, 열심히 노력하신다. 우리는 그의 사랑을 느낄 수 있다.

20 오늘은 나의 생일이었다. 저녁에 나의 가족은 나를 위해 집에서 생일 파티를 열어주었다. 나의 엄마는 나에게 딸기 케이크를 만들어 주셨다. 그것은 정말 맛있었다. 나의 아빠는 나에게 책을 주셨다. 나는 그것이 아주 좋았다. 나의 오빠는 나에게 생일 카드를 써줬다. 우리는 아주 멋진 밤을 보냈다. 나의 가족은 항상 나를 행복하게 만든다.

(1) 당신의 엄마는 당신에게 무엇을 만들어 주셨나요?
→ 그녀는 저에게 딸기 케이크를 만들어 주셨어요.
(2) 딸기 케이크는 맛이 어땠나요?
→ 그것은 정말 맛있었어요.
(3) 당신의 오빠는 당신에게 무엇을 써 주었나요?
→ 그는 나에게 생일 카드를 써 주었어요.
(4) 당신의 기분은 어땠나요?
→ 저는 행복했어요.

21 아이들은 잔디 위에서 뛰어다니고 있다. 그들은 매우 신나 보인다.
[어휘] excited 신이 난, 들뜬

22 우리 마을에는 새로운 공원이 있다. 휴식을 취하기에, 사람들은 그 새로운 공원이 좋은 장소라는 것을 알게 되었다.
[어휘] rest 쉬다, 휴식을 취하다

23 나는 오늘 내 도시락을 집에 두고 갔다. 다행히, 내 남동생이 나에게 도시락을 가져다주었다.
[어휘] fortunately 다행스럽게도

24 지난 토요일, 우리 자원봉사 동아리는 Blue 보육원에 방문했다. 우리는 아이들을 위해 공연을 열었다. 우리는 함께 노래를 부르고 춤을 췄다. 아이들의 웃음소리가 모두를 즐겁게 했다. 우리도 신이 났다. 정말 멋진 날이었다.
[어휘] volunteer 자원봉사자; 자원봉사를 하다   children's home 보육원   hold 열다, 개최하다   laugh 웃음; 웃다   joyful 즐거운, 기쁜

25 (1) I named it Brown
(2) it gives me a warm hug
(3) keeps our house clean
(4) cooks my family meals
(5) makes our lives easy

26 ⓐ → of you
ⓒ → feel bad

25 (1) 저의 새 로봇 친구를 소개합니다. 저는 그것을 Brown이라고 이름 지었습니다.
(2) Brown은 로봇이지만, 그것은 우리의 기분을 보살핍니다. 제가 기분이 좋지 않을 때, 그것은 저에게 따뜻한 포옹을 해 줍니다.
(3) Brown은 우리 집을 깨끗하게 유지합니다.
(4) Brown은 나의 가족에게 식사를 요리해 줍니다.
(5) Brown은 우리의 삶을 쉽게 만들어 줍니다.
[어휘] hug 포옹; 포옹하다

26 Mike: Jane, 너에게 부탁 좀 해도 될까?
Jane: 무엇이니, Mike?
Mike: 나에게 저 책을 빌려줄 수 있니? 나는 내 숙제를 위해 그 책이 필요해.
Jane: 미안해. 나도 내 숙제를 위해서 그것이 필요해. 정말 유감이야.
Mike: 아, 알겠어. 괜찮아.
Jane: Jenny에게 네 문제를 말해보는 게 어때? 그녀도 이 책을 가지고 있어.
Mike: 응, 그럴게.
[해설] ⓐ ask a favor 표현은 간접목적어를 뒤로 보낼 때 전치사 of를 쓴다.
ⓒ 감각동사 feel의 보어 자리이므로 부사가 아닌 형용사 bad를 써야 한다.

Challenge!

27 ⓑ → You exercise regularly, don't you?
ⓔ → Her story made all the students in the class happy.

 ⓐ 나는 파티에 무엇을 입고 가야 할까?
ⓑ 너는 운동을 규칙적으로 하는구나, 그렇지 않니?
ⓒ 나는 슈퍼마켓에서 사과 몇 개를 샀다.
ⓓ 그는 매일 저녁 그의 아들에게 책을 읽어준다.
ⓔ 그녀의 이야기는 학급의 모든 학생들을 행복하게 만들었다.
해설 ⓑ 일반동사 현재형의 긍정문이 쓰였으므로 부가의문문은
aren't가 아닌 don't로 써야 한다.

ⓔ '~을 …하게 만들다'의 의미를 나타내려면 「make+목적어+형
용사 보어」의 형태로 써야 하므로, 부사 happily를 형용사 happy
로 써야 한다.
어휘 regularly 규칙적으로

Chapter 08 | to부정사

Unit 01 to부정사의 명사적 쓰임

POINT 1   p.131

1 To eat vegetables is good
2 to throw a party for Tyler
3 To go swimming is really exciting
4 My wish is to travel around the world
5 To exercise regularly is important
6 To play musical instruments is
7 His job is to take care of children.
8 To stay at home all day is
9 My sister's dream is to become a cook.
10 my goal is to finish this book

10 A: 너는 주말에 무슨 계획이 있니?
   B: 응, 내 목표는 이 책을 끝내는 거야.

POINT 2   p.133

1 decided to buy new shoes
2 like to spend time with my family
3 need to finish their homework
4 promised to come
5 hates to wake up
6 I hope to sing
7 We plan to visit the history museum
8 Mia learned to bake bread
9 I want to visit Busan with my friends.

9 A: 너는 다음 방학 때 어디에 가고 싶니?
   B: 나는 나의 친구들과 부산에 방문하고 싶어.

Unit 02 to부정사의 부사적 쓰임

POINT 3   p.135

1 saved money to buy concert tickets
2 raised my hand to ask a question
3 were happy to get good scores
4 To improve your writing
5 The girl was glad to see a play.
6 They were very sad to hear the news.
7 went to the playground to play badminton
8 (1) to study English
   (2) to borrow a book
   (3) to do his homework

8 (1) Joe는 영어 공부를 하려고 도서관에 갔다.
   (2) Max는 책 한 권을 빌리기 위해 도서관에 갔다.
   (3) Tim은 그의 숙제를 하려고 도서관에 갔다.

Unit 03 to부정사의 형용사적 쓰임

POINT 4   p.137

1 I don't have a coat to wear
2 He found a place to stay
3 They picked a movie to watch together
4 We need someone to help us
5 There are many musicals to watch
6 I need time to take a rest.
7 Justin got a chance to travel Paris.
8 My parents bought a car to drive.
9 Sumi wrote some letters to give
10 It was a perfect way to relax.

10 John은 방학 때 읽을 책을 찾았다. 그는 그것을 이틀 만에 끝냈다.
   그것은 휴식을 취하는 완벽한 방법이었다.

STAGE 1

1 want to buy a new cap
2 is to live in England
3 student to finish the exam
4 happy to go to the amusement park
5 To play with friends is fun
6 My mom is planning to start a new job
7 Can you give me something to drink
8 She makes cookies to give to her friends

2 어휘 England 영국
3 어휘 exam 시험
4 어휘 amusement park 놀이공원
7 해설 -thing, -one, -body로 끝나는 대명사는 to부정사가 뒤에서 수식한다.
8 Ruby는 빵 굽는 것을 좋아한다. 그녀는 그녀의 친구들에게 나누어 주기 위해 쿠키를 만든다. 그들은 이 선물들을 항상 좋아한다.

STAGE 2

9 to wear glasses
10 to lose her book
11 to open the door
12 to meet my friend
13 to be[become] an actor
14 To watch a soccer game
15 to jog around the lake
16 to buy some eggs
17 (1) Lena began to save money
   (2) is to read ten books
18 travels → travel
19 visit → to visit
20 missing → miss
21 use → to use
22 were → was
23 stayed → to stay
24 lend → to lend
25 (1) I want to help sick people
   (2) I decided to be[become] a nurse
26 (1) He likes to learn new languages.
   (2) His goal is to use these languages
27 (1) wants to play board games with his friends on Saturday
   (2) wants to go skating on Sunday

15 A: Clara, 너 오늘 아침에 어디에 있었니?
  B: 나는 공원에 있었어. 나는 호수 주변을 조깅했어.
  Q: Clara는 왜 공원에 갔었니?
  A: 그녀는 호수 주변을 조깅하려고 공원에 갔다.
  해설 목적을 나타내는 to부정사를 사용해 질문에 대답한다.
  어휘 jog 조깅하다
16 A: 왜 늦었어, 진호야?
  B: 나는 오는 길에 슈퍼마켓에 잠시 들렀어. 나는 달걀을 좀 샀어.
  Q: 진호는 왜 늦었나?
  A: 그는 달걀을 좀 사기 위해 슈퍼마켓에 잠시 들렀다.
  어휘 stop by (~에) 잠시 들르다 on one's way 가는 길에, 도중에
18 Linda는 내년에 아시아로 여행하길 바란다.
19 우리는 우리 마을에 있는 사과 농장을 방문하기로 선택했다.
20 그들은 그 콘서트를 놓쳐서 슬펐다.
21 그 남자아이는 세탁기를 사용하는 것을 배웠다.
  어휘 washing machine 세탁기

22 이 문제를 푸는 것은 어려웠다.
  해설 to부정사 주어는 단수 취급하므로 동사로 was를 써야 한다.
23 그녀는 오늘 방과 후에 집에 머물기로 약속했다.
24 너는 나에게 빌려줄 연필이 있니?
  해설 의미상 명사 a pencil을 꾸며 주는 to부정사인 to lend를 써야 한다.
  어휘 lend 빌려주다
25 오늘 나는 나의 미래 목표에 관해 이야기할 것이다. 나는 미래에 아픈 사람들을 돕길 원한다. 어느 날, 나는 플로렌스 나이팅게일에 관해 읽었고 그녀는 나의 롤 모델이 되었다. 그래서 나는 간호사가 되기로 결심했다.
  어휘 role model 본보기, 롤 모델
26 호민이는 13살이다. 그는 새로운 언어들을 배우기를 좋아한다. 그의 목표는 많은 나라에서 이 언어들을 사용하는 것이다. 준비하기 위해서, 그는 매일 다른 언어로 된 영화를 본다.

27

하고 싶은 것	토요일에	일요일에
친구들과 함께 보드게임 하기	○	×
스케이트 타러 가기	×	○

(1) Liam은 토요일에 그의 친구들과 함께 보드게임을 하고 싶다.
(2) Liam은 일요일에 스케이트를 타러 가고 싶다.

STAGE 3

28 (1) likes to eat
   (2) to buy
   (3) happy to receive
   (4) to invite
29 (1) To take a plane[To go to New York]
   (2) to travel abroad
   (3) to visit
   (4) want to visit

28

Jina의 생일 파티를 위한 계획	
Jina가 가장 좋아하는 케이크	치즈케이크
살 것들	장미 몇 송이
초대할 친구들	다섯 명

  Jina는 나의 가장 친구이고 내일은 그녀의 생일이다. 나의 친구들과 나는 생일 파티를 열어줄 것이다.
  Jina는 치즈케이크를 먹는 것을 좋아한다. 그래서 우리는 유명한 빵집에서 치즈케이크를 하나 샀다. 그다음 나는 장미를 몇 송이 사기 위해 꽃집에 갔다. Jina는 그것들을 받고 행복해할 것이다. 우리는 파티를 위한 초대장도 만들었다. 파티에 초대할 다섯 명의 친구들이 있다. Jina는 굉장한 생일을 보내게 될 것이다.
  어휘 receive 받다, 얻다 hold 열다, 개최하다 invitation 초대장, 초대
29   나는 지난여름 나의 가족과 함께 뉴욕에 갔다. 우리는 공항에 가서 비행기를 탔다. 나는 처음으로 해외여행을 했고 매우 신이 났다.
  나는 많은 미술관과 박물관들을 방문했다. 뉴욕 사람들은 너무 빨리 말해서 나는 그들을 잘 이해할 수 없었다. 모든 것이 도전이었지만, 신나는 도전이었다. 나는 정말로 내년에 그 도시를 다시 방문하고 싶다.
(1) 비행기를 타기 위해서[뉴욕에 가기 위해서] 우리는 공항에 갔다.
(2) 나는 해외여행을 해서 매우 신이 났다.
(3) 뉴욕에는 방문할 많은 미술관과 박물관들이 있다.
(4) 내년에, 나는 그 도시를 다시 방문하길 원한다.
  해설 (1) 목적을 나타내는 to부정사는 문장 맨 앞에 올 수 있다.
  어휘 airport 공항 abroad 해외로 excited 신이 난, 흥분한 gallery 미술관, 화랑 New Yorker 뉴욕 시민 challenge 도전

Challenge!

30 ⓑ → I didn't expect to see you here.
  ⓒ → The chocolate cake tasted sweet.

30 ⓐ Ted는 그의 엄마를 위해 저녁을 만들었다.
ⓑ 나는 너를 여기서 보게 될 거라고 예상하지 못했다.
ⓒ 초콜릿 케이크는 달콤한 맛이 났다.
ⓓ 너무 음악을 크게 듣지 마.
ⓔ 사람들은 날씨를 확인하기 위해 스마트폰을 사용한다.

해설 ⓑ expect는 to부정사를 목적어로 취하는 동사이므로 seeing 을 to see로 고쳐 써야 한다.
ⓒ 감각동사 taste는 보어로 형용사를 취하므로 sweetly를 sweet 로 고쳐 써야 한다.

Chapter 09 | 동명사

Unit 01 명사로 쓰이는 동명사

POINT 1   p.145

1 Taking a trip by train is
2 Biting your nails is
3 is improving my cooking skills
4 Eating fruits and vegetables is
5 Waiting in line is boring
6 Being on time is important.
7 Learning foreign languages is not[isn't] easy.
8 Reading a book builds your vocabulary.
9 (1) Her[Olivia's] job is taking care of pets.
또는 Taking care of pets is her[Olivia's] job.
(2) Her[Olivia's] hobby is playing the piano.
또는 Playing the piano is her[Olivia's] hobby.

9 Olivia는 동물 병원에서 반려동물들을 돌본다. 그것이 그녀의 직업이다. 여가 시간에 그녀는 피아노 연주하는 것을 좋아한다. 그것은 그녀의 취미이다.
(1) Olivia의 직업은 무엇인가요?
→ 그녀의[Olivia의] 직업은 반려동물들을 돌보는 것이다.
반려동물들을 돌보는 것이 그녀의[Olivia의] 직업이다.
(2) Olivia의 취미는 무엇인가요?
→ 그녀의[Olivia의] 취미는 피아노를 연주하는 것이다.
피아노를 연주하는 것이 그녀의[Olivia의] 취미이다.

POINT 2   p.147

1 Anna gave up finding her watch
2 We finished building a sandcastle
3 Erica avoids taking a bus
4 suggested watching a movie
5 practice speaking English
6 mind turning on the air conditioner
7 The soccer team keeps winning.
8 I love trying out[to try out] new things.
9 (1) He[My brother] enjoys singing songs.
(2) She[My sister] practices riding a bike.

9

	형	여동생
자전거 타기		○
노래 부르기	○	

A: 너의 형은 여가 시간에 무엇을 즐기니?
B: 그는[나의 형은] 노래 부르는 것을 즐겨.
A: 너의 여동생은 무엇을 연습하니?
B: 그녀는[나의 여동생은] 자전거 타는 것을 연습해.

Unit 02 자주 쓰이는 동명사 표현

POINT 3   p.149

1 went skiing last weekend
2 are good at seeing
3 Thank you for lending me a book
4 am excited about going on vacation
5 How about visiting the museum
6 We celebrate Chuseok by having
7 He is[He's] afraid of riding roller coasters.
8 Andy is interested in studying
9 left the party without saying goodbye
10 is good at playing basketball

10 나는 Bella이다. 나는 노래는 잘 못 부르지만, 나는 농구를 매우 잘한다. 나는 모든 경기에서 가장 많은 점수를 득점하고, 나의 팀은 농구 경기에서 항상 이긴다.
→ 그녀는 농구를 잘한다.

Chapter Test   p.150

STAGE 1

1 is reading fashion magazines
2 Ethan stopped drinking soda
3 Making cookies with friends is enjoyable
4 He avoids eating too late

  5 Traveling[Travelling, To travel] to new places is interesting.
  6 Mom practices driving her car
  7 Thank you for telling me
  8 playing, dancing, taking[to take]

1 어휘 magazine 잡지
2 어휘 soda 탄산음료
3 어휘 enjoyable 즐거운
6 어휘 these days 요즘
7 어휘 information 정보
8 학교 축제가 다음 주이다. 나는 피아노 치는 것을 즐겨서, 나는 내가 가장 좋아하는 곡을 연주할 것이다. Jacob은 춤을 잘 춰서, 그는 친구들과 함께 공연을 할 것이다. Emily의 취미는 사진 찍는 것이어서, 그녀는 축제에 카메라를 가져올 것이다.
   어휘 perform 공연[연주]하다

STAGE 2

 9 to take → taking   10 aren't → isn't
11 to ask → asking   12 to take → taking
13 Watch → Watching[To watch]
14 break → breaking   15 to bake → baking
16 show → showing   17 to put → putting
18 He is[He's, Dean is] considering cooking dinner
19 She[Judy] gave up learning Spanish
20 (1) He likes making things with his hands.
   (2) She is interested in learning pottery.
21 Going[To go] to college is
22 I finished writing it
23 be afraid of trying new things
24 Thank you for fixing it
25 How about going fishing
26 (1) I am[I'm] considering getting a puppy
   (2) I kept persuading them.
27 ⓒ → Watching sports is fun and exciting.
   ⓔ → I love walking[to walk] my dog on the weekend.

 9 너는 나중에 산책하는 것을 꺼리니?
   해설 mind는 동명사를 목적어로 취하는 동사이다.
10 만화책을 읽는 것은 나에게 재미가 없다.
   해설 동명사 주어는 단수 취급한다.
11 나의 남동생은 자연에 대해서 질문하는 것을 계속했다.
   해설 keep은 동명사를 목적어로 취하는 동사이다.
12 나의 사촌은 다른 나라로 여행을 가는 것을 즐긴다.
   해설 enjoy는 동명사를 목적어로 취하는 동사이다.
13 무서운 영화를 보는 것은 흥미진진하다.
   해설 주어 자리에는 동사원형이 올 수 없다.
14 Jim은 교칙을 어기는 것을 피했다.
   해설 avoid는 동명사를 목적어로 취하는 동사이다.
   어휘 break a rule 규칙을 어기다
15 Jessica는 사과 파이를 굽는 것을 끝냈다.
   해설 finish는 동명사를 목적어로 취하는 동사이다.
16 나는 나의 학생증을 보여줌으로써 도서관에 들어갔다.
   해설 전치사 by 뒤에 동사를 쓸 때는 동명사 형태로 써야 한다.
   어휘 ID card 신분증 (= identification card)
17 Sue는 퍼즐을 맞추는 것을 포기했다.
   해설 give up은 동명사를 목적어로 취하는 동사이다.
   어휘 put A together (이것저것 모아) A를 만들다

[18~19]

	Dean	Alex	Judy
축구를 하다		○	
스페인어를 배우다			○
저녁 식사를 만들다	○		

18 A: Dean은 무엇을 생각하고 있니?
   B: 그는[Dean은] 자신의 가족을 위해 저녁을 요리할 것을 고려하고 있어.
19 A: Judy는 무엇을 포기했니?
   B: 그녀는[Judy는] 스페인어를 배우는 것을 포기했어.
20 해설 (1) like는 목적어로 동명사와 to부정사 모두 취하는 동사이다. 제시된 단어 수에 맞게 동사 make를 동명사 형태로 쓴다.
   (2) '~에 관심이 있다'는 「be interested in+동명사」로 표현한다.
   어휘 pottery 도예; 도자기
21 A: 너희 오빠의 고등학교 졸업 후 계획은 무엇이니?
   B: 대학에 가는 것이 그의 다음 단계야.
22 A: 너는 너의 독후감을 끝냈니?
   B: 응, 나는 그것을 쓰는 것을 어제 마쳤어.
   어휘 be done 끝나다, 종료되다
23 A: 나는 처음으로 캠핑을 하는 것에 대해 걱정돼.
   B: 새로운 것들을 시도하는 것을 무서워하지 마.
24 A: 와, 너는 정말 나의 자전거를 빨리 고쳤구나!
   B: 별일 아니었어.
   A: 그것을 고쳐줘서 고마워. 나는 이제 학교에 타고 갈 수 있어!
   어휘 no big deal 별일 아니다, 대수롭지 않다
25 A: 너는 이번 주말에 무엇을 하고 싶니?
   B: 낚시하러 가는 거 어때? 강 옆에 조용한 장소가 있어.
   어휘 spot 장소; 점
26 Leo에게,
      안녕, Leo야. 오랫동안 이야기를 못 했구나! 너의 새 학교는 어때?
      요즘, 나는 강아지를 키우는 것을 고려하고 있어. 하지만 나의 부모님은 처음에는 그것을 허락하지 않으셨어. 나는 그분들을 설득하는 것을 계속했어. 그리고 그들은 마침내 동의하셨어! 내가 강아지를 집에 데려오면 너에게 강아지 사진을 보내줄게.
      나는 너를 곧 만나길 바라!

   몸 건강해,
   Serena
   해설 (1) consider는 동명사를 목적어로 취하는 동사이다.
   (2) keep은 동명사를 목적어로 취하는 동사이다.
   어휘 chat 이야기, 대화   soon 곧   persuade 설득하다
27 ⓐ 너는 집을 청소하는 것을 끝냈니?
   ⓑ 엄마는 소풍 가는 것을 제안하셨다.
   ⓒ 스포츠를 보는 것은 재미있고 흥미롭다.
   ⓓ Noah는 늘 결정하는 것을 피한다.
   ⓔ 나는 주말에 내 개를 산책시키는 것을 아주 좋아한다.
   해설 ⓒ 동명사 주어는 단수 취급한다.
   ⓔ love는 목적어로 동명사와 to부정사를 모두 취할 수 있다.
   어휘 make a decision 결정하다   walk (동물을) 산책시키다

STAGE 3

28 (1) She enjoys taking a walk
   (2) She avoids being late to school
   (3) She practices playing the violin
   (4) She is[She's] good at dancing
   (5) She minds watching scary movies
29 ⓑ → He enjoys helping other people.
   ⓔ → When he finished volunteering, he was very proud of himself.

28 나의 친구 Amelia를 소개해. 그녀는 미국에서 왔어.
   (1) 그녀는 공원에서 산책하는 것을 즐겨.
   (2) 그녀는 학교에 늦는 것을 피해.
   (3) 그녀는 바이올린 연주하는 것을 연습해.
   (4) 그녀는 춤추는 것을 잘해.
   (5) 그녀는 무서운 영화 보는 것을 꺼려.
   [어휘] the United States 미국

29   나의 남동생은 지난여름에 특별한 방학을 보내기를 원했다. 그는 다른 사람들을 돕는 것을 즐긴다. 그래서 그는 병원에서 자원봉사 활동을 시작했다. 그는 사람들을 행복하게 만드는 것을 아주 좋아한다. 그는 아픈 사람들에게 흥미로운 이야기들을 들려주었다. 그들은 그에게 고마워했다. 그가 자원봉사 활동하는 것을 마쳤을 때, 그는 자기 자신을 매우 자랑스러워했다.
   [해설] enjoy와 finish는 동명사를 목적어로 취하는 동사이다.
   [어휘] voluteer work 자원봉사   thankful 감사하는, 고마워하는   volunteer 자원봉사를 하다   be proud of ~을 자랑스러워하다

30 ⓑ → He hopes to go to England next year.
   ⓒ → Can you teach French to me[teach me French] after school?

30 ⓐ 빵집에 있는 그 빵은 좋은 냄새가 났다.
   ⓑ 그는 내년에 영국에 가기를 바란다.
   ⓒ 방과 후에 나에게 프랑스어를 가르쳐줄 수 있니?
   ⓓ 근육을 키우기 위해서, 그는 매일 운동한다.
   ⓔ 그녀는 연극을 위해 대사를 암기하는 것을 포기하지 않았다.
   [해설] ⓑ hope는 to부정사를 목적어로 취하는 동사이다.
   ⓒ teach는 간접목적어를 뒤로 보낼 때 전치사 to를 쓴다. 또는 「teach+간접목적어+직접목적어」의 형태로도 쓸 수 있다.
   [어휘] muscle 근육   memorize 암기하다   line (연극·영화의) 대사; 선, 줄   play 연극

Chapter 10 | 전치사와 접속사

Unit 01 전치사

POINT 1   p.157

1 is next to the library
2 are singing in the sky
3 were many pictures on the wall
4 found my wallet at the bus stop
5 The Earth goes around the Sun.
6 A butterfly flew into his room.
7 I will[I'll] wait for you at the main gate.
8 is a big yard behind our house
9 (1) is between two chairs
   (2) is on the table
   (3) are in the vase

9 (1) 탁자가 두 의자 사이에 있다.
   (2) 꽃병 하나가 탁자 위에 있다.
   (3) 꽃 몇 송이가 꽃병 안에 있다.

POINT 2   p.159

1 on Tuesday
2 in 2023
3 for five years
4 Susan called me before dinner
5 The Australians enjoy Christmas in summer
6 She visited her hometown during the vacation
7 watches a movie on Saturdays
8 moved to Busan in July

9 saw the full moon at night
10 Greg always gets up at seven in

10 [해설] 시각을 나타내는 말 앞에는 전치사 at을, 아침, 점심 등과 같이 하루를 이루는 말 앞에는 전치사 in을 쓴다.

POINT 3   p.161

1 like an angel   **2** with many pockets
3 as a photographer   **4** by subway
5 about the service
6 France is famous for the Eiffel Tower
7 Henry was happy with his exam results
8 He studied math from morning to evening
9 Her story is different from the truth.
10 Thanks to Hans, people can get things

10 Hans는 그린란드에 산다. 개썰매는 그의 일상의 일부이다. 겨울에 그의 개들은 사람들에게 많은 물건들을 배달한다. Hans 덕분에, 사람들은 물건들을 쉽게 받을 수 있다.

Unit 02 접속사

POINT 4   p.163

1 played soccer and changed clothes
2 plan to play board games and have lunch
3 You can take the bus or walk to the school
4 outside or watching TV
5 The story was interesting but too long.

6 My sister went to the park and rode a bike

7 he cleans the house and does laundry

8 He and I will visit Japan or Hong Kong

9 but I didn't have an umbrella

9 방과 후에 비가 많이 왔지만, 나는 우산이 없었다.

POINT 5　p.165

1 before you go to bed

2 If it is sunny tomorrow

3 so I went to another store

4 when I went to the museum

5 After my dad read a newspaper

6 If you know the answer

7 when he goes to Italy

8 Because Julia lost her cell phone

9 was happy because my team won the game

9 나는 나의 팀이 경기에서 이겼기 때문에 행복했다.

POINT 6　p.167

1 thought that it was the answer

2 believe that Victor will help me

3 hope that I become a good student

4 knows that Tim is very honest

5 said we must clean the classroom

6 I remember (that) he was a singer

7 Emily said (that) the musical was interesting.

8 People think (that) the restaurant is the best

9 I believe that he will be the school president.

9 Adam은 학교의 모든 사람들에게 항상 친절하다. 그는 예의 바르고 다른 사람들의 말을 주의 깊게 듣는다. Adam은 다음 달에 학생회장 선거에 출마할 것이다. 나는 그가 학생회장이 될 거라고 믿는다.

Chapter Test　p.168

STAGE 1

1 If it rains tomorrow

2 remember that Mike has a younger sister

3 when he arrives at the hotel

4 but she finished her homework

5 on the desk

6 cold or snowy

7 in July and August

8 I think that he can solve it

1 어휘 cancel 취소하다

7 해설 월 앞에는 전치사 in을 쓴다.

8 A: 너는 나를 위해 이 수학 문제를 풀어줄 수 있니?
B: 미안해. 나는 할 수 없어. Mike에게 물어보는 게 어때?
A: 그는 수학을 잘하니?
B: 응, 맞아. 나는 그가 그것을 풀 수 있다고 생각해.

STAGE 2

9 for　　　**10** in

11 during　　**12** by

13 until　　**14** When

15 because　　**16** so

17 (1) is lying on the bed

(2) is beside the bed

(3) is sitting under the table

(4) is behind the dog

18 (1) The library opens from 8 a.m. to 5 p.m.

(2) is famous for its newest books

19 when I have a cold

20 because I did not[didn't] sleep well

21 When she waits for the bus

22 after he gets home

23 Because I missed the subway

24 at → on　　**25** because of → because

26 during → for　　**27** in → on

28 go → went

29 (1) always wash my hands before I eat dinner

(2) waited until the rain stopped

9 우리는 두 시간 동안 줄을 서서 기다렸다.
해설 숫자를 포함한 구체적인 기간 two hours가 쓰였으므로 전치사 for를 쓴다.

10 그 영화는 2024년에 개봉했다.
해설 연도 앞에는 전치사 in을 쓴다.

11 Fred는 클래식 음악 콘서트를 보는 동안 잠이 들었다.
해설 특정한 때를 나타내는 the classical music concert가 쓰였으므로 전치사 during을 쓴다.
어휘 fall asleep 잠이 들다　classical music 클래식 음악

12 너는 다음 주 금요일까지 도서관에 그 책들을 반납해야 한다.
해설 '반납'이라는 일회성의 행동이 완료되는 기한을 나타낼 때는 전치사 by를 쓴다.

13 나의 아빠는 내일까지 집에 오지 않으실 것이다. 아빠는 지금 출장 중이시다.
해설 계속되던 동작이 끝나는 시점을 나타낼 때는 until을 쓴다.
어휘 business trip 출장

14 비가 올 때, 나는 주로 집에 머무른다.

15 나는 저 식당이 너무 시끄럽기 때문에 좋아하지 않는다.

16 우리는 버스를 놓쳐서 학교까지 걸어가야 했다.

17 (1) 여자아이 한 명이 침대 위에 누워 있다.
(2) 탁자 하나가 침대 옆에 있다.
(3) 개 한 마리가 탁자 아래에 앉아 있다.
(4) 상자 하나가 개 뒤에 있다.

18 나의 집 근처에 도서관이 하나 있다. 그 도서관은 오전 8시부터 오후 5시까지 문을 연다. 그곳은 최신 책들로 유명하다. 그래서 나는 그곳에 가는 것을 아주 좋아한다.

24 금요일에 야구 시합이 있을 것이다.

25 나는 지난밤 늦게까지 깨어있어서 지금 피곤하다.
해설 뒤에 주어와 동사가 있는 완전한 문장이 나오므로 접속사 because를 써야 한다. because of 뒤에는 명사구가 온다.

26 한 시간 동안 비가 많이 내렸다.
어휘 heavily 심하게, 아주 많이

27 그녀는 벽에 달력을 걸었다.
어휘 calendar 달력

28 나는 일주일 전에 친구를 만나서 영화를 보러 갔다.
해설 동사가 접속사 and로 연결될 때는 시제를 동일하게 써야 하므로 go를 went로 고쳐 써야 한다.

29 (1) ・나는 항상 나의 손을 씻는다.
・나는 저녁 식사를 한다.

→ 나는 저녁 식사를 하기 전에 항상 나의 손을 씻는다.
(2) • 우리는 기다렸다.
　　• 비가 그쳤다.
　　→ 우리는 비가 그칠 때까지 기다렸다.

STAGE 3

30 (1) If　　　　(2) after
　　(3) Before　　　(4) because
31 believe that he[Suho] will be the best player

30

> ### 컵케이크 만드는 방법
> 1. 그릇에 버터와 설탕을 넣고 휘저어라.
> 2. 밀가루, 계란, 베이킹파우더, 그리고 소금을 넣고 잘 저어라.
> 3. 반죽을 제빵용 컵에 부어라.
> 4. 오븐에 컵케이크를 10분 동안 구워라.
> 5. 컵케이크가 식을 때까지 10분을 더 기다려라.
> 　이제 너의 컵케이크를 즐겨라!

단것을 좋아한다면, 컵케이크를 만들어 보는 건 어떨까요?
먼저, 그릇에 버터와 설탕을 넣고 휘저으세요! 그러고 나서 그릇에 밀가루, 달걀, 베이킹파우더 그리고 소금을 넣은 후에 잘 저어주세요.
반죽을 구울 때 제빵용 컵이 필요해요. 컵케이크를 즐기기 전에 10분을 기다려야 하는데, 컵케이크가 너무 뜨거울 것이기 때문이에요.

어휘 **bowl** (우묵한) 그릇　**beat** 휘젓다　**flour** 밀가루　**stir** 젓다
mix 반죽; 섞다　**sweet** 단것; 달콤한

31 나의 가장 친한 친구인 수호는 축구 선수가 되길 원한다. 그가 열 살이었을 때, 그는 경기장에서 축구 경기를 봤다. 그때 이후로, 그는 축구 선수가 되는 꿈을 꾸기 시작했다. 방과 후에 그는 항상 열심히 연습한다. 그래서 나는 미래에 그개[수호가] 최고의 선수가 될 것이라고 믿는다.
해설 동사 believe 뒤에 명사절을 이끄는 접속사 that이 와야 한다. 이때, that은 생략 가능하지만 8 단어로 써야 하므로 that을 써줘야 한다.
어휘 **stadium** 경기장

32 ⓑ → My mom and I are good at singing songs.
　　ⓓ → He travels a lot and meets many people.

32 ⓐ 나는 살을 빼기 위해 규칙적으로 운동한다.
　　ⓑ 나의 엄마와 나는 노래 부르는 것을 잘한다.
　　ⓒ 나는 네가 너 자신을 자랑스러워해야 한다고 생각해.
　　ⓓ 그는 여행을 많이 다니고 많은 사람들을 만난다.
　　ⓔ 그녀는 뱀을 보았을 때 비명을 질렀다.
해설 ⓑ 전치사가 포함된 be good at 표현 뒤에 동사를 쓸 때는 동명사 형태로 써야 한다.
ⓓ 접속사 and가 동사를 연결할 때는 동사의 수를 일치시켜야 한다.
어휘 **regularly** 규칙적으로　**scream** 비명을 지르다; 비명
snake 뱀

Unit 01　be동사　　p.02

1 He is a talented singer
2 Brian and I are on the same soccer team
3 She was not happy with the result
4 Were you　　　　5 Yes, I am
6 No, it isn't 또는 No, it's not
7 These gloves are very warm.
8 We are not[We aren't, We're not] late for the movie.
9 Was she angry with me
10 (1) No, I wasn't. (2) I was in Korea.

4 A: 너는 긴 여행 후에 피곤했니?
　 B: 응, 맞아. 난 하루 종일 집에 있었어.
5 A: 넌 지금 졸리니?
　 B: 응, 맞아. 난 휴식을 취하고 싶어.
6 A: 네 휴대전화는 주머니에 있니?
　 B: 아니, 그렇지 않아. 내 책상 위에 있어.
10 A: 넌 2년 전에 영국에 있었니?
　 B: 아니, 그렇지 않아. 나는 한국에 있었어.
　 [해설] (1) be동사 과거형의 의문문으로 묻고 있으므로, 부정(no)의 응답은 「No, 주어+과거형 be동사+not.」으로 써야 한다. 의문문의 주어가 you이므로 응답문의 주어는 I를 써야 한다.
　 (2) 주어가 I이며, 과거의 일에 대해 얘기하고 있으므로 be동사로는 was를 써야 한다.

Unit 02　일반동사의 현재형과 과거형　　p.03

1 teaches　　　　2 carries
3 planned　　　　4 kept
5 Carol speaks three languages
6 We heard a strange noise
7 My friends and I watched a movie
8 He misses his friends
9 I caught a cold
10 Jamie and I have different ideas
11 ⓐ have　ⓑ makes　ⓒ sets　ⓓ washes

11 우리 집에서는 우리 모두 각자의 일이 있다. 매일 아침, 나의 아빠는 모두를 위해 아침 식사를 만드신다. 내 여동생은 식탁을 차린다. 나의 엄마는 설거지하신다. 나는 쓰레기를 버린다. 우리는 함께 우리 집을 청소한다.

Unit 03　일반동사의 부정문과 의문문　　p.04

1 does not[doesn't] spend
2 did not[didn't] go
3 Does Sally's mom read
4 I do not[don't] play computer games
5 This book does not[doesn't] belong
6 She did not[didn't] listen to my advice.
7 Do you like broccoli
8 No, they didn't
9 (1) Does he like science fiction books?
　 (2) Yes, he does.

1 그는 스마트폰에 시간을 많이 쓴다.
　→ 그는 스마트폰에 시간을 많이 쓰지 않는다.
2 작년에 우리는 싱가포르로 여행을 갔다.
　→ 작년에 우리는 싱가포르로 여행을 가지 않았다.
3 Sally의 엄마는 매일 신문을 읽으신다.
　→ Sally의 엄마는 매일 신문을 읽으시니?
7 A: 너는 브로콜리를 좋아하니?
　 B: 아니, 그렇지 않아. 나는 채소를 싫어해.
8 A: 그 학생들은 버스 터미널에 제때 도착했니?
　 B: 아니, 그렇지 않아. 그들은 버스를 놓쳤어.
9 A: Samuel에게 생일 선물을 사 주자.
　 B: 좋은 생각이야.
　 A: 그는 공상 과학 소설책을 좋아하니?
　 B: 응, 맞아. 그는 우주 이야기를 아주 좋아해.
　 A: 그럼 그에게 새로운 공상 과학책을 사 주자!
　 [해설] (1) 주어(he)가 3인칭 단수인 일반동사(like) 현재형 의문문은 「Does+주어+동사원형 ~?」의 형태로 써야 한다.
　 (2) Does로 시작하는 일반동사 의문문에 대한 긍정의 대답은 「Yes, 주어+does.」로 쓴다.

Unit 01　현재진행형　　p.05

1 I am[I'm] packing my bag
2 She is[She's] drawing a picture
3 The Sun is rising
4 The students are planning a field trip
5 He is not[He isn't, He's not] riding his bike
6 Are you talking on the phone
7 The cars are not[aren't] stopping
8 Is our team winning the game?
9 (1) are sleeping on the sofa
　 (2) is making a sandwich for lunch

5 그는 지금 자전거를 타고 있지 않다.
6 너는 지금 통화하는 중이니?
7 그 차들은 빨간불에 멈추고 있지 않다.
8 우리 팀은 그 경기를 이기고 있니?
9 (1) 그 고양이들은 소파 위에서 자고 있다.
　 (2) 그녀는 점심 식사로 샌드위치를 만들고 있다.
　 [해설] (1) 주어(The cats)가 3인칭 복수인 현재진행형은 「are+동사의 -ing형」으로 쓴다.
　 (2) 주어(She)가 3인칭 단수인 현재진행형은 「is+동사의 -ing형」으로 쓴다.

1 I will clean my room
2 She will not take the bus
3 Will you come to the class meeting
4 We are going to visit our aunt
5 Is the city going to build a library
6 Taylor will order pizza
7 I will not[won't] wear the dress
8 They are not[They aren't, They're not] going to change
9 Is he going to start a new job
10 I will make Korean traditional snacks.

10 A: 너는 학교 축제에서 무엇을 할 거니?
   B: 나는 한국의 전통 간식을 만들 거야. 그다음, 우리 문화를 소개하기 위해 그것들을 판매할 거야.
   A: 좋은 생각이야!

Chapter 03 조동사

1 He can solve complex puzzles
2 Can you turn down the volume
3 You may not talk on the phone
4 can swim   5 Can[May], borrow
6 may close   7 may not be true
8 Can[May] I take a look at the menu?
9 I cannot[can't] remember her name.
10 (1) They can run very fast.
   (2) they cannot[can't] run fast

10 내가 가장 좋아하는 동물은 치타이다. 그것들의 몸에는 아름다운 반점이 있다. 그것들은 매우 빠르게 달릴 수 있다. 하지만 그것들은 장거리를 빨리 달리지 못한다.

1 must arrive   2 have to wear
3 must not lie   4 has to wait
5 don't have to buy
6 You must show your ID card.
7 We should not[shouldn't] waste food.
8 My family had to move to a new city
9 My mom doesn't[does not] have to cook dinner
10 (1) You don't have to wear your school uniforms
   (2) You must wear comfortable clothes

10 A: 내일 현장 학습에 무엇을 입어야 할까?
   B: 너는 내일 교복을 입을 필요가 없어. 너는 편안한 옷을 입어야 돼. 우리는 스포츠 활동들을 할 예정이거든.

해설 (1) '~할 필요가 없다'라는 의미는 don't have to를 사용해 나타낼 수 있으며, 그 뒤에는 동사원형 wear를 써야 한다.
(2) '~해야 한다'라는 의미는 must를 사용해 나타낼 수 있다.

총괄평가 1회 Chapter 01~03

1 I can climb tall mountains
2 You must not take a picture here
3 Sora has to practice the piano
4 were sick   5 goes to school
6 left home   7 are going to ride
8 She washes her dog
9 Aaron and I are drawing a picture
10 I will not[won't] watch TV
11 Is Mr. Kim a firefighter?
12 He is[He's] taking a nap in his room.
13 I do not[don't] eat breakfast at eight-thirty.
14 Did she go to the jazz concert?
15 Did you finish   16 No, it isn't[is not]
17 is picking some vegetables
18 are going to go shopping
19 Can   20 should
21 May
22 doesn't → don't 또는 My parents → My parent
23 see → saw   24 fly → flying
25 is → be
26 (1) made a cake for Mom
   (2) am swimming in the pool
   (3) will[am going to] be in the movie theater
27 (1) should study English
   (2) have to wash the cat
   (3) don't[do not] have to clean the living room
   (4) don't[do not] have to go to the market
   (5) must not play computer games

4 해설 주어 My brother and I는 복수이고 과거시제이므로 be동사는 were를 써야 한다.
  어휘 cold 감기; 차가운
11 김 씨 아저씨는 소방관이시다.
   → 김 씨 아저씨는 소방관이시니?
   어휘 firefighter 소방관
12 그는 그의 방에서 낮잠을 잔다.
   → 그는 그의 방에서 낮잠을 자고 있다.
   어휘 take a nap 낮잠을 자다
13 나는 8시 30분에 아침 식사를 한다.
   → 나는 8시 30분에 아침 식사를 하지 않는다.
14 그녀는 재즈 콘서트에 갔다.
   → 그녀는 재즈 콘서트에 갔었니?
   어휘 jazz 재즈
15 A: 너는 숙제를 마쳤니?
   B: 네, 맞아요. 저 지금 밖에 나가서 놀아도 될까요?
   해설 B의 응답의 주어가 I이고 did로 답했으므로 A의 질문은 「Did you ~?」가 알맞다.
   어휘 go out 나가다, 외출하다
16 A: Lilly, 네가 가장 좋아하는 디저트는 치즈케이크니?
   B: 아니, 그렇지 않아. 내가 가장 좋아하는 디저트는 푸딩이야.
   어휘 dessert 디저트   pudding 푸딩

17 A: 수진이는 지금 정원에서 무엇을 하고 있니?
B: 그녀는 야채를 좀 따고 있어.
[해설] 현재진행형 시제로 묻고 있으므로 대답도 현재진행형으로 한다.

18 A: 너와 Tom은 이번 주말에 무엇을 할 거니?
B: 우리는 쇼핑을 갈 거야.

19 A: 나에게 소금을 좀 건네줄래?
B: 물론이지. 여기 있어. 다른 것도 필요하니?
[해설] '~해줄래?'와 같은 '요청'의 의미를 나타낼 수 있는 표현은
「Can you+동사원형 ~?」이다.
[어휘] pass 건네주다; 지나가다

20 A: 나는 실수로 민호의 휴대 전화를 고장 냈어. 그는 나에게 정말
화가 났어.
B: 아, 저런. 너는 그에게 사과를 해야 해.
[어휘] accidentally 실수로   be mad at ~에게 화가 나다
apologize 사과하다

21 A: 제가 한 시간 동안 컴퓨터 게임을 해도 될까요?
B: 아니. 너는 네 방을 먼저 청소해야 해.
[해설] '~해도 되나요?'와 같은 '허가'의 의미를 나타낼 수 있는 표현
은 「May I+동사원형 ~?」이다.

22 나의 부모님은 운전을 하지 않으신다.
[해설] 주어 My parents는 복수이므로 doesn't를 don't로 쓰거나,
주어를 단수인 My parent로 고쳐 써야 한다.

23 나는 어젯밤에 공원에서 나의 친구를 보았다.
[해설] 과거를 나타내는 last night이 있으므로 see를 과거형 saw로
고쳐 써야 한다.

24 새 한 마리가 지금 하늘을 날고 있다.
[해설] right now로 보아 현재진행형으로 써야 하므로 be동사 뒤의
fly는 flying으로 고쳐야 한다.

25 날씨가 곧 좋아질까?
[해설] will 의문문은 「Will+주어+동사원형~?」으로 써야 하므로 is
는 be로 고쳐 써야 한다.
[어휘] soon 곧

26

이번 주 일정	
월요일	미술관 방문하기
화요일	엄마를 위해 케이크 만들기
수요일 (오늘)	수영장에서 수영하기
목요일	영화관에 가기

〈보기〉 나는 월요일에 미술관을 방문했다.
(1) 나는 화요일에 엄마를 위해 케이크를 만들었다.
(2) 나는 지금 수영장에서 수영을 하고 있다.
(3) 나는 목요일에 영화관에 갈 것이다.
[해설] (3) 일정표로 보아 Thursday(목요일)는 미래의 일을 나타내므
로 「will[be going to]+동사원형」을 사용해 쓴다.

27   애들아, 미안하구나.
나는 회의 때문에 나왔고, 밤 10시까지 돌아올 거란다.
미나야. 너는 영어 공부를 해야 해. 태민아, 너는 고양이를 씻겨
야 해. 미나야, 너는 거실을 청소할 필요가 없어. 태민아, 너는 시장
에 갈 필요가 없어.
그리고 기억하렴, 너희 둘은 컴퓨터 게임을 하면 안 된단다.
[해설] (3) '~할 필요가 없다'라는 의미는 don't[do not] have to를
사용해 나타낼 수 있으며, 그 뒤에는 동사원형 clean을 써야 한다.

Unit 01 명사
p.12

1 I found two watches
2 She read three stories
3 He posted five photos
4 There isn't a cloud in the sky
5 Is there a problem with the Wi-Fi
6 She took a bottle of juice
7 Mom baked three loaves of banana bread
8 There are five pieces of paper
9 (1) There is a picture on the wall.
   (2) There are two mice under the table.

9 (1) 벽에 그림 한 점이 걸려 있다.
   (2) 탁자 아래에 두 마리의 쥐가 있다.

Unit 02 인칭대명사와 재귀대명사
p.13

1 He, my   **2** They, us   **3** my, his
4 People don't know about themselves
5 We should protect ourselves from stress
6 His puppy follows him everywhere.
7 You should treat yourself well.
8 she challenges herself with a new goal.
9 I expressed myself

9 A: 네가 직접 이 사진을 찍었니?
B: 응, 맞아. 나는 사진을 통해 나 자신을 표현해 보았어.
A: 정말 아름답다!
B: 고마워.

Unit 03 지시대명사와 부정대명사
p.14

1 I bought these sneakers
2 It takes thirty minutes to the beach
3 I found some money in my old coat
4 That → Those 또는 mountains are → mountain is
5 are → is
6 some → any 또는 aren't → are
7 It gets really hot
8 Nobody believes his story.
9 Are there any good restaurants
10 (1) It is[It's] rainy outside.
   (2) Do you have any favorite activities

4 봐! 저 산들은[산은] 아름다워.
[해설] 지시대명사(That) 뒤에 오는 명사가 mountains로 복수명사
이므로 Those로 고쳐 쓰거나, mountains are를 mountain is로
고쳐야 한다.

5 Kate, 누군가가 너를 찾고 있어.
[해설] someone이 주어로 쓰일 때는 항상 3인칭 단수 취급하므로

are를 is로 고쳐야 한다.

6 그 병에는 쿠키가 하나도 없다[좀 있다].
해설 부정문이므로 some을 any로 쓰거나 aren't를 are로 고쳐 긍정문으로 써야 한다.

10 밖에 비가 와요. 저는 비 오는 날을 좋아해요. 저는 보통 비 오는 날에는 책을 읽어요. 저는 빗방울 소리도 좋아해요. 여러분은 비 오는 날에 가장 좋아하는 활동이 있나요?

Chapter 05 형용사, 부사, 비교

Unit 01 형용사   p.15

1 She bought some fresh vegetables
2 Aiden keeps his desk clean
3 He wanted something sweet for dessert
4 There is little water
5 Jay spent much money
6 Mr. White got a few emails
7 Few students understood today's lesson.
8 (1) Did you invite many guests
   (2) a few friends will come

8 A: 엄마, 저는 친구들을 오늘 파티에 초대했어요.
B: 너는 파티에 많은 손님들을 초대했니?
A: 아니요. 몇 명의 친구들만 올 거예요.
B: 알겠단다. 그들을 위해 맛있는 음식을 좀 준비해 줄게.
A: 감사해요, 엄마.
해설 (1) 셀 수 있는 명사(guest) 앞에는 many, a few가 올 수 있으며, 의미상 many를 써야 한다. 이때 셀 수 있는 명사는 복수형(guests)으로 써야 한다.
(2) 셀 수 있는 명사(friend) 앞에는 의미상 a few가 와야 하며, 셀 수 있는 명사는 복수형(friends)으로 써야 한다.

Unit 02 부사   p.16

1 The sunset was so beautiful
2 The snow fell very heavily
3 Surprisingly, the baby fell asleep quickly[quickly fell asleep]
4 Jake often asks questions
5 Most students usually come to school
6 My little sister is always curious
7 You must never lose your passport.
8 (1) he sometimes goes to the park
   (2) He spends his weekends busily[busily spends his weekends].

8 주말에 민호는 아침 8시에 일어난다. 아침 식사 후, 그는 때때로 그의 강아지 Molly와 공원에 간다. 오후에 그는 보통 엄마나 아빠의 집안일을 돕는다. 그는 그의 주말을 바쁘게 보낸다.

Unit 03 비교급과 최상급   p.17

1 are sweeter than the green ones
2 plays the piano better than his brother
3 are the newest headphones in the shop
4 Tony's backpack is heavier than mine.
5 Today's weather is hotter than yesterday's.
6 This mountain is the highest in East Asia.
7 Tim trains the hardest of his teammates.
8 (1) is the most popular
   (2) is more popular than
   (3) is cheaper than

Chapter 06 여러 가지 문장 종류

Unit 01 명령문, 제안문, 감탄문   p.18

1 Bring your notebook to class
2 Don't touch the artworks in the museum
3 Let's have a barbecue party
4 Why don't we start a book club
5 How comfortable the sofa is
6 What a talented singer he is
7 What a cute puppy it is!
8 How quickly the time flies!
9 How about going to the concert
10 (1) Turn off the light in your room
   (2) don't[do not] forget the family gathering

10 A: 외출할 때는 네 방의 불을 끄렴.
B: 알겠어요, 엄마.
A: 그리고 오늘 가족 모임을 잊지 마렴.
B: 물론이죠. 잊지 않을게요.
해설 (1) 긍정 명령문이므로 동사원형인 Turn off로 시작해야 한다.
(2) 부정 명령문이므로 「Don't[Do not]+동사원형」으로 써야 한다.

Unit 02 의문사 의문문   p.19

1 Who is your role model
2 What does she want
3 How often do you exercise
4 What kind of movie do you like
5 Where can we find the nearest bus stop
6 Why does Jim study English
7 When did the fireworks finish
8 Whose jacket is it
9 (1) What is[What's] your plan for the vacation?
   (2) Why do you like that island?

6 A: Jim은 왜 영어 공부를 열심히 하니?
B: 왜냐하면 그는 유학 가는 것을 계획하기 때문이야.

7 A: 불꽃놀이가 언제 끝났니?
B: 5분 전에 막 끝났어.
8 A: 의자 위의 그것은 누구의 재킷이니?
B: 그것은 Elly의 것이야. 그녀는 오늘 아침 그것을 거기에 두고 갔어.
9 A: 네 휴가 계획은 무엇이니?
B: 나는 제주도에 갈 거야. 거기는 내가 가장 좋아하는 곳이야.
A: 너는 왜 그 섬을 좋아하니?
B: 왜냐하면 그곳에는 아름다운 해변과 산이 있기 때문이야.

Unit 03 부가의문문
p.20

1 aren't you
2 doesn't it
3 did she
4 can he
5 shall we
6 is, isn't she
7 don't have, do we
8 aren't, are they
9 invited, didn't he
10 Pass, will you
11 You didn't watch that movie, did you

11 A: 너는 어제 그 코미디 영화를 재미있게 봤니?
B: 응. 정말 재밌었어. 넌 그 영화를 보지 않았지, 그렇지?
A: 아니, 난 봤어. 나도 많이 웃었어.

총괄평가 2회 Chapter 04~06
p.21

1 There was someone strange
2 She has a cup of coffee and an apple
3 What a huge lake it is
4 many passengers
5 little water
6 any special plans
7 should love ourselves
8 Your advice is always helpful
9 Don't[Do not] use your cell phone in class.
10 Why don't we study math together?
11 a few
12 few
13 little
14 (1) There is a baseball
(2) There are two chairs
(3) There are three sheets of paper
15 yours, mine
16 sometimes play tennis
17 Where did you leave
18 What kind of food do you want
19 (1) It is[It's] November 17th, It is[It's] rainy and cold
(2) It is[It's] November 16th, It is[It's] sunny and clear
20 quiet → quietly
21 drink never → never drink
22 is the baby → the baby is
23 don't → aren't
24 wrong anything → anything wrong
25 (1) is lighter than (2) is the heaviest
(3) is shorter than

26 (1) How often do you travel?
(2) Where did you visit
(3) Why did you choose Busan
(4) What did you do

3 해설 What 감탄문은 「What＋a/an＋형용사＋명사(＋주어＋동사)」의 어순으로 쓴다.
어휘 huge 큰, 거대한
4 어휘 passenger 승객
8 해설 be동사가 있을 때 빈도부사는 be동사 뒤에 쓴다.
어휘 helpful 도움이 되는, 유용한　advice 충고
11 A: 너는 네 방에 책을 많이 가지고 있니?
B: 몇 권 있지만 많지는 않아.
12 A: Brain, 너 오늘 일찍 왔구나!
B: 응. 도로에 차가 거의 없었어.
13 A: 내 과학 프로젝트를 도와줄 수 있니?
B: 미안. 나는 오늘 시간이 거의 없어.
14 〈보기〉 침대 옆에 상자 한 개가 있다.
(1) 상자 안에 야구공 한 개가 있다.
(2) 책상 옆에 의자 두 개가 있다.
(3) 책상 위에 종이 세 장이 있다.
해설 단수명사와 셀 수 없는 명사 앞에는 There is를 쓰고, 복수명사 앞에는 There are를 쓴다.
15 A: 어느 것이 내 선물이니?
B: 빨간색 상자가 네 것이고, 파란색 상자는 내 것이야.
16 A: 너는 운동을 자주 하니?
B: 나는 가끔 테니스를 치지만, 매주는 아니야.
17 A: 너는 어디에 열쇠를 뒀니? 나는 그것을 못 찾겠어.
B: 나는 그것을 탁자 위에 뒀어.
해설 B의 대답에서 on the table이 장소를 설명해 주고 있으므로 장소를 묻는 의문사 where를 쓴다.
18 A: 너는 어떤 종류의 음식을 원하니?
B: 음, 스파게티. 그건 내가 가장 좋아하는 거야.
해설 좋아하는 음식에 대해 응답하는 것으로 보아 어떤 종류의 음식(what kind of food)을 좋아하는지 묻는 것이 자연스럽다.

19

	서울	런던
날짜	11월 17일	11월 16일
날씨	비가 오고 추움	화창하고 맑음

(1) 11월 17일이다. 오늘은 비가 오고 춥다.
(2) 11월 16일이다. 오늘은 화창하고 맑다.
20 Nick은 그의 친구에게 조용히 말했다.
21 나의 남동생과 나는 탄산음료를 절대 마시지 않는다.
22 정말 귀여운 아기구나!
해설 How 감탄문은 「How＋형용사/부사(＋주어＋동사)」의 어순으로 쓴다.
23 Tom과 Brian은 형제야, 그렇지 않니?
해설 문장의 동사가 are이므로 부가의문문은 don't가 아닌 aren't로 써야 한다.
24 네 자전거에 무슨 문제가 있니?

25

	말	코끼리	곰	기린
키 (m)	1.6	3	2	5
몸무게 (kg)	600	5,000	800	1,300

(1) 말은 곰보다 더 가볍다.
(2) 코끼리는 모든 동물들 중에 가장 무거운 동물이다.
(3) 곰은 기린보다 키가 더 작다.
어휘 height 키
26 A: 네 취미는 무엇이니?
B: 나는 여행을 좋아해!
A: 너는 얼마나 자주 여행을 하니?
B: 나는 보통 매달 여행을 해.
A: 멋지다! 지난달에는 어디를 방문했니?

B: 나는 나의 가족과 함께 부산을 방문했어.
A: 너는 여행지로 왜 부산을 선택했어?
B: 멋진 해변이 있기 때문이야.
A: 그렇구나. 너는 그곳에서 무엇을 했니?
B: 나는 바다에서 수영을 했고, 밤에는 불꽃놀이를 즐겼어.

해설 (1) B가 여행을 다니는 '빈도'에 대해 응답하고 있으므로, How often을 사용하여 의문사 의문문을 쓴다.
(3) B가 Because를 사용해 '이유'에 대해 응답하고 있으므로 Why를 사용해 의문사 의문문을 만든다.
(4) B가 '무엇'을 했는지에 대해 응답하고 있으므로, What을 사용해 의문사 의문문을 만든다.

어휘 fireworks (복수형) 불꽃놀이

Chapter 07 문장의 여러 형식

Unit 01 SVC(2형식) p.24

1 The weather got cold
2 Your voice sounds low
3 The floor feels very slippery
4 His face looks quite familiar
5 These cookies smell sweet.
6 I became very nervous
7 The lemonade tasted too sour.
8 The blanket feels soft and warm.
9 (1) It looks great on you!
　 (2) It tastes bitter.

9 (1) A: 내 새 셔츠는 어때 보여?
　　 B: 그것은 너에게 잘 어울려 보여!
　 (2) A: 차 맛이 어때?
　　 B: 그것은 쓴맛이 나.
　　 A: 그럼 꿀을 좀 넣으면 돼.

Unit 02 SVOO(4형식) p.25

1 showed me his photo album
2 taught her dog some tricks
3 will bring the bestseller to you
4 He will buy a new watch for his wife
5 Ann asked a favor of her neighbor
6 Joseph sent a package of snacks to me
7 Emma wrote her brother a letter
8 Jim told his opinion to the teacher
9 (1) I showed David my painting
　 (2) I gave the painting to him

4 그는 그의 아내에게 새 손목시계를 사 줄 것이다.
5 Ann은 그녀의 이웃에게 부탁을 했다.
6 Joseph은 지난 주말에 나에게 간식 꾸러미를 보내주었다.
9 A: 난 어제 David에게 내 그림을 보여주었어.
　 B: 오, 그랬어? 그가 뭐라고 말했어?
　 A: 그는 그것이 아주 맘에 든다고 말했어! 그래서 난 그에게
　　　 그 그림을 선물로 주었어.
　 B: 그는 분명히 너에게 고마워할 거야.

Unit 03 SVOC(5형식) p.26

1 We found Ben's idea creative
2 My friends and I call him a superhero
3 We should keep our environment clean
4 I left the window open
5 The parents named their baby Oliver.
6 Jane's smile makes everyone happy.
7 Exercise keeps muscles strong.
8 She leaves her bed messy
9 The song made him a famous singer.

9 여러분께 제가 가장 좋아하는 가수를 소개하겠습니다. Charlie는 가수이자 작곡가입니다. 그는 좋은 목소리를 갖고 있고, 기타를 매우 잘 칩니다. 그의 첫 곡이 제가 가장 좋아하는 것입니다. 그 노래가 그를 유명한 가수로 만들었습니다.

Chapter 08 to부정사

Unit 01 to부정사의 명사적 쓰임 p.27

1 is to run a marathon next year
2 I want to adopt a puppy
3 To have breakfast daily is important
4 is to become a pilot
5 Chris likes to make model airplanes
6 Lily promised to send the files
7 We decided to plant some roses
8 (1) planned to have a barbecue party
　 (2) To go camping is very enjoyable

8 나의 사촌인 Tommy가 지난주에 한국을 방문했다. 그는 한국식 바비큐를 아주 좋아한다. 그래서, 나의 부모님은 캠핑장에서 바비큐 파티를 열기로 계획하셨다. Tommy와 나는 캠핑 가는 것을 정말 좋아한다. 캠핑을 가는 것은 우리에게 매우 즐겁다.

Unit 02 to부정사의 부사적 쓰임 p.28

1 was sad to say goodbye
2 practices yoga to reduce stress
3 is studying hard to pass the exam
4 were very excited to see the aurora
5 To sleep well at night
6 She was nervous to give a presentation
7 takes notes to remember important things.
8 I am[I'm] pleased to join the dance club.

9 (1) I began it to express my feelings.
　또는 To express my feelings, I began it.
　(2) I am[I'm] happy to make my own artwork.

9　A: 너는 왜 그림을 그리는 것을 시작했니?
　　B: 난 내 감정을 표현하려고 그것을 시작했어.
　　A: 네 새로운 취미는 어때?
　　B: 정말 좋아! 난 나만의 예술 작품을 만들게 돼서 행복해.
　　해설 (1) '~하려고'라는 '목적'을 나타내는 부사적 쓰임의 to부정사
　　구(to express my feelings)는 문장의 맨 앞이나 뒤에 써야 한다.
　　(2) '~해서(원인) …한 감정을 느낀다'라는 의미의 부사적 쓰임의
　　to부정사(to make)는 감정을 나타내는 형용사(happy) 뒤에 써야
　　한다.

Unit 03　to부정사의 형용사적 쓰임　p.29

1 I have a lot of homework to do
2 They have some guests to invite
3 My parents need someone to drive them
4 Lisa is looking for a quiet place to study
5 time to go to bed
6 lost the key to unlock
7 know any comedy movies to watch
8 have some questions to ask you
9 I bought a new board game to play

9　A: 난 주말에 할 새로운 보드게임을 샀어.
　　B: 재밌겠다! 그게 뭔데?
　　A: '모노폴리' 게임이야. 나랑 함께 할래?
　　B: 물론이지, 난 하고 싶어!

Chapter 09　동명사

Unit 01　명사로 쓰이는 동명사　p.30

1 is taking care of sick patients
2 Henry practices playing the guitar
3 Making new friends is not easy
4 is snowboarding
5 Mastering a new language takes
6 I finished editing the video
7 She kept shaking her leg.
8 My brother gave up fixing his bike.
9 I enjoy playing adventure games

9　A: 비디오 게임을 하는 것은 항상 재미있어.
　　B: 동의해! 너는 어떤 게임을 가장 좋아하니?
　　A: 사실, 난 모험 게임을 하는 것을 즐겨.
　　B: 나도!
　　해설 '~하는 것을 즐기다'라는 의미는 「enjoy -ing」 형태로 쓴다.

Unit 02　자주 쓰이는 동명사 표현　p.31

1 How about playing tennis
2 Thank you for coming
3 Emma is good at leading people
4 He eats healthy food by cooking
5 I will[I'll] go surfing at the beach
6 without making any mistakes
7 by using less plastic
8 is interested in trying new recipes
9 (1) He[Martin] is good at swimming.
　(2) He[Martin] is afraid of jumping[diving] from
　　high places.

9　Martin은 수영을 매우 잘한다. 그는 작년에 수영 대회에서 우승했
　　다. 그러나 그는 높은 곳에서 다이빙하는 것을 좋아하지 않는다. 그
　　는 높은 곳에서 점프하는 것을 무서워한다.
　　(1) Martin은 무엇을 잘하는가?
　　　→ 그는[Martin은] 수영하는 것을 잘한다.
　　(2) Martin은 무엇을 무서워하는가?
　　　→ 그는[Martin은] 높은 곳에서 점프하는 것을[다이빙하는 것
　　　을] 무서워한다.

Chapter 10　전치사와 접속사

Unit 01　전치사　p.32

1 at midnight　　　2 to London
3 by train　　　　4 for two weeks
5 in the gym
6 We decorated our tent with lights.
7 I felt nervous in front of the audience.
8 The train goes from Seoul to Busan
9 We cannot[can't] live without water.

9　A: 우리가 화성에서 살 수 있을까?
　　B: 아마 아닐 거야. 그곳에는 충분한 물이 있지 않아. 우리는 물
　　　없이 살 수 없어.
　　A: 맞아. 하지만 우리는 언젠가 다른 행성에서 살지도 몰라.
　　B: 나도 동의해.

Unit 02　접속사　p.33

1 You can choose tea or coffee
2 We decided to watch a movie and eat out
3 Mark thinks that spring is the best season
4 when the weather is nice
5 because I did not[didn't] feel well
6 If you want more information
7 I hope (that) you have a safe trip.
8 I believe (that) money can't buy happiness.
9 (1) after he ran this morning, he felt pain
　(2) he took out some ice and put it

9 조깅하는 것은 인호의 취미이다. 하지만 그는 오늘 아침에 달리고 난 후, 그는 다리에 통증을 느꼈다. 그래서 그는 얼음을 좀 꺼내 그 것을 다리에 두었다.

총괄평가 3회 Chapter 07~10 p.34

1 Those tulips smell wonderful
2 We called the puppy Coco
3 I know that Han is an honest person
4 walk or take a bus
5 showed us her garden
6 sent a text message to me
7 before he goes to bed
8 wants to be a popular singer
9 finished decorating the house
10 is considering visiting his cousin
11 in **12** on
13 until **14** by
15 during **16** time to wait
17 Hiking every Sunday
18 Thank you for lending
19 by joining a club
20 to hear the loud noise **21** to find my umbrella
22 greatly → great **23** to got → to get
24 to turn → turning **25** are → is
26 (1) I needed to buy a gift[present]
(2) I chose to buy a necklace
27 (1) My sister loves drawing.
(2) Her dream is to be an artist.
28 (1) because she was very tired
(2) after she had dinner
(3) if it rains
29 ⓒ → made her sleepy
ⓔ → asked a question of her
[asked her a question]
30 (1) Jay wrote our teacher a poem.
(2) Kevin showed interesting magic tricks to us.
(3) Eric made some sandwiches for everyone.
(4) Everyone made our teacher happy.
31 (1) was good at running
(2) decided to have a rest
(3) enjoyed taking a nap
(4) kept going
(5) was proud of

1 어휘 tulip 튤립
11 미나는 더 큰 집에서 살기를 원한다.
12 Tom의 가족은 매년 크리스마스에 놀이공원에 간다.
13 나의 사촌은 다음 달까지 우리 집에 머물 것이다.
해설 다음 달까지 머무는 행위가 계속되는 것이므로 전치사 until 을 쓴다.
14 너는 내일까지 콘서트 표를 사야 한다.
해설 어떠한 행위가 완료되어야 하는 기한을 의미하므로 전치사 by를 쓴다.
15 Susan은 핼러윈 파티 동안 마녀 복장을 입고 있었다.

해설 특정한 때를 나타내는 the Halloween party가 쓰였으므로 전치사 during을 쓴다.
어휘 witch 마녀 costume 의상, 복장
17 해설 to부정사와 동명사 모두 주어로 쓰일 수 있지만, 조건에 맞게 3 단어로 쓰기 위해 동명사를 쓴다.
22 그 복숭아 파이는 맛이 좋다.
해설 감각동사 taste 뒤에 오는 주격보어 자리에는 형용사를 쓴다.
어휘 peach 복숭아
23 그는 올해 좋은 성적을 받기로 약속했다.
24 음량을 올리는 것을 꺼리시나요? (음량을 올려도 될까요?)
어휘 turn up (소리 등을) 높이다 volume 음량, 볼륨
25 사진을 찍는 것은 무언가를 기억하는 좋은 방식이다.
해설 동명사구 주어는 단수 취급하므로 are를 is로 고쳐 써야 한다.
26 어제는 어머니의 날이어서, 나는 선물을 하나 사야 했다. 그래 서, 나는 쇼핑몰에 갔다. 몇 시간 후, 나는 목걸이를 사는 것을 선택 했다. 엄마는 나의 선물을 아주 좋아하셨다.
27 내 이름은 호진이다. 나는 중학생이다. 나는 과학자가 되는 것 을 희망한다. 오늘, 나는 도서관에 가서 과학에 관한 책을 좀 빌릴 것이다. 내 여동생은 그리는 것을 아주 좋아한다. 그녀는 매우 잘 그린다. 그녀의 꿈은 예술가가 되는 것이다.
28 〈보기〉 비가 온다. 그녀는 매우 피곤했다. 그녀는 저녁을 먹었다.
(1) Lily는 매우 피곤했기 때문에 일찍 자러 갔다.
(2) Lily는 저녁을 먹은 후에 이를 닦았다.
(3) Lily는 만약 비가 온다면 밖에 나가지 않을 것이다.
29 Sue는 어제 두통이 있었다. 그녀는 몸이 좋지 않아서 수업 전 에 보건실에 갔다. 보건 선생님께서 그녀에게 약을 좀 주셨다. 그것 은 그녀를 졸리게 만들었다.
과학 수업 동안, 그녀는 수업에 집중할 수가 없었다. 선생님은 그녀의 행동이 이상하다는 것을 알게 되셨다. 그는 그녀에게 질문 을 했지만, 그녀는 듣지 못했다.
해설 ⓒ make는 목적격보어로 형용사를 쓰는 동사이므로 sleepily 가 아닌 sleepy로 고쳐 쓴다.
ⓔ ask는 「ask+직접목적어+of+간접목적어」 또는 「ask+간접목 적어+직접목적어」의 어순으로 쓸 수 있다.
어휘 headache 두통 school clinic 보건실 school nurse 보건 선생님 behavior 행동 strange 이상한, 낯선
30 오늘은 스승의 날이었다! 우리 반은 우리 선생님을 위한 파티 를 열었다. 모든 학생은 그를 위해 무언가를 준비했다. Jay는 우리 선생님에게 시를 써 드렸다. Kevin은 우리에게 흥미로운 마술 묘기 를 보여주었다. Eric은 모두에게 샌드위치를 좀 만들어 주었다. 모 두는 우리 선생님을 행복하게 만들어 드렸다.
그는 우리에게 아이스크림을 좀 사주셨다. 최고의 날이었다!
해설 (2) 「show+간접목적어+직접목적어」 구조를 3형식 문장으로 쓸 때 간접목적어 앞에는 전치사 to를 쓴다.
(3) 「make+간접목적어+직접목적어」 구조를 3형식 문장으로 쓸 때 간접목적어 앞에는 전치사 for를 쓴다.
어휘 poem (한 편의) 시
31 어느 날, 토끼와 거북이는 경주를 했다. 토끼는 달리기를 잘했 지만, 거북이는 아니었다.
토끼는 그 경주를 이길 것이라고 예상해서, 그녀는 잠깐 쉬기 로 결정했다. 토끼는 나무 아래에 누워서 낮잠을 즐겼다. 그러나, 토끼가 잠을 자고 있던 동안, 거북이는 계속 나아갔다. 그는 결승선 까지 달리는 것을 절대 멈추지 않았다.
결과적으로, 거북이가 경주를 이겼다. 그는 스스로가 자랑스러 웠다.
해설 (1) '～하는 것을 잘하다'라는 의미는 「be good at -ing」 형태 로 쓴다.
(2) decide는 to부정사를 목적어로 취하는 동사이다.
(3) enjoy는 동명사를 목적어로 취하는 동사이다.
(4) keep은 동명사를 목적어로 취하는 동사이다.
(5) '～을 자랑스러워하다'라는 의미는 전치사 표현인 「be proud of」로 쓴다.
어휘 moment 잠깐, 잠시 as a result 결과적으로

쎄듀 초·중등 커리큘럼

초등 (예비초 / 초1 / 초2 / 초3 / 초4 / 초5 / 초6)

구문
- 천일문 365 일력 | 초1-3 | 교육부 지정 초등 필수 영어 문장
- 개정 초등 천일문 SENTENCE 1 / 2 / 3 — 1001개 통문장 암기로 완성하는 초등 영어의 기초

문법
- 왓츠 Grammar — Start (초등 기초 영문법) / Plus (초등 영문법 마무리)

독해
- 왓츠 리딩 30/40 / 50 / 60 / 70 / 80 / 90 / 100 — 쉽고 재미있게 완성되는 영어 독해력

어휘
- 개정 초등 천일문 VOCA&STORY — 한 권으로 끝내는 초등 필수 영단어 1000개
- 패턴으로 말하는 초등 필수 영단어 1 / 2 — 문장 패턴으로 완성하는 초등 필수 영단어

ELT
- Oh! My PHONICS 1 / 2 / 3 / 4 — 유·초등학생을 위한 첫 영어 파닉스
- Oh! My SPEAKING 1 / 2 / 3 / 4 / 5 / 6 — 핵심 문장 패턴으로 더욱 쉬운 영어 말하기
- Oh! My GRAMMAR 1 / 2 / 3 — 쓰기로 완성하는 첫 초등 영문법

중등 (예비중 / 중1 / 중2 / 중3)

구문
- 천일문 STARTER 1 / 2 — 중등 필수 구문 & 문법 총정리

문법
- 천일문 중등 GRAMMAR LEVEL 1 / 2 / 3 — 예문 중심 문법 기본서
- GRAMMAR Q Starter 1, 2 / Intermediate 1, 2 / Advanced 1, 2 — 학기별 문법 기본서
- 잘 풀리는 영문법 1 / 2 / 3 — 문제 중심 문법 적용서
- GRAMMAR PIC 1 / 2 / 3 / 4 — 이해가 쉬운 도식화된 문법서
- 1센치 영문법 — 1권으로 핵심 문법 정리

문법+어법
- 개정 미리 수능 영어 문법·어법 1, 2 *첫단추 BASIC 개정 — 중학생을 위한 수능 문법·어법 입문

문법+쓰기
- EGU 영단어&품사 / 문장 형식 / 동사 써먹기 / 문법 써먹기 / 구문 써먹기 — 서술형 기초 세우기와 문법 다지기

쓰기
- 개정 천일문 중등 WRITING LEVEL 1 / 2 / 3 *거침없이 Writing 개정 — 중등 교과서 내신 기출 서술형
- 중학 영어 쓰작 1 / 2 / 3 — 중등 교과서 패턴 드릴 서술형

어휘
- 개정 천일문 VOCA 중등 스타트 / 필수 / 마스터 — 2800개 중등 3개년 필수 어휘
- 개정 어휘끝 중학 필수편 — 중학 필수어휘 1000개
- 개정 어휘끝 중학 마스터편 — 고난도 중학어휘 +고등기초 어휘 1000개

독해
- ReadingGraphy LEVEL 1 / 2 / 3 / 4 / 신간 5 / 신간 6 — 중·고등 필수 구문까지 잡는 흥미로운 소재 독해
- Reading Relay Starter 1, 2 / Challenger 1, 2 / Master 1, 2 — 타교과 연계 배경 지식 독해
- READING Q Starter 1, 2 / Intermediate 1, 2 / Advanced 1, 2 — 예측/추론/요약 사고력 독해

독해전략
- 리딩 플랫폼 1 / 2 / 3 — 논픽션 지문 독해

독해유형
- Reading 16 LEVEL 1 / 2 / 3 — 수능 유형 맛보기 + 내신 대비
- 개정 미리 수능 영어 기초 독해 / 유형 독해 *첫단추 BASIC 개정 — 중학생을 위한 수능 독해 입문

듣기
- Listening Q 유형편 / 1 / 2 / 3 — 유형별 듣기 전략 및 실전 대비
- 쎄듀 빠르게 중학영어듣기 모의고사 1 / 2 / 3 — 교육청 듣기평가 대비